JOHN ASHBERY

阿什贝利自选诗集
I
（汉英对照）

马永波 译

著作权合同登记号　图字 01-2018-3336

SELECTED POEMS by John Ashbery
Copyright © John Ashbery，1985
Published by arrangement with Georges Borchardt, Inc.
through Bardon-Chinese Media Agency.
Simplified Chinese translation copyright © 2018 by
Shanghai 99 Readers' Culture Co., Ltd.
ALL RIGHTS RESERVED

图书在版编目(CIP)数据

阿什贝利自选诗集：全三卷：汉英对照/（美）约翰·阿什贝利著；马永波译. —北京：人民文学出版社，2018
ISBN 978-7-02-014477-8

Ⅰ．①阿…　Ⅱ．①约…　②马…　Ⅲ．①诗集-美国-现代　Ⅳ．①I712.25

中国版本图书馆 CIP 数据核字(2018)第 187370 号

责任编辑　卜艳冰　何炜宏　邰莉莉
装帧设计　高静芳

出版发行	人民文学出版社
社　　址	北京市朝内大街 166 号
邮　　编	100705
网　　址	http://www.rw-cn.com
印　　刷	上海利丰雅高印刷有限公司
经　　销	全国新华书店等
字　　数	180 千字
开　　本	889×1194 毫米　1/32
印　　张	26.75
版　　次	2019 年 4 月北京第 1 版
印　　次	2019 年 4 月第 1 次印刷
书　　号	978-7-02-014477-8
定　　价	168.00 元

如有印装质量问题，请与本社图书销售中心调换。电话：010－65233595

SELECTED POEMS

JOHN ASHBERY

Contents

From *SOME TREES*	001
Two Scenes	002
Popular Songs	004
The Instruction Manual	008
The Grapevine	016
A Boy	018
Glazunoviana	022
The Picture of Little J. A. in a Prospect of Flowers	024
Sonnet	030
The Young Son	032
Errors	034
Illustration	036
Some Trees	042
The Painter	044
And You Know	048
He	054
A Long Novel	060
The Pied Piper	064
Le Livre Est Sur La Table	066

目录

一些树（1956） 001
 两个场景 003
 流行歌曲 005
 使用说明书 009
 葡萄藤 017
 男　孩 019
 格拉祖诺瓦娜 023
 以鲜花为景的小约翰·阿什贝利的照片 025
 十四行 031
 年轻的儿子 033
 错　误 035
 插　图 037
 一些树 043
 画　家 045
 而你知道 049
 他 055
 一部长篇小说 061
 花衣魔笛手 065
 生活在桌面上 067

From *THE TENNIS COURT OATH*	071
Thoughts of a Young Girl	072
"How Much Longer Will I Be Able	
to Inhabit the Divine Sepulcher…"	074
White Roses	084
Our Youth	086
An Additional Poem	090
Faust	092
A Last World	096
From The New Realism	106
From *RIVERS AND MOUNTAINS*	111
Rivers and Mountains	112
Last Month	120
If the Birds Knew	122
Into the Dusk-charged Air	126
The Ecclesiast	140
The Recent Past	144
A Blessing in Disguise	146
Clepsydra	150
From The Skaters	172
From *THE DOUBLE DREAM OF SPRING*	195
The Task	196

网球场宣言（1962） 071
一个年轻姑娘的想法 073
"还要多久我才能继承那神圣的坟墓……" 075
白玫瑰 085
我们的青春 087
一首附加的诗 091
浮士德 093
最后的世界 097
新现实主义 107

山山水水（1966） 111
山山水水 113
上个月 121
如果鸟儿们知道 123
在黄昏弥漫的天空中 127
传教士 141
最近以来 145
貌似灾祸的福音 147
滴 漏 151
滑冰者（节选） 173

春天的双重梦幻（1970） 195
工 作 197

Spring Day	200
Plainness in Diversity	206
Soonest Mended	208
Summer	214
It Was Raining in the Capital	218
Variations, Calypso and Fugue on a Theme of Ella Wheeler Wilcox	226
Song	240
Decoy	244
For John Clare	248
Farm Implements and Rutabagas in a Landscape	252
Papergon	256
Some Words	260
The Bungalows	272
The Chateau Hardware	280
Sortes Vergilianae	282
From *THREE POEMS*	289
The System	290
From *SELF-PORTRAIT IN A CONVEX MIRROR*	379
As One Put Drunk into the Packet-boat	380
Worsening Situation	384
Forties Flick	388

春　日	201
差异中的清晰	207
最快速修补	209
夏　天	215
首都正在下雨	219
有关埃拉·惠勒·威尔科克斯的一个主题的变奏曲、卡里普索和赋格曲	227
歌	241
诱　饵	245
致约翰·克莱尔	249
风景中的农具和芜菁	253
文学小品	257
一些词语	261
平　房	273
庄园硬件	281
以维吉尔诗句占卜	283

三首诗（1972） 289
　　系　统 291

凸面镜中的自画像（1975） 379
　　当一个人把醉鬼放入邮船 381
　　恶化的事态 385
　　四十年代的电影 389

As You Came from the Holy Land	390
Scheherazade	396
Grand Galop	404
Hop O' My Thumb	424
Mixed Feelings	430
Märchenbilder	434
Oleum Misericordiae	438
Self-Portrait in a Convex Mirror	444
From *HOUSEBOAT DAYS*	491
Street Musicians	492
The Other Tradition	496
Variant	500
Wooden Buildings	502
Pyrography	504
The Gazing Grain	512
Unctuous Platitudes	514
The Couple in the Next Room	518
Business Personals	520
Crazy Weather	528
On the Townpath	530
Bird's-Eye View of the Tool and Die Co.	536
Wet Casements	538
Saying It to Keep It from Happening	542

因为你来自圣地	391
山鲁佐德	397
大加洛普舞曲	405
小矮人	425
混杂的情感	431
童话场景	435
慈悲之油	439
凸面镜中的自画像	445

船屋的日子（1977） 491

街头音乐家	493
另外的传统	497
变　量	501
木　楼	503
烙　画	505
注目的谷物	513
虚情假意的陈词滥调	515
隔壁的夫妻	519
商业人事广告	521
疯狂的天气	529
牵　道	531
鸟瞰工具及冲模公司	537
潮湿的地下室	539
说它是为了阻止它发生	543

Daffy Duck in Hollywood	546
Houseboat Days	558
The Lament Upon the Waters	564
And *Ut Pictura Poesis* Is Her Name	568
What Is Poetry	572
And Others, Vaguer Presences	574
The Wrong Kind of Insurance	576
Friends	582
The Ice-Cream Wars	586
Blue Sonata	590
Syringa	594
From Fantasia on "The Nut-Brown Maid"	602

From *AS WE KNOW*	607
From Litany	608
Silhouette	618
Many Wagons Ago	622
As We Know	624
Otherwise	628
Flowering Death	630
Haunted Landscape	632
My Erotic Double	638
Train Rising out of the Sea	640
Late Echo	644

达菲鸭在好莱坞　　547

　　船屋的日子　　559

　　水上的哀悼　　565

　　而诗如画是她的名字　　569

　　什么是诗歌　　573

　　而其他人，模糊的存在　　575

　　投错的保险　　577

　　朋友们　　583

　　冰淇淋战争　　587

　　蓝色奏鸣曲　　591

　　紫丁香　　595

　　有关"栗色头发的少女"的幻想曲　　603

正如我们所知（1979）　　607

　　连　祷　　609

　　剪　影　　619

　　许多马车前　　623

　　正如我们所知　　625

　　否　则　　629

　　开花的死亡　　631

　　闹鬼的风景　　633

　　我好色的替身演员　　639

　　海中升起的列车　　641

　　迟到的回声　　645

And I'd Love You to Be in It	646
Tapestry	650
A Love Poem	654
This Configuration	656
Their Day	660
A Tone Poem	664
The Other Cindy	666
The Plural of "Jack in the Box"	670

From *SHADOW TRAIN* — 673

The Pursuit of Happiness	674
Punishing the Myth	676
Paradoxes and Oxymorons	678
Another Chain Letter	680
The Ivory Tower	682
At the Inn	684
The Absence of a Noble Presence	686
Qualm	688
Here Everything Is Still Floating	690
Some Old Tires	692
Something Similar	694
Or in My Throat	696
Untilted	698
The Leasing of September	700

而我喜欢你在它里面	647
织　锦	651
一首爱情诗	655
结　构	657
他们的日子	661
一首音诗	665
另一个辛迪	667
玩偶盒的复数	671

影子列车（1981） 673

对幸福的追求	675
惩罚神话	677
悖论与矛盾修辞	679
另一封连锁信	681
象牙塔	683
在旅馆	685
一个高贵存在的缺席	687
疑　虑	689
这里的一切仍在漂浮	691
一些旧轮胎	693
类似的事物	695
或者在我的喉咙里	697
非倾斜	699
九月的出租	701

Unusual Precautions	702
We Hesitate	704
Frontispiece	706
The Vegetarians	708

From *A WAVE*   711

At North Farm	712
The Songs We Know Best	714
Landscape (After Baudelaire)	722
Just Walking Around	726
The Ongoing Story	730
Thank You for Not Cooperating	734
More Pleasant Adventures	738
Purists Will Object	742
37 Haiku	744
The Lonedale Operator	752
Darlene's Hospital	756
Whatever It Is, Wherever You Are	764
A Wave	770

不同寻常的预防措施 703

我们在犹豫 705

卷首插图 707

素食者 709

一排浪（1984） 711

在北方农场 713

我们最熟悉的歌曲 715

风景 723

只是在周围走走 727

正在进行的故事 731

谢谢你的不合作 735

更愉快的冒险 739

纯粹主义者会反对 743

三十七俳句 745

隆台尔的报务员 753

达莲娜医院 757

无论它是什么，无论你在哪儿 765

波　浪 771

From
SOME TREES
一些树
(1956)

Two Scenes

I

We see us as we truly behave:

From every corner comes a distinctive offering.

The train comes bearing joy;

The sparks it strikes illuminate the table.

Destiny guides the water-pilot, and it is destiny.

For long we hadn't heard so much news, such noise.

The day was warm and pleasant.

"We see you in your hair,

Air resting around the tips of mountains."

II

A fine rain anoints the canal machinery.

This is perhaps a day of general honesty

Without example in the world's history

Though the fumes are not of a singular authority

And indeed are dry as poverty.

Terrific units are on an old man

In the blue shadow of some paint cans

As laughing cadets say, "In the evening

Everything has a schedule, if you can find out what it is."

两个场景

1

我们在真正行动时才看见自己：
每个角落都贡献出一份独特的礼物。
火车满载快乐而来；
它撞击出的火花照亮了桌子。
命运引导着领航员，这就是命运。
我们已很久没有听到这么多新闻，这样的喧嚣。
日子温暖而愉快。
"我们看见你在自己的发间，
空气绕着群山之巅休憩。"

2

一场细雨为运河的机器涂油。
这也许是大体忠诚的一天
在世界历史中绝无仅有
虽然烟气不是唯一的权威
甚至如贫穷一般干燥。
可怕的部位在一个老人那里
在一些油漆桶的蓝色阴影中
就像军校生笑着说，"晚上
每件事都有安排，只要你能发现它是什么。"

Popular Songs

He continued to consult her for her beauty

(The host gone to a longing grave).

The story then resumed in day coaches

Both bravely eyed the finer dust on the blue. That summer

("The worst ever") she stayed in the car with the cur.

That was something between her legs.

Alton had been getting letters from his mother

About the payments—half the flood

Over and what about the net rest of the year?

Who cares? Anyway (you know how thirsty they were)

The extra worry began it—on the

Blue blue mountain—she never set foot

And then and there. Meanwhile the host

Mourned her quiet tenure. They all stayed chatting.

No one did much about eating.

The tears came and stopped, came and stopped, until

Becoming the guano-lightened summer night landscape,

All one glow, one mild laugh lasting ages.

Some precision, he fumed into his soup.

You laugh. There is no peace in the fountain.

流行歌曲

他继续为她的美向她请教

(主人走向一座渴望的坟墓)。

而后故事在坐席客车中重新开始

两个人都勇敢地注视着蓝天上更细的灰尘。那个夏天

("糟糕至极")她和杂种狗留在车里。

那是她两腿之间的某个东西。

阿尔顿收到了他母亲的信

关于付款的事——一半的洪水

已经过去,今年干脆休息怎么样?

谁在意呢?无论如何(你知道他们多么干渴)

多余的忧虑开始了——在蓝色的

蓝色的山上——她从未涉足

彼时彼地。与此同时,主人

为她安静的任期深感遗憾。他们在闲聊。

没有人怎么吃东西。

眼泪流了又止,流了又止,直到

变成海鸟粪照亮的夏夜风景,

一切都在发光,一阵微弱的笑声持续了数年。

有点刻板,他冲着他的汤发怒。

你在笑。喷泉动荡不宁。

The footmen smile and shift. The mountain

Rises nightly to disappointed stands

Dining in "The Gardens of the Moon."

There is no way to prevent this

Or the expectation of disappointment.

All are aware, some carry a secret

Better, of hands emulating deeds

Of days untrustworthy. But these may decide.

The face extended its sorrowing light

Far out over them. And now silent as a group

The actors prepare their first decline.

男仆微笑,轮班。山峰
每晚向失望的看台上升
在"月亮的花园"进餐。
无法预防此事的发生
或者对失望的预期。
大家都知道,有人携带一个秘密,
那样更好,知道双手在模仿动作
日子不值得信任。可这些人会做出决定。
面孔拉长了它悲哀的光
远远地越过他们。现在寂静得像一群人
演员们在准备他们的第一次谢幕。

The Instruction Manual

As I sit looking out of a window of the building
I wish I did not have to write the instruction manual on the uses of a new metal.
I look down into the street and see people, each walking with an inner peace,
And envy them—they are so far away from me!
Not one of them has to worry about getting out this manual on schedule.
And, as my way is, I begin to dream, resting my elbows on the desk and leaning out of the window a little,
Of dim Guadalajara! City of rose-colored flowers!
City I wanted most to see, and most did not see, in Mexico!
But I fancy I see, under the press of having to write the instruction manual,
Your public square, city, with its elaborate little bandstand!
The band is playing *Scheherazade* by Rimsky-Korsakov.
Around stand the flower girls, handing out rose- and lemon- colored flowers,
Each attractive in her rose-and-blue striped dress (Oh! such shades of rose and blue),
And nearby is the little white booth where women in green serve you green and yellow fruit.
The couples are parading; everyone is in a holiday mood.
First, leading the parade, is a dapper fellow
Clothed in deep blue. On his head sits a white hat
And he wears a mustache, which has been trimmed for the occasion.

使用说明书

当我坐在大楼中望着窗外

我希望我无需写一份新的金属制品的使用说明书。

我俯视下面的街道,看见每一个人都带着内在的安宁行走,

我羡慕他们——他们离我那么遥远!

他们不需要为按时完成这份说明书而操心。

于是,我以自己的方式开始做梦,把肘支在桌子上

    倾斜着稍微探出窗外,

梦见黯淡的瓜达拉哈拉!玫瑰色的鲜花之城!

我最想看见,又从未去过的,墨西哥的城!

但是我幻想我看见了,在必须写使用说明书的压力下,

你的公共广场,城市,它精致的小乐台!

乐队正在演奏里姆斯基·科萨科夫的《天方夜谭》。

在乐台周围卖花的少女,举着玫瑰色和柠檬色的鲜花,

每个人都被她玫瑰和蓝色的条纹装所吸引(哦!如此的玫瑰

  与蓝色的阴影),

而附近是白色的小货摊,身穿绿衣的妇女为你供应绿色黄色的

  水果。

夫妇们在游行;每个人都沉浸在节日的气氛中。

首先,走在队伍前面的,是一个衣冠楚楚的小伙子

穿着深蓝色的服装。头戴一顶白帽子

留着胡须,为这个场合特意修剪过。

His dear one, his wife, is young and pretty; her shawl is rose, pink, and white.
Her slippers are patent leather, in the American fashion,
And she carries a fan, for she is modest, and does not want the crowd to see her face too often.
But everybody is so busy with his wife or loved one

I doubt they would notice the mustachioed man's wife.
Here come the boys! They are skipping, and throwing little things on the sidewalk
Which is made of gray tile. One of them, a little older, has a toothpick in his teeth.
He is silenter than the rest, and affects not to notice the pretty young girls in white.
But his friends notice them, and shout their jeers at the laughing girls.
Yet soon all this will cease, with the deepening of their years,
And love bring each to the parade grounds for another reason.
But I have lost sight of the young fellow with the toothpick.
Wait—there he is —on the other side of the bandstand,
Secluded from his friends, in earnest talk with a young girl
Of fourteen or fifteen. I try to hear what they are saying
But it seems they are just mumbling something—shy words of love, probably.
She is slightly taller than he, and looks quietly down into his sincere eyes.
She is wearing white. The breeze ruffles her long fine black hair against her olive cheek.
Obviously she is in love. The boy, the young boy with the toothpick, he is in love too;
His eyes show it. Turning from this couple,
I see there is an intermission in the concert.
The paraders are resting and sipping drinks through straws
(The drinks are dispensed from a large glass crock by a lady in dark blue),

010

他可爱的妻子,年轻漂亮;她的方形披肩是玫瑰、粉色和白色。
她的拖鞋是新颖的皮革制成,美国时髦样式,
她还带着一柄扇子,因为生性谦逊不想让人过多看到她的脸。
但每个人都忙着照料自己的妻子或心爱的人

我怀疑他们是否会注意到这个留胡子的男人的妻子。
现在男孩们过来了!他们跳跃着向铺了灰瓷砖的人行道上
抛撒着细屑。其中一个,年纪稍大一些,嘴里衔着一根牙签。
他比其他人要沉静,装做没有注意到穿白衣的漂亮姑娘。
但是他的朋友们注意到了她们,嘲笑着欢笑的姑娘们。
但这一切不久便会终止,随着他们年岁加深,
爱会以另一种理由把每个人带到游行的广场。
但是我已看不见那衔着牙签的小伙子。
等等——他在那里——在乐台的另一侧,
与他的朋友们隔开了,正在与一个十四五岁的少女
一本正经地谈话。我试着听听他们在谈什么
但是他们似乎只是在窃窃私语——很可能,是羞答答的情话。
她比他稍高一些,平静地俯视着他真诚的眼睛。
她穿着白衣服。微风拂弄着她橄榄色颊边的黑色长发。
很显然她在恋爱。那男孩,那咬着牙签的小伙子,也在恋爱;
他的眼睛说明了这点。将视线从这一对身上挪开,
我看见音乐会进入了幕间休息。
游行的人停下来休息,用吸管吸着饮料
(饮料由一名穿深蓝色衣服的女士用一只大玻璃罐子分发),

And the musicians mingle among them, in their creamy white
   uniforms, and talk
About the weather, perhaps, or how their kids are doing at school.

Let us take this opportunity to tiptoe into one of the side streets.
Here you may see one of those white houses with green trim
That are so popular here. Look—I told you!
It is cool and dim inside, but the patio is sunny.
An old woman in gray sits there, fanning herself with a palm leaf fan.
She welcomes us to her patio, and offers us a cooling drink.
"My son is in Mexico City," she says. "He would welcome you too
If he were here. But his job is with a bank there.
Look, here is a photograph of him."
And a dark-skinned lad with pearly teeth grins out at us from the
   worn leather frame.
We thank her for her hospitality, for it is getting late
And we must catch a view of the city, before we leave, from a good
   high place.
That church tower will do—the faded pink one, there against the
   fierce blue of the sky. Slowly we enter.
The caretaker, an old man dressed in brown and gray, asks us how
   long we have been in the city, and how we like it here.
His daughter is scrubbing the steps—she nods to us as we pass into
   the tower.
Soon we have reached the top, and the whole network of the city
   extends before us.
There is the rich quarter, with its houses of pink and white, and its
   crumbling, leafy terraces.
There is the poorer quarter, its homes a deep blue.
There is the market, where men are selling hats and swatting flies

而乐手们混在人群中间，穿着油腻的白制服，
谈着天气，也许，或谈着他们孩子在学校的表现。

让我们趁此机会溜到一条小巷去。
这里你可以看见一座带绿边的白房子
这样的房子此地非常流行。看——我告诉过你！
屋子里凉爽而幽暗，但是院子里阳光明媚。
一个穿灰衣服的老妇人坐在那里，用一把棕榈叶扇子扇凉。
她欢迎我们来到她家，为我们奉上冷饮。
"我儿子在墨西哥城，"她说，"如果他在他会欢迎你们。
但是他在那里的一家银行工作。
瞧，这是他的照片。"
一个黑皮肤的小伙子从磨损的皮相框里向我们露齿微笑。
我们感谢她的款待，因为天色已晚
我们必须找一个高处，在离开前眺望一下城市的全景。
那座教堂塔楼就行——那座褪色的粉色塔楼，对着蓝天。
我们慢慢走进去。
看守人，一个穿棕灰衣服的老人，问我们在城里已经多久了，
我们喜不喜欢这里。
她的女儿正在擦楼梯——当我们进来时她向我们点头致意。
不久我们就到了塔顶，整个城市之网在我们面前展开。
那是富人区，有粉色和白色的房子，还有覆盖绿叶的零散的平台
那是穷人区，那里的房子是深蓝色的。
那是市场，男人们在卖帽子，拍苍蝇，

And there is the public library, painted several shades of pale green and beige.
Look! There is the square we just came from, with the promenaders.
There are fewer of them, now that the heat of the day has increased,
But the young boy and girl still lurk in the shadows of the bandstand.
And there is the home of the little old lady—
She is still sitting in the patio, fanning herself.
How limited, but how complete withal, has been our experience of Guadalajara!
We have seen young love, married love, and the love of an aged mother for her son.
We have heard the music, tasted the drinks, and looked at colored houses.
What more is there to do, except stay? And that we cannot do.
And as a last breeze freshens the top of the weathered old tower, I turn my gaze
Back to the instruction manual which has made me dream of Guadalajara.

还有公共图书馆,漆成几种灰绿色和米色。

瞧!那是我们刚才去过的广场,有人在散步。

只是人少了一些,现在白昼的热气在消退,

但是少男少女仍藏在乐台的阴影中。

那里是那瘦小老妇人的家——

她仍坐在院子里,扇着扇子。

多么有限,但又是多么完整,我们游览了瓜达拉哈拉!

我们看见了年轻人的爱,已婚夫妇的爱,和一个老母亲对儿子
的爱。

我们听到了音乐,品尝了饮料,看到了彩色的房子。

除了在这儿留下来,还有什么要做的?而这我们又办不到。

当最后一阵微风吹过风雨剥蚀的古老塔顶,我把目光

转回到使我梦见瓜达拉哈拉的使用说明书上。

The Grapevine

Of who we and all they are
You all now know. But you know
After they began to find us out we grew
Before they died thinking us the causes

Of their acts. Now we'll not know
The truth of some still at the piano, though
They often date from us, causing
These changes we think we are. We don't care

Though, so tall up there
In young air. But things get darker as we move
To ask them: Whom must we get to know
To die, so you live and we know?

葡萄藤

关于我们和他们是谁
你现在全都知道了。但是你知道
在他们发现我们长大之后
在他们临死之前,把我们认做

他们行为的起因。现在我们不知道
有些真理还在钢琴上,尽管
它们往往起源于我们,导致
这些我们所认为的变化。我们不在乎

而是高耸在那里
在年轻的天空中。事物变得更暗
当我们走过去问它们:我们必须认识谁
谁必须死去,以便你活着,我们知道?

A Boy

I'll do what the raids suggest,

Dad, and that other livid window,

But the tide pushes an awful lot of monsters

And I think it's my true fate.

It had been raining but

It had not been raining.

No one could begin to mop up this particular mess.

Thunder lay down in the heart.

"My child, I love any vast electrical disturbance."

Disturbance! Could the old man, face in the rainweed,

Ask more smuttily? By night it charged over plains,

Driven from Dallas and Oregon, always *whither*,

Why not now? The boy seemed to have fallen

From shelf to shelf of someone's rage.

That night it rained on the boxcars, explaining

The thought of the pensive cabbage roses near the boxcars.

My boy. Isn't there something I asked you once?

男　孩

我将按照突然搜捕所暗示的去做，
爹爹，还有那另一扇铅色的窗户，
但是潮汐卷来相当多的一群怪物
我认为这是我真正的命运。

天一直在下雨但是
天没有一直在下雨。

没人能着手清理这特定的混乱。
雷打在心脏上。
"我的孩子，我爱巨大的电子干扰。"
干扰！那把脸藏在雨衣中的老人

能下流地要求更多吗？夜里它充满平原，
从达拉斯和俄勒冈吹打而来，无论去往何处，
为什么不是现在？男孩似乎
从某人愤怒的架子上跌落。

那一晚雨落在货运车厢上，解释着
车厢旁沉思的百叶蔷薇的思想。
我的男孩。我没有问过你什么事情吗？

What happened? It's also farther to the corner

Aboard the maple furniture. *He*

Couldn't lie. He'd tell'em by their syntax.

But listen now in the flood.

They're throwing up behind the lines.

Dry fields of lightning rise to receive

The observer, the mincing flag. *An unendurable age.*

发生了什么？它离角落更远了

在枫木家具上。他

不能撒谎。他会用他们的语法告诉他们。

但是现在偷偷地听那洪水。

他们在航线后面呕吐。

闪电照亮的干燥田野升起，接受

观察者，破碎的旗帜。一个不可忍受的时代。

Glazunoviana

The man with the red hat

And the polar bear, is he here too?

The window giving on shade,

Is that here too?

And all the little helps,

My initials in the sky,

The hay of an arctic summer night?

The bear

Drops dead in sight of the window.

Lovely tribes have just moved to the north.

In the flickering evening the martins grow denser.

Rivers of wings surround us and vast tribulation.

格拉祖诺瓦娜

戴红帽子的男人
和北极熊,他也在这里吗?
对着阴影的窗户,
它也在这里吗?
还有所有小小的帮助,
我的开始在天空中,
一个北极夏夜的干草?

熊
在窗户的注视下倒地而亡。
可爱的部落刚刚迁向了北方。
在闪烁的傍晚燕子变得密集。
翅膀的河流环绕着我们和巨大的苦难。

The Picture of Little J. A. in a Prospect of Flowers

> He was spoilt from childhood
> by the future, which he mastered
> rather early and apparently
> without great difficulty.
> BORIS PASTERNAK

I
Darkness falls like a wet sponge
And Dick gives Genevieve a swift punch
In the pajamas. "Aroint thee, witch."
Her tongue from previous ecstasy
Releases thoughts like little hats.

"He clap'd me first during the eclipse.
Afterwards I noted his manner
Much altered. But he sending
At that time certain handsome jewels
I durst not seem to take offence."

In a far recess of summer
Monks are playing soccer.

以鲜花为景的
小约翰·阿什贝利的照片

他从童年起就被未来
宠坏了,他很早就
征服了它并且显然
没有太大的困难。
　　　——帕斯捷尔纳克

1
黑暗像潮湿的海绵一样落下
迪克轻轻戳了一下穿睡衣的
吉纳维芙。"走开,巫婆。"
她的舌头从先前的狂喜中
释放出小帽子一样的思想。

"在日蚀期间他首先为我鼓掌。
后来我注意到他的方式
有了很大的改变。但他在那时
送了我一些漂亮的宝石
我不敢显出见怪的样子。"

遥远的夏天深处
僧侣们在踢足球。

II

So far is goodness a mere memory

Or naming of recent scenes of badness

That even these lives, children,

You may pass through to be blessed,

So fair does each invent his virtue.

And coming from a white world, music

Will sparkle at the lips of many who are

Beloved. Then these, as dirty handmaidens

To some transparent witch, will dream

Of a white hero's subtle wooing,

And time shall force a gift on each.

That beggar to whom you gave no cent

Striped the night with his strange descant.

III

Yet I cannot escape the picture

Of my small self in that bank of flowers:

My head among the blazing phlox

Seemed a pale and gigantic fungus.

I had a hard stare, accepting

2
如此遥远的是仁慈,一份纯粹的记忆
或者历数最近的邪恶景象
孩子们,甚至这样的生活,
你们也会经历,受到祝福,
如此公平,每个人都发明他自己的美德。

而来自一个白色世界的音乐,
将在许多被热爱的人的唇上
释放出火花。那时,对于某个透明的女巫
这些脏得像女仆的人,将梦见
一个白色的英雄在狡猾地求爱,
而时间将给每个人强加一份礼物。

你分文不予的那个乞丐
用他陌生的旋律,脱去夜晚的衣服。

3
我依然不能避开
小小的自我在花丛中的这张照片:
我的头在闪耀的福禄考花中间
像一枚巨大的灰色真菌。
我的目光坚定,接纳着

Everything, taking nothing,

As though the rolled-up future might stink

As loud as stood the sick moment

The shutter clicked. Though I was wrong,

Still, as the loveliest feelings

Must soon find words, and these, yes,

Displace them, so I am not wrong

In calling this comic version of myself

The true one. For as change is horror,

Virtue is really stubbornness

And only in the light of lost words

Can we imagine our rewards.

一切，吸收着虚无，
仿佛卷起来的未来会发出臭味
这厌倦的时辰伫立
像快门一样响亮。虽然我错了，
但是，如同最美妙的感觉

必须尽快找到词语，是的，那些词语，
代替了它们，因此我没有错
把自我的这个喜剧版本
称为真正的我。因为像变化一样可怕，
美德是真正的顽固

并且仅仅在无语的光中
我们才能想象我们的回报。

Sonnet

Each servant stamps the reader with a look.
After many years he has been brought nothing.
The servant's frown is the reader's patience.
The servant goes to bed.
The patience rambles on
Musing on the library's lofty holes.

His pain is the servant's alive.
It pushes to the top stain of the wall
Its tree-top's head of excitement:
Baskets, birds, beetles, spools.
The light walls collapse next day.
Traffic is the reader's pictured face.
Dear, be the tree your sleep awaits;
Worms be your words, you not safe from ours.

十四行

每个仆人都用表情给读者盖章。

多年以后他带来的只是虚无。

仆人的皱眉是读者的耐心。

仆人上床了。

耐心继续闲逛

若有所思地望着图书馆高高的窟窿。

他的痛苦是仆人的活力。

它将激动的树顶

推向有污迹的墙头:

篮子,鸟,甲虫,线轴。

轻盈的墙第二天就会坍塌。

交通是读者画下的脸。

亲爱的,你的睡眠在等待变成树;

蚯蚓是你的词语,你离开我们不安全。

The Young Son

The screen of supreme good fortune curved his absolute smile into a celestial scream. These things (the most arbitrary that could exist) wakened denials, thoughts of putrid reversals as he traced the green paths to and fro. Here and there a bird sang, a rose silenced her expression of him, and all the gaga flowers wondered. But they puzzled the wanderer with their vague wearinesses. Is the conclusion, he asked, the road forced by concubines from exact meters of strategy? Surely the trees are hinged to no definite purpose or surface. Yet now a wonder would shoot up, all one hue, and virtues would jostle each other to get a view of nothing—the crowded house, two faces glued fast to the mirror, corners and the bustling forest ever preparing, ever menacing its own shape with a shadow of the evil defenses gotten up and in fact already exhausted in some void of darkness, some kingdom he knew the earth could not even bother to avoid if the minutes arranged and divine lettermen with smiling cries were to come in the evening of administration and night which no cure, no bird ever more compulsory, no subject apparently intent on its heart's own demon would forestall even if the truths she told of were now being seriously lit, one by one, in the hushed and fast darkening room.

年轻的儿子

　　超级好运的屏幕把他专制的微笑弯曲成天上的尖叫。当他来回追踪绿色的小径时，这些事物（最武断的才能存在）唤来背弃，堕落逆转的思想。这里和那里，一只鸟歌唱，一朵玫瑰压抑下她对他的态度，所有天真的花都感到奇怪。但是它们以模糊的疲惫困扰漫游者。他问，这就是道路被情妇们以精确的战略逼出的结论吗？树木肯定不以确定的意图或表面为转移。不过，现在又一个奇迹会发芽，只有一种色彩，为了看一眼虚无，众美德会彼此拥挤——拥挤的房屋，两张紧粘在镜子上的面孔，角落和一直在做准备的忙乱的树林，用业已增强的防御邪恶的影子威胁它自己的形状，事实上它已经在黑暗的空虚中消耗殆尽，他知道连地球都无法费心避开的某个王国，如果安排好备忘录，非凡的优秀运动员又哭又笑地在行政管理的傍晚到达，而夜晚无药可救，鸟儿没有更多的义务，明显专注于心中魔鬼的主体不会占先一步，即便她所说的真相正在被严肃地照亮，一个接一个，在寂静而迅速变暗的房间。

Errors

Jealousy. Whispered weather reports.

In the street we found boxes

Littered with snow, to burn at home.

What flower tolling on the waters,

You stupefied me. We waxed,

Carnivores, late and alight

In the beaded winter. All was ominous, luminous.

Beyond the bed's veils the white walls danced

Some violent compunction. Promises,

We thought then of your dry portals,

Bright cornices of eavesdropping palaces,

You were painfully stitched to hours

The moon now tears up, scoffing at the unrinsed portions.

And loves adopted realm. Flees to water,

The coach dissolving in mists.

      A wish

Refines the lines around the mouth

At these ten-year intervals. It fumed

Clear air of wars. It desired

Excess of core in all things. From all things sucked

A glossy denial. But look, pale day:

We fly hence. To return if sketched

In the prophet's silence. Who doubts it is true?

错　误

嫉妒。低语的天气预报。
我们在街上找到一些盒子
乱丢在雪中，在家里烧。
是什么花在水面上引诱
你麻醉我。我们在变大，
食肉动物，迟到了，发亮
在缀有小珠的冬天。一切都明亮而不祥。
床帏之上白墙舞蹈
某种强烈的内疚。许诺，
我们于是想到你干燥的大门，
宫殿明亮的滴水飞檐，
你痛苦地被时间固定
现在月亮飞奔而来，嘲笑未漂洗的部分。
而爱情接受了王国。溜向水边，
马车溶解在雾中。
　　　　　一个希望
提炼嘴边的线条
在十年之间。它发出
战争清晰的气味。它渴望
万物多余的核心。从万物中吸取
圆滑的拒绝。可是看，灰色的日子：
我们由此飞走。如果在先知的沉默中
留下轮廓，那就折返。谁怀疑这是真的？

Illustration

I

A novice was sitting on a cornice

High over the city. Angels

Combined their prayers with those

Of the police, begging her to come off it.

One lady promised to be her friend.

"I do not want a friend," she said.

A mother offered her some nylons

Stripped from her very legs. Others brought

Little offerings of fruit and candy,

The blind man all his flowers. If any

Could be called successful, these were,

For that the scene should be a ceremony

Was what she wanted. "I desire

Monuments," she said. "I want to move

插　图

1
一个见习修女坐在飞檐上
高居于城市之上。天使们

用祷告配合
那些警察，祈求她下来。

一位女士许诺做她的朋友。
"我不需要朋友。"她说。

一位母亲给她一些尼龙袜
是刚从她腿上脱下来的。其他人拿来

水果和糖作为小礼物，
盲人献上他所有的花。

如果有人堪称成功者，这些人便是，
因为她所需要的场面

应该是一场加冕典礼。"我渴望
纪念碑，"她说，"我要象征性地

Figuratively, as waves caress

The thoughtless shore. You people I know

Will offer me every good thing

I do not want. But please remember

I died accepting them." With that, the wind

Unpinned her bulky robes, and naked

As a roc's egg, she drifted softly downward

Out of the angels' tenderness and the minds of men.

II

Much that is beautiful must be discarded

So that we may resemble a taller

Impression of ourselves. Moths climb in the flame,

Alas, that wish only to be the flame:

They do not lessen our stature

We twinkle under the weight

Of indiscretions. But how could we tell

移动,像波浪爱抚着
淡漠的岸。我知道你们这些人

会为我提供我不需要的
所有好处。但请记住

接受了它们我就会死掉。"随着这些话
风吹掉了她笨重的长袍,使她赤裸

像一只大鹏的卵,柔软地滚下来
从天使的温柔与男人的心灵中消失。

2
必须抛弃大部分的美,我们
才能配得上,自我更高的

印象。蛾子在火焰中攀登,
唉,仅仅是希望成为火焰:

它们不会减少我们的身高。
我们在轻率的重压下

闪耀。但我们如何能够说出

That of the truth we know, she was

The somber vestment? For that night, rockets sighed

Elegantly over the city, and there was feasting:

There is so much in that moment!

So many attitudes toward that flame,

We might have soared from earth, watching her glide

Aloft, in her peplum of bright leaves.

But she, of course, was only an effigy

Of indifference, a miracle

Not meant for us, as the leaves are not

Winter's because it is the end.

我们知道的真相，她是

阴森的法衣？为那个夜晚，火箭
在城市上空优雅地叹息，城市在盛宴：

那时刻如此辉煌！
关于火焰有如此多不同的态度，

我们应该从地上升腾，看着她
在半空滑翔，穿着明丽的树叶裙。

当然，她只是一幅冷漠的
肖像，一个奇迹

并非为我们而显现，就像树叶
不属于冬天，因为这就是终结。

Some Trees

These are amazing: each
Joining a neighbor, as though speech
Were a still performance.
Arranging by chance

To meet as far this morning
From the world as agreeing
With it, you and I
Are suddenly what the trees try

To tell us we are:
That their merely being there
Means something; that soon
We may touch, love, explain.

And glad not to have invented
Such comeliness, we are surrounded:
A silence already filled with noises,
A canvas on which emerges

A chorus of smiles, a winter morning.
Placed in a puzzling light, and moving,
Our days put on such reticence
These accents seem their own defense.

一些树

这些树令人惊奇:每一棵
都与邻树相连,似乎言语
是一次静止的表演。
偶然做出这样的安排

今晨我们相会
远离这个世界,似乎
心有默契,你和我
突然变成这些树

想告诉我们的那个样子:
仅仅它们在这里的存在
就有某种意味;不久
我们就会触摸,相爱,解释。

高兴的是我们从未发明
这样的美,我们被包围:
一种寂静已充满喧嚣,
一幅油画,里面涌出

一支微笑的合唱曲,一个冬天的早晨。
安置在令人迷惑的光中,移动,
我们的岁月裹在这样的沉默中
似乎用这些话音就能自卫。

The Painter

Sitting between the sea and the buildings
He enjoyed painting the sea's portrait.
But just as children imagine a prayer
Is merely silence, he expected his subject
To rush up the sand, and, seizing a brush,
Plaster its own portrait on the canvas.

So there was never any paint on his canvas
Until the people who lived in the buildings
Put him to work: "Try using the brush
As a means to an end. Select, for a portrait,
Something less angry and large, and more subject
To a painter's moods, or, perhaps, to a prayer."

How could he explain to them his prayer
That nature, not art, might usurp the canvas?
He chose his wife for a new subject,
Making her vast, like ruined buildings,
As if, forgetting itself, the portrait
Had expressed itself without a brush.

画　家

坐在大海与楼群之间
他愉快地描绘大海的画像。
但正如孩子们将祈祷
仅仅想象为静默,他希望他的主题
冲上沙滩,抓起画笔,
在画布上涂抹出自己的形象。

于是他的画布上什么也没有出现
直到住在楼中的人们
催促他开始工作:"试着把画笔
当作达到目的的手段。为一幅画像,选择一个
不太强烈也不太庞大但在一位画家
或一个祈祷者的心头常出现的主题。"

他怎样向他们解释,他祈求的
是自然而不是艺术,来占领他的画布?
他把他的妻子当成一个新主题,
把她画得很大,像倒塌的楼群,
那画像仿佛已经忘记了自身
不用画笔便把自己表现出来。

Slightly encouraged, he dipped his brush

In the sea, murmuring a heartfelt prayer:

"My soul, when I paint this next portrait

Let it be you who wrecks the canvas."

The news spread like wildfire through the buildings:

He had gone back to the sea for his subject.

Imagine a painter crucified by his subject!

Too exhausted even to lift his brush,

He provoked some artists leaning from the buildings

To malicious mirth: "We haven't a prayer

Now, of putting ourselves on canvas,

Or getting the sea to sit for a portrait!"

Others declared it a self-portrait.

Finally all indications of a subject

Began to fade, leaving the canvas

Perfectly white. He put down the brush.

At once a howl, that was also a prayer,

Arose from the overcrowded buildings.

They tossed him, the portrait, from the tallest of the buildings;

And the sea devoured the canvas and the brush

As though his subject had decided to remain a prayer.

稍感鼓舞，他把画笔浸入
海中，喃喃念诵一个由衷的祈祷：
"我的灵魂，当我画下一张画像时
愿那毁坏我的画布的就是你。"
这消息像野火在楼群间蔓延：
为了找主题，他已经回到大海。

想一想一个画家被他的主题所折磨，
精疲力竭甚至举不起他的画笔
他引起楼上探身观望的艺术家
不怀好意的嬉笑："我们可没有祈祷
把我们自己画到画布上去
或者让大海坐下来等待被画成肖像！"

其他人宣称那是一幅自画像。
最后所有标志一个主题的东西
都开始消失，画面上只留下
完全的空白。他放下画笔。
突然一声嚎叫，那也是一种祈祷，
从挤满了人的大楼升起。

他们从大楼的最高处，把他和画像抛起；
而大海吞没了他的画布和画笔
仿佛他的主题已经决定继续保持这个祈求。

And You Know

The girls, protected by gold wire from the gaze
Of the onrushing students, live in an atmosphere of vacuum
In the old schoolhouse covered with nasturtiums.
At night, comets, shootings stars, twirling planets,
Suns, bits of illuminated pumice, and spooks hang over the old place;
The atmosphere is breathless. Some find the summer light
Nauseous and damp, but there are those
Who are charmed by it, going out into the morning.
We must rest here, for this is where the teacher comes.
On his desk stands a vase of tears.
A quiet feeling pervades the playroom. His voice clears
Through the interminable afternoon: "I was a child once
Under the spangled sun. Now I do what must be done.
I teach reading and writing and flaming arithmetic. Those
In my home come to me anxiously at night, asking how it goes.
My door is always open. I never lie, and the great heat warms me."

His door is always open, the fond schoolmaster!
We ought to imitate him in our lives,
For as a man lives, he dies. To pass away
In the afternoon, on the vast vapid bank
You think is coming to crown you with hollyhocks and lilacs, or in
    gold at the opera,
Requires that one shall have lived so much! And not merely

而你知道

少女们,由金色的铁丝网保护着
避开汹涌的学生们的注视,她们住在真空中
在刷成橙黄色的老校舍中。
夜晚,彗星,闪射的流星,旋转的行星,
太阳们,明亮的浮石碎片,以及幽灵悬挂在老地方的上空;
空中没有一丝微风。有人发现夏天的光
潮湿而令人恶心,但仍有
被它迷住的人,早上出门。
我们必须停在这里,因为那教师要到这里来。
在他的桌子上站着一花瓶的眼泪。
一种安宁感弥漫在游戏室中。他的声音清晰地
穿过漫长的下午:"我曾是一个孩子
站在闪闪发光的太阳下。现在我做我必须做的。
我教阅读写作和讨厌的算术。那些人
晚上焦虑地来到我家,询问情况如何。
我的门一直开着。我从不撒谎,伟大的激情温暖着我。"

他的门一直开着,这温柔的校长!
我们应该在自己的生活中模仿他,
因为他作为男人活着,死去。离开
下午,在巨大单调的行列中

Asking questions and giving answers, but grandly sitting,

Like a great rock, through many years.

It is the erratic path of time we trace

On the globe, with moist fingertip, and surely, the globe stops;

We are pointing to England, to Africa, to Nigeria;

And we shall visit these places, you and I, and other places,

Including heavenly Naples, queen of the sea, where I shall be king and you will be queen,

And all the places around Naples.

So the good old teacher is right, to stop with his finger on Naples, gazing out into the mild December afternoon

As his star pupil enters the classroom in that elaborate black and yellow creation.

He is thinking of her flounces, and is caught in them as if they were made of iron, they will crush him to death!

Goodbye, old teacher, we must travel on, not to a better land, perhaps,

But to the England of the sonnets, Paris, Colombia, and Switzerland

And all the places with names, that we wish to visit—

Strasbourg, Albania,

The coast of Holland, Madrid, Singapore, Naples, Salonika, Liberia, and Turkey.

So we leave you behind with her of the black and yellow flounces.

You were always a good friend, but a special one.

Now as we brush through the clinging leaves we seem to hear you crying;

You want us to come back, but it is too late to come back, isn't it?

It is too late to go to the places with the names (what were they,

你以为蜀葵和丁香要为你加冕，或者在歌剧中穿着金色衣服，
要求那个活得这么长久的人！并且不仅仅
提出问题，回答，而是庄严地坐着，
像巨大的岩石，历经许多岁月。
在这星球上我们遵循的
是游移不定的道路，用潮湿的指尖，而星球肯定已经停止；
我们正指向英格兰，非洲，尼日利亚；
我们将访问这些地方，你和我，还有其他地方，
包括神圣的那不勒斯，海的女王，我将在那里称王而你是王后，
以及所有那不勒斯周围的地方。
所以善良的老教师是对的，他的手指停在那不勒斯，
凝视着外面十二月温暖的下午
当他杰出的小学生穿着精心制作的黑黄相间的衣服进入教室。
他正在琢磨她裙子的荷叶边，并为之吸引，
仿佛它们是铁做的，它们将把他碾死！
再见，老教师，我们必须继续旅行，
也许，不是朝向一片更美好的土地，
而是去十四行诗的英格兰、巴黎、哥伦比亚和瑞士
以及所有有名字的地方，我们盼望去那里旅行——
斯特拉斯堡、阿尔巴尼亚、荷兰海岸，
马德里、新加坡、那不勒斯、萨洛尼卡、利比亚和土耳其。
于是我们把你留下，留给她黑黄相间的荷叶裙边。
你一直是个好朋友，但是十分特殊。
现在当我们掠过悬挂的叶子，我们似乎听见了你的叫喊；

anyway? just names).
It is too late to go anywhere but to the nearest star, that one, that
    hangs just over the hill, beckoning
Like a hand of which the arm is not visible. Goodbye, Father!
    Goodbye, pupils. Goodbye, my master and my dame.
We fly to the nearest star, whether it be red like a furnace, or yellow,
And we carry your lessons in our hearts (the lessons and our hearts
    are the same)
Out of the humid classroom, into the forever. Goodbye, Old Dog
    Tray.

And so they have left us feeling tired and old.
They never cared for school anyway.
And they have left us with the things pinned on the bulletin board,
And the night, the endless, muggy night that is invading our school.

你要我们回来,可是已经太晚了,不是吗?

去有名字的地方已经太晚了(它们是什么?只是名字)。

去任何地方都已经太晚,除了最近的星星,

那一颗星星,就挂在山冈上,召唤我们

像一只看不见的手。再见,父亲!再见,

小学生们。再见,我的主人和我的夫人。

我们飞往最近的星星,无论它红得像一只火炉,还是黄色的,

我们在心中把你的课程(那课程和我们的心是一体的)

带出潮湿的教室,带入永恒。再见,老狗伴。

于是他们就这样离开又老又疲倦的我们。

他们从不在乎学校。

他们把钉在布告板上的东西留给我们,

而夜晚,无尽闷热的夜晚正侵入我们的学校。

He

He cuts down the lakes so they appear straight

He smiles at his feet in their tired mules.

He turns up the music much louder.

He takes down the vaseline from the pantry shelf.

He is the capricious smile behind the colored bottles.

He eats not lest the poor want some.

He breathes of attitudes the piney altitudes.

He indeed is the White Cliffs of Dover.

He knows that his neck is frozen.

He snorts in the vale of dim wolves.

He writes to say, "If ever you visit this island,

He'll grow you back to your childhood.

"He is the liar behind the hedge

He grew one morning out of candor.

He is his own consolation prize.

He has had his eye on you from the beginning."

He hears the weak cut down with a smile.

他

他切下湖泊于是湖泊径直出现
他向拖鞋中疲倦的脚微笑。
他把音乐开得更响。
他从餐具架上取下凡士林。

他是彩色瓶子后变幻的微笑。
他吃,不担心穷人向他讨要。
他摆出松树那样的高姿态。
他的行为是多佛的白色峭壁。

他知道他的脖子冻僵了。
他在幽暗的狼谷中哼鼻子。
他写下,"如果你访问过这座岛,
他会使你回到童年。

他是树篱后的说谎者
他从真诚中培养出一个早晨。
他是他自己的安慰奖。
他从一开始就盯住了你。"

他听到虚弱的人被一个微笑砍倒。

He waltzes tragically on the spitting housetops.

He is never near. What you need

He cancels with the air of one making a salad.

He is always the last to know.

He is strength you once said was your bonnet.

He has appeared in "Carmen."

He is after us. If you decide

He is important, it will get you nowhere.

He is the source of much bitter reflection.

He used to be pretty for a rat.

He is now over-proud of his Etruscan appearance.

He walks in his sleep into your life.

He is worth knowing only for the children

He has reared as savages in Utah.

He helps his mother take in the clothes-line.

He is unforgettable as a shooting star.

He is known as "Liverlips."

He will tell you he has had a bad time of it.

He will try to pretend his pressagent is a temptress.

他在喷火的屋顶上悲惨地跳华尔兹。
他从不在附近。你需要的东西
他用一个人做沙拉的空气把它们删掉。

他总是最后一个知道。
他是你曾经称为呢帽的力量。
他已经在"卡门"中出现。
他模仿你。如果你认为

他重要,这会使你无处容身。
他是更苦涩的影像的来源。
他习惯于美化一只老鼠。
他现在为他伊特鲁里亚人的外表而骄傲。

他在他的睡眠中走进你的生活。
他只配让孩子们知道。
他在犹他州被当做野蛮人饲养。
他帮助他母亲接受晾衣绳。

他作为明星不能被忘记。
他以"边缘人"而闻名。
他会告诉你他有过艰难的日子。
他会试着把他的发表欲伪装成一个妖妇。

He looks terrible on the stairs.

He cuts himself on what he eats.

He was last seen flying to New York.

He was handing out cards which read:

"He wears a question in his left eye.

He dislikes the police but will associate with them.

He will demand something not on the menu.

He is invisible to the eyes of beauty and culture.

"He prevented the murder of Mistinguett in Mexico.

He has a knack for abortions. If you see

He is following you, forget him immediately:

He is dangerous even though asleep and unarmed."

他恐惧地注视着楼梯。

他不再吃东西。

最后有人看见他飞去了纽约。

他举起写着这样字句的卡片：

"他的左眼中呈现出一个问题。

他不喜欢警察但将与他们联合起来。

他将点一道菜单上没有的菜。

他是美与文化之眼所看不见的。

他阻止了墨西哥米斯廷盖特的谋杀。

他有堕胎的本领。如果你看见

他跟着你，马上把他忘掉：

他很危险，即便睡着时手无寸铁。"

A Long Novel

What will his crimes become, now that her hands

Have gone to sleep? He gathers deeds

In the pure air, the agent

Of their factual excesses. He laughs as she inhales.

If it could have ended before

It began—the sorrow, the snow

Dropping, dropping its fine regrets.

The myrtle dries about his lavish brow.

He stands quieter than the day, a breath

In which all evils are one.

He is the purest air. But her patience,

The imperative Become, trembles

Where hands have been before. In the foul air

Each snowflake seems a Piranesi

一部长篇小说

他的罪行会变成什么,既然她的手
已坠入睡眠?他收集事迹

在纯净的空气中,它们实际上
过剩的媒介。她一吸气他就笑。

如果它在开始之前
便已结束——这悲哀,这雪

坠下,坠下它美丽的遗憾。
爱神木在他慷慨的眉毛边干燥。

他比日子还要宁静地站立,一种呼吸
在其中所有的罪都是同一种罪。

他是最纯净的空气。但她的耐心,
必不可少。变得颤抖,

从前双手在那里。在发臭的空气中
每片雪花都仿佛一个皮拉内西

Dropping in the past; his words are heavy

With their final meaning. Milady! Mimosa! So the end

Was the same: the discharge of spittle

Into frozen air. Except that, in a new

Humorous landscape, without music,

Written by music, he knew he was a saint,

While she touched all goodness

As golden hair, knowing its goodness

Impossible, and waking and waking

As it grew in the eyes of the beloved.

在过去中坠落；他的话
因最终的含义而沉重。夫人！含羞草！所以

结局是一样的：不负责的唾沫
喷入冻结的空气。除了那个，在一片

滑稽的新风景中，没有音乐，
用音乐书写，他知道他是个圣人，

当她触摸所有的善
像触摸金发，知道它的善

是不可能的，醒来，醒来
当它在爱人的眼中生长。

The Pied Piper

Under the day's crust a half-eaten child
And further sores which eyesight shall reveal
And they live. But what of dark elders
Whose touch at nightfall must now be
To keep their promise? Misery
Starches the host's one bed, his hand
Falls like an axe on her curls:
"Come in, come in! Better that the winter
Blaze unseen, than we two sleep apart!"

Who in old age will often part
From single sleep at the murmur
Of acerb revels under the hill;
Whose children couple as the earth crumbles
In vanity forever going down
A sunlit road, for his love was strongest
Who never loved them at all, and his notes
Most civil, laughing not to return.

花衣魔笛手

日子的硬壳下面，一个被吃掉一半的孩子
以及眼睛会看透的更深的痛苦
他们活着。可是什么样阴郁的老人
他们入夜的触摸现在必须
要信守承诺？悲惨
给主人的一张床上浆，他的手
像一把斧子落在她的鬓发上：
"进来，进来！冬天无形的燃烧
胜过了我们两个分开睡！"

在古代谁会经常告别
单独一个人的睡眠，为了
山脚下苦涩的狂欢的低语；
谁的孩子们成双结对，当大地崩溃
徒劳地永远走在
一条阳光照亮的路上，因为他的爱最为强烈
谁从未爱过他们，他的音符
最为文雅，笑着不再返回。

Le Livre Est Sur La Table

I

All beauty, resonance, integrity,

Exist by deprivation or logic

Of strange position. This being so,

We can only imagine a world in which a woman

Walks and wears her hair and knows

All that she does not know. Yet we know

What her breasts are. And we give fullness

To the dream. The table supports the book,

The plume leaps in the hand. But what

Dismal scene is this? The old man pouting

At a black cloud, the woman gone

Into the house, from which the wailing starts?

II

The young man places a bird-house

Against the blue sea. He walks away

And it remains. Now other

生活在桌面上

1
所有的美,回声,正直,
都凭借匮乏或陌生立场的
逻辑而存在。确实如此,

我们只能想象一个这样的世界
一个女人在其中行走,披着头发,知道
她不知道的一切。而我们知道

她的乳房是什么。我们使梦
圆满。桌子支撑着书籍,
羽毛在掌中跳跃。可是

这是怎样凄凉的景象?老人
因一朵黑云而不快,女人回到
屋中,开始在里面恸哭?

2
年轻人把一只鸟笼
放在大海边。他走开
鸟笼留了下来。现在

Men appear, but they live in boxes.

The sea protects them like a wall.

The gods worship a line-drawing

Of a woman, in the shadow of the sea

Which goes on writing. Are there

Collisions, communications on the shore

Or did all secrets vanish when

The woman left? Is the bird mentioned

In the waves' minutes, or did the land advance?

其他人出现，可他们住在盒子里。
海像一堵墙保护着他们。
众神崇拜一个女人画下的

一条线，它在海的阴影中
继续延伸。岸上
有碰撞和交流吗

还是当那女人离去，所有的秘密
都告消失？是波浪提到了鸟
还是陆地在前进？

From
THE TENNIS COURT OATH
网球场宣言
(1962)

Thoughts of a Young Girl

"It is such a beautiful day I had to write you a letter

From the tower, and to show I'm not mad:

I only slipped on the cake of soap of the air

And drowned in the bathtub of the world.

You were too good to cry much over me.

And now I let you go. Signed, The Dwarf."

I passed by late in the afternoon

And the smile still played about her lips

As it has for centuries. She always knows

How to be utterly delightful. Oh my daughter,

My sweetheart, daughter of my late employer, princess,

May you not be long on the way!

一个年轻姑娘的想法

"这是多么美丽的一天我应该从塔里
给你写封信,来表明我并不疯:
我只是滑倒在空气肥皂的蛋糕上
并在世界的澡盆中溺了水。
你善良得无法为我过分地哭泣。
现在我让你走开。签名,侏儒。"

下午的晚些时候我经过那里
微笑依然装扮在她的唇边
仿佛已经几个世纪。她始终知道
怎样彻底地快乐。哦!我的女儿,
我的甜心,我逝去的雇主的女儿,公主,
但愿你不会在路上那么久!

"How Much Longer Will I Be Able to Inhabit the Divine Sepulcher..."

How much longer will I be able to inhabit the divine sepulcher

Of life, my great love? Do dolphins plunge bottomward

To find the light? Or is it rock

That is searched? Unrelentingly? Hull. And if some day

Men with orange shovels come to break open the rock

Which encases me, what about the light that comes in then?

What about the smell of the light?

What about the moss?

In pilgrim times he wounded me

Since then I only lie

My bed of light is a furnace choking me

With hell (and sometimes I hear salt water dripping).

I mean it—because I'm one of the few

To have held my breath under the house. I'll trade

One red sucker for two blue ones. I'm

Named Tom. The

Light bounces off mossy rocks down to me

"还要多久我才能继承
那神圣的坟墓……"

还要多久我才能继承生活那神圣的
坟墓,我伟大的爱?海豚投向水底
是去寻找光吗?或者寻找的
是岩石?坚定地?哈。如果有一天

带着橘色铁锹的男人到来打碎了封闭我的
岩石,随后进入的光会怎么样?
光的气味怎么样?
苔藓怎么样?

在朝圣者的时代他伤害了我
自那时起我只好躺着
我光的床榻是一座用地狱
窒息我的熔炉(有时我听见咸涩的水在滴落)。

我是故意的——因为我是少数中的一个
在房屋下面扼住呼吸的人。我将
用一个红色吸盘交换两个蓝色的。我
名叫汤姆。光

从生苔的岩石上跳向我

In this glen (the neat villa! which

When he'd had he would not had he of

And jests under the smarting of privet

Which on hot spring nights perfumes the empty rooms

With the smell of sperm flushed down toilets

On hot summer afternoons within sight of the sea.

If you knew why then professor) reads

To his friends: Drink to me only with

And the reader is carried away

By a great shadow under the sea.

Behind the steering wheel

The boy took out his own forehead.

His girlfriend's head was a green bag

Of narcissus stems. "OK you win

But meet me anyway at Cohen's Drug Store

In 22 minutes." What a marvel is ancient man!

Under the tulip roots he has figured out a way to be a religious animal

And would be a mathematician. But where in unsuitable heaven

Can he get the heat that will make him grow?

在这幽谷中（整洁的别墅！
当他拥有他不愿拥有的
在剧痛的水蜡树下讲笑话

在灼热的春夜空旷的房间弥漫着
厕所里泛滥而下的精液的气味
在灼热的夏日午后可以看见大海。
教授你是否知道为什么）向他的朋友

朗读：只和我一同饮酒
读者被带走了
被海下面一个巨大的影子
在舵轮后

男孩挪开他的前额。
他的女友的头是一袋绿色的
水仙花梗。"好吧你赢了
但无论如何二十二分钟后

在科亨的药店见。"古人是个什么样的奇迹！
在郁金香根下他画出一条成为虔诚动物的道路
并且将成为一个数学家。但在何处不相称的天堂
他能获得使他成长的热量？

For he needs something or will forever remain a dwarf,

Though a perfect one, and possessing a normal-sized brain

But he has got to be released by giants from things.

And as the plant grows older it realizes it will never be a tree,

Will probably always be haunted by a bee

And cultivates stupid impressions

So as not to become part of the dirt. The dirt

Is mounting like a sea. And we say goodbye

Shaking hands in front of the crashing of the waves

That give our words lonesomeness, and make these flabby hands seem ours—

Hands that are always writing things

On mirrors for people to see later—

Do you want them to water

Plant, tear listlessly among the exchangeable ivy—

Carrying food to mouth, touching genitals—

But no doubt you have understood

It all now and I am a fool. It remains

For me to get better, and to understand you so

Like a chair-sized man. Boots

因为他需要某种东西否则他将永远是个侏儒,
虽然是完整的一个人,拥有正常大小的脑袋
但必须由巨人们来使他挣脱事物。
当植物变老认识到它永远不会成为一棵树,

也许将始终被一只蜜蜂纠缠
并收获愚蠢的印象
为了不变成泥土的一部分。泥土
像海一样上升。我们说再见

在飞溅的波浪前握手
给我们的词语赋予了孤寂,使这些无力的手
显得是我们的——
那总是在镜子上写下事物
给后来者看的手——

你要它们去浇灌植物,
在可更换的常春藤中没精打采地撕扯——
把食物拿到嘴边,抚摸生殖器——
无疑现在你已经全然明白了它

而我是个傻瓜。它存留
为了让我变好,并这样理解你
像一个椅子大小的人。靴子声

Were heard on the floor above. In the garden the sunlight was still purple

But what buzzed in it had changed slightly

But not forever...but casting its shadow

On sticks, and looking around for an opening in the air, was quite as

    if it had never refused to exist differently. Guys

In the yard handled the belt he had made

Stars

Painted the garage roof crimson and black

He is not a man

Who can read these signs . . . his bones were stays . . .

And even refused to live

In a world and refunded the hiss

Of all that exists terribly near us

Like you, my love, and light.

For what is obedience but the air around us

To the house? For which the federal men came

In a minute after the sidewalk

Had taken you home? ("Latin . . . blossom . . .")

After which you led me to water

在上面的地板上传来。花园里阳光仍是紫色的

但是在里面嗡鸣的已经微微改变
不是永远……只是把它的影子投掷在
树枝上，在周围的空气中寻找空隙，仿佛
它从未拒绝不同的存在。人们
在院子里摆弄他做的皮带

群星
把车库顶涂成深红色和黑色
他不是一个
能阅读这些标志的人……他的骨头是支柱……

甚至拒绝
在世上生活，偿还
所有在我们附近存在的可怕的嘘声
像你一样，我的爱，和光。

为什么只有我们周围的空气
服从房屋？为什么那些联邦人员
在人行道把你带回家一分钟后
到来？（"拉丁语……开花……"）

在那之后你领我去水边

And bade me drink, which I did, owing to your kindness.

You would not let me out for two days and three nights,

Bringing me books bound in wild thyme and scented wild grasses

As if reading had any interest for me, you . . .

Now you are laughing.

Darkness interrupts my story.

Turn on the light.

Meanwhile what am I going to do?

I am growing up again, in school, the crisis will be very soon.

And you twist the darkness in your fingers, you

Who are slightly older . . .

Who are you, anyway?

And it is the color of sand,

The darkness, as it sifts through your hand

Because what does anything mean,

The ivy and the sand? That boat

Pulled up on the shore? Am I wonder,

Strategically, and in the light

Of the long sepulcher that hid death and hides me?

命令我饮水,我做了,归于你的善良。
你不会让我出去过上两天三夜,
带给我百里香捆着的散发野草味的书

仿佛我有兴趣阅读,你……
现在你在笑。
黑暗打断了我的故事。
把灯打开。

这时我打算做什么?
我再次长大,在学校里,难关将近。
你把黑暗绕在指头上,你
只比我大上一点……

无论如何,你是谁?
而这是沙子的颜色,
黑暗,当它穿过你的手筛下
任何事都意味着,

常春藤和沙子?那只船
拖到了岸上?从战略观点看,
我是奇迹吗,在那隐藏起死亡
隐藏起我的长长坟墓的光中?

White Roses

The worst side of it all—

The white sunlight on the polished floor—

Pressed into service,

And then the window closed

And the night ends and begins again.

Her face goes green, her eyes are green,

In the dark corner playing "The Stars and Stripes Forever." I try to describe for you,

But you will not listen, you are like the swan.

No stars are there,

No stripes,

But a blind man's cane poking, however clumsily, into the inmost corners of the house.

Nothing can be harmed! Night and day are beginning again!

So put away the book,

The flowers you were keeping to give someone:

Only the white, tremendous foam of the street has any importance,

The new white flowers that are beginning to shoot up about now.

白玫瑰

它最糟糕的一面——
白色阳光照在擦亮的地板上——
用来应急,
然后窗子关上
夜晚结束并再次开始。
她的脸变绿,她的眼睛是绿的;
在黑暗的角落里奏着"星条旗永不落"。
我试图为你描述,
但你不会听,你像天鹅。

那里没有星星,
没有条纹,
只有一个老瞎子的藤杖刺戳着,笨拙地,
　　刺入房子最内里的角落。
没有什么能被伤害!夜与昼正在再次开始!
所以把书放下,
也放下你为某人留下来的花:
只有白色的,街道巨大的泡沫拥有重要性,
白色的新花此刻正开始发芽。

Our Youth

Of bricks... Who built it? Like some crazy balloon
When love leans on us
Its nights... The velvety pavement sticks to our feet.
The dead puppies turn us back on love.

Where we are. Sometimes
The brick arches led to a room like a bubble, that broke when you entered it
And sometimes to a fallen leaf.
We got crazy with emotion, showing how much we knew.

The Arabs took us. We knew
The dead horses. We were discovering coffee,
How it is to be drunk hot, with bare feet
In Canada. And the immortal music of Chopin

Which we had been discovering for several months
Since we were fourteen years old. And coffee grounds,
And the wonder of hands, and the wonder of the day
When the child discovers her first dead hand.

Do you know it? Hasn't she
Observed you too? Haven't you been observed to her?
My, haven't the flowers been? Is the evil

我们的青春

(我们)砖块的青春……谁建造了它?像一些疯狂的气球
当爱倾斜在我们之上
它的黑夜……天鹅绒般的人行道贴着我们的脚。
死去的幼犬出于爱而回到我们这里。

我们在哪儿。有时
砖的拱廊通向一间气泡般的屋子,当你进入时破碎了
而有时则是一片落叶。
我们因激情而疯癫,这表明我们知道得多么多。

阿拉伯人带走了我们。我们了解
那些死马。我们发现,
怎样热着喝咖啡,在加拿大
赤脚。而肖邦永恒的乐曲

我们已发现几个月了
因为我们十四岁。咖啡粉,
手的奇迹,和日子的奇迹
当那孩子发现了她最早无生命的手。

你知道它吗?她没有
谈论过你吗?你不是一直被谈论着吗?
我的,不一直是花吗?罪

In't? What window? What did you say there?

Heh? Eh? Our youth is dead.
From the minute we discover it with eyes closed
Advancing into mountain light.
Ouch. . . You will never have that young boy,

That boy with the monocle
Could have been your father
He is passing by. No, that other one,
Upstairs. He is the one who wanted to see you.

He is dead. Green and yellow handkerchiefs cover him.
Perhaps he will never rot, I see
That my clothes are dry. I will go.
The naked girl crosses the street.

Blue hampers. . . Explosions,
Ice. . . The ridiculous
Vases of porphyry. All that our youth
Can't use, that it was created for.

It's true we have not avoided our destiny
By weeding out the old people.
Our faces have filled with smoke. We escape
Down the cloud ladder, but the problem has not been solved.

是在它里面吗？什么窗户？你在那里说什么？

嗨？哦？我们的青春死了。
从我们用闭上的眼睛发现它的时候起
便在向山光之中前进。
哎呀……你将再不能拥有那个年轻的男孩，

那戴着单眼镜的男孩
可能是你的父亲
他正在经过。不，那另一个
在楼上。他要见你。

他死了。黄绿色的手帕盖住他。
也许他永不腐烂，我知道
我的衣服是干的。我将走开。
裸体的少女穿过街道。

蓝色的饭盒……爆炸，
冰……可笑的
斑岩花瓶。那一切我们的青春
都不能使用，那为它创造的一切。

我们真的没能避开我们的命运
凭淘汰老人。
我们的脸已填满了烟雾。我们逃下
云梯，可是问题还没有解决。

An Additional Poem

Where then shall hope and fear their objects find?

The harbor cold to the mating ships,

And you have lost as you stand by the balcony

With the forest of the sea calm and gray beneath.

A strong impression torn from the descending light

But night is guilty. You knew the shadow

In the trunk was raving

But as you keep growing hungry you forget.

The distant box is open. A sound of grain

Poured over the floor in some eagerness—we

Rise with the night let out of the box of wind.

一首附加的诗

那么希望和恐惧会在哪里发现它们的目标?
港口冷对成双结对的船只,
你已迷失,你站在阳台边
下面是沉静灰暗的海的森林。
一个强烈的印象从下降的光上剥离
夜是有罪的。你知道影子
正在躯体里咆哮
可随着你的饥饿越来越深,你就忘了。
遥远的盒子打开。谷子的声音
焦急地倾泻在地板上——我们
随同夜晚从风的盒子里升起。

Faust

If only the phantom would stop reappearing!
Business, if you wanted to know, was punk at the opera.
The heroine no longer appeared in *Faust*.
The crowds strolled sadly away. The phantom
Watched them from the roof, not guessing the hungers
That must be stirred before disappointment can begin.

One day as morning was about to begin
A man in brown with a white shirt reappearing
At the bottom of his yellow vest, was talking hungers
With the silver-haired director of the opera.
On the green-carpeted floor no phantom
Appeared, except yellow squares of sunlight, like those in *Faust*.

That night as the musicians for *Faust*
Were about to go on strike, lest darkness begin
In the corridors, and through them the phantom
Glide unobstructed, the vision reappearing
Of blonde Marguerite practicing a new opera
At her window awoke terrible new hungers

浮士德

但愿幽灵不会再次出现!
交易,如果你想知道,无助于歌剧。
女主角不再出现在《浮士德》中。
人群悲哀地漫步走开。幽灵
在屋顶上观察他们,没有猜到渴望
一定会被激起,在开始失望之前。

一天当早晨即将开始
一个穿棕色衣服白衬衫的人再次出现
在他的黄背心底下,和银发的歌剧
导演谈着渴望。
在铺绿地毯的地板上没有幽灵
出现,除了阳光的黄色方块,仿佛在《浮士德》中。

那天晚上乐师准备为《浮士德》
继续演奏,以免黑暗开始
在走廊中,从他们中间穿过的是幽灵
不受阻碍地滑行,幻象再次出现
金发碧眼的玛格丽特演出了一幕新歌剧
她在窗边唤醒了新的可怕的渴望

In the already starving tenor. But hungers

Are just another topic, like the new Faust

Drifting through the tunnels of the opera

(In search of lost old age? For they begin

To notice a twinkle in his eye. It is cold daylight reappearing

At the window behind him, itself a phantom

Window, painted by the phantom

Scene painters, sick of not getting paid, of hungers

For a scene below of tiny, reappearing

Dancers, with a sandbag falling like a note in *Faust*

Through purple air. And the spectators begin

To understand the bleeding tenor star of the opera.)

That night the opera

Was crowded to the rafters. The phantom

Took twenty-nine curtain calls. "Begin!

Begin!" In the wings the tenor hungers

For the heroine's convulsive kiss, and Faust

Moves forward, no longer young, reappearing

And reappearing for the last time. The opera

Faust would no longer need its phantom.

On the bare, sunlit stage the hungers could begin.

男高音已经在挨饿。但是渴望
只是另一个主题,像新的《浮士德》
飘过隧道般的歌剧院
(寻找失去的旧时代?因为他们开始
注意到他的一只眼睛在闪光。寒冷的日光再次出现
在他身后的窗户上,它自身就是一个幽灵

窗户,被幽灵
的风景画家涂抹,倦于得不到报偿,倦于渴望
下面小小的景象,正在再次出现
舞者,像一个音符带着沙袋倒在《浮士德》中
穿过紫色的空气。而观众开始
理解流血的男高音的歌剧。)

那天晚上歌剧院
拥挤异常。幽灵
二十九次谢幕。"开始!
开始!"男高音在侧幕中渴望
女主角痉挛的吻,而浮士德
向前,不再年轻,再次出现

最后一次出现。歌剧
《浮士德》将不再需要它的幽灵。
在光秃,阳光照亮的舞台上渴望可以开始了。

A Last World

These wonderful things
Were planted on the surface of a round mind that was to become our present time.
The mark of things belongs to someone
But if that somebody was wise
Then the whole of things might be different
From what it was thought to be in the beginning, before an angel bandaged the field glasses.
Then one could say nothing hear nothing
Of what the great time spoke to its divisors.
All borders between men were closed.
Now all is different without having changed
As though one were to pass through the same street at different times
And nothing that is old can prefer the new.
An enormous merit has been placed on the head of all things
Which, bowing down, arrive near the region of their feet
So that the earth-stone has stared at them in memory at the approach of an error.
Still it is not too late for these things to die
Provided that an anemone will grab them and rush them to the wildest heaven.
But having plucked oneself, who could live in the sunlight?
And the truth is cold, as a giant's knee
Will seem cold.

最后的世界

这些美妙的事物

被种在一个将要变成我们现时代的圆形心灵表面。

万物的标记属于某人

但如果那人足够聪明

一切便会不同于

开始时认为的样子,在一个天使把望远镜用绷带包扎起来之前。

那时,一个人就可以什么都不说

也听不见伟大时代对它的因子说了什么。

男人之间的所有边境都被关闭了。

现在一切不同了,但又没有改变

仿佛一个人要在不同的时刻穿过同一街道

没有任何旧事物能够喜欢新事物。

一项重大价值已落在万物头上

它们鞠躬,几乎低到脚面

以至于土石在记忆中凝视它们,当一个错误即将发生。

这些事物现在去死还不太晚

假如一枝银莲花能抓住它们,把它们抛到最荒凉的天堂。

但是把自己拔出来,谁能在阳光中活下去?

真理是寒冷的,像巨人的膝盖

将显得寒冷。

Yet having once played with tawny truth
Having once looked at a cold mullet on a plate on a table supported
    by the weight of the inconstant universe
He wished to go far away from himself.
There were no baskets in those jovial pine-tree forests, and the waves
    pushed without whitecaps
In that foam where he wished to be.

Man is never without woman, the neuter sex
Casting up her equations, looks to her lord for loving kindness
For man smiles never at woman.
In the forests a night landslide could disclose that she smiled.
Guns were fired to discourage dogs into the interior
But woman—never. She is completely out of this world.
She climbs a tree to see if he is coming
Sunlight breaks at the edges of the wet lakes
And she is happy, if free
For the power he forces down at her like a storm of lightning.

Once a happy old man
One can never change the core of things, and light burns you the
    harder for it.
Glad of the changes already and if there are more it will never be
    you that minds
Since it will not be you to be changed, but in the evening in the severe
    lamplight doubts come
From many scattered distances, and do not come too near.
As it falls along the house, your treasure

而你曾经玩弄茶色的真理

曾经注视由不连续的宇宙的重量支撑的桌子上的一个盘子里的
　　一条冷鲻鱼

他希望远离自己。

那些快乐的松林中没有篮子,没有白帽浪的浪花

在他希望存在的泡沫中涌动。

男人永远不能没有女人,中性

计算她的方程式,向她的主人寻求爱的温存

因为男人从不对女人微笑。

林中一次夜晚的滑坡就能泄露她的微笑。

开枪是为了吓唬进来的狗

但女人——永远不是这样。她完全超出了这个世界。

她爬上一棵树去看他来了没有

阳光在潮湿的湖边破碎

她是幸福的,如果像一场雷电

摆脱了他施加给她的权力。

曾有一个幸福的老人

一个人永不能改变事物的核,光为了它更猛烈地燃烧你。

悦于已有的变化而如果有更多的变化在乎的也永远不是你

既然将被改变的不是你,但在傍晚严厉的灯光中疑虑

从许多四散的远方而来,并不靠得太近。

当它沿房屋坠落,你珍爱的人

Cries to the other men; the darkness will have none of you, and you
    are folded into it like mint into the sound of haying.
It was ninety-five years ago that you strolled in the serene little port;
    under an enormous cornice six boys in black slowly stood.
Six frock coats today, six black fungi tomorrow,
And the day after tomorrow—but the day after tomorrow itself is
    blackening dust.
You court obsidian pools
And from a tremendous height twilight falls like a stone and hits you.

You who were always in the way
Flower
Are you afraid of trembling like breath

But there is no breath in seriousness; the lake howls for it.
Swiftly sky covers earth, the wrong breast for a child to suck, and
    that,
What have you got there in your hand?
It is a stone

So the passions are divided into tiniest units
And of these many are lost, and those that remain are given at
    nightfall to the uneasy old man
The old man who goes skipping along the roadbed.
In a dumb harvest
Passions are locked away, and states of creation are used instead, that
    is to say synonyms are used.

Honey

对其他男人哭泣；黑暗将与你无关，你被折叠进黑暗中像薄荷
　　折进割干草的声音。
九十五年前你闲逛在宁静的小港口；在一个巨大飞檐下六个穿
　　黑衣的男孩慢慢站住。
今天的六件童装，明日的六只黑色真菌，
而后天——后天本身是变黑的灰尘。
你向黑曜岩池塘献殷勤
微光从高空坠落像一块石头击中你。

你这始终在碍事的人
花
你害怕呼吸般的颤抖吗
但在肃穆中没有呼吸；湖为它怒号。
天空即刻覆盖了大地，给孩子吮的假乳房，还有，
你手里拿着什么？
是一块石头

于是激情被分成最小的单元
丢失了许多，剩下的在日暮时送给了不安的老人
那沿着路基跳跃而行的老人。
在沉默的收获中
激情被锁起来，代之以创造的状态，也就是使用了同义词。

蜂蜜

On the lips of elders is not contenting, so

A firebrand is made. Woman carries it,

She who thought herself good only for bearing children is decked out in the lace of fire

And this is exactly the way she wanted it, the trees coming to place themselves in her

In a rite of torpor, dust.

A bug carries the elixir

Naked men pray the ground and chew it with their hands

The fire lives

Men are nabbed

She her bonnet half off, is sobbing there while the massacre yet continues with a terrific thin energy

A silver blaze calms the darkness.

Rest undisturbed on the dry of the beach

Flower

And night stand suddenly sideways to observe your bones

Vixen

Do men later go home

Because we wanted to travel

Under the kettle of trees

We thought the sky would melt to see us

But to tell the truth the air turned to smoke,

We were forced back onto a foul pillow that was another place.

Or were lost by our comrades

Somewhere between heaven and no place, and were growing smaller.

In another place a mysterious mist shot up like a wall, down which

长者唇上的蜂蜜让人不满足,于是

造一个火把。女人带着它,

认为自己只适合养孩子的她装饰着火的项链

这正是她希望的样子,树木逐渐把自己安置在她内部

在冬眠的仪式中,灰尘。

一只甲虫带着长生不老药

裸体的男人们向土地祈祷,用双手玩味它

火活着

男人们被捉住

软帽半垂的她在啜泣,大屠杀仍在继续,以一种可怕的细弱能量

一片银色火焰使黑暗平静下来。

未受打扰地歇在干燥的海滩上

花

和夜晚突然站在小路上观察你的骨头

泼妇

男人们后来回家了

因为我们要在

林中洼地旅行

我们以为天空看见我们就会融化

可说实话空气变成了烟,

我们被迫退回一个污秽的枕头那是另一个地方。

或是被我们的同志抛弃在

天堂和乌有之乡的中间,变得越来越小。

trickled the tears of our loved ones.

Bananas rotten with their ripeness hung from the leaves, and cakes and jewels covered the sand.

But these were not the best men

But there were moments of the others

Seen through indifference, only bare methods

But we can remember them and so we are saved.

A last world moves on the figures;

They are smaller than when we last saw them caring about them.

The sky is a giant rocking horse

And of the other things death is a new office building filled with modern furniture,

A wise thing, but which has no purpose for us.

Everything is being blown away;

A little horse trots up with a letter in its mouth, which is read with eagerness

As we gallop into the flame.

在另一个地方一阵神秘的雾像墙一样高耸,淌下我们所爱之人
　　的眼泪。
成熟而腐烂的香蕉从叶子上垂下,蛋糕和宝石覆盖了沙子。
但这些不是最好的男人
有些时候其他人
透过冷漠看见的,只是赤裸的手段
我们能够回忆起它们来,于是我们得救了。

一个最后的世界在数字上移动;
它们比我们最后一次看见并为之忧虑时还要小。
天空是一匹巨大摇晃的马
对于其他事物,死亡是一座充满时髦家具的新办公楼,
一件聪明之物,但对我们毫无用处。

一切都被吹走了;
一匹小马嘴里衔着一封信小跑过来,那信被迫不及待地阅读
当我们飞驰进火焰之中。

From *The New Realism*

There was calm rapture in the way she spoke

Perhaps I would get over the way the joke

Always turned against me, in the end.

The bars had been removed from all the windows

There was something quiet in the way the light entered

Her trousseau. Wine fished out of the sea—they hadn't known

We were coming relaxed forever

We stood off the land because if you get too far

From a perfume you can squeeze the life out of it

One seal came into view and then the others

Yellow in the vast sun.

A watchdog performed and they triumphed

The day was bleak—ice had replaced air

The sigh of the children to former music

Supplanting the mutt's yelps.

This was as far as she would go—

A tavern with plants.

Dynamite out over the horizon

And a sequel, and a racket. Dolphins repelling

The sand. Squads of bulldozers

Wrecked the site, and she died laughing

新现实主义

她说话的方式中有一种冷静的狂喜
也许我会结束这种方式,玩笑
最后总是冲着我来。
所有窗上的栅栏都已拆除
光进入她妆奁的样子有某种
宁静意味。酒取自大海——他们不知道
我们永远是轻松而来
我们悬空而立因为如果你离一种香水太远
你可以从生活中去榨取
一只海豹出现了,然后是其他的
在空旷的阳光中发黄。
一条看门狗尽忠职守,而它们却得逞了
日子阴冷——冰取代了空气
孩子们为从前的音乐叹息
取代了杂种狗的吠叫。
这就是她走得最远的地方——
一个有植物的小酒馆。
在地平线上炸开
又炸了一次,然后一片喧闹。海豚厌恶
沙子。一排排推土机
破坏了现场,而她大笑着死去

Because only once does prosperity let you get away

On your doorstep she used to explain

How if the returning merchants in the morning hitched the rim of the van

In the evening one must be very quick to give them the slip.

The judge knocked. The zinnias

Had never looked better—red, yellow, and blue

They were, and the forget-me-nots and dahlias

At least sixty different varieties

As the shade went up

And the ambulance came crashing through the dust

Of the new day, the moon and the sun and the stars,

And the iceberg slowly sank

In the volcano and the sea ran far away

Yellow over the hot sand, green as the green trees.

因为只有一次幸运让你离开

在你的门阶上她经常解释

如果商人们早上回来就像攀住货车的边

傍晚时一个人又多么容易犯错。

一锤定音。百日草

从未这么好看过——红的，黄的，蓝的

它们原本如此，勿忘我和大丽花

至少有六十个不同品种

当树荫上升

救护车碾过新一天的尘土

月亮太阳和星星，

冰山缓缓沉入

火山，而大海远远地展开

在灼热的黄沙上，树木一样葱绿。

From
RIVERS AND MOUNTAINS
山山水水
(1966)

Rivers and Mountains

On the secret map the assassins

Cloistered, the Moon River was marked

Near the eighteen peaks and the city

Of humiliation and defeat—wan ending

Of the trail among dry, papery leaves

Gray-brown quills like thoughts

In the melodious but vast mass of today's

Writing through fields and swamps

Marked, on the map, with little bunches of weeds.

Certainly squirrels lived in the woods

But devastation and dull sleep still

Hung over the land, quelled

The rioters turned out of sleep in the peace of prisons

Singing on marble factory walls

Deaf consolation of minor tunes that pack

The air with heavy invisible rods

Pent in some sand valley from

Which only quiet walking ever instructs.

The bird flew over and

Sat—there was nothing else to do.

Do not mistake its silence for pride or strength

山山水水

在刺客隐居的秘密

地图上,月亮河标在

十八座山峰和耻辱

与失败之城附近——道路

暗淡地终结在干燥的纸一般的落叶中

棕灰色的羽毛像思想

在悦耳的大量当代写作中

穿过地图上用小捆杂草

标出的田野和沼泽。

松鼠当然住在林中

但是破坏和沉闷的睡眠依然

悬挂在陆地之上,镇压着

在监狱的和平中辗转难眠的暴徒

在大理石工厂的墙上唱歌

无人愿听的安慰的小调

用沉重无形的枝条塞满空气

关在某座沙谷中

那里发令的只有宁静的散步。

鸟儿飞过

栖息——此外没什么可做。

不要把它的沉默误认为骄傲或力量

Or the waterfall for a harbor

Full of light boats that is there

Performing for thousands of people

In clothes some with places to go

Or games. Sometimes over the pillar

Of square stones its impact

Makes a light print.

So going around cities

To get to other places you found

It all on paper but the land

Was made of paper processed

To look like ferns, mud or other

Whose sea unrolled its magic

Distances and then rolled them up

Its secret was only a pocket

After all but some corners are darker

Than these moonless nights spent as on a raft

In the seclusion of a melody heard

As though through trees

And you can never ignite their touch

Long but there were homes

Flung far out near the asperities

Of a sharp, rocky pinnacle

或者把瀑布误认为港口

充满了轻盈的船只,在那里

正为成千上万的人表演

有些人穿着衣服要去什么地方

或是去比赛。有时在方形石柱上

它的碰撞

留下轻微的印迹。

就这样绕城而行

为到达其他地方,你发现

那全然是在纸上,而陆地

是用纸做成的,加工成

羊齿植物的样子,泥浆或其他什么

它的海洋展开魔术般的

远方,然后又卷起来

它的秘密仅仅是一只口袋

终归有一些角落

比这些仿佛木筏上度过的无月之夜更黑

在一首仿佛隔着树林

传来的幽幽乐曲中

你无法长久激发它们的作用

但有一些人家

远远抛在一座粗糙尖锐的

岩石峰顶附近

And other collective places

Shadows of vineyards whose wine

Tasted of the forest floor

Fisheries and oyster beds

Tides under the pole

Seminaries of instruction, public

Places for electric light

And the major tax assessment area

Wrinkled on the plan

Of election to public office

Sixty-two years old bath and breakfast

The formal traffic, shadows

To make it not worth joining

After the ox had pulled away the cart.

Your plan was to separate the enemy into two groups

With the razor-edged mountains between.

It worked well on paper

But their camp had grown

To be the mountains and the map

Carefully peeled away and not torn

Was the light, a tender but tough bark

On everything. Fortunately the war was solved

In another way by isolating the two sections

以及其他共同之处

葡萄园的阴影,那里的酒

有森林地表的味道

渔场和牡蛎养殖场

极地的潮汐

训练学院,为电灯而设的

公共场所

以及主要的税收区

在公职竞选计划上

是皱巴巴的

六十二岁的沐浴和早餐

正常的交通,阴影

使它不值得加入

在公牛把大车拖走之后。

你的计划是把敌人分隔成两群

用剃刀般的山峰。

它在纸上进展顺利

但是他们的帐篷长成了

山峰,地图

被小心地剥去,没有撕掉的

是这灯光,万物之上

一层柔韧的树皮。

幸运的是,战争

Of the enemy's navy so that the mainland

Warded away the big floating ships.

Light bounced off the ends

Of the small gray waves to tell

Them in the observatory

About the great drama that was being won

To turn off the machinery

And quietly move among the rustic landscape

Scooping snow off the mountains rinsing

The coarser ones that love had

Slowly risen in the night to overflow

Wetting pillow and petal

Determined to place the letter

On the unassassinated president's desk

So that a stamp could reproduce all this

In detail, down to the last autumn leaf

And the affliction of June ride

Slowly out into the sun-blackened landscape.

以另一种方式解决了,把敌人海军的
两部分隔开,于是,大陆
便挡住了漂浮的大船。
光在灰色细浪的尾部
跳跃,在天文台里
向他们讲述
赢得胜利的伟大戏剧
关掉机器
在纯朴的风景中安静地移动
舀来山峰上的积雪冲洗
更为粗糙的山脉,爱
在夜里缓缓升起,溢出
弄湿枕头和花瓣
决定把信放在
没有被刺杀的总统的桌上
以便一张邮票就能复制这一切
细节,直到秋天最后的叶子
和六月的痛苦
慢慢驶进太阳变黑的风景。

Last Month

No changes of support—only

Patches of gray, here where sunlight fell.

The house seems heavier

Now that they have gone away.

In fact it emptied in record time.

When the flat table used to result

A match recedes, slowly, into the night.

The academy of the future is

Opening its doors and willing

The fruitless sunlight streams into domes,

The chairs piled high with books and papers.

The sedate one is this month's skittish one

Confirming the property that,

A timeless value, has changed hands.

And you could have a new automobile

Ping pong set and garage, but the thief

Stole everything like a miracle.

In his book there was a picture of treason only

And in the garden, cries and colors.

上个月

支撑没有改变——只有
灰色的斑点,在阳光坠落之处。
房子显得更沉重了
既然他们已经离开。
事实上有史以来它就是空的。
当扁平的桌子常常
使一个对手,缓慢地,退入夜晚。
未来的学院
将打开它的门户,希望
徒劳的阳光涌进圆顶,
椅子和书本纸张高高堆在一起。

镇静的是这个月的善变者
证实产权,
一种永恒的价值,已经易手。
而你可以拥有一部新汽车
乒乓球拍和车库,但是小偷
像一个奇迹偷走了一切。
在他的书里只有一幅叛徒的画像
而在花园里,是哭泣和色彩。

If the Birds Knew

It is better this year.

And the clothes they wear

In the gray unweeded sky of our earth

There is no possibility of change

Because all of the true fragments are here.

So I was glad of the fog's

Taking me to you

Undetermined summer thing eaten

Of grief and passage—where you stay.

The wheel is ready to turn again.

When you have gone it will light up,

The shadow of the spokes to drown

Your departure where the summer knells

Speak to grown dawn.

There is after all a kind of promise

To the affair of the waiting weather.

We have learned not to be tired

Among the lanterns of this year of sleep

But someone pays—no transparency

Has ever hardened us before

To long piers of silence, and hedges

如果鸟儿们知道

今年更好一些。

它们穿的衣服

在我们地球灰色的未除草的天空中

没有更换的可能

因为所有真实的片段都在这里。

于是我欣喜于浓雾

把我带给你

莫名的夏天之物吞噬了

悲伤和片段——在你停留之处。

车轮准备再次启动。

当你离开,它将燃亮。

轮辐的影子淹没了

你的离别,夏天的丧钟

向成熟的黎明倾诉。

对于等待着的天气的风流韵事

毕竟有着一种许诺。

我们已学会不要累着

在这一年睡眠的灯笼中间

但有人付出了代价——不是为了

以前使我们为难的透明性

而是为了寂静的长堤,

Of understanding, difficult passing

From one lesson to the next and the coldness

Of the consistency of our lives'

Devotion to immaculate danger.

A leaf would have settled the disturbance

Of the atmosphere, but at that high

Valley's point disbanded

Clouds that rocks smote newly

The person or persons involved

Parading slowly through the sunlit fields

Not only as though the danger did not exist

But as though the birds were in on the secret.

理解的树篱，
从一课向另一课的艰难传递，
以及我们生活的一致性的寒冷
对纯洁的危险的热爱。
一片叶子就会平息大气的
骚动，但在那个高度
山谷顶端驱散了
岩石刚刚打败的云
一个人或一群人卷了进来
缓慢地穿过太阳照亮的田野游行
似乎不仅没有危险
似乎鸟儿也知道了内情。

Into the Dusk-charged Air

Far from the Rappahannock, the silent
Danube moves along toward the sea.
The brown and green Nile rolls slowly
Like the Niagara's welling descent.
Tractors stood on the green banks of the Loire
Near where it joined the Cher.
The St. Lawrence prods among black stones
And mud. But the Arno is all stones.
Wind ruffles the Hudson's
Surface. The Irawaddy is overflowing.
But the yellowish, gray Tiber
Is contained within steep banks. The Isar
Flows too fast to swim in, the Jordan's water
Courses over the flat land. The Allegheny and its boats
Were dark blue. The Moskowa is
Gray boats. The Amstel flows slowly.
Leaves fall into the Connecticut as it passes
Underneath. The Liffey is full of sewage,
Like the Seine, but unlike
The brownish-yellow Dordogne.
Mountains hem in the Colorado

在黄昏弥漫的天空中

远离拉帕汉诺克港,沉静的
多瑙河驶向大海,
棕绿色的尼罗河缓慢流动
像尼亚加拉一样源源不断地坠落。
拖拉机立在卢瓦尔河绿色的岸边
在它与切尔河交汇之处。
圣劳伦斯在黑色的石头和泥浆中
刺戳。但亚诺河中全是石头。
风吹皱哈德逊河面。
伊拉瓦迪河正在溢出河堤。
黄灰色的台伯河
包容在陡峭的河岸之间。伊萨河
流速快得无法在里面游泳,约旦河水
流过平坦的土地。阿勒格尼和它上面的船
都是深蓝色的。莫斯科瓦河上
是灰色的船。阿姆斯特尔缓慢流动。
树叶落进康涅狄格河
当它在下面经过。利弗雷河里满是排污管,
像塞纳河一样,但与
棕黄色的多尔多涅河不同。
群山包围了科罗拉多河

And the Oder is very deep, almost

As deep as the Congo is wide.

The plain banks of the Neva are

Gray. The dark Saône flows silently.

And the Volga is long and wide

As it flows across the brownish land. The Ebro

Is blue, and slow. The Shannon flows

Swiftly between its banks. The Mississippi

Is one of the world's longest rivers, like the Amazon.

It has the Missouri for a tributary.

The Harlem flows amid factories

And buildings. The Nelson is in Canada,

Flowing. Through hard banks the Dubawnt

Forces its way. People walk near the Trent.

The landscape around the Mohawk stretches away;

The Rubicon is merely a brook.

In winter the Main

Surges; the Rhine sings its eternal song.

The Rhône slogs along through whitish banks

And the Rio Grande spins tales of the past.

The Loir bursts its frozen shackles

But the Moldau's wet mud ensnares it.

The East catches the light.

Near the Escaut the noise of factories echoes

奥德河非常之深，几乎

和刚果河一样深一样宽。

涅瓦河平坦的河岸

呈灰色。黑色的索恩河沉静地流淌。

而伏尔加河又长又宽

流过棕色的土地。埃布罗河

是蓝色的，流速缓慢。香农河

在两岸之间平静地流淌。密西西比河

是世界最长的河流之一，像亚马逊河一样。

密苏里河是它的支流。

哈莱姆河在工厂和建筑物中间

流过。纳尔逊河在加拿大，

流动。穿过坚硬的河岸，杜班特河

奋力前进。人们在特伦特河附近散步。

风景在莫霍克河周边延伸开去；

卢比孔河仅是一条小溪。

在冬天，美因河汹涌澎湃；

莱茵河唱着它永恒的歌。

罗纳河穿过发白的堤岸跋涉

而格兰德河编织着过去的故事。

洛尔河打破了它结冻的枷锁

莫尔道河却陷入了湿泥。

东方捕捉住光线。

埃斯考河附近回响着工厂的噪声

And the sinuous Humboldt gurgles wildly.
The Po too flows, and the many-colored
Thames. Into the Atlantic Ocean
Pours the Garonne. Few ships navigate
On the Housatonic, but quite a few can be seen
On the Elbe. For centuries
The Afton has flowed.
      If the Rio Negro
Could abandon its song, and the Magdalena
The jungle flowers, the Tagus
Would still flow serenely, and the Ohio
Abrade its slate banks. The tan Euphrates would
Sidle silently across the world. The Yukon
Was choked with ice, but the Susquehanna still pushed
Bravely along. The Dee caught the day's last flares
Like the Pilcomayo's carrion rose.
The Peace offered eternal fragrance
Perhaps, but the Mackenzie churned livid mud
Like tan chalk-marks. Near where
The Brahmaputra slapped swollen dikes
Was an opening through which the Limmat
Could have trickled. A young man strode the Churchill's
Banks, thinking of night. The Vistula seized
The shadows. The Theiss, stark mad, bubbled

蜿蜒的哈姆波尔特河狂野地轰隆作响。

波河也在流动，还有色彩多变的

泰晤士河。加龙河

倾入大西洋。很少有船

在豪萨托尼克河上航行，在易北河上

却可以看见许多条船。阿夫顿河

已流淌了几个世纪。

　　　　　是否内格罗河

能放弃它的歌，而马格达雷那河

丛林之花塔霍河

仍可以宁静地流淌，俄亥俄河

仍在磨损它的页岩河岸。棕色的幼发拉底河

静悄悄地滑过世界。育空河

被冰堵塞了，但萨斯奎哈纳河

仍勇敢向前。迪伊河捉住白昼最后的闪光

像皮尔科马约的腐肉玫瑰。

也许皮斯河在贡献永恒的芳香，

但马更些河剧烈搅动乌青色的泥浆

像粉笔印。布拉马普特拉河

拍打涨水的堤坝，附近

是利马特河渐渐干涸的

一片开阔地。一个年轻人沿丘吉尔河

大步行走，思考着夜晚。维斯瓦河

捉住了阴影。蒂萨河，完全疯了，

In the windy evening. And the Ob shuffled

Crazily along. Fat billows encrusted the Dniester's

Pallid flood, and the Fraser's porous surface.

Fish gasped amid the Spree's reeds. A boat

Descended the bobbing Orinoco. When the

Marne flowed by the plants nodded

And above the glistering Gila

A sunset as beautiful as the Athabasca

Stammered. The Zambezi chimed. The Oxus

Flowed somewhere. The Paranaíba

Is flowing, like the wind-washed Cumberland.

The Araguaia flows in the rain.

And, through overlying rocks the Isère

Cascades gently. The Guadalquivir sputtered.

Someday time will confound the Indre,

Making a rill of the Huang Ho. And

The Potomac rumbles softly. Crested birds

Watch the Ucayali go

Through dreaming night. You cannot stop

The Yenisei. And afterwards

The White flows strongly to its. . .

Goal. If the Tyne's shores

Hold you, and the Albany

Arrest your development, can you resist the Red's

在有风的傍晚吐着泡沫。而鄂毕河

疯狂地拖曳着步伐。肥硕的巨浪装饰着

德涅斯特河苍白的洪水,以及弗雷泽河多孔的河面。

鱼在斯普里河的芦苇中喘息。一艘船

在奥里诺科河上漂来漂去。

当马恩河在摇曳的植物旁流过

在闪耀的希拉河上

日落像口吃的阿萨巴斯卡人

一样美丽。赞比西河水声悦耳。

奥修斯河在某处流动。帕纳伊巴河

在流动,像风吹的坎伯兰河。

阿拉瓜河在雨中流淌。

而穿过密布的岩石,伊瑟尔河

优雅地倾泻。瓜达尔基维尔河噼啪作响。

有一天时间将使因德尔河困惑,

使它变成另一条黄河。

波托马克河柔和地鸣响。

羽冠的鸟注视乌卡亚利河

穿过梦幻的夜。你不能阻止

叶尼塞河。而后来

怀特河将汹涌奔向

它的目标。如果泰恩河畔

阻挡了你,奥尔巴尼河

抑制了你的进展,你能抗拒红河的

Musk, the Meuse's situation?

A particle of mud in the Neckar

Does not turn it black. You cannot

Like the Saskatchewan, nor refuse

The meandering Yangtze, unleash

The Genesee. Does the Scamander

Still irrigate crimson plains? And the Durance

And the Pechora? The São Francisco

Skulks amid gray, rubbery nettles. The Liard's

Reflexes are slow, and the Arkansas erodes

Anthracite hummocks. The Paraná stinks.

The Ottawa is light emerald green

Among grays. Better that the Indus fade

In steaming sands! Let the Brazos

Freeze solid! And the Wabash turn to a leaden

Cinder of ice! The Marañón is too tepid, we must

Find a way to freeze it hard. The Ural

Is freezing slowly in the blasts. The black Yonne

Congeals nicely. And the Petit-Morin

Curls up on the solid earth. The Inn

Does not remember better times, and the Merrimack's

Galvanized. The Ganges is liquid snow by now;

The Vyatka's ice-gray. The once-molten Tennessee's

Curdled. The Japurá is a pack of ice. Gelid

麝香,控制默兹河的局面吗?

尼卡河的一滴泥浆

不能将它变黑。你不能

像萨斯克彻温河一样,也不能拒绝

曲折的扬子江,解放

热尼西河。斯卡芒德河

仍在灌溉着深红色的平原吗?还有杜兰斯河

与伯朝拉河?圣弗兰西斯科河

在灰色、坚韧的荨麻中隐伏着。利亚德河的

反应很慢,阿肯色河侵蚀着

无烟煤山岗。巴拉那河发出恶臭。

渥太华河在一片灰色中

呈淡淡的祖母绿。印度河最好是

消失在冒着蒸汽的沙子里!让布拉佐斯河

冻得结结实实!让瓦巴什河变成一片铅灰色的

冰煤渣!马腊尼翁河太不热情了,我们必须

找到一种方法把它冻僵。乌拉尔河

在风暴中慢慢结冻。黑色的约纳河

冻得很美。而皮特莫林河

蜷缩在坚硬的土地上。因河

不记得曾有过更好的时光,梅里马克河

振奋起来。恒河现在是液体的雪;

维亚特卡河呈冰灰色。曾经炽热的田纳西河

凝结了。贾普拉河是一块冰。杰里德

The Columbia's gray loam banks. The Don's merely

A giant icicle. The Niger freezes, slowly.

The interminable Lena plods on

But the Purus' mercurial waters are icy, grim

With cold. The Loing is choked with fragments of ice.

The Weser is frozen, like liquid air.

And so is the Kama. And the beige, thickly flowing

Tocantins. The rivers bask in the cold.

The stern Uruguay chafes its banks,

A mass of ice. The Hooghly is solid

Ice. The Adour is silent, motionless.

The lovely Tigris is nothing but scratchy ice

Like the Yellowstone, with its osier-clustered banks.

The Mekong is beginning to thaw out a little

And the Donets gurgles beneath the

Huge blocks of ice. The Manzanares gushes free.

The Illinois darts through the sunny air again.

But the Dnieper is still ice-bound. Somewhere

The Salado propels its floes, but the Roosevelt's

Frozen. The Oka is frozen solider

Than the Somme. The Minho slumbers

In winter, nor does the Snake

Remember August. Hilarious, the Canadian

Is solid ice. The Madeira slavers

哥伦比亚灰色的土岸。顿河仅仅是

一根巨大的冰柱。尼日尔河正在结冻,缓慢地。

漫无尽头的勒拿河沉重而缓慢

但是普鲁斯河活泼的水面满是冰碴,

阴森寒冷。劳因河被碎冰块堵住了。

威悉河结冻了,像液体的空气。

卡马河也是如此。还有那米色的水量充沛的

托坎汀斯河。这些河流在寒冷中晒太阳。

严厉的乌拉圭河磨损着它的河岸,

一块巨冰。胡利河是坚固的冰。

阿多尔河沉静,一动不动。

可爱的底格里斯河只不过是炫目的冰

像黄石河一样,岸上柳树成行。

湄公河开始融化了一点

而顿涅茨河在巨大的冰层下

汩汩流淌。曼赞那尔斯河自由喷涌。

伊利诺依河再次飞过阳光明媚的空气。

但是第聂伯河依然冰封雪裹。某处

萨拉多河推动它的浮冰,而罗斯福河

已结冻。奥卡河冻得

比索姆河还结实。敏霍河

在冬天微睡,斯内克河

也忘记了八月。兴高采烈的加拿大河

成了坚冰。马代拉河淌着口水

Across the thawing fields, and the Plata laughs.
The Dvina soaks up the snow. The Sava's
Temperature is above freezing. The Avon
Carols noiselessly. The Drôme presses
Grass banks; the Adige's frozen
Surface is like gray pebbles.

Birds circle the Ticino. In winter
The Var was dark blue, unfrozen. The
Thwaite, cold, is choked with sandy ice;
The Ardèche glistens feebly through the freezing rain.

穿过解冻的田野，而普拉塔河在笑。
德维那河浸湿了积雪。萨瓦河
温度到了冰点以上。艾冯河
无声地欢唱。德罗米河压迫着
长草的堤岸；阿迪杰河
结冻的河面像灰色的卵石。

鸟群在提西诺河上空盘旋。冬天
瓦尔河呈深蓝色，没有结冻。
斯维特河，寒冷，被含沙的冰窒息；
阿戴彻河虚弱地闪烁着穿过冷雨。

The Ecclesiast

"Worse than the sunflower," she had said.
But the new dimension of truth had only recently
Burst in on us. Now it was to be condemned.
And in vagrant shadow her mothball truth is eaten.
In cool, like-it-or-not shadow the humdrum is consumed.
Tired housewives begat it some decades ago,
A small piece of truth that if it was honey to the lips
Was also millions of miles from filling the place reserved for it.
You see how honey crumbles your universe
Which seems like an institution—how many walls?

Then everything, in her belief, was to be submerged
And soon. There was no life you could live out to its end
And no attitude which, in the end, would save you.
The monkish and the frivolous alike were to be trapped in death's
    capacious claw
But listen while I tell you about the wallpaper—
There was a key to everything in that oak forest
But a sad one. Ever since childhood there
Has been this special meaning to everything.
You smile at your friend's joke, but only later, through tears.

传教士

"比向日葵还差劲,"她说。
可是真理的新维度只是最近
才突然出现在我们面前。现在它将受到谴责。
在游移的阴影中她的卫生球真理被吃掉了。
在不管你喜不喜欢的阴凉中单调被耗尽。
疲惫的主妇几十年前招惹了它,
一小片真理即便对嘴唇来说是蜜
也填不满留给它的几百万公里。
你明白蜂蜜如何瓦解你的宇宙
就像一个公共机构——有多少面墙?

于是,她相信一切都会很快
被淹没。没有任何生活你能过到头
也没有任何态度,最后,能够救你。
苦行僧和琐碎无聊之人同样会落入死亡的巨爪
可是听着,我告诉你关于墙纸的事——
对于一切,有一把钥匙在那片橡树林里
却是一把悲哀的钥匙。从童年起
一切便有着这种特殊的意义。
朋友的玩笑,只是在后来,才让你通过眼泪微笑。

For the shoe pinches, even though it fits perfectly.
Apples were made to be gathered, also the whole host of the world's
    ailments and troubles.
There is no time like the present for giving in to this temptation.
Tomorrow you'll weep—what of it? There is time enough
Once the harvest is in and the animals put away for the winter
To stand at the uncomprehending window cultivating the desert
With salt tears which will never do anyone any good.
My dearest I am as a galleon on salt billows.
Perfume my head with forgetting all about me.

For some day these projects will return.
The funereal voyage over ice-strewn seas is ended.
You wake up forgetting. Already
Daylight shakes you in the yard.
The hands remain empty. They are constructing an osier basket
Just now, and across the sunlight darkness is taking root anew
In intense activity. You shall never have seen it just this way
And that is to be your one reward.

Fine vapors escape from whatever is doing the living.
The night is cold and delicate and full of angels
Pounding down the living. The factories are all lit up,
The chime goes unheard.
We are together at last, though far apart.

至于鞋子夹脚，就当它完全合脚吧。

苹果造来是为了摘的，还有整个世界的不安与麻烦。

没有任何时代像现在这样屈服于这种诱惑。

明天你将啜泣——又能怎么样呢？时间够了

一旦收完庄稼，把野兽推给冬天

就站在不明所以的窗边耕作沙漠

用对任何人都永远无益的咸涩的眼泪。

我最亲爱的，我就像咸涩巨浪上的一艘大帆船。

全然忘我让我的脑袋香喷喷。

有一天这些计划将返回。

在撒满冰块的海上，送葬的航行结束了。

你醒来就忘了。白昼的光

已经在院子里摇撼你。

双手仍是空的。它们组成一只柳条篮

就是现在，穿过阳光，黑暗扎下新根

紧张地活动。你再也不会看到它这个样子

而那将是你的一份回报。

任何忙于生存的活物都释放出纤细的蒸汽。

夜晚寒冷而怡人，充满了天使

捣毁着活物。工厂全都点亮了灯，

钟声敲响，无人听见。

我们最后聚在一起，尽管远远分开。

The Recent Past

Perhaps we ought to feel with more imagination.
As today the sky 70 degrees above zero with lines falling
The way September moves a lace curtain to be near a pear,
The oddest device can't be usual. And that is where
The pejorative sense of fear moves axles. In the stars
There is no longer any peace, emptied like a cup of coffee
Between the blinding rain that interviews.

You were my quintuplets when I decided to leave you
Opening a picture book the pictures were all of grass
Slowly the book was on fire, you the reader
Sitting with specs full of smoke exclaimed
How it was a rhyme for "brick" or "redder."
The next chapter told all about a brook.
You were beginning to see the relation when a tidal wave
Arrived with sinking ships that spelled out "Aladdin."
I thought about the Arab boy in his cave
But the thoughts came faster than advice.
If you knew that snow was a still toboggan in space
The print could rhyme with "fallen star."

最近以来

也许我们应该带着更多的想象去感受。
因为今天天空零上七十度,线条在坠落
九月移动花边窗帘的方式近乎于一只梨,
最奇特的装置不可能是普通的。就在那里
恐惧的轻蔑感在移动车轴。在群星中
不再有和平,空得像一杯咖啡
在正在采访的炫目的雨之间。

你是我的五胞胎,当我决定把你留下
打开一本图画书,画里都是草
书慢慢燃烧起来,你这个读者
与说明书坐在一起,充满了烟,惊叫
它怎么能和"砖"或"更红"一个韵。
下一章讲的全都是一条小溪的事儿。
你开始明白其中的关系,当一个波浪
带着沉船到达,拼写出"阿拉丁"。
我想着洞穴中的阿拉伯少年
但是思想比建议来得快。
如果你知道雪在宇宙中仍是一只平底雪橇
书上的字便可以和"坠落的星星"押韵。

A Blessing in Disguise

Yes, they are alive and can have those colors,

But I, in my soul, am alive too.

I feel I must sing and dance, to tell

Of this in a way, that knowing you may be drawn to me.

And I sing amid despair and isolation

Of the chance to know you, to sing of me

Which are you. You see,

You hold me up to the light in a way

I should never have expected, or suspected, perhaps

Because you always tell me I am you,

And right. The great spruces loom.

I am yours to die with, to desire.

I cannot ever think of me, I desire you

For a room in which the chairs ever

Have their backs turned to the light

Inflicted on the stone and paths, the real trees

That seem to shine at me through a lattice toward you.

貌似灾祸的福音

是的,他们活着并可以拥有那些色彩,
但是我,我的灵魂,也在活着。
我觉得我必须又唱又跳,以一种方式
讲讲这个,知道你可能会被我吸引。

于是我在绝望和孤独中
歌唱认识你的机缘,歌唱我自己
我就是你。你看,
你以一种方式把我举向光明

我从未期待过,或怀疑过,也许
是因为你总是告诉我我就是你,
那就对了。巨大的云杉隐约出现。
我是你渴望一同死去的人。

我无法想到自己,我渴望为你
拥有一个房间,里面的椅子
把它们的背转向光明
那光打在石头和小径上,真正的树

似乎穿过你面前的格子窗向我闪耀。

If the wild light of this January day is true

I pledge me to be truthful unto you

Whom I cannot ever stop remembering.

Remembering to forgive. Remember to pass beyond you into the day

On the wings of the secret you will never know.

Taking me from myself, in the path

Which the pastel girth of the day has assigned to me.

I prefer "you" in the plural, I want "you,"

You must come to me, all golden and pale

Like the dew and the air.

And then I start getting this feeling of exaltation.

如果这一月荒凉的光线是真的
我向自己保证要真诚待你
我不曾有片刻忘记的人。

记得要原谅。记得要超越你进入日子
利用你永远不会知道的秘密的翅膀。
带我离开自我,在日子
分配给我的蜡笔宽的路上。

我选择复数的"你",我需要"你",
你必须到我这里来,全身金灰色
像露水和空气。
那时我将获得这种兴奋的感觉。

Clepsydra

Hasn't the sky? Returned from moving the other

Authority recently dropped, wrested as much of

That severe sunshine as you need now on the way

You go. The reason why it happened only since

You woke up is letting the steam disappear

From those clouds when the landscape all around

Is hilly sites that will have to be reckoned

Into the total for there to be more air: that is,

More fitness read into the undeduced result, than land.

This means never getting any closer to the basic

Principle operating behind it than to the distracted

Entity of a mirage. The half-meant, half-perceived

Motions of fronds out of idle depths that are

Summer. And expansion into little draughts.

The reply wakens easily, darting from

Untruth to willed moment, scarcely called into being

Before it swells, the way a waterfall

Drums at different levels. Each moment

Of utterance is the true one; likewise none are true,

Only is the bounding from air to air, a serpentine

Gesture which hides the truth behind a congruent

滴　漏

难道没有天空吗？自移开另一个最近
堕落的权威归来，扭曲得有如
你现在走路需要的严酷的阳光。
它仅仅在你醒来之后发生
其中的原因正在促使蒸汽
从那些云彩里消失，当周围的风景
满是山丘，它们必须要计入总数
为了能有更多的天空：亦即，
它们比土地更适合计入未经推断的结果。
这意味着永远不要再靠近它后面起作用的
基本原理，不要超过那让人分心的
海市蜃楼的实体。从停滞的深渊中
复叶半主动半被动的运动便是
夏天。还有膨胀出来的小小的气流。
很容易唤来的回答，从虚假不实
射向意志坚强的瞬间，在它膨胀之前
几乎没有形成，瀑布在不同层面
击鼓的方式。每一个说话的瞬间
都是真实的瞬间；同样也无一真实，
只有从空气到空气的跳跃，一种
蛇一般蜿蜒的姿势将真实隐藏在一个

Message, the way air hides the sky, is, in fact,

Tearing it limb from limb this very moment: but

The sky has pleaded already and this is about

As graceful a kind of non-absence as either

Has a right to expect: whether it's the form of

Some creator who has momentarily turned away,

Marrying detachment with respect, so that the pieces

Are seen as parts of a spectrum, independent

Yet symbolic of their staggered times of arrival;

Whether on the other hand all of it is to be

Seen as no luck. A recurring whiteness like

The face of stone pleasure, urging forward as

Nostrils what only meant dust. But the argument,

That is its way, has already left these behind: it

Is, it would have you believe, the white din up ahead

That matters: unformed yells, rocketings,

Affected turns, and tones of voice called

By upper shadows toward some cloud of belief

Or its unstated circumference. But the light

Has already gone from there too and it may be that

It is lines contracting into a plane. We hear so much

Of its further action that at last it seems that

It is we, our taking it into account rather, that are

The reply that prompted the question, and

一致的信息背后,空气隐藏起天空的方式,事实上,
恰恰将这个瞬间的肢体撕裂;但是
天空已经有了借口,这关乎于
一种同样优雅的不缺席,
也有权利表达:它是不是某个
暂时避开的创造者的形式,
将超然与尊敬合一,以便使片段
被视为一个频谱的部分,独立
但依然象征着它们蹒跚到达的时刻;
是否在另一方面它的全部要被视为
运气不佳。一种反复出现的白色
如同石头的欢乐的脸,敦促向前
就像只想要灰尘的鼻孔。但是争论,
是它的方式,已经把这些留在后面:
它会让你相信,要紧的是在头上
喧闹不已的白色:无形的叫喊,火箭发射,
假装的转折,以及一些声调
凭借上方的影子呼唤某朵信仰之云
或是它未加说明的圆周。但是光
同样从那里消失了,也许那是
收缩成一个平面的线条。我们甚至听见
它进一步的运动,以至于到最后
似乎是我们,是我们宁可认为,
那激起问题的回答,以及

That the latter, like a person waking on a pillow

Has the sensation of having dreamt the whole thing,

Of returning to participate in that dream, until

The last word is exhausted; certainly this is

Peace of a sort, like nets drying in the sun,

That we must progress toward the whole thing

About an hour ago. As long as it is there

You will desire it as its tag of wall sinks

Deeper as though hollowed by sunlight that

Just fits over it; it is both mirage and the little

That was present, the miserable totality

Mustered at any given moment, like your eyes

And all they speak of, such as your hands, in lost

Accents beyond any dream of ever wanting them again.

To have this to be constantly coming back from—

Nothing more, really, than surprise at your absence

And preparing to continue the dialogue into

Those mysterious and near regions that are

Precisely the time of its being furthered.

Seeing it, as it was, dividing that time,

Casting colored paddles against the welter

Of a future of disunion just to abolish confusion

And permit level walks into the gaze of its standing

Around admiringly, it was then, that it was these

问题本身,像一个人从枕头上醒来

觉得自己正在梦见整件事情,

正在重新参与到那个梦中,直到

最后的词语耗尽;这当然是

一种和平,像渔网在阳光下晒干,

我们必须向大约一小时前的

整件事情前进。只要它存在

你就渴望得到它,它墙壁上的标签沉得更深

仿佛被正好适合它的阳光

所掏空;它既是海市蜃楼,又是小人物

那曾是礼物,悲惨的总体

在任何给定时刻集合起来,像你的眼睛

和他们说到的一切,像你的双手,在失去的口音中

超越了任何希望再次存在的梦。

让此事不断地返回——

实际上,无非是为你的缺席吃惊

并准备将对话延续到

那些神秘的相邻区域

那恰好是助长其存在的时刻。

像过去那样看着它,将那时刻分开,

将彩色船桨投向分裂的未来

那起伏的波浪,只是为了消除混乱

并允许标准不知不觉地凝视起自己的地位

欣赏着周围,那时,这些瞬间

Moments that were the truth, although each tapered
Into the distant surrounding night. But
Wasn't it their blindness, instead, and wasn't this
The fact of being so turned in on each other that
Neither would ever see his way clear again? It
Did not stagger the imagination so long as it stayed
This way, comparable to exclusion from the light of the stars
That drenched every instant of that being, in an egoistic way,
As though their round time were only the reverse
Of some more concealable, vengeful purpose to become known
Once its result had more or less established
The look of the horizon. But the condition
Of those moments of timeless elasticity and blindness
Was being joined secretly so
That their paths would cross again and be separated
Only to join again in a final assumption rising like a shout
And be endless in the discovery of the declamatory
Nature of the distance traveled. All this is
Not without small variations and surprises, yet
An invisible fountain continually destroys and refreshes the previsions.
Then is their permanence merely a function of
The assurance with which it's understood, assurance
Which, you might say, goes a long way toward conditioning
Whatever result? But there was no statement

才是真实，尽管每一个都逐渐变弱

成为遥远的环绕的夜晚。但是

难道不正是它们的盲目，不正是这个

存在的事实，反而互相出卖

两者都不曾再次看清他的方式？

它没有使想象力犹豫，只要它保持

这种方式，比得上从群星之光中排除

那存在的每一个湿透的瞬间，以一种自我中心的方式，

仿佛它们每回合的时间不过是颠倒了

某个更隐蔽更有报复性的意图，使其为人所知

一旦它的结果或多或少确定了

地平线的样子。但是那些瞬间

保持永恒弹性和盲目的条件

被如此秘密地连接在一起

它们的路径将再次交叉，并被分开

只为了再次连接，在一个最终的假定中

如同一声叫喊升起并不断地发现

行经旅途的雄辩家性质。这一切

并非没有细小的变数和意外，却依然

有一个无形的喷泉在持续地摧毁和更新着预言。

它们的持久仅仅具有一种担保功能

以此使它获得理解，这担保

你可以说，为了控制任何结果

要经过一个漫长的过程？可在一开始

At the beginning. There was only a breathless waste,
A dumb cry shaping everything in projected
After-effects orphaned by playing the part intended for them,
Though one must not forget that the nature of this
Emptiness, these previsions,
Was that it could only happen here, on this page held
Too close to be legible, sprouting erasures, except that they
Ended everything in the transparent sphere of what was
Intended only a moment ago, spiraling further out, its
Gesture finally dissolving in the weather.
It was the long way back out of sadness
Of that first meeting: a half-triumph, an imaginary feeling
Which still protected its events and pauses, the way
A telescope protects its view of distant mountains
And all they include, the coming and going,
Moving correctly up to other levels, preparing to spend the night
There where the tiny figures halt as darkness comes on,
Beside some loud torrent in an empty yet personal
Landscape, which has the further advantage of being
What surrounds without insisting, the very breath so
Honorably offered, and accepted in the same spirit.
There was in fact pleasure in those high walls.
Each moment seemed to bore back into the centuries
For profit and manners, and an old way of looking that

没有任何声明。有的只是一个没有呼吸的废物,
一种无声的哭泣塑造着一切,以计划好的
结果,孤立于扮演指定给它们的角色,
尽管一个人不可以忘记
这种空虚的性质,这些预言,
只能发生于此处,在这一页上
举得太近而看不清楚,发芽的擦痕,除非它们
在透明领域中结束一切
片刻前才想要的东西,更远地盘旋而出,
它的姿势最终融解在天气中。
它是收回那初遇之悲哀的漫漫
长途:胜负参半,一种想象的情感
依然保护着它的事件和暂停,
以一架望远镜保护它远山视野的方式
以及它们所包含的一切,来来去去,
正确地升向其他层次,准备度过夜晚
那里有小小的人影停顿,当黑暗降临,
除了一片空虚而个人化的风景中
一条响亮的湍流,拥有进一步的优势
无需坚持地围绕着一切,奉献出
如此体面的气息,并以同样的精神接受。
实际上那些高墙中存在着乐趣。
每个瞬间似乎都带回诸多世纪
为了利益和风俗,一种古老的观看方式

Continually shaped those lips into a smile. Or it was
Like standing at the edge of a harbor early on a summer morning
With the discreet shadows cast by the water all around
And a feeling, again, of emptiness, but of richness in the way
The whole thing is organized, on what a miraculous scale,
Really what is meant by a human level, with the figures of giants
Not too much bigger than the men who have come to petition them:
A moment that gave not only itself, but
Also the means of keeping it, of not turning to dust
Or gestures somewhere up ahead
But of becoming complicated like the torrent
In new dark passages, tears and laughter which
Are a sign of life, of distant life in this case.
And yet, as always happens, there would come a moment when
Acts no longer sufficed and the calm
Of this true progression hardened into shreds
Of another kind of calm, returning to the conclusion, its premises
Undertaken before any formal agreement had been reached, hence
A writ that was the shadow of the colossal reason behind all this
Like a second, rigid body behind the one you know is yours.
And it was in vain that tears blotted the contract now, because
It had been freely drawn up and consented to as insurance
Against the very condition it was now so efficiently
Seeking to establish. It had reduced that other world,

持续地将那些嘴唇塑造成微笑。或者
就像夏日一大早站在海港边上
周遭的墙壁投下谨慎的影子
一种空虚感,再次,以丰富感的方式出现
整件事情以何其不可思议的规模组织起来,
实际上何谓人类层面,和巨人的身影在一起
比前来向他们请愿的人大不了多少:
一个瞬间不仅仅贡献出它自身,
也贡献出保持它自身的方式,不是变成灰尘
或者在某处升起在头顶的姿势
而是变得复杂,如同激流进入
黑暗的新流域,这种情况下
眼泪和笑声是生命的标志,一种遥远的生命。
不过,经常会出现一个瞬间,那时
行为不再足够,这真实进程的沉静
硬化成了另一种
沉静的碎片,返回结局,它的前提
在取得任何正式的共识之前就被接受了,
因此,一份文书便是这一切背后巨大原因的影子
如同另一个僵硬的身体,在你知道是你自己身体的后面。
现在用眼泪弄脏那契约已属徒劳,因为
它是随意起草的,一致赞成,作为保险
防备的正是现在如此有效地寻求确立的
这种情况。它将那个另外的世界,

The round one of the telescope, to a kind of very fine powder or dust
So small that space could not remember it.
Thereafter any signs of feeling were cut short by
The comfort and security, a certain elegance even,
Like the fittings of a ship, that are after all
The most normal things in the world. Yes, perhaps, but the words
"After all" are important for understanding the almost
Exaggerated strictness of the condition, and why, in spite of this,
It seemed the validity of the former continuing was
Not likely to be reinstated for a long time.
"After all," that too might be possible, as indeed
All kinds of things are possible in the widening angle of
The day, as it comes to blush with pleasure and increase,
So that light sinks into itself, becomes dark and heavy
Like a surface stained with ink: there was something
Not quite good or correct about the way
Things were looking recently: hadn't the point
Of all this new construction been to provide
A protected medium for the exchanges each felt of such vital
Concern, and wasn't it now giving itself the airs of a palace?
And yet her hair had never been so long.
It was a feeling of well-being, if you will, as though a smallest
Distant impulse had rendered the whole surface ultra-sensitive
But its fierceness was still acquiescence

望远镜的浑圆世界，缩小成一种很细的粉尘
小得连空间都记不住它。
其后任何情感的迹象都被安慰和安全措施
所削减，一种典雅，甚至，
像船上的装备一样，在这世界上
终归事属平常。是的，也许如此，但是
"终归"这个词对于理解这种情况
那近乎夸张的严重性是很重要的，尽管如此，
为何前者的有效性似乎还在延续
在很长时间里不太可能复原。
"终归"，也有可能这样，实际上
各种东西都有可能置身于不断扩大的白昼的
角度里，当它快乐得满脸通红并且逐渐增长，
以至于光明沉入自身，变得黑暗而沉重
如同一个墨水玷污的表面：有某种东西
对于近期观看事物的方式
没多大益处，也不恰当：这个全新结构的关键
难道没有提供一种受到保护的媒介
让每一个人交换这切身的忧虑之感，
难道现在也没有使自己显出宫殿的样子？
她的头发还从来没有这么长过。
它是一种康乐的感觉，如果你愿意，仿佛
一个最小的遥远的脉冲致使整个表面格外敏感
但是它的凶猛依然默许于

To the nature of this goodness already past
And it was a kind of sweet acknowledgment of how
The past is yours, to keep invisible if you wish
But also to make absurd elaborations with
And in this way prolong your dance of non-discovery
In brittle, useless architecture that is nevertheless
The map of your desires, irreproachable, beyond
Madness and the toe of approaching night, if only
You desire to arrange it this way. Your acts
Are sentinels against this quiet
Invasion. Long may you prosper, and may your years
Be the throes of what is even now exhausting itself
In one last effort to outwit us; it could only be a map
Of the world: in their defeat such peninsulas as become
Prolongations of our reluctance to approach, but also
Fine days on whose memorable successions of events
We shall be ever afterwards tempted to dwell. I am
Not speaking of a partially successful attempt to be
Opposite; anybody at all can read that page, it has only
To be thrust in front of him. I mean now something much broader,
The sum total of all the private aspects that can ever
Become legible in what is outside, as much in the rocks
And foliage as in the invisible look of the distant
Ether and in the iron fist that suddenly closes over your own.

这已成过去的善的本质

它是一种甜蜜的认知,知道

过去如何属于你,如果你愿意,就会保持无形

但是以这种方式进行荒谬的细化

也会拖长你无所发现的舞蹈

在脆弱易碎、无用的建筑中,然而

那就是你欲望的地图,无可指责,

越过疯狂和正在靠近的夜晚的脚趾,只要

你渴望以这种方式将它安排。你的行为

便是抵挡这无声入侵的哨兵。

愿你兴盛,愿你的年岁

成为甚至正在耗尽自身的一切的冠冕

在最后一次努力中骗过我们;它可能只是一幅

世界的地图:在它们的失败中,这样的半岛

成了我们不愿接近的延长部分,但也是

美好的日子,其中值得回忆的一连串事件

随后会始终诱使我们流连忘返。我

说的不是一次部分成功的反对的尝试;

任何人都能读懂那一页,只需要

把它推到他的面前。我现在指的是某种更宽阔的事物,

所有私人方面的总和都随时可以

在外面的一切中变得清晰可辨,在岩石

和叶簇中就像在遥远的以太那无形的

面貌中,在突然握住你手的铁拳中一样。

I see myself in this totality, and meanwhile

I am only a transparent diagram, of manners and

Private words with the certainty of being about to fall.

And even this crumb of life I also owe to you

For being so close as to seal out knowledge of that other

Voluntary life, and so keep its root in darkness until your

Maturity when your hair will actually be the branches

Of a tree with the light pouring through them.

It intensifies echoes in such a way as to

Form a channel to absorb every correct motion.

In this way any direction taken was the right one,

Leading first to you, and through you to

Myself that is beyond you and which is the same thing as space,

That is the stammering vehicles that remain unknown,

Eating the sky in all sincerity because the difference

Can never be made up: therefore, why not examine the distance?

It seemed he had been repeating the same stupid phrase

Over and over throughout his life; meanwhile

Infant destinies had suavely matured; there was

To be a meeting or collection of them that very evening.

He was out of it of course for having lain happily awake

On the tepid fringes of that field or whatever

Whose center was beginning to churn darkly, but even more for having

The progression of minutes by accepting them, as one accepts drops of rain

在这总体中我看见自己，与此同时

我只是一个透明的图表，关乎礼貌

和私人话语，伴随着即将坠落的必然性。

甚至这生活的碎屑我也要归功于你

它严严实实，密封住我们关于那自愿的

另一种生活的知识，由此存其根于黑暗，

直到你成熟，那时你的头发实际上会成为

一棵树的枝条，有光线倾注其中。

它以这样的方式强化了回声

形成一个通道，吸收每一个正确的运动。

在这种方式中任何方向都被当作是正确的，

先是通向你，然后穿过你，到达

在你之外的我自己，那是等同于空间的东西，

那是始终陌生的结结巴巴的工具，

竭尽忠诚地侵蚀着天空，因为永远确定不了

区别何在：所以，为什么不检查下距离？

似乎他一直在重复同一个愚蠢的短语

在他的一生中反复不断；与此同时

幼稚的命运完美地成熟了；每天傍晚

它们都有一次集会或是募捐。

他幸福地醒着躺在那里，因而置身其外

在那片田野或是随便什么微温的边缘

它的中心开始模糊地搅动，但更重要的是

它凭接受它们而取得微小的进步，就像一个人接受雨滴

As they form a shower, and without worrying about the fine weather
    that will come after.
Why shouldn't all climate and all music be equal
Without growing? There should be an invariable balance of
Contentment to hold everything in place, ministering
To stunted memories, helping them stand alone
And return into the world, without ever looking back at
What they might have become, even though in doing so they
Might just once have been the truth that, invisible,
Still surrounds us like the air and is the dividing force
Between our slightest steps and the notes taken on them.
It is because everything is relative
That we shall never see in that sphere of pure wisdom and
Entertainment much more than groping shadows of an incomplete
Former existence so close it burns like the mouth that
Closes down over all your effort like the moment
Of death, but stays, raging and burning the design of
Its intentions into the house of your brain, until
You wake up alone, the certainty that it
Wasn't a dream your only clue to why the walls
Are turning on you and why the windows no longer speak
Of time but are themselves, transparent guardians you
Invented for what there was to hide. Which has now
Grown up, or moved away, as a jewel
Exists when there is no one to look at it, and this

当它们形成阵雨，无需担心随后将会出现的好天气。

为什么所有气候和音乐没有发展

就不应该平等？应该有一种不变的满足的平衡

固定每一件事物，照看

发育不良的记忆，帮助它们独自站立

并返回世界，从不曾回望

它们应该变成的东西，即便在这么做时

它们可能只有一次是真实的，无形的，

依然像空气围绕着我们，是将我们

最为轻微的脚步和脚步声区分开来的力量。

这是因为万事都有关联

我们永远不会看见那纯智慧的领域和消遣

更胜过先前未完成的存在那摸索着的阴影，

它如此靠近，像嘴巴一样燃烧

对你的全部努力闭而不言，像死亡的瞬间一样

但是停下吧，怒斥和焚烧它企图进入

你大脑房间的谋划，直到

你独自醒来，要确定这不是梦

为什么墙壁在对你发怒，为什么窗户

不再谈论时间，而是它们自己

你仅有的线索是你为藏在那里的东西

虚构的透明守卫。它现在

长大了，或是走开了，像一块宝石

在没有宝石可以注视的时刻存在

Existence saps your own. Perhaps you are being kept here
Only so that somewhere else the peculiar light of someone's
Purpose can blaze unexpectedly in the acute
Angles of the rooms. It is not a question, then,
Of having not lived in vain. What is meant is that this distant
Image of you, the way you really are, is the test
Of how you see yourself, and regardless of whether or not
You hesitate, it may be assumed that you have won, that this
Wooden and external representation
Returns the full echo of what you meant
With nothing left over, from that circumference now alight
With ex-possibilities become present fact, and you
Must wear them like clothing, moving in the shadow of
Your single and twin existence, waking in intact
Appreciation of it, while morning is still and before the body
Is changed by the faces of evening.

这存在让你衰竭。也许你被保存在这里
只是为了在其他某处，让某人意图的独特之光
可以在房间的锐角里出乎意料地
燃烧。那么，它就不是一个有关
不在徒劳中生活的问题。它的意义在于
这遥远的你的形象，你真正的样子，
是对你如何看待自己的测试，
不管你是否犹豫，可以假定你已获胜，
这呆板而外在的表象
送回了你意欲的完整的回声
无一遗漏，现在从那圆周中飞落下来
所有不可能性都变为当下的事实，而你
必须像衣服一样穿上它们，在你单独又成双的
存在的阴影中移动，完整无损地醒来
对它心存感激，当早晨寂然不动，当身体
被傍晚的面孔改变之前。

From *The Skaters*

From II

Old heavens, you used to tweak above us,
Standing like rain whenever a salvo... Old heavens,
You lying there above the old, but not ruined, fort,
Can you hear, there, what I am saying?

For it is you I am parodying,
Your invisible denials. And the almost correct impressions
Corroborated by newsprint, which is so fine.
I call to you there, but I do not think that you will answer me.

For I am condemned to drum my fingers
On the closed lid of this piano, this tedious planet, earth
As it winks to you through the aspiring, growing distances,
A last spark before the night.

There was much to be said in favor of storms
But you seem to have abandoned them in favor of endless light.
I cannot say that I think the change much of an improvement.
There is something fearful in these summer nights that go on forever...

We are nearing the Moorish coast, I think, in a *bateau*.
I wonder if I will have any friends there
Whether the future will be kinder to me than the past, for example,
And am all set to be put out, finding it to be not.

滑冰者（节选）

II
古老的天空，你习惯在我们上方扭曲，
每逢一阵齐鸣便雨一样伫立……古老的天空，
你躺在古老但又没有倾颓的堡垒上方，
你能听见，我在说些什么吗？

因为我戏仿的是你，
你无形的背弃。几乎正确的印象
被报纸证实，那报纸如此精美。
我向你呼唤，但是我不认为你会回答。

因为我已被定罪，用我的手指擂响
这钢琴紧闭的盖子，这沉闷的行星，这地球
当它向你眨眼，穿过高耸而增长着的距离，
夜晚之前最后的一点火花。

为了有利于风暴，有很多话要说
可你似乎放弃了它们，为了支持无尽的光。
我不能说我认为变化更是一种改善。
在这些夏夜中有某种可怕的东西在永远持续……

Still, I am prepared for this voyage, and for anything else you may care to mention.
Not that I am not afraid, but there is very little time left.
You have probably made travel arrangements, and know the feeling.
Suddenly, one morning, the little train arrives in the station, but oh, so big

It is! Much bigger and faster than anyone told you.
A bearded student in an old baggy overcoat is waiting to take it.
"Why do you want to go *there*," they all say. "It is better in the other direction."
And so it is. There people are free, at any rate. But where you are going no one is.

Still there are parks and libraries to be visited, "la Bibliothèque Municipale,"
Hotel reservations and all that rot. Old American films dubbed into the foreign language,
Coffee and whiskey and cigar stubs. Nobody minds. And rain on the bristly wool of your topcoat.
I realize that I never knew why I wanted to come.

Yet I shall never return to the past, that attic.
Its sailboats are perhaps more beautiful than these, these I am leaning against,
Spangled with diamonds and orange and purple stains,
Bearing me once again in quest of the unknown. These sails are life itself to me.

I heard a girl say this once, and cried, and brought her fresh fruit and fishes,
Olives and golden baked loaves. She dried her tears and thanked me.

我们正在靠近摩尔人的海岸,我想,我们是在平底驳船上。
我怀疑我在那里是否会有朋友
未来是否会比过去对我仁慈一些,例如,
我已准备出航,发现情况并非如此。

我已准备好航行,准备好了你提及的其他一切。
不是我不害怕,而是剩下的时间已经不多。
你也许做过旅行安排,知道那种感觉。
突然,一天早晨,小火车到站了,可是啊,它如此

巨大!比任何人告诉你的都又大又快。
一个留胡子的学生穿着宽松旧大衣在候车。
"为什么你想去那儿,"他们都这样说,"反方向更好。"
就是这样。无论如何,那里的人是自由的。但是你要去的地方
　　不是这样。

还有一些公园和图书馆要去参观。"市政图书馆,"
旅馆预定和那一套胡说。美国老电影以外语配音,
咖啡、威士忌和雪茄烟蒂。无人在意。你外套粗毛上的雨珠。
我意识到我从来不知道我为什么要来。

但我也永远不会回到过去,那个阁楼。
它的帆船也许比这些,这些我正倚靠着的要美,
装饰着宝石,橘色和紫色的斑点,

Now we are both setting sail into the purplish evening.
I love it! This cruise can never last long enough for me.

But once more, office desks, radiators—No! That is behind me.
No more dullness, only movies and love and laughter, sex and fun.
The ticket seller is blowing his little horn—hurry before the window slams down.
The train we are getting onto is a boat train, and the boats are really boats this time.

But I heard the heavens say—Is it right? This continual changing back and forth?
Laughter and tears and so on? Mightn't just plain sadness be sufficient for him?
No! I'll not accept that any more, you bewhiskered old caverns of blue!
This is just right for me. I am cozily ensconced in the balcony of my face

Looking out over the whole darn countryside, a beacon of satisfaction
I am. I'll not trade places with a king. Here I am then, continuing but ever beginning
My perennial voyage, into new memories, new hope and flowers
The way the coasts glide past you. I shall never forget this moment

Because it consists of purest ecstasy. I am happier now than I ever dared believe
Anyone could be. And we finger down the dog-eared coasts. . .
It is all passing! It is past! No, I am here,
Bellow the coasts, and even the heavens roar their assent

支撑我再次探索未知。这些船帆对于我就是生活本身。

我听见一个少女又说起这个,还哭了,便带给她新鲜水果和鱼,
橄榄和大块金色的烤面包。她擦干眼泪,向我致谢。
现在我们全都准备驶进紫色的傍晚。
我爱它!在我看来,这巡航永远无法持续足够长的时间。

但是再一次,办公桌,散热器——不!那是在我后面。
不再有沉闷,只有电影、爱和欢笑,性和娱乐。
售票员在吹他的小喇叭——赶在窗口使劲合上之前。
我们要乘的火车是港口联运火车,这次的船是真正的船。

但是我听见天空说——这对吗?这持续往复的变化?
笑声和眼泪和其他?难道朴素的悲哀对他还够吗?
不!我不会再接受,你这络腮胡子的蓝色旧洞穴!
在我这刚好是对的。我安逸地隐藏在我面孔的阳台里

向外俯视整个可恶的农村,我是一个满足的灯塔。
我不会和国王换位置。我在这里,继续着但总是开始
我四季不断的航行,进入新的记忆,新的希望和花朵
以海岸从你身边滑过的方式。我永远不会忘记这个时刻

因为它由最纯粹的狂喜组成。我不相信任何人
能比我现在还幸福。我们拨弄折角的海岸……

As we pick up a lemon-colored light horizontally
projected into the night, the night that heaven
Was kind enough to send, and I launch into the happiest dreams,
Happier once again, because tomorrow is already here.

Yet certain kernels remain. Clouds that drift past sheds—
Read it in the official bulletin. We shan't be putting out today.
The old stove smoked worse than ever because rain was coming down
    its chimney.
Only the bleary eye of fog accosted one through the mended pane.

Outside, the swamp water lapped the broken wood step.
A rowboat was moored in the alligator-infested swamp.
Somewhere, from deep in the interior of the jungle, a groan was
    heard.
Could it be. . . ? Anyway, a rainy day—wet weather.

The whole voyage will have to be canceled.
It would be impossible to make different connections.
Besides, the hotels are all full at this season. The junks packed with
    refugees
Returning from the islands. Sea-bream and flounder abound in the
    muddied waters. . .

They in fact represent the backbone of the island economy.
That, and cigar rolling. Please leave your papers at the desk as you
    pass out,
You know. "The Wedding March." Ah yes, that's the way. The couple
    descend

一切都在过去！已成过去！不，我在这里，
对海岸嚎叫，甚至天空也在咆哮着赞成

当我们捡起一束柠檬色的光
水平投射进夜晚，那天空足够仁慈地
送来的夜晚，我扎进最为幸福的梦幻，
再次快乐起来，因为明天已经到了。

可还有一些精髓留下。云彩飘过棚屋——
在官方公告中看到它。我们今天不会出航。
老炉子比以往冒烟更狠，因为雨正落在烟囱里
只有雾的朦胧之眼通过修补过的窗格勾引人。

外面，沼泽里的水拍打破碎的木头台阶。
一艘划艇停泊在鳄鱼出没的沼泽。
某处，丛林深处，传来一声呻吟。
那可能是……？总之，一个雨天——潮湿的天气。

整个航程将被迫取消。
不可能做出不同的关联。
此外，这个季节旅馆客满。垃圾和难民堆在一起
从岛上返回，泥水中满是海鲤和比目鱼……

它们事实上代表了岛屿经济的支柱。

The steps of the little old church. Ribbons are flung, ribbons of cloud

And the sun seems to be coming out. But there have been so many false alarms...
No, it's happened! The storm is over. Again the weather is fine and clear.
And the voyage? It's on! Listen everybody, the ship is starting,
I can hear its whistle's roar! We have just time enough to make it to the dock!

And away they pour, in the sulfurous sunlight,
To the aqua and silver waters where stands the glistening white ship
And into the great vessel they flood, a motley and happy crowd
Chanting and pouring down hymns on the surface of the ocean...

Pulling, tugging us along with them, by means of streamers,
Golden and silver confetti. Smiling, we laugh and sing with the revelers
But are not quite certain that we want to go—the dock is so sunny and warm.
That majestic ship will pull up anchor who knows where?

And full of laughter and tears, we sidle once again with the other passengers.
The ground is heaving under foot. Is it the ship? It could be the dock...
And with a great whoosh all the sails go up... Hideous black smoke belches forth from the funnels
Smudging the gold carnival costumes with the gaiety of its jet-black soot

雪茄滚动。你昏倒时请把你的报纸留在桌子上，
你知道，"婚礼进行曲。"哦是的，就是那样。一对儿新人
走下古老小教堂的台阶。丝带飞扬，云彩的丝带

太阳似乎就要出来了。可是有这么多假警报……
不，它发生了！风暴过去了。天又放晴了。
而航行呢？它在继续！大家听着，船在启动，
我能听见汽笛的呼啸！我们刚好有时间让它靠上码头！

他们倾泻而去，在硫黄色的阳光中，
倒进浅绿色和银色的水中，水中矗立着闪光的白船
他们涌进大船，五色杂陈快乐的一群
唱着歌，将圣歌倾泻在洋面……

牵引，拖曳着我们，用彩色的纸带，
金色和银色的纸屑。微笑着，我们与欢宴者一同又笑又唱
但是不太确定我们想走——码头如此温暖，阳光明媚。
谁知道那宏伟的大船将在何处起锚？

充满笑声和眼泪，我们再次挨近其他的旅客，
大地在脚下起伏。它是船吗？它可能是码头……
所有的船帆都嗖嗖地升起……烟囱里喷出可怕的黑烟
黑亮的煤烟的欢乐熏脏了金色的狂欢节服装

And, as into a tunnel the voyage starts

Only, as I said, to be continued. The eyes of those left standing on the dock are wet

But ours are dry. Into the secretive, vaporous night with all of us!

Into the unknown, the unknown that loves us, the great unknown!

IV

The wind thrashes the maple seed-pods,

The whole brilliant mass comes spattering down.

This is my fourteenth year as governor of C province.

I was little more than a lad when I first came here.

Now I am old but scarcely any wiser.

So little are white hair and a wrinkled forehead a sign of wisdom!

To slowly raise oneself

Hand over hand, lifting one's entire weight;

To forget there was a possibility

Of some more politic movement. That freedom, courage

And pleasant company could exist.

That has always been behind you.

An earlier litigation: wind hard in the tops

Of the baggy eucalyptus branches.

Today I wrote, "The spring is late this year.

还有，当航行开始进入一条隧道

如我所言，只能继续。那些留在码头上的人眼睛潮湿

可是我们的眼睛干巴巴的。我们全都进入了秘密的、蒸汽弥漫
　　的夜晚！

进入未知，而未知爱着我们，那伟大的未知！

IV

风抽打着枫树的种荚，

灿烂的一大群飞溅而下。

这是我做C省省长的第十四个年头。

刚来时我还是个小伙子。

现在我老了，但几乎没有变得更聪明。

白发和布满皱纹的前额很少是智慧的标志！

要慢慢提升自己

双手交替，把全部的重量提起来；

要忘记还有更为精明的

运动的可能性。自由，勇气

和可能存在的怡人的伙伴。

那一切始终在支持着你。

早些时候的一起诉讼：强硬的风

在松松垮垮的桉树枝头。

In the early mornings there is hoarfrost on the water meadows.

And on the highway the frozen ruts are papered over with ice."

The day was gloves.

How far from the usual statement

About time, ice—the weather itself had gone.

I mean this. Through the years

You have approached an inventory

And it is now that tomorrow

Is going to be the climax of your casual

Statement about yourself, begun

So long ago in humility and false quietude.

The sands are frantic

In the hourglass. But there is time

To change, to utterly destroy

That too-familiar image

Lurking in the glass

Each morning, at the edge of the mirror.

The train is still sitting in the station.

You only dreamed it was in motion.

今天我写道,"今年的春天迟了。
早晨河边的湿草地上还有白霜。
公路上结冻的车辙覆盖着薄冰。"

日子是手套。

多么有别于关于时间的常规
表达,冰——天气本身已经消失。

我指的是这个。经过重重岁月
你接近了一份存货
正是现在,明天
将达到你有关自身的
随意表达的顶点,开始于
很久以前的谦卑和虚假平静之中。

沙漏中的沙子
疯狂了。但还有时间
去改变,去最终摧毁
那过于熟悉的形象
每个早晨,它潜伏在
玻璃中,在镜子的边缘。

There are a few travelers on Z high road.

Behind a shutter, two black eyes are watching them.

They belong to the wife of P, the high-school principal.

The screen door bangs in the wind, one of the hinges is loose.

And together we look back at the house.

It could use a coat of paint

Except that I am too poor to hire a workman.

I have all I can do to keep body and soul together

And soon, even that relatively simple task may prove to be beyond my

    powers.

That was a good joke you played on the other guests.

A joke of silence.

One seizes these moments as they come along, afraid

To believe too much in the happiness that might result

Or confide too much of one's love and fear, even in

Oneself.

The spring, though mild, is incredibly wet.

I have spent the afternoon blowing soap bubbles

火车仍然坐在车站里。
你只是梦见它在运动。

Z 号公路上有几个旅行者。
一扇百叶窗后，两只黑眼睛在观察他们。
它们属于中学校长 P 的妻子。

纱门在风中砰砰作响，一个铰链松了。
我们一起回头望着房子。
它可以用一层油漆
除非我穷得一个工人都雇不起。

为了使身体和灵魂合一我已竭尽所能
很快，那相对简单的任务最终也会超出我的能力。

你给其他客人讲的那个笑话不错。
一个有关寂静的笑话。

当这些时刻出现，有人抓住了它们，担心
过于相信可能引发的幸福
或是过多吐露自己的爱与恐惧，即便
对他自己。

春天温和，却难以置信地潮湿。

And it is with a feeling of delight I realize I am
All alone in the skittish darkness.
The birch-pods come clattering down on the weed-grown marble pavement.
And a curl of smoke stands above the triangular wooden roof.

Seventeen years in the capital of Foo-Yung province!
Surely woman was born for something
Besides continual fornication, retarded only by menstrual cramps.

I had thought of announcing my engagement to you
On the day of the first full moon of X month.

The wind has stopped, but the magnolia blossoms still
Fall with a plop onto the dry, spongy earth.
The evening air is pestiferous with midges.

There is only one way of completing the puzzle:
By finding a hog-shaped piece that is light green shading to buff at one side.

It is the beginning of March, a few
Russet and yellow wallflowers are blooming in the border
Protected by moss-grown, fragmentary masonry.

我用吹肥皂泡消磨下午
伴随着一种愉快之感我认识到
在不安的黑暗中我是全然孤独的。
桦树豆荚哗啦啦落在杂草丛生的大理石人行道上。
一缕烟直立在三角形的木头屋顶上。

在芙蓉省的省会待了十七年！
女人肯定是为了什么东西才生的
除了持续的通奸，只被月经的痉挛所阻止。

我曾想宣布我和你的婚约
在 X 月的第一个满月之日。

风已经停了，可木兰花依然
扑通落在干燥松软的土地上。
傍晚的空气因蚊蝱而恼人。

只有一个办法才能完成拼图：
找到猪形的一块，它的一边从淡绿渐变为浅黄。

这是三月的开端，一些
赤褐色和黄色的桂竹香正在狭长花坛上开放
被生苔的、断断续续的石砌建筑保护着。

One morning you appear at breakfast

Dressed, as for a journey, in your worst suit of clothes.

And over a pot of coffee, or, more accurately, rusted water

Announce your intention of leaving me alone in this cistern-like house.

In your own best interests I shall decide not to believe you.

I think there is a funny sand bar

Beyond the old boardwalk

Your intrigue makes you understand.

"At thirty-two I came up to take my examination at the university.

The U wax factory, it seemed, wanted a new general manager.

I was the sole applicant for the job, but it was refused me.

So I have preferred to finish my life

In the quietude of this floral retreat."

The tiresome old man is telling us his life story.

Trout are circling under water—

Masters of eloquence

Glisten on the pages of your book

Like mountains veiled by water or the sky.

一天早晨吃饭时你出现了
打扮齐整,像是要出门旅行,穿着你最差的套装。
你俯身在咖啡壶上,或者毋宁说,是生锈的水上
宣布你打算把我一个人留在这座水箱般的房子里。
为了你的利益考虑,我决定不去相信你。

我以为有一片有趣的沙洲
在旧木板路那边
你的阴谋让你明白了。

"我三十二岁时通过了大学考试。
U 蜡厂,似乎需要一个新的总经理。
我是这个职位的唯一申请者,但我被拒绝了。
于是我选择在这隐退之地
开花的寂静中了此一生。"

厌倦的老人正在向我们讲述他的生活故事。

鲑鱼在水下绕圈——

雄辩术的大师们
在你的书页上闪光
像被水或是天空笼罩的群山。

The "second position"

Comes in the seventeenth year

Watching the meaningless gyrations of flies above a sill.

Heads in hands, waterfall of simplicity.

The delta of living into everything.

The pump is busted. I shall have to get it fixed.

Your knotted hair

Around your shoulders

A shawl the color of the spectrum

Like that marvelous thing you haven't learned yet.

To refuse the square hive,

                      postpone the highest . . .

The apples are all getting tinted

In the cool light of autumn.

The constellations are rising

In perfect order: Taurus, Leo, Gemini.

"第二个岗位"
在第十七年来了
观察窗台上的苍蝇那无意义的螺旋。

双手抱头,简约性的瀑布。
生存的三角洲进入万物。
水泵爆裂了。我必须把它修好。

你打结的头发
环绕你的双肩
一条光谱颜色的围巾

像你还不懂的那件神奇之物。

拒绝正方形的蜂巢,
    推迟最高的……

苹果全都上了色
在秋天的冷光中。

星座正以完美的秩序
升起:金牛座,狮子座,双子座。

From
THE DOUBLE DREAM OF SPRING
春天的双重梦幻
(1970)

The Task

They are preparing to begin again:

Problems, new pennant up the flagpole

In a predicated romance.

About the time the sun begins to cut laterally across

The western hemisphere with its shadows, its carnival echoes,

The fugitive lands crowd under separate names.

It is the blankness that follows gaiety, and Everyman must depart

Out there into stranded night, for his destiny

Is to return unfruitful out of the lightness

That passing time evokes. It was only

Cloud-castles, adept to seize the past

And possess it, through hurting. And the way is clear

Now for linear acting into that time

In whose corrosive mass he first discovered how to breathe.

Just look at the filth you've made,

See what you've done.

Yet if these are regrets they stir only lightly

The children playing after supper,

Promise of the pillow and so much in the night to come.

工 作

他们准备再次开始:
问题,新的三角旗升上旗杆
在可以预料的浪漫曲中。

大约此时,太阳开始用它的影子
它游艺场的回声,从侧面切开西半球,
在各自的名字下,无常的国土拥挤不堪。
欢乐之后是空白,每个人必须分离
进入无助的夜,因为他的命运
是一无所获地返回,超越
时间流逝产生的光亮。只有
云彩的城堡,擅长捉住过去
通过伤害占有它。现在道路畅通
为了直线进入那个时刻
在其腐蚀物中他第一次发现如何呼吸。

只要看看你造成的污秽,
看看你干了什么。
如果这些是遗憾,他们只略微打扰了
晚饭后儿童们的游戏,
枕头的许诺,和许多将在夜晚到来的东西。

I plan to stay here a little while

For these are moments only, moments of insight,

And there are reaches to be attained,

A last level of anxiety that melts

In becoming, like miles under the pilgrim's feet.

我计划在这里停留片刻

因为这些只是瞬间,洞察的瞬间,

还有些河段需要抵达,

焦虑的最后一层一边出现

一边融化,像朝圣者脚下的远方。

Spring Day

The immense hope, and forbearance

Trailing out of night, to sidewalks of the day

Like air breathed into a paper city, exhaled

As night returns bringing doubts

That swarm around the sleeper's head

But are fended off with clubs and knives, so that morning

Installs again in cold hope

The air that was yesterday, is what you are,

In so many phases the head slips from the hand.

The tears ride freely, laughs or sobs:

What do they matter? There is free giving and taking;

The giant body relaxed as though beside a stream

Wakens to the force of it and has to recognize

The secret sweetness before it turns into life—

Sucked out of many exchanges, torn from the womb,

Disinterred before completely dead—and heaves

Its mountain-broad chest. "They were long in coming,

春　日

巨大的希望，耐心
从夜晚拖出，来到白昼的人行道上
像空气吹进一座纸城，呼出
当夜晚带着怀疑返回

蜂拥在睡眠者的脑袋周围
但是被棍棒和刀子击退，以至于早晨
又在寒冷的希望中
安置下昨天的空气，昨天的你，

在如此多的方面，脑袋从手中滑落。
自由地驾驭眼泪，或哭或笑：
它们有什么要紧？有免费的给予和索取；
巨大的躯体松弛下来仿佛在一条激流边

醒悟到它的力量并不得不辨识
秘密的甜蜜，在它变成生命之前——
吮干很多交易，扯离子宫，
在彻底死掉以前被掘出——起伏着

它山一样宽广的胸膛。"他们渴望来，

Those others, and mattered so little that it slowed them

To almost nothing. They were presumed dead,

Their names honorably grafted on the landscape

To be a memory to men. Until today

We have been living in their shell.

Now we break forth like a river breaking through a dam,

Pausing over the puzzled, frightened plain,

And our further progress shall be terrible,

Turning fresh knives in the wounds

In that gulf of recreation, that bare canvas

As matter-of-fact as the traffic and the day's noise."

The mountain stopped shaking; its body

Arched into its own contradiction, its enjoyment,

As far from us lights were put out, memories of boys and girls

Who walked here before the great change,

Before the air mirrored us,

Taking the opposite shape of our effort,

Its inseparable comment and corollary

But casting us farther and farther out.

那些其他人,无关紧要,他们慢得
几乎成了虚无。假定他们死了,
他们的名字体面地嫁接在风景上

成为男人们的记忆。直到今天
我们还生活在他们的壳里。
现在我们像一条河冲破大堤,
停顿在迷惑的,惊呆了的平原上,

我们下一步的进展将是可怕的,
在伤口中转动新鲜的刀子
在那游戏的海湾中,光秃的画布
平淡得有如交通和白昼的噪音。"

山停止了颤抖;它的躯体
在它固有的矛盾中拱起,它的快乐,
像离我们很远的灯熄灭,像男孩女孩的记忆
在剧变之前,他们在这里散步,

在空气映照我们之前,
我们的努力取得相反的形式,
它不可分的说明和必然结果
将我们更远更远地投射出去。

What—what happened? You are with

The orange tree, so that its summer produce

Can go back to where we got it wrong, then drip gently

Into history, if it wants to. A page turned; we were

Just now floundering in the wind of its colossal death.

And whether it is Thursday, or the day is stormy,

With thunder and rain, or the birds attack each other,

We have rolled into another dream.

No use charging the barriers of that other:

It no longer exists. But you,

Gracious and growing thing, with those leaves like stars,

We shall soon give all our attention to you.

发——发生了什么？你和橘子树
在一起，所以它夏天的出产
可以返回我们拿错的地方，然后在需要时
轻轻滴进历史。一页翻过；我们

此刻在它死亡的大风中挣扎。
无论是星期三，还是暴风雨
雷电交加，还是鸟儿互相攻击，
我们已经卷进了又一个梦。

给别的电池充电也无济于事：
它不再存在。但是你，
生长的妙物，有着星星般的叶子，
我们很快就会全部钟情于你。

Plainness in Diversity

Silly girls your heads full of boys
There is a last sample of talk on the outer side
Your stand at last lifts to dumb evening.
It is reflected in the steep blue sides of the crater,
So much water shall wash over these our breaths
Yet shall remain unwashed at the end. The fine
Branches of the fir tree catch at it, ebbing.
Not on our planet is the destiny
That can make you one.

To be placed on the side of some mountain
Is the truer story, with the breath only
Coming in patches at first, and then the little spurt
The way a steam engine starts up eventually.
The sagas purposely ignore how better off it was next day,
The feeling in between the chapters, like fins.
There is so much they must say, and it is important
About all the swimming motions, and the way the hands
Came up out of the ocean with original fronds,
The famous arrow, the girls who came at dawn
To pay a visit to the young child, and how, when he grew up to be a man
The same restive ceremony replaced the limited years between,
Only now he was old, and forced to begin the journey to the sun.

差异中的清晰

愚蠢的少女你们满脑子男孩
最后一段谈话在外面
你的站姿最后举向沉默的黄昏。
它反射在火山口陡峭的蓝色侧面,
这么多的水将这些冲刷,我们的呼吸
最后仍会留下不被冲走。冷杉树
美丽的枝条捉住它,落潮。
那可以使你成为一个人的命运
不在我们的行星上。

被放在某座山侧面的
是更真实的故事,只有风
起初断续地吹来,然后是小冲刺
以一架蒸汽引擎终于启动的方式。
英雄传奇有意忽略了更加美好的明天,
各章之间的感觉,像一些鱼鳍。
他们有这么多话要说,重要的是
关于游泳运动的一切,以及双手
带着原始藻类从海洋中升起的方式,
著名的箭,少女们在黎明到达
拜访一个少年,当他长大成人
同样不耐烦的仪式怎样取代了中间有限的岁月,
只不过现在他老了,并被迫开始朝向太阳的旅程。

Soonest Mended

Barely tolerated, living on the margin
In our technological society, we were always having to be rescued
On the brink of destruction, like heroines in *Orlando Furioso*
Before it was time to start all over again.
There would be thunder in the bushes, a rustling of coils,
And Angelica, in the Ingres painting, was considering
The colorful but small monster near her toe, as though wondering whether forgetting
The whole thing might not, in the end, be the only solution.
And then there always came a time when
Happy Hooligan in his rusted green automobile
Came plowing down the course, just to make sure everything was O. K.,
Only by that time we were in another chapter and confused
About how to receive this latest piece of information.
Was it information? Weren't we rather acting this out
For someone else's benefit, thoughts in a mind
With room enough and to spare for our little problems (so they began to seem),
Our daily quandary about food and the rent and bills to be paid?
To reduce all this to a small variant,
To step free at last, minuscule on the gigantic plateau—
This was our ambition: to be small and clear and free.
Alas, the summer's energy wanes quickly,
A moment and it is gone. And no longer

最快速修补

勉强能够忍受,生活在边缘
在我们的技术社会,我们始终需要
在毁灭的边缘被拯救,像"失常的奥兰多"中的女杰们
在一切重新开始之前。
灌木丛中将响起雷声,线圈的沙沙声,
安吉莉卡,在安格尔的绘画中,正在思考
她脚边彩色斑斓的小怪物,仿佛在奇怪
是否忘记整件事情,是最后的唯一解决。
那时总会有一个时刻出现
快乐阿飞驾着他生锈的绿色汽车
在路上逡巡,只为了确证一切正常,
只是那时我们已在另一章中,困惑于
如何接收这最后的信息。
它是信息吗?为了使其他人受益
我们宁可不这样做,为了头脑中的思想
有足够的空间,而是去省略我们的小问题(它们开始显得如此),
我们要对付食物、房租和账单的日常窘境?
把这一切减少到一个小变量,
最终摆脱出来,小写在巨大的高原上——
这是我们的野心:变得小而清晰且又自由。
上帝,夏天的能量迅速衰减,
一瞬间便耗尽了。我们不再

May we make the necessary arrangements, simple as they are.
Our star was brighter perhaps when it had water in it.
Now there is no question even of that, but only
Of holding on to the hard earth so as not to get thrown off,
With an occasional dream, a vision: a robin flies across
The upper corner of the window, you brush your hair away
And cannot quite see, or a wound will flash
Against the sweet faces of the others, something like:
This is what you wanted to hear, so why
Did you think of listening to something else? We are all talkers
It is true, but underneath the talk lies
The moving and not wanting to be moved, the loose
Meaning, untidy and simple like a threshing floor.

These then were some hazards of the course,
Yet though we knew the course *was* hazards and nothing else
It was still a shock when, almost a quarter of a century later,
The clarity of the rules dawned on you for the first time.
They were the players, and we who had struggled at the game
Were merely spectators, though subject to its vicissitudes
And moving with it out of the tearful stadium, borne on shoulders, at
    last.
Night after night this message returns, repeated
In the flickering bulbs of the sky, raised past us, taken away from us,
Yet ours over and over until the end that is past truth,
The being of our sentences, in the climate that fostered them,
Not ours to own, like a book, but to be with, and sometimes

做出必要的安排，像它们一样简单。
我们的星在它里面有水的时候也许更亮。
现在那也不成问题，关键在于
抱住坚硬的大地，不被抛出去，
随着偶尔的梦，一个幻象：一只知更鸟飞过
窗户的上角，你撩开头发
也看不太清，或者是一个伤口
对着其他人甜蜜的脸闪烁，诸如此类：
这就是你想听的，那为什么
你以为自己正在听的是别的东西？我们都很健谈
这是真的，但在谈话下面存在的
是移动和不想被移动的东西，是松散的
意义，杂乱无章，简单得像一块打谷场。

那么这就是谈话的风险，
虽然我们知道谈话是冒险而非其他
几乎四分之一世纪之后，你才明白
规则的透明性，你仍然感到震惊。
他们是游戏者，而我们这些努力游戏的人
却仅仅是观众，虽然心系其兴衰
与它一同离开悲痛的竞技场，最后，把它放在肩上。
这个信息夜复一夜返回，
在天空闪烁的灯泡中重复，升起，离开我们，
而我们的游戏一再重复，直到最后，那过去的真理，
我们的句子，在培养它们的气候中存在，

To be without, alone and desperate.
But the fantasy makes it ours, a kind of fence-sitting
Raised to the level of an esthetic ideal. These were moments, years,
Solid with reality, faces, namable events, kisses, heroic acts,
But like the friendly beginning of a geometrical progression
Not too reassuring, as though meaning could be cast aside some day
When it had been outgrown. Better, you said, to stay cowering
Like this in the early lessons, since the promise of learning
Is a delusion, and I agreed, adding that
Tomorrow would alter the sense of what had already been learned,
That the learning process is extended in this way, so that from this
    standpoint
None of us ever graduates from college,
For time is an emulsion, and probably thinking not to grow up
Is the brightest kind of maturity for us, right now at any rate.
And you see, both of us were right, though nothing
Has somehow come to nothing; the avatars
Of our conforming to the rules and living
Around the home have made—well, in a sense, "good citizens" of us,
Brushing the teeth and all that, and learning to accept
The charity of the hard moments as they are doled out,
For this is action, this not being sure, this careless
Preparing, sowing the seeds crooked in the furrow,
Making ready to forget, and always coming back
To the mooring of starting out, that day so long ago.

不属于我们，而是像一本书，有时和我们在一起，
有时不在一起，孤独而绝望。
但是幻想它属于我们，一种中立态度
被提高到审美典范的水平。这些是瞬间，年月，
因真实，面孔，可命名的事件，亲吻，英雄的行为而坚固，
但是像一个几何级数的友好开端
不太可靠，仿佛有一天可以把意义废除
在它已经过时的时候。你说，最好继续这样
畏缩在早期课程中，既然学习的许诺
是一个幻想，我同意这点，而且
明天会改变已经学会了什么的感觉
学习过程以这种方式延伸，从这一点来说
我们任何人都无法从学校中毕业，
因为时间是乳剂，也许不想长大
对于我们是成年的最大仁慈，
你明白，我们都是对的，虽则虚无
终归是虚无；我们的替身
对规则的遵守以及围绕着家的生活，
已经在某种意义上，使我们成了"好公民"，
学会刷牙那一套，学会接受
艰难时刻所分发的施舍，
因为这是行动，不是确定，这是漫不经心的
准备，在犁沟中播下弯曲的种子，
准备遗忘，并经常回到
出发的泊位，很久以前的那一天。

Summer

There is that sound like the wind
Forgetting in the branches that means something
Nobody can translate. And there is the sobering "later on,"
When you consider what a thing meant, and put it down.

For the time being the shadow is ample
And hardly seen, divided among the twigs of a tree,
The trees of a forest, just as life is divided up
Between you and me, and among all the others out there.

And the thinning-out phase follows
The period of reflection. And suddenly, to be dying
Is not a little or mean or cheap thing,
Only wearying, the heat unbearable,

And also the little mindless constructions put upon
Our fantasies of what we did: summer, the ball of pine needles,
The loose fates serving our acts, with token smiles,
Carrying out their instructions too accurately—

Too late to cancel them now—and winter, the twitter

夏　天

那里有像风一样的声音
遗忘在树枝间,它意味着什么
无人能解。有人镇静地说着"以后吧",
当你思忖着一件事的含意,并把它放下。

因为影子暂时是足够的
几乎看不见,在一棵树的细枝间分裂,
一片树林中的树木,就像生活被分开
在你我之间,在外面的所有其他人中间。

逐渐变得稀疏的阶段之后
便是沉思的阶段。突然,死灭的
不是一点儿,也不是卑贱或便宜之物,
只是疲倦的,不可忍受的热量,

还有漫不经心的结构附加在
我们对自己做过什么的幻想之上:夏天,松针的球,
为我们行动服务的松懈的命运,用象征性的微笑,
执行着它们过于精确的指令——

现在取消它们已经太晚——冬天,

Of cold stars at the pane, that describes with broad gestures
This state of being that is not so big after all.
Summer involves going down as a steep flight of steps

To a narrow ledge over the water. Is this it, then,
This iron comfort, these reasonable taboos,
Or did you mean it when you stopped? And the face
Resembles yours, the one reflected in the water.

寒冷的星星在窗上啁啾,用宽容的姿态描述着
终究并不怎么伟大的这种存在状态。
夏天卷进来像一面陡峭的台阶继续向下

通往狭窄的水上暗礁。那么,这就是它吗,
这铁的安慰,这些合理的禁忌,
当你停下时,你指的是它吗?还有
那与你相似的,水中映出的那张面孔。

It Was Raining in the Capital

It was raining in the capital
And for many days and nights
The one they called the Aquarian
Had stayed alone with her delight.

What with the winter and its business
It had fallen to one side
And she had only recently picked it up
Where the other had died.

Between the pages of the newspaper
It smiled like a face.
Next to the drugstore on the corner
It looked to another place.

Or it would just hang around
Like sullen clouds over the sun.
But—this was the point—it was real
To her and to everyone.

For spring had entered the capital

首都正在下雨

首都正在下雨
日夜不息,持续多时
他们称做宝瓶座的人
怡然独处。

随着冬天和它的事务
它落在一边
她只是最近才把它捡起
在其他的乐趣消失之处。

在报纸的各版之间
它微笑如一张面孔。
在角落的药店旁边
它看着另一个地方。

或是仅仅在周围闲荡
像阴云在太阳之上。
但是——这是关键——它是真实的
对于她,对于每一个人。

因为春天已经进入了首都

Walking on gigantic feet.

The smell of witch hazel indoors

Changed to narcissus in the street.

She thought she had seen all this before:

Bundles of new, fresh flowers,

All changing, pressing upward

To the distant office towers.

Until now nothing had been easy,

Hemmed in by all that shit—

Horseshit, dogshit, birdshit, manshit—

Yes, she remembered having said it,

Having spoken in that way, thinking

There could be no road ahead,

Sobbing into the intractable presence of it

As one weeps alone in bed.

Its chamber was narrower than a seed

Yet when the doorbell rang

It reduced all that living to air

As *"kyrie eleison"* it sang.

迈着巨大的双脚。
女巫淡褐色内室的气味
在街道上变成了水仙。

她想起以前见过这一切：
成束清新的鲜花，
都在变化，努力向上
朝向遥远的办公室塔楼。

到目前一切都不容易，
被各种粪便包围——
马粪，狗粪，鸟粪，人粪——
是的，她记起曾经说过，

以那种方式说过，想着
前面可能没有路了，
为它难以应付的存在而哭泣
就像一个人独自在床上流泪。

它的房间比一粒种子还狭小
不过，当门铃响起
它把所有的生活缩成空气
像它唱"求怜经"的时候。

Hearing that music he had once known

But now forgotten, the man,

The one who had waited casually in the dark

Turned to smile at the door's span.

He smiled and shrugged—a lesson

In the newspaper no longer

But fed by the ink and paper

Into a sign of something stronger

Who reads the news and takes the bus

Going to work each day

But who was never born of woman

Nor formed of the earth's clay.

Then what unholy bridegroom

Did the Aquarian foretell?

Or was such lively intelligence

Only the breath of hell?

It scarcely mattered at the moment

And it shall never matter at all

Since the moment will not be replaced

But stand, poised for its fall,

听着他曾经熟悉

但业已遗忘的音乐,那男人,

那在黑暗中漫不经心等待的男人

转身对着门的跨度微笑。

他微笑,耸肩——一门

报纸上不再有的课程

却被墨水和纸张喂养

成了更强大的东西的符号

谁每天读着新闻

乘公交车去上班

谁就不是女人生的

也不是由大地的黏土做的。

这宝瓶座人预言的

又是什么邪恶的新郎?

或许这如此生动的智慧

仅仅是地狱的呼吸?

这一刻它几乎无关紧要

它永远也不会有什么要紧

既然这一刻不会被替代

而是留驻,永远保持着

Forever. "This is what my learning
Teaches," the Aquarian said,
"To absorb life through the pores
For the life around you is dead."

The sun came out in the capital
Just before it set.
The lovely death's head shone in the sky
As though these two had never met.

平衡。"这就是我学会的
教训,"宝瓶座人说,
"通过毛孔吸收生命
因为你周围的生活是死的。"

首都出太阳了
就在它落下之前。
死亡可爱的头颅在天空闪耀
仿佛这两个从未相遇过。

Variations, Calypso and Fugue on a Theme of Ella Wheeler Wilcox

"For the pleasures of the many

May be ofttimes traced to one

As the hand that plants an acorn

Shelters armies from the sun."

And in places where the annual rainfall is . 0071 inches

What a pleasure to lie under the tree, to sit, stand, and get up under the tree!

Im wunderschönen Monat Mai

The feeling is of never wanting to leave the tree,

Of predominantly peace and relaxation.

Do you step out from under the shade a moment,

It is only to return with renewed expectation, of expectation fulfilled.

Insecurity be damned! There is something to all this, that will not elude us:

Growing up under the shade of friendly trees, with our brothers all around.

And truly, young adulthood was never like this:

Such delight, such consideration, such affirmation in the way the day

    goes round together.

Yes, the world goes round a good deal faster

When there are highlights on the lips, unspoken and true words in the heart,

And the hand keeps brushing away a strand of chestnut hair, only to

    have it fall back into place again.

But all good things must come to an end, and so one must move forward

有关埃拉·惠勒·威尔科克斯的一个主题的变奏曲、卡里普索和赋格曲

"因为众人的快乐

往往源自一个人

就像种植一棵橡树的手

为一支军队遮阳。"

在每年降雨量为 0.0071 英寸的地方

躺在树下是多么惬意,在树下或坐,或立,或是站起身来!

在灿烂的五月里

永远不想离开树的感觉

是支配一切的和平与放松。

你从树荫下走出来一会儿,

只是为了带着复苏的期待,圆满的期待返回。

心神不定真是该死!对于这一切有什么东西,不会回避我们:

在友善的树影下成长,我们的兄弟们都在身边。

真的,年轻的成人从来不这样:

这欢乐,这考虑,这主张,以日子一同进出的方式。

是的,世界旋转的速度快多了

当嘴唇上有要闻,心里有未说出的真话,

当手一直在梳理一绺栗色的头发,只是为了让它再回到原位。

但是所有的好事都必定终结,一个人必须向前

进入一个人的结局所留下的空间。这就是变老吗?

Into the space left by one's conclusions. Is this growing old?
Well, it is a good experience, to divest oneself of some tested ideals,
    some old standbys,
And even finding nothing to put in their place is a good experience,
Preparing one, as it does, for the consternation that is to come.
But—and this is the gist of it—what if I dreamed it all,
The branches, the late afternoon sun,

The trusting camaraderie, the love that watered all,
Disappearing promptly down into the roots as it should?
For later in the vast gloom of cities, only there you learn
How the ideas were good only because they had to die,
Leaving you alone and skinless, a drawing by Vesalius.
This is what was meant, and toward which everything directs:
That the tree should shrivel in 120-degree heat, the acorns
Lie around on the worn earth like eyeballs, and the lead soldiers
    shrug and slink off.

So my youth was spent, underneath the trees
I always moved around with perfect ease

I voyaged to Paris at the age of ten
And met many prominent literary men

好吧，这是个好经验，迫使自己放弃一些经过考验的理想，一
　　些旧的备用品，
甚至发现没有什么来取代它们也是个好经验，
实际上，这是为即将到来的惊愕做准备。
但是——这是它的主旨——万一我梦见了它，
树枝，午后晚些时候的太阳，

信任的友情，浇灌一切的爱，
理当立即消失在根须之中吗？
因为后来在城市的巨大阴郁中，只有你知道
思想有多么好，只是因为它们不得不死掉，
把你独自留下，没有皮肤，维萨里的一幅画。
这就是意图所在，朝向一切所指的方向：
那棵树应该在一百二十度的高温中枯萎，橡树
躺在眼球一样磨损的大地上，尖兵们耸肩，溜走。

你的青春就这样消磨了，在树下
我总是安逸无比地在周围转悠

我十岁时去巴黎旅行
遇见许多杰出的文人

凝视阿尔卑斯山是相当棒的景色
我感觉眼泪无比有力地涌流出来

Gazing at the Alps was quite a sight
I felt the tears flow forth with all their might

A climb to the Acropolis meant a lot to me
I had read the Greek philosophers you see

In the Colosseum I thought my heart would burst
Thinking of all the victims who had been there first

On Mount Ararat's side I began to grow
Remembering the Flood there, so long ago

On the banks of the Ganges I stood in mud
And watched the water light up like blood

The Great Wall of China is really a thrill
It cleaves through the air like a silver pill

It was built by the hand of man for good or ill
Showing what he can do when he decides not to kill

But of all the sights that were seen by me
In the East or West, on land or sea,
The best was the place that is spelled H-O-M-E.

攀登卫城对我意义重大
我读过希腊的那些哲学家你知道

在罗马大斗兽场我以为我的心会爆炸
想着那里曾经存在的所有牺牲者

第一次在阿勒山的山坡我开始逐渐
回忆起那里的洪水，很久以前

在恒河岸边我站在淤泥中
观察河水像血一样亮了起来

中国的长城果真惊险
它像一颗银弹劈开空气

无论好歹，它是由一个男人的手所建
表明他决定不杀人的时候他能做什么

但在我见过的所有景色之中
无论东西，无论水陆，
最好的地方叫做"家"。

现在我再次抵达了家
我将克制住继续漫游的冲动

Now that once again I have achieved home
I shall forbear all further urge to roam

There is a hole of truth in the green earth's rug
Once you find it you are as snug as a bug

Maybe some do not like it quite as much as you
That isn't all you're going to do.

You must remember that it is yours
Which is why nobody is sending you flowers

This age-old truth I to thee impart
Act according to the dictates of your art

Because if you don't no one else is going to
And that person isn't likely to be you.

It is the wind that comes from afar
It is the truth of the farthest star

In all likelihood you will not need these
So take it easy and learn your ABC's

And trust in the dream that will never come true
'Cause that is the scheme that is best for you
And the gleam that is the most suitable too.

在绿色大地的地毯上有一个真理的洞
一旦你发现它你就像虫子一样藏起来

也许有人像你一样不喜欢它
那并不是你要做的全部。

你必须记住它是你的
记住为什么没人给你送花

我传授给你这个古老的真理
依据你的艺术的命令行事

因为如果你不做，就没人会做
人们不可能和你一样。

它是风从远方而来
它是最远的星辰的真理

在所有可能性中你都不会需要这些
那就别紧张了，学你的 ABC 吧

相信永远不会成真的梦
因为那是对你最有利的计划

"MAKE MY DREAM COME TRUE." This message, set in 84-point Hobo type, startled in the morning editions of the paper: the old, half-won security troubles the new pause. And with the approach of the holidays, the present is clearly here to stay: the big brass band of its particular moment's consciousness invades the plazas and the narrow alleys. Three-fourths of the houses in this city are on narrow stilts, finer than a girl's wrists: it is largely a question of keeping one's feet dry, and of privacy. In the morning you forget what the punishment was. Probably it was something like eating a pretzel or going into the back yard. Still, you can't tell. These things could be a lot clearer without hurting anybody. But it does not follow that such issues will produce the most dynamic capital gains for you.

Friday. We are really missing you.

"The most suitable," however, was not the one specially asked for nor the one hanging around the lobby. It was just the one asked after, day after day—what spilled over, claimed by the spillway. The distinction of a dog, of how a dog walks. The thought of a dog walking. No one ever referred to the incident again. The case was officially closed. Maybe there were choruses of silent gratitude, welling up in the spring night like a column of cloud, reaching to the very rafters of the sky—but this was their own business. The point is no ear ever heard them. Thus, the incident, to call it by one of its names—choice, conduct, absent-minded frown might be others—came to be not only as though it had never happened, but as though it never *could* have happened. Sealed into the wall of all that season's coming on. And thus,

也是最为适宜的微光。

"让我的梦想成真。"这个信息，以八十四磅艺术字体，赫然出现在晨报上：即将成功的旧证券干扰着新的暂停。随着假期的临近，礼物显然要留在这里：它特定瞬间的意识的大铜管乐队侵占了广场和狭窄的胡同。这个城市四分之三的房子都立在细细的支柱上，比少女的手腕还细：这主要涉及如何保持一个人双脚干爽和隐私的问题。早晨你忘记了过去遭受的惩罚。也许它就像是吃椒盐脆饼干或是去后院。不过，你不能说。这些事情可能要清晰得多而又不伤害任何人。但是这样的问题随后并没有为你取得最具活力的资本。

星期五。我们真的想念你。

然而，"最合适的"不是特别要求的那个，也不是在大厅晃荡的那个。仅仅是日复一日探问的那一个——由溢洪道认领的溢出物。一条狗的特性，在于它如何走路。一条狗的思想在走路。没有人再提这件事。这个案子已经正式终结。也许有沉默感恩的合唱，在春夜里涌起，如同一排云彩，抵达天空的橡子——但这是它们自己的事儿。关键是没有任何耳朵听到过它们。于是，这事件，以其名之一来称呼——选择，行为，心不在焉的皱眉可能是别人——它最后不仅仅是好像从未发生过，而且是好像永远不可能发生。密封在墙壁里的季节即将出现。于是，为了区区少数

for a mere handful of people—roustabouts and degenerates, most of them—it became the only true version. Nothing else mattered. It was bread by morning and night, the dates falling listlessly from the trees—man, woman, child, festering glistening in a single orb. The reply to "hello."

    Pink purple and blue

    The way you used to do

The next two days passed oddly for Peter and Christine, and were among the most absorbing they had ever known. On the one hand, a vast open basin—or sea; on the other a narrow spit of land, terminating in a copse, with a few broken down outbuildings lying here and there. It made no difference that the bey—b-e-y this time, oriental potentate—had ordained their release, there was this funny feeling that they should always be there, sustained by looks out over the ether, missing Mother and Alan and the others but really quiet, in a kind of activity that offers its own way of life, sunflower chained to the sun. Can it ever be resolved? Or are the forms of a person's thoughts controlled by inexorable laws, as in Dürer's Adam and Eve? So mutually exclusive, and so steep—Himalayas jammed side by side like New York apartment buildings. Oh the blame of it, the de-crescendo. My vice is worry. Forget it. The continual splitting up, the ear-shattering volumes of a polar ice-cap breaking up are just what you wanted. You've got it, so shut up.

    The crystal haze

    For days and days

Lots of sleep is an important factor, and rubbing the eyes. Getting off the subway he suddenly felt hungry. He went into one place,

人——大部分都是码头工人和堕落的人——它成了唯一真实的版本。别的都不要紧。凭借晨昏的面包，从树上无精打采坠落的年代——男人，女人，孩子，在一个天体中溃烂和闪耀。对"喂"的回答。

粉红色和蓝色
你习惯的方式

彼得和克里斯汀接下来的两天过得很奇妙，他们置身于自己熟识的最有趣的人群当中。在一边，是一个巨大敞开的盆——或者是大海；另一边是一条狭长的岬角，终结于一片杂树林，到处躺着一些倒塌的附属建筑。它不起作用，省长——这次是东方的统治者——已经颁发了赦免令，这才有了这种滑稽的感觉，他们应该始终待在那里，以向外望着苍天，想念着母亲和艾伦作为支撑，其他人真是安静，以一种提供自己的生活方式的活动，把向日葵和太阳拴在一起。它能解决吗？还是一个人的思维方式受控于铁律，就像丢勒的亚当和夏娃？就这样互相排斥，如此陡峭——喜马拉雅群山并排挤在一起，就像纽约的公寓楼。啊那是它的责任，声音渐弱。我的罪在于焦虑。忘记它。持续不断的分裂，北极冰帽炸裂的震耳欲聋，正是你需要的。你已经得到了，那就住口吧。

水晶的薄雾
为了日子和日子

a place he knew, and ordered a hamburger and a cup of coffee. He hadn't been in this neighborhood in a long time—not since he was a kid. He used to play stickball in the vacant lot across the street. Sometimes his bunch would get into a fight with some of the older boys, and he'd go home tired and bleeding. Most days were the same though. He'd say "Hi" to the other kids and they'd say "Hi" to him. Nice bunch of guys. Finally he decided to take a turn past the old grade school he'd attended as a kid. It was a rambling structure of yellow brick, now gone in seediness and shabbiness which the late-afternoon shadows mercifully softened. The gravel playground in front was choked with weeds. Large trees and shrubbery would do no harm flanking the main entrance. Time farted.

    The first shock rattles the cruets in their stand,

    The second rips the door from its hinges.

"My dear friend," he said gently, "you said you were Professor Hertz. You must pardon me if I say that the information startles and mystifies me. When you are stronger I have some questions to ask you, if you will be kind enough to answer them."

No one was prepared for the man's answer to that apparently harmless statement.

Weak as he was, Gustavus Hertz raised himself on his elbow. He stared wildly about him, peering fearfully into the shadowy corners of the room.

"I will tell you nothing! Nothing, do you hear? he shrieked. "Go away! Go away!"

睡得很多是一个重要因素,擦着眼睛。下地铁后他突然感到饿了。他走进一个地方,一个他认识的地方,叫了一份汉堡和一杯咖啡。很长时间他没到这附近来了——从他还是个孩子起就不来了。他习惯在街对过的空场玩棍子球。有时他那伙人会和年纪更大的男孩们打起来,他就会疲倦地流着血回家去。大多数日子都是一个样。他会对其他孩子说"嘿",他们会对他说"嘿"。很棒的一伙儿家伙。最后他决定转一圈,经过他孩提时上过的旧小学。那是一座不规则的黄砖建筑,现在破旧而褴褛,午后的阴影仁慈地使它变得柔和。前面碎石的操场被杂草窒息了。主入口侧翼的大树和灌木丛不会有任何危害。时间放屁了。

        第一次震动使立着的调味瓶咯咯作响,
        第二次震动将门从铰链上撕裂下来。

"我亲爱的朋友,"他温和地说,"你说你是赫兹教授。你必须原谅我,如果我说那信息让我吃惊和困惑。在你变得更坚强的时候,我有些问题要问你,如果你能好心地予以回答。"
没有一个人准备聆听那个人对那个明显无害的声明的回答。
尽管还很虚弱,古斯塔夫斯·赫兹还是用肘撑起身体。他狂暴地盯着他,看着他恐惧地溜进房间荫翳的角落。
"我什么都不会告诉你!什么都不会,你听见了吗?"他尖叫道。
    "走开!走开"

Song

The song tells us of our old way of living,

Of life in former times. Fragrance of florals,

How things merely ended when they ended,

Of beginning again into a sigh. Later

Some movement is reversed and the urgent masks

Speed toward a totally unexpected end

Like clocks out of control. Is this the gesture

That was meant, long ago, the curving in

Of frustrated denials, like jungle foliage

And the simplicity of the ending all to be let go

In quick, suffocating sweetness? The day

Puts toward a nothingness of sky

Its face of rusticated brick. Sooner or later,

The cars lament, the whole business will be hurled down.

Meanwhile we sit, scarcely daring to speak,

To breathe, as though this closeness cost us life.

The pretensions of a past will some day

歌

歌向我们诉说我们古老的生活方式,
诉说从前的生活。花的芳香,
事物如何只在结束时结束,
在一声叹息中再次开始。后来

某种运动被颠倒,急迫的面具
加速驶向一个完全没有料到的终结
像钟表失去了控制。很久以前
这种姿势意味着,在沮丧的否弃中

蜷缩起来,像丛林的树叶
在短暂、遏制的甜蜜中
放弃终结的全部单纯?日子
将交出满天的空虚

它质朴砖头的脸。或早或晚,
汽车将悔恨,整桩交易将被推翻。
同时我们坐着,几乎不敢说话,
不敢呼吸,仿佛这种结局会要了我们的命。

某一天,过去的自负

Make it over into progress, a growing up,

As beautiful as a new history book

With uncut pages, unseen illustrations,

And the purpose of the many stops and starts will be made clear:

Backing into the old affair of not wanting to grow

Into the night, which becomes a house, a parting of the ways

Taking us far into sleep. A dumb love.

将使它进步，一种成长，
美得像一本新历史书
有着未切开的书页，未见过的插图，

许多终止与开始的目的将变得清晰：
返回不需要长成夜晚的古老的
事态，它变成了一座房子，一个岔路口
把我们带入更深的睡眠。一份沉默的爱。

Decoy

We hold these truths to be self-evident:
That ostracism, both political and moral, has
Its place in the twentieth-century scheme of things;
That urban chaos is the problem we have been seeing into and seeing into,
For the factory, deadpanned by its very existence into a
Descending code of values, has moved right across the road from total financial upheaval
And caught regression head-on. The descending scale does not imply
A corresponding deterioration of moral values, punctuated
By acts of corporate vandalism every five years,
Like a bunch of violets pinned to a dress, that knows and ignores its own standing.
There is every reason to rejoice with those self-styled prophets of commercial disaster, those harbingers of gloom,
Over the imminent lateness of the denouement that, advancing slowly, never arrives,
At the same time keeping the door open to a tongue-in-cheek attitude on the part of the perpetrators,
The men who sit down to their vast desks on Monday to begin planning the week's notations, jotting memoranda that take
Invisible form in the air, like flocks of sparrows
Above the city pavements, turning and wheeling aimlessly
But on the average directed by discernible motives.

To sum up: We are fond of plotting itineraries
And our pyramiding memories, alert as dandelion fuzz, dart from one

诱　饵

我们占有这些真理是为了自我证明：
在政治和道德两方面，放逐，
在二十世纪的事物格局中都有其位置；
城市的混乱是我们一直关注的问题，
因为工厂，不动声色地凭其存在本身
成了价值衰退的代码，从整体的金融剧变中径直穿过道路
迎头赶上了衰退。衰退的规模并不意味着
道德价值上相应的堕落，
被五年一次全体的蓄意破坏不时打断，
像一束紫罗兰别在连衣裙上，了解又无视它自己的身份。
有各种理由与那些自称的商业灾难预言家同欢，阴暗的先兆，
笼罩着逼近的结局，那结局进展缓慢，从未到来，
同时向有关犯罪者的半开玩笑的态度敞开大门，
星期一在大桌子边坐下的人们开始规划一周的乐谱，潦草的备
　　忘录
空气中的无形之形，像一群群麻雀
在城市人行道上空，漫无目的地旋转打滚
但却普遍受到可辨动机的指引。

总而言之：我们喜欢制定旅行日程
我们金字塔形的记忆，像蒲公英的绒毛一样警觉，从一个借口

      pretext to the next
Seeking in occasions new sources of memories, for memory is profit
Until the day it spreads out all its accumulation, delta-like, on the plain
For that day no good can come of remembering, and the anomalies
      cancel each other out.
But until then foreshortened memories will keep us going, alive, one
      to the other.

There was never any excuse for this and perhaps there need be none,
For kicking out into the morning, on the wide bed,
Waking far apart on the bed, the two of them:
Husband and wife
Man and wife

飞向下一个借口
在偶然中搜寻记忆的新源泉，因为记忆就是利润
直到有一天它把所有积累，像三角洲一样，在平原上展开
因为到那天记忆将无济于事，反常事物将彼此取消。
但在那之前，缩短的记忆会维持我们，活着，从一个到另一个。

对此，从来没有任何借口，或许也根本不需要，
被踢进早晨的借口，在宽大的床上，
离得远远地醒来，他们两个：
丈夫和妻子
男人和妻子

For John Clare

Kind of empty in the way it sees everything, the earth gets to its feet and salutes the sky. More of a success at it this time than most others it is. The feeling that the sky might be in the back of someone's mind. Then there is no telling how many there are. They grace everything—bush and tree—to take the roisterer's mind off his caroling—so it's like a smooth switch back. To what was aired in their previous conniption fit. There is so much to be seen everywhere that it's like not getting used to it, only there is so much it never feels new, never any different. You ate standing looking at that building and you cannot take it all in, certain details are already hazy and the mind boggles. What will it all be like in five years' time when you try to remember? Will there have been boards in between the grass part and the edge of the street? As long as that couple is stopping to look in that Window over there we cannot go. We feel like they have to tell us we can, but they never look our way and they are already gone, gone far into the future—the night of time. If we could look at a photograph of it and say there they are, they never really stopped but there they are. There is so much to be said, and on the surface of it very little gets said.

There ought to be room for more things, for a spreading out, like. Being immersed in the details of rock and field and slope— letting them come to you for once, and then meeting them halfway would be so much easier—if they took an ingenuous pride in being in one's blood. Alas, we perceive them if at all as those things that were meant to be put aside— costumes of the supporting actors or voice trilling at the end of a narrow enclosed street. You can do nothing

致约翰·克莱尔

它看待一切的方式中有一种空虚,大地站起来向天空致敬。这种时候它比其他大多数时候更要成功。感觉天空可能在某个人思想的后面。所以就说不清有多少这样的时刻了。他们使一切优美——灌木和树——使喧闹的饮酒者不再想着他的欢唱——这就像是一次平稳切换。回到他们先前大吵大闹时所夸耀的东西。到处都有这么多的东西要看,很容易变得不习惯,只要有这么多它从来不觉得新鲜、从来没有变化的东西。你正站着,注视那座建筑,你无法看见它的全貌,一些细节已经模糊,思想开始退缩。五年后你尝试回忆的时候它会是什么样子?在草坪和街道边缘之间会有木板吗?只要那对夫妇停下来向那扇窗户里看,我们就不能去那里。我们觉得他们不得不告诉我们能去,但是他们从来不向我们这边看,他们已经走了,远远地走进了未来——时间的夜晚。如果我们能看一看它的一张照片,说他们在那儿,他们从未真地停下来,但是他们在那儿。有这么多东西要说,它表面上说出来的很少。

应该有房间容纳更多的东西,比如,为了传播出去。沉浸在岩石、田野和斜坡的细节之中——让它们再次向你而来,而后中途相遇,这样会容易得多——如果它们因为在一个人的血液里存在而感到天真的自豪。唉,我们感知到它们,如果它们完全像那些有意要撇开的东西——男配角的服装,或是一条封闭的窄街尽头的颤声。你对它们什么也做不了。甚至主动付费

with them. Not even offer to pay.

It is possible that finally, like coming to the end of a long, barely perceptible rise, there is mutual cohesion and interaction. The whole scene is fixed in your mind, the music all present, as though you could see each note as well as hear it. I say this because there is an uneasiness in things just now. Waiting for something to be over before you are forced to notice it. The pollarded trees scarcely bucking the wind—and yet it's keen, it makes you fall over. Clabbered sky. Seasons that pass with a rush. After all it's their time too—nothing says they aren't to make something of it. As for Jenny Wren, she cares, hopping about on her little twig like she was tryin' to tell us somethin', but that's just it, she couldn't even if she wanted to—dumb bird. But the others—and they in some way must know too—it would never occur to them to want to, even if they could take the first step of the terrible journey toward feeling somebody should act, that ends in utter confusion and hopelessness, east of the sun and west of the moon. So their comment is: "No comment." Meanwhile the whole history of probabilities is coming to life, starting in the upper left-hand corner, like a sail.

也不行。

有可能到最后,就如同一个漫长、勉强可觉察的上升过程抵达终点,其间存在着互相的衔接与作用。整个场景固定在你的思想中,音乐全部呈现,仿佛你可以像听见那样看见每个音符。我这么说是因为目前的事物中存在着一种不安。在你被迫注意到它之前,等待某件事过去。截去树梢的树木简直抗不住风——可它依然敏捷,让你跌倒。凝结的天空。四季匆匆而过。这毕竟也是它们的时间——没有任何东西说它们不想利用它。至于鹩鹩,她在乎,她在自己的嫩枝附近跳跃,像要告诉我们什么事,可恰恰是这事儿,她想说也无法说出来——哑鸟。但是其他的鸟——在某种程度上一定也知道——它们永远不会想要这样,即便能够在可怕的旅程上迈出第一步,去感受人应该怎么做,这旅程的终点还是乱作一团,毫无希望,是日出东方和月出西方。于是,它们的评论是:"不做评论。"与此同时,整个可能性的历史正在走向生活,在左上角开始,像一次航行。

Farm Implements and Rutabagas in a Landscape

The first of the undecoded messages read: "Popeye sits in thunder,
Unthought of. From that shoebox of an apartment,
From livid curtain's hue, a tangram emerges: a country."
Meanwhile the Sea Hag was relaxing on a green couch: "How pleasant
To spend one's vacation *en la casa de Popeye*," she scratched
Her cleft chin's solitary hair. She remembered spinach

And was going to ask Wimpy if he had bought any spinach.
"M'love," he intercepted, "the plains are decked out in thunder
Today, and it shall be as you wish." He scratched
The part of his head under his hat. The apartment
Seemed to grow smaller. "But what if no pleasant
Inspiration plunge us now to the stars? For *this is my country*."

Suddenly they remembered how it was cheaper in the country.
Wimpy was thoughtfully cutting open a number 2 can of spinach
When the door opened and Swee'pea crept in. "How pleasant!"
But Swee'pea looked morose. A note was pinned to his bib. "Thunder
And tears are unavailing," it read. "Henceforth shall Popeye's apartment
Be but remembered space, toxic or salubrious, whole or scratched."

Olive came hurtling through the window; its geraniums scratched
Her long thigh. "I have news!" she gasped. "Popeye, forced as you know to flee the country

风景中的农具和芜菁

未解码的信息是这样开头的:"卜派坐在雷电中,
出乎意料。从房间的那个鞋盒子,
从铅色的窗帘,出现了一个七巧板:一片田野。"
这时,海巫婆松弛地坐在绿色长沙发上:
"在卜派的房子里度假是多么愉快,"她搔着
裂开的下巴上孤独的毛。她想起了菠菜

想去问问维姆派他买了菠菜没有。
"亲爱的,"他阻拦道,"今天平原上布满雷电,
你会如愿以偿的。"他搔着
帽子下的脑袋。房间似乎变得更小了。
"可万一没有美妙的灵感现在就把我们
投向群星呢?因为这是我的乡野。"

他们突然想起乡下的菠菜有多么便宜。
维姆派沉思着打开二号菠菜罐头
这时门开了,甜豌豆溜进来。"多么美妙!"
但是甜豌豆显得闷闷不乐。一张纸条钉在他的围嘴上。
上面写着,"雷电和眼泪无济于事,卜派的房间
今后将被记住,无论有害还是有益,全部还是碎片。"

奥莉芙探进窗户;天竺葵搔着她的长腿。

One musty gusty evening, by the schemes of his wizened, duplicate
    father, jealous of the apartment
And all that it contains, myself and spinach
In particular, heaves bolts of loving thunder
At his own astonished becoming, rupturing the pleasant

Arpeggio of our years. No more shall pleasant
Rays of the sun refresh your sense of growing old, nor the scratched
Tree-trunks and mossy foliage, only immaculate darkness and
    thunder."

She grabbed Swee'pea. "I'm taking the brat to the country."
"But you can't do that—he hasn't even finished his spinach,"
Urged the Sea Hag, looking fearfully around at the apartment.

But Olive was already out of earshot. Now the apartment
Succumbed to a strange new hush. "Actually it's quite pleasant
Here," thought the Sea Hag. "If this is all we need fear from spinach
Then I don't mind so much. Perhaps we could invite Alice the Goon
    over"—she scratched
One dug pensively—"but Wimpy is such a country
Bumpkin, always burping like that." Minute at first, the thunder

Soon filled the apartment. It was domestic thunder,
The color of spinach. Popeye chuckled and scratched
His balls: it sure was pleasant to spend a day in the country.

"我有消息!"她喘息道,"卜派,你知道我们被迫逃到乡下
在一个散发霉味的暴风雨的傍晚,迫于他干瘪的
一模一样的父亲的阴谋,对公寓的嫉妒
以及它里面的一切,我自己和菠菜
尤其是,可爱的暴风雨投掷的霹雳
让他震惊,撕裂了

我们岁月的琶音。不再有美妙的阳光
刷新你老去的感觉,也没有擦破的树干
和青苔般的绿叶,只有纯洁的黑暗和雷电。"
她抱住甜豌豆。"我要把小鬼带到乡下去。"
"可你不能那么做——他还没吃完菠菜呢,"
焦急的海巫婆,恐惧地环顾着房间。

但是已经听不见奥莉芙了。现在
房间屈服于新的陌生的寂静。"实际上这里十分怡人,"
海巫婆想,"如果这就是我们需要害怕菠菜的全部原因
我就不会这么在意了。也许我们可以邀请艾丽丝那个呆子"——
　　她悲哀地
搔着一只乳房——"可维姆派简直是个乡巴佬
总是那样打嗝。"雷声,起初很小

不久便充满了房间。那是家中的雷电,
菠菜的颜色。卜派轻笑,抓搔着
他的裆部:在乡下度过一天确实愉快。

Papergon

We are happy in our way of life.

It doesn't make much sense to others. We sit about,

Read, and are restless. Occasionally it becomes time

To lower the dark shade over it all.

Our entity pivots on a self-induced trance

Like sleep. Noiseless our living stops

And one strays as in a dream

Into those respectable purlieus where life is motionless and alive

To utter the few words one knows:

"O woebegone people! Why so much crying,

Such desolation in the streets?

Is it the present of flesh, that each of you

At your jagged casement window should handle,

Nervous unto thirst and ultimate death?

Meanwhile the true way is sleeping;

Your lawful acts drink an unhealthy repose

From the upturned lip of this vessel, secretly,

But it is always time for a change.

That certain sins of omission go unpunished

Does not weaken your position

文学小品

我们对自己的生活方式很满意。
它对别人没什么意义。我们坐下,
阅读,不安。偶尔时间到了
便用黑色的阴影笼罩住它。
我们的实体在自我导致的恍惚中旋转
像睡眠一样。我们的生活无声地停止
一个人像在梦中迷失在
那些可敬的郊区,生活在那里停滞了
说着一个人知道的那么几句话:

"哦!悲伤的人们!为什么如此哭泣,
为什么街上如此荒凉?
在你们锯齿状的竖铰链窗边,你们每个人
应该触摸的,是肉体的礼物,
为渴望和最后的死亡而焦虑不安?
同时那真正的路正在沉睡;
你合法的行动,从这容器倒置的边缘,
秘密地汲取一种有害的安息,
但是总有时间去改变。
有些疏忽之罪不会受到惩罚
不会动摇你的位置

But this underbrush in which you are secure

Is its doing. Farewell then,

Until, under a better sky

We may meet expended, for just doing it

Is only an excuse. We need the tether

Of entering each other's lives, eyes wide apart, crying."

As one who moves forward from a dream

The stranger left that house on hastening feet

Leaving behind the woman with the face shaped like an arrowhead,

And all who gazed upon him wondered at

The strange activity around him.

How fast the faces kindled as he passed!

It was a marvel that no one spoke

To stem the river of his passing

Now grown to flood proportions, as on the sunlit mall

Or in the enclosure of some court

He took his pleasure, savage

And mild with the contemplating.

Yet each knew he saw only aspects,

That the continuity was fierce beyond all dream of enduring,

And turned his head away, and so

The lesson eddied far into the night:

Joyful its beams, and in the blackness blacker still,

Though undying joyousness, caught in that trap.

可你藏身其中的下层灌木
是它的所为。那么再见吧,
直到,在一片更美好的天空下
我们再次相遇,因为说做就做
只是个借口。我们需要栓绳
进入彼此的生活,双眼分得很开,哭泣。"

像一个人在梦中向前走去
陌生人匆忙离开那所房子
把脸孔形如箭头的女人留下,
以及所有盯着他
对他的奇怪活动感到好奇的人。
当他经过时那些面孔亮得多快!
这是个奇迹,无人对树干说起
他正在经过的河流
现在涨成了洪水,像在阳光照亮的林荫道上
或者某个法院的围墙内
他自娱自乐,野蛮
又因为沉思而变得温和。
但每个人都知道他仅仅看见了现象,
所有痛苦的梦都摆脱了连续性,
于是他转过头,于是
这一课打着漩涡远远地进入夜晚:
它愉快的光线,黑色中静止的擦皮鞋的人,
仿佛尚未消失的欢乐,落入陷阱。

Some Words

from the French of Arthur Cravan

Life is not at all what you might think it to be
A simple tale where each thing has its history
    It's much more than its scuffle and anything goes
Both evil and good, subject to the same laws.
    Each hour has its color and forever gives place
Leaving less than yon bird of itself a trace.
In vain does memory attempt to store away
The scent of its colors in a single bouquet
Memory can but shift cold ashes around
When the depths of time it endeavors to sound.
    Never think that you may be allowed, at the end,
To say to yourself, "I am of myself the friend,"
Or make with yourself a last reconciliation.
You will remain the victim of your hesitation
You will forget today before tomorrow is here
And disavow yourself while much is still far from clear.
    The defunct days will offer you their images
Only so that you may read of former outrages
And the days to come will mar with their complaints
The splendor that in your honor dejected evening paints.
    Wishing to collect in your heart the feelings

一些词语

生活根本不是你想的那样

是一个简单的故事,每件事都有来历

　　它不仅仅是混战和任何进行中的事

恶与善,都受制于相同的法律。

　　每个时辰都有自己的色彩和永远给定的地点

留下比远处的鸟还少的痕迹。

记忆徒劳地试图在一束花中

贮藏起它色彩的香味

记忆只能在周围移动寒冷的灰烬

当它竭力抵达的时间的深渊开始鸣响。

　　不要以为你会获得准许,在最后,

对自己说,"我是我自己的朋友,"

或者与你自己做最后的和解。

你将继续成为你的犹豫的牺牲品

你将在明天到达此处之前忘记今天

在大体上还不清楚时就否认自己。

　　那失效的日子将给你提供它们的形象

只为了让你能了解从前的暴行

未来的日子将用它们的抱怨玷污

沮丧的傍晚在你的荣誉中画出的光辉。

　　希望在你心中收集

Scattered in the meadows of misfortune's hard dealings
You will be the shepherd whose dog has run away
You will know even less whence comes your dismay
Than you know the hour your boredom first saw the light.

    Weary of seeking day you will relish the night
In night's dim orchards you will find some rest
The counsels of the trees of night are best
Better than those of the tree of knowledge, which corrupts us at birth
And which you allowed to flourish in the accursèd earth.

    When your most arduous labors grow pale as death
And you begin to inhale autumn's chilly breath
Winter will come soon to batter with his mace
Your precious moments, scattering them all over the place.

    You will always be having to get up from your chairs
To move on to other heartbreaks, be caught in other snares.

    The seasons will revolve on their scented course
Solar or devastated you will perforce
Be perfumed at their tepid passing, and not know
Whether their fragrance brings you joy or woe.

    At the moment when your life becomes a total shambles
You will have to resume your hopeless rambles
You have left everything behind and you still are eligible
And all alone, as the gulf becomes unbridgeable
You will have to earn your daily bread

艰难交易抛弃在不幸草坪上的感情
你将是牧犬跑走了的牧人
你将对你的绝望自何而来所知甚少
比不过你的厌倦初露端倪的时辰。

　　倦于追寻白昼你将喜爱夜晚
在夜晚幽暗的果园你将安歇
夜色中树木的忠告是最好的
胜过了使我们一出生就堕落的知识之树
你允许它们在受诅咒的尘世中繁荣茂盛。

　　当你最艰苦的劳动变得死一般苍白
你开始吸入秋天冷冽的气息
冬天不久就会到来，用狼牙棒捣毁
你珍贵的瞬间，将它们到处抛撒。

　　你将常常被迫从椅子中起身
移向其他的伤心事，落入其他的陷阱。

　　季节将在它们芳香的进程中旋转
通往太阳或者毁灭，你将被迫
在它们淡漠地经过时喷洒香水，不知道
它们的芳香带给你的是快乐还是悲伤。

　　当你的生活变成完全的废墟
你将被迫重新开始无望的闲逛
你留下了一切，你依然有资格
全然孤独，当海湾变得不可逾越
你将被迫挣到每日的面包

Although you feel you'd be better off dead.

    They'll hurt you, and you'd like to put up some resistance
Because you know that your very existence
Depends on others as unworthy of you
As you are of God, and when it's time to review
Your wrongs, you will feel no pain, they will seem a joke
For you will have ceased to suffer under their yoke.

    Whether you pass through fields, towns or across the sea
You will always retain your melancholy
And look after it; you will have to think of your career
Not live it, as in a game where the best player
Is he who forgets himself, and cannot say
What spurs him on, and makes him win the day.

    When weary henceforth of wishing to gaze
At the sinuous path of your spread-out days
You return to the place where your stables used to tower
You will find nothing left but some fetid manure
Your steeds beneath other horsemen will have fled
To autumn's far country, all rusted and red.

    Like an ardent rose in the September sun
You will feel the flesh sag from your limbs, one by one,
Less of you than of a pruned rosebush will remain,
That spring lies in wait for, to clothe once again.

    If you wish to love you won't know whom to choose

尽管你觉得你死了才好。

　　他们将伤害你，你愿意做一些抵抗
因为你知道你的存在
依赖于配不上你的别人
因为你属于上帝，到了评论你的错误之时
你将感觉不到痛苦，它们似乎是个笑话
因为你将不再忍受它们的束缚。

　　无论你经过田野、城镇，还是越过大海
你将始终保持着你的忧郁
照看它；你将被迫想起你的事业
不是生活，就像在一个游戏中
最好的游戏者是忘我的人，不能说
是什么鼓舞他，使他赢得了日子。

　　从此以后厌倦了渴望地注视
你度过的日子那蜿蜒的道路
你返回你的马棚过去曾是塔的地方
你将发现什么都没有了，除了恶臭的粪便
你的马在其他马夫脚下溜走，溜向
秋天遥远的乡野，全都生锈发红。

　　像七月阳光下一朵热情的玫瑰
你将感到肉体从你的四肢垂下，一个接一个，
你留下的东西将比修剪过的玫瑰丛还少，
躺着等待的春天，再次穿上衣服。

　　如果你想恋爱又不知该选谁

There are none whose love you'd be sorry to lose

Not to love at all would be the better part

Lest another seize and confiscate your heart.

    When evening descends on your deserted routes

You won't be afraid and will say, "What boots

It to worry and fret? To rail at my luck?

Since time my actions like an apple will pluck."

    You would like of yourself to curtail certain features

That you dislike, making allowances for this creature,

Giving that other one a chance to show his fettle,

Confining yet another behind bars of metal:

That rebel will soon become an armèd titan.

    Then let yourself love all that you take delight in

Accept yourself whole, accept the heritage

That shaped you and is passed on from age to age

Down to your entity. Remain mysterious;

Rather than be pure, accept yourself as numerous.

The wave of heredity will not be denied:

Best, then, on a lover's silken breast to abide

And be wafted by her to Nirvana's blue shoals

Where the self is abolished and renounces its goals.

    In you all things must live and procreate

Forget about the harvest and its sheaves of wheat

You are the harvest and not the reaper

那么失去任何人的爱你都不会难过
根本就别去爱可能更好
以免另一个人捉住并没收你的心。

　　当黄昏降临在你荒废的路上
你不必害怕,你会说,"什么样的靴子
要去焦虑和烦恼?抱怨我的运气?
既然我的行为像一只将要摘下的苹果。"

　　你情愿减少某些你不喜欢的
特征,体谅这个生灵,
给那个生灵提供展示强健的机会,
将另一个关在铁栅栏后面;
那个造反者不久会变成一个武装的泰坦。

　　然后让自己爱上让你欢喜的一切
接受你自己的全部,接受
那塑造你并代代相传的
由你来负责的遗产。保持神秘;
不是变得纯粹,而是接受众多的你。
遗传的波浪不会被否定:
最好是在爱人丝一样的胸脯上逗留
让她把你飘送到天堂蓝色的浅滩
在那里自我将被废除,并放弃它的目的。

　　万物必须在你内部生息繁衍
忘记丰收和一束束麦捆
你就是丰收本身而不是收获者

And of your domain another is the keeper.

    When you see the lapsed dreams that childhood invents
Salute your adolescence and fold their tents
Virginal, tall and slim beside the jasmine tree
An adorable girl is plaiting tenderly
The bouquet of love, which will stick in your memory
As the final vision and the final story.

    Henceforth you will burn with lascivious fire
Accursèd passion will strum its lyre
At the charming crossroads where day is on the wane
As the curve of a hill dissolves in a plain.

    The tacit beauty of the sacred plateau
Will be spoiled for you and you will never know
Henceforth the peace a pious heart bestows
To the soul its gentle sister in whom it echoes;
Anxiety will have called everything into question
And you will be tempted to the wildest actions.

    Then let all fade at the edge of our days!
No God emerges to dream our destinies.
The days depart, only boredom does not retreat
It's like a path that flies beneath one's feet
Whose horizon shifts while as we trudge
The dust and mud stick to us and do not budge.

    In vain do we speak, provoke actions or think,

你的领土由另一个人来看管。

　　当你看见童年发明的流逝的梦
迎接你的成年，折起他们的帐篷
贞洁，高挑，纤细，在素馨花树旁
一个可爱的少女正在温柔地编织
爱的花束，它将插在你的记忆中
如同最后的幻象和最后的故事。
　　从此你将为淫荡之火所焚烧
遭谴的激情将拨动它的里拉琴
在迷惘的十字路口白昼在衰退
像一座山的曲线渐渐融入平原。
　　神圣高原的缄默之美
将是你的渴望，此后你永远不会知道
一颗虔诚的心把和平赠给了灵魂
它那优雅的姐妹，并在其中回响；
焦虑将会把万事万物加以质询
你将被野蛮至极的行为所吸引。
　　那就让一切在日子的边缘消失！
没有上帝出现，梦见我们的命运。
日子离去，只有厌倦还没有撤离
它像一条在脚下飞舞的路
当我们艰难跋涉，地平线在移动
灰尘和烂泥粘在我们身上一动不动。
　　我们在徒劳中说话，挑逗，思考，

We are prisoners of the world's demented sink.

    The soft enchantments of our years of innocence
Are harvested by accredited experience
Our fondest memories soon turn to poison
And only oblivion remains in season.

    When, beside a window, one feels evening prevail
Who is there who can receive its slanting veil
And not regret day that bore it on its stream
Whether day was joy or under evil's regime
Drawing us to the one and deploring the other
Regretting the departure of all our brothers
And all that made the day, including its stains.

    Whoever you may be O man who complains
Not at your destiny, can you then doubt,
When the moment arrives for you to stretch out,
That remorse, a stinking jackal with subtle nose,
Will come at the end to devour your repose?

    ... Something gentle and something sad eftsoons
In the flanks of our pale and realistic noons
Holds with our soul a discourse without end
The curtain rises on the afternoon wind
Day sheds its leaves and now will soon be gone
And already my adulthood seems to mourn
Beside the reddish sunsets of the hollow vase
As gently it starts to deepen and slowly to increase.

我们是世界疯狂污水池的囚犯。

　　我们纯真年代那温柔的狂喜
被普遍认可的经验所收割
我们最珍爱的记忆很快就变成毒素
只有遗忘在季节中存留。

　　何时，在窗边，谁感到黄昏占了上风
谁在那里就能得到它倾斜的面纱
毫不遗憾那以激流承载它的日子
无论日子是快乐还是处于罪恶的统治之下
它都把我们拖向一个日子并哀叹另一个日子
悔恨着与我们所有兄弟的分离
那一切形成了日子，包括它的污迹。

　　无论你是谁，人啊，都不要抱怨
你的命运，你怎么可以怀疑，
你手脚摊开躺下的时刻何时到来，
痛悔，那鼻子发臭的狡诈的胡狼，
最后将前来吞噬你的安息？

　　……很快，优雅的事物和悲哀的事物
就会在我们苍白而真实的中午的侧翼
与我们的灵魂举行无休止的交谈
窗帘将在下午的风中升起
白昼脱落它的叶子，不久就会消失
我的成年时代已然在悲悼
傍着红色落日那空洞的花瓶
当它开始悄悄地变深，缓慢地扩大。

The Bungalows

Impatient as we were for all of them to join us,
The land had not yet risen into view: gulls had swept the gray steel
    towers away
So that it profited less to go searching, away over the humming earth
Than to stay in immediate relation to these other things—boxes,
    store parts, whatever you wanted to call them—
Whose installedness was the price of further revolutions, so you
    knew this combat was the last.
And still the relationship waxed, billowed like scenery on the breeze.

They are the same aren't they,
The presumed landscape and the dream of home
Because the people are all homesick today or desperately sleeping,
Trying to remember how those rectangular shapes
Became so extraneous and so near
To create a foreground of quiet knowledge
In which youth had grown old, chanting and singing wise hymns that
Will sign for old age
And so lift up the past to be persuaded, and be put down again.

The warning is nothing more than an aspirate "h";
The problem is sketched completely, like fireworks mounted on poles:
Complexion of evening, the accurate voices of the others.

平　房

我们像过去那样渴望它们全都加入我们，
大陆还未进入视野：海鸥卷走了灰色铁塔
让它无益于继续搜索，离开嗡嗡响的地球
不如与其他事物保持直接的联系——盒子，备件，无论你怎么
　　称呼——
安装它们的代价是进一步的革命，所以你知道这是最后的战斗。
关系还在加强，汹涌如同微风中的景色。

它们是同样的，难道不是吗？
假设的风景和关于家乡的梦
因为人们今天都患了思乡病或是在无望地沉睡，
试图回忆那些长方形是如何
变得如此不相干，如此靠近
为了创造一个宁静知识的前景
青春在其中老去，不停地唱着智慧的圣歌
为古老的时代叹息
并这样举起被说服的过去，然后又放下。

警告只不过是一个呼气音"h"；
难题被完整勾勒下来，像烟火攀上极地：
黄昏的面貌，其他人谨慎的声音。

During Coca-Cola lessons it becomes patent
Of noise on the left, and we had so skipped a stage that
The great wave of the past, compounded in derision,
Submerged idea and non-dreamer alike
In falsetto starlight like "purity"
Of design that had been the first danger sign
To wash the sticky, icky stuff down the drain—pfui!

How does it feel to be outside and inside at the same time,
The delicious feeling of the air contradicting and secretly abetting
The interior warmth? But land curdles the dismay in which it's
    written
Bearing to a final point of folly and doom
The wisdom of these generations.
Look at what you've done to the landscape—
The ice cube, the olive—
There is a perfect tri-city mesh of things
Extending all the way along the river on both sides
With the end left for thoughts on construction
That are always turning to alps and thresholds
Above the tide of others, feeding a European moss rose without
    glory.

We shall very soon have the pleasure of recording
A period of unanimous tergiversation in this respect
And to make that pleasure the greater, it is worth while

在可口可乐讲座上,它在左侧变成了
噪音的专利,我们就这样溜过舞台
过去的巨浪,在嘲笑中增高,
将思想和无梦之人同样淹没
在用假声的星光中像"纯净"的意图
那最初的危险信号
把黏乎乎冰凉的材料冲下水管——扑通!

同时在外面也在里面是什么感觉,
对空气的珍贵感觉否认又秘密煽动着
内部的温暖?但是土地凝固了将它写在其中的沮丧
向一个荒唐的终点移动
毁灭这些时代的智慧。
看看你对风景都干了什么——
冰块,橄榄树——
有一个万物组成的完美的三城之网
沿河的两岸一路伸展开来
将末端留给关于建筑的思想
它常常变成高山和门槛
在另外的潮汐上,哺育没有荣耀的一朵欧洲百叶蔷薇。

在这个方面,我们很快就会有幸记录
一个一致背弃的时期
值得花些时间,使那快乐增加

At the risk of tedious iteration, to put first upon record a final
    protest:
Rather decaying art, genius, inspiration to hold to
An impossible "calque" of reality, than
"The new school of the trivial, rising up on the field of battle,
A thing of sludge and leaf-mold," and life
Goes trickling out through the holes, like water through a sieve,
All in one direction.

You who were directionless, and thought it would solve everything if
    you found one,
What do you make of this? Just because a thing is immortal
Is that any reason to worship it? Death, after all, is immortal.
But you have gone into your houses and shut the doors, meaning
There can be no further discussion.
And the river pursues its lonely course
With the sky and the trees cast up from the landscape
For green brings unhappiness—*le vert porte malheur*.
"The chartreuse mountain on the absinthe plain
Makes the strong man's tears tumble down like rain."

All this came to pass eons ago.
Your program worked out perfectly. You even avoided
The monotony of perfection by leaving in certain flaws:
A backward way of becoming, a forced handshake,
An absent-minded smile, though in fact nothing was left to chance.

冒着乏味重复的风险，把最初的记录置于最后的拒绝：
宁可荒废艺术，天赋，灵感，去阻止
一个不可能的对真实的"仿造"，胜过了
"琐碎的新族类，在战场上升起，
某种烂泥和树叶腐植土似的东西"，而生活
继续渗过小孔，像水从一个方向，
透过筛子。

漫无方向的你，以为找到一个方向一切就会迎刃而解，
你利用这个干了什么？只是因为一件事物是不朽的
就有理由崇拜它？毕竟，死亡，就是不朽。
但你已经进屋，关上了门，那意味着
不再有商量的余地了。
河流继续它孤独的旅程
带着天空和风景中所有的树木
绿色带来不幸——面色发青的不祥之人
"淡绿色平原上嫩黄色的山
使坚强的男人泪落如雨。"

这些都是万古以前的事了。
你的程序效果完美。你甚至留下瑕疵
避免了完美的单调：
一条合适的退路，一次有力的握手，
一个无心的微笑，虽然事实上没有留下什么机会。

Each detail was startlingly clear, as though seen through a
    magnifying glass,
Or would have been to an ideal observer, namely yourself—
For only you could watch yourself so patiently from afar
The way God watches a sinner on the path to redemption,
Sometimes disappearing into valleys, but always *on the way*,
For it all builds up into something, meaningless or meaningful
As architecture, because planned and then abandoned when
    completed,
To live afterwards, in sunlight and shadow, a certain amount of years.
Who cares about what was there before? There is no going back,
For standing still means death, and life is moving on,
Moving on towards death. But sometimes standing still is also life.

每个细节都出奇地清晰,仿佛透过放大镜去看,
或许你自己,就是一个理想的观察者——
因为只有你能从远处如此耐心地观察自己
就像上帝观察一个走向救赎之途的罪人,
有时消失在峡谷中,但始终是在路上,
为此万有合为一物,毫无意义或者意味深长
就像建筑,经过规划,完成后便被放弃,
后来,在阳光和阴影中,又存在了若干年月。
谁在意从前那里有过什么?没有人回来,
因为静止意味着死亡,生命在于运动,
朝向死亡的运动。但有时静止也是生命。

The Chateau Hardware

It was always November there. The farms

Were a kind of precinct; a certain control

Had been exercised. The little birds

Used to collect along the fence.   ·

It was the great "as though," the how the day went,

The excursions of the police

As I pursued my bodily functions, wanting

Neither fire nor water,

Vibrating to the distant pinch

And turning out the way I am, turning out to greet you.

庄园硬件

那里总是十一月。农场

是一种院落；施加了

某种控制。小鸟们

习惯于在篱边觅食。

那是伟大的"仿佛"，是日子流逝的方式，

警察的远足

当我行使我的肉体功能，需要的

既非火也非水，

颤抖于遥远的指控

从我走的路上拐出来，拐出来迎接你。

Sortes Vergilianae

You have been living now for a long time and there is nothing you do
 not know.
Perhaps something you read in the newspaper influenced you and that
 was very frequently.
They have left you to think along these lines and you have gone your
 own way because you guessed that
Under their hiding was the secret, casual as breath, betrayed for the asking.
Then the sky opened up, revealing much more than any of you were
 intended to know.
It is a strange thing how fast the growth is, almost as fast as the light
 from polar regions
Reflected off the arctic ice-cap in summer. When you know where it
 is heading
You have to follow it, though at a sadly reduced rate of speed,
Hence folly and idleness, raging at the confines of some miserable
 sunlit alley or court.
It is the nature of these people to embrace each other, they know no
 other kind but themselves.
Things pass quickly out of sight and the best is to be forgotten quickly
For it is wretchedness that endures, shedding its cancerous light on
 all it approaches:
Words spoken in the heat of passion, that might have been retracted
 in good time,
All good intentions, all that was arguable. These are stilled now, as
 the embrace in the hollow of its flux
And can never be revived except as perverse notations on an
 indisputable state of things,
As conduct in the past, vanished from the reckoning long before it
 was time.
Lately you've found the dull fevers still inflict their round, only they

以维吉尔诗句占卜

你已经活了很久,没有什么你不知道的。
也许你在报纸上看到的东西影响了你,那很常见。
他们留下你思考这些句子而你走了自己的路因为你猜测
在它们下面藏着秘密,呼吸一般随意,一问就泄露。
于是天空打开,暴露的东西比你想知道的还多。
长得快是件怪事,几乎和来自极地的光一样快
从夏天的北极冰帽上反射回来。当你知道它往哪里去时
你必须跟随它,尽管悲惨地降低了速度,
愚蠢而懒惰,因局限于阳光惨淡的小巷或庭院而生气。
这些人的本性就是彼此拥抱,他们除了自己不知道别样的人
  存在。
事物迅速经过,超出视野,最好是被迅速遗忘
因为悲惨的是忍受,把它有癌的光洒在它接触的一切之上:
在炽热激情中说出的话,会在美好的时刻收回,
所有良好的意图,都是有疑问的。现在这些是静止的,仿佛拥
  抱在变迁的空洞中
永远不能复活,除非作为事物在无争状态下的荒谬符号,
像过去的行为,早在时间到来之前,就从计算中消失。
最近你发现沉闷的热病仍在损害着周围,只有它们是不可同化的
既然新奇或重要性已经消失。它像日夜一样与我们同在,
巨浪穿过小学涌起,定位并爆裂成柔软的灰色花朵

are unassimilable
Now that newness or importance has worn away. It is with us like day
and night,
The surge upward through the grade-school positioning and bursting
into soft gray blooms
Like vacuum-cleaner sweepings, the opulent fuzz of our cage, or like
an excited insect
In nervous scrimmage for the head, etching its none-too-complex
ordinances into the matter of the day.
Presently all will go off satisfied, leaving the millpond bare, a site for
new picnics,
As they came, naked, to explore all the possible grounds on which
exchanges could be set up.
It is "No Fishing" in modest capital letters, and getting out from
under the major weight of the thing
As it was being indoctrinated and dropped, heavy as a branch with apples,
And as it started to sigh, just before tumbling into your lap, chagrined
and satisfied at the same time,
Knowing its day over and your patience only beginning, toward what
marvels of speculation, auscultation, world-view,
Satisfied with the entourage. It is this blank carcass of whims and
tentative afterthoughts
Which is being delivered into your hand like a letter some forty-odd
years after the day it was posted.
Strange, isn't it, that the message makes some sense, if only a relative
one in the larger context of message-receiving
That you will be called to account for just as the purpose of it is
becoming plain,
Being one and the same with the day it set out, though you cannot
imagine this.
There was a time when the words dug in, and you laughed and joked,
accomplice
Of all the possibilities of their journey through the night and the
stars, creature

像吸尘器正在打扫，我们笼子里的众多细毛，或者像一只兴奋
　　的昆虫
为脑袋而挣扎，把它绝不复杂的法令蚀刻在今天的事物上。
现在所有人将满意地离开，留下空水池，一个新的野餐地点，
当他们到达，赤身裸体，探索所有可能进行交易的地方。
这是大写字母的"禁止垂钓"，从事物的压迫下取出
当它被教导和丢下，沉重如一根结满苹果的树枝，
当它开始叹息，在跌到你腿上之前，同时感到懊恼和满足，
知道它的日子结束了而你的耐心刚刚开始，朝向怎样神奇的思
　　索、听诊和世界观，
满足于周围的环境。这幻想的空虚尸骸和事后的追悔
被邮递到你的手中，像一封四十多年前发出的信。
陌生，不是吗，那信息有某种意义，只要它与接收信息的更大
　　语境有关系
你就会被叫去为之做出解释，就在它的目的变得清晰，
和它发出时一模一样，尽管你无法想象。
有一段时间词语固执己见，你嘲笑、揶揄，
承认所有它们穿过夜晚和群星旅行的可能性
这生灵渴望放弃如此陈旧的形式，同时
又支持它们，像成全了你的工具。性冲动到后来才变得明显
那时去检查如此宽泛的方面为时已晚，比如在等待别人表演时
要做什么：很不幸，没有成堆的破杂志作为证据，
这样的戏剧沉睡在日常机器的表面之下；此外
不是每个人都被赋予了才能，你是谁，你一直以为你有才？

285

Who looked to the abandonment of such archaic forms as these, and meanwhile
Supported them as the tools that made you. The rut became apparent only later
And by then it was too late to check such expansive aspects as what to do while waiting
For the others to show: unfortunately no pile of tattered magazines was in evidence,
Such dramas sleeping below the surface of the everyday machinery; besides
Quality is not given to everybody, and who are you to have been supposing you had it?
So the journey grew ever slower; the battlements of the city could now be discerned from afar
But meanwhile the water was giving out and malaria had decimated their ranks and undermined their morale,
You know the story, so that if turning back was unthinkable, so was victorious conquest of the great brazen gates.
Best perhaps to fold up right here, but even that was not to be granted.
Some days later in the pulsating of orchestras someone asked for a drink:
The music stopped and those who had been confidently counting the rhythms grew pale.
This is just a footnote, though a microcosmic one perhaps, to the greater curve
Of the elaboration; it asks no place in it, only insertion *hors-texte* as the invisible notion of how that day grew
From planisphere to heaven, and what part in it all the "I" had, the insatiable researcher of learned trivia, bookworm,
And one who marched along with, "made common cause" yet had neither the gumption nor the desire to trick the thing into happening,
Only long patience, as the star climbs and sinks, leaving illumination to the setting sun.

于是旅行变得更慢；现在可以从远处看清城墙了
可这时水就要用完了，疟疾摧毁了他们的队列，破坏了士气，
你知道这故事，所以，如果回去是不能考虑的，
胜利征服巨大的黄铜大门也是如此。
也许最好是在这里放弃，可甚至那也不成。
若干天后在悠扬的管弦乐中有人要了杯酒：
音乐停了，那些一直在自信地数拍子的人脸色白了。
这只是一个注脚，尽管对于更大的精心设计的弧线来说
它也许是很小的一个注脚；它不占地方，仅仅插在正文以外
作为那一天如何从星座图成长为天体的无形的想法，
而"我"，这熟知琐事的不知餍足的研究者，书虫子，
一个和它一同进军的人，我在其中的角色，"形成了普遍原因"，
但既没有气概也没有欲望去诱使事情发生，
只有长久的耐心，当星星升起又落下，把启示留给落日。

JOHN ASHBERY

阿什贝利自选诗集
II
（汉英对照）

马永波 译

人民文学出版社
PEOPLE'S LITERATURE PUBLISHING HOUSE

From
THREE POEMS
三首诗
(1972)

The System

The system was breaking down. The one who had wandered alone past so many happenings and events began to feel, backing up along the primal vein that led to his center, the beginning of a hiccup that would, if left to gather, explode the center to the extremities of life, the suburbs through which one makes one's way to where the country is.

At this time of life whatever being there is is doing a lot of listening, as though to the feeling of the wind before it starts, and it slides down this anticipation of itself, already full-fledged, a lightning existence that has come into our own. The trees and the streets are there merely to divide it up, to prevent it from getting all over itself, from retreating into itself instead of logically unshuffling into this morning that had to be, of the day of temptation. It is with some playfulness that we actually sit down to the business of mastering the many pauses and the abrupt, sharp accretions of regular being in the clotted sphere of today's activities. As though this were just any old day. There is no need for setting out, to advertise one's destination. All the facts are here and it remains only to use them in the right combinations, but that building will be the size of today, the rooms habitable and leading into one another in a lasting sequence, eternal and of the greatest timeliness.

It is all that. But there was time for others, that were to have got under way, sequences that now can exist only in memory, for there were other times for them. Yet they really existed. For instance a jagged kind of mood that comes at the end of the day, lifting life into the truth of real pain for a few moments before subsiding in

系　统

　　系统正在崩溃。独自漫游的那个人经历了这么多事件和变故，开始有所感觉，沿着通向他的中心的主静脉倒退，一个正在开始的呃逆，如果任由其发展，就会把中心炸到生活的尽头，那些一个人从中摸索着穿过走向乡村的郊区。

　　在生活的这个时刻，无论如何，都要学会经常倾听，就像在风起之前感受到风一样，而风从这种对自身的预感中滑下，业已完备，一个闪电般的存在已进入我们的生命。那里的树木和街道仅仅将风分开，防止它不断增强，防止它撤回自身，而不是合乎逻辑地迅捷进入这个早晨，这个注定充满诱惑的日子。实际上，带着某种玩闹的心态，我们坐下来，忙着处理众多的停顿和突然剧增的常规事务，在今日活动凝结的球体里。仿佛这只是随便一个过去的日子。不需要出发，让自己的目的广为人知。所有事实都在这里，剩下的只是以正确的组合使用它们，但是那建筑将是今天的规模，房间可以居住并彼此连通成一个持续的序列，永恒又最为及时。

　　这就是一切。可其他人还有时间，去发动现在只能在记忆中存在的序列，因为它们还有其他时机。不过，它们真的存在过。例如，一天结束时出现的一种锯齿状的情绪，在和万物一样消退于惯例庸常之前，片刻之间，将生命提升，进入真实痛

the usual irregular way, as things do. These were as much there as anything, things to be fumbled with, cringed before: dry churrings of no timbre, hysterical staccato passages that one cannot master or turn away from. These things led into life. Now they are gone but it remains, calm, lucid, but weightless, drifting above everything and everybody like a light in the sky, no more to be surmised, only remembered as so many things that remain at equal distances from us are remembered. The light drinks the dark and sinks down, not on top of us as we had expected but far, far from us in some other, unrelated sphere. This was not even the life that was going to happen to us. It was different in those days, though. Men felt things differently and their reactions were different. It was all life, this truth, you forgot about it and it was there. No need to collect your thoughts at every moment before putting forth a hesitant feeler into the rank and file of their sensations: the truth was obstinately itself, so much so that it always seemed about to harden and shrink, to grow hard and dark and vanish into itself anxiously but stubbornly, but this was just the other side of the coin of its intense conviction. It really knew what it *was*. Meanwhile the life uncurled around it in calm waves, unimpressed by the severity and yet not paying much mind, also very much itself. It seemed as though innumerable transparent tissues hovered around these two entities and joined them in some way, and yet when one looked there was nothing special to be seen, only miles and miles of buoyancy, the way the mild blue sky of a summer afternoon seems to support a distant soaring bird. This was the outside reality. Inside there was like a bare room, or an alphabet, an alphabet of clemency. Now at last you knew what you were supposed to know. The words formed from it and the sentences formed from them were dry and clear, as though made of wood. There wasn't too much of any one thing. The feelings never wandered off into a

苦的真理。这些事和任何事一样重要，是要加以摸索的事物，以前畏畏缩缩的事物：一个人无法掌握或是避开的没有音色的枯燥的颤鸣声，歇斯底里的断奏乐段。这些事物通向生命。现在它们消失了，但是它留了下来，沉静、明晰，没有重量，漂浮在万事与众人之上，像天空中的一束光，不再遭到臆测，只是被人们记住，就像这么多与我们保持同等距离的事物被记住一样。这光畅饮黑暗，沉落下来，不是像我们期望的那样降在我们头顶，而是降落在远处，远离我们，落在其他某个不相干的领域。这甚至不是那即将落在我们头上的生活。尽管在那些日子里它有所不同。人们对事物的感受不同，他们的反应也不同。这就是全部的生活，这个真理，你忘记了，而它就在那里。在将一根犹豫的触角伸进队列，将它们的感觉归档之前，不需要每一次都整理好你的思想：真理固执于自身，如此固执，以至于始终在硬化和收缩，变硬变黑，不安而倔强地消失在自身之中，但这仅仅是它的强烈信念的硬币的另一面。它的确知道它过去是什么。与此同时，生活在沉静的波浪中围绕它展开，不为这严重性所动，也不太在乎，对自己也是如此。那似乎是无数透明的组织盘旋在这两个实体周围，以某种方式把它们联合起来，一个人看去，又看不到任何特殊的东西，只有一英里又一英里的浮力，就像夏日午后温柔的蓝天支撑着一只远翔的鸟儿。这是外在的真实。内在的真实就像一个空房间，或一个字母表，一个仁慈的字母表。现在你终于知道了你应该知道的东西。用它构成的词语和用它们构成的句子干燥而清晰，仿佛是用木头做的。凡事都没有什么要紧。这些感情永远不会游走，

private song or tried to present the procession of straightforward facts as something like a pageant: the gorgeous was still unknown. There was, however, a residue, a kind of fiction that developed parallel to the classic truths of daily life (as it was in that heroic but commonplace age) as they unfolded with the foreseeable majesty of a holocaust, an unfrightening one, and went unrecognized, drawing force and grandeur from this like the illegitimate offspring of a king. It is this "other tradition" which we propose to explore. The facts of history have been too well rehearsed (I'm speaking needless to say not of written history but the oral kind that goes on in you without your having to do anything about it) to require further elucidation here. But the other, unrelated happenings that form a kind of sequence of fantastic reflections as they succeed each other at a pace and according to an inner necessity of their own—these, I say, have hardly ever been looked at from a vantage point other than the historian's and an arcane historian's at that. The living aspect of these obscure phenomena has never to my knowledge been examined from a point of view like the painter's: in the round, bathed in a sufficient flow of overhead light, with "all its imperfections on its head" and yet without prejudice of the exaggerations either of the anathematist or the eulogist: quietly, in short, and I hope succinctly. Judged from this angle the whole affair will, I think, partake of and benefit from the enthusiasm not of the religious fanatic but of the average, open-minded, intelligent person who has never interested himself before in these matters either from not having had the leisure to do so or from ignorance of their existence.

  From the outset it was apparent that someone had played a colossal trick on something. The switches had been tripped, as it were; the entire world or one's limited but accurate idea of it was bathed in glowing love, of a sort that need never have come into being but was now indispensable

进入一首隐秘的歌曲，或是试图将一队简单的事实表现成游行那样的东西：华丽依然是陌生的。然而，有一种残渣，一种虚构，与日常生活的经典真理平行发展（仿佛那是英雄的时代，而非平凡时代），那时，这些真理随着并不恐惧、尚未得到认识的大屠杀那可预见的威严一同展开，从这一切中吸取力量和庄严，像一个国王的私生子。我们打算探索的正是这"另外的传统"。历史事实排练得太好了（不用说，我现在说的不是书面的历史，而是正在你身上继续而又不需要你和它有任何关系的口述历史），在这里无需进一步的说明。但是其他不相干的事件构成了一系列完美的倒影，它们步调一致，彼此接续，服从于自己内在的需求——这些，我说，几乎不能从历史学家之外的一个有利位置来予以看待，只能从一个神秘难懂的历史学家的位置来看待。这些晦涩现象的活性我从来没有从画家的观点进行研究：全身心沐浴在头顶充沛的光流之中，"所有缺点都在它的头上"，又对诅咒者和赞颂者的夸大不存偏见：简而言之，我希望一切都是安静而简便的。从这个角度判断，我认为，整件事将分享和受益于并非来自宗教幻想的热忱，而是来自心胸开放、头脑明智的普通人，他以前从不会对这些事情感兴趣，因为没有闲暇于此，或是不知道它们的存在。

一开始显然就有人在某事上耍了个大阴谋。像过去一样，开关已经触发；整个世界或者一个人对世界有限但精确的想法沐浴灼热的爱，这爱永远不需要存在，可现在却不可或缺，有如空气之于活物。它充满整个宇宙，提升万物的温度。任何一

as air is to living creatures. It filled up the whole universe, raising the temperature of all things. Not an atom but did not feel obscurely compelled to set out in search of a mate; not a living creature, no insect or rodent, that didn't feel the obscure twitchings of dormant love, that didn' t ache to join in the universal turmoil and hullabaloo that fell over the earth, roiling the clear waters of the reflective intellect, getting it into all kinds of messes that could have been avoided if only, as Pascal says, we had the sense to stay in our room, but the individual will condenms this notion and sallies forth full of ardor and *hubris*, bent on self-discovery in the guise of an attractive partner who is *the* heaven-sent one, the convex one with whom he has had the urge to mate all these seasons without realizing it. Thus a state of positively sinful disquiet began to prevail wherein men's eyes could be averted from the truth by the passing of a romantic stranger whose perfume set in motion all kinds of idle and frivolous trains of thought leading who knows where—to hell, most likely, or at very best to a position of blankness and ill-conceived repose on the edge of the flood, so that looking down into it one no longer saw the comforting reflection of one's own face and felt secure in the knowledge that, whatever the outcome, the struggle was going on in the arena of one's own breast. The bases for true reflective thinking had been annihilated by the scourge, and at the same time there was the undeniable fact of exaltation on many fronts, of a sense of holiness growing up through the many kinds of passion like a tree with branches bearing candelabra higher and higher up until they almost vanish from sight and are confused with the stars whose earthly avatars they are: the celestial promise of delights to come in another world and still lovely to look at in this one. Thus, in a half-baked kind of way, this cosmic welter of attractions was coming to stand for the real thing, which has to be colorless and featureless if it is to be the true reflection of the primeval energy from which it issued forth, once a salient force capable of assuming the shape of any of the great impulses struggling to accomplish the universal task,

个原子无不模糊地觉得必须出发寻找一个配偶；任何活物，昆虫或是啮齿动物，无不感觉到休眠的爱在模糊地抽搐，无不渴望加入大地之上普遍的骚动和喧嚣，搅浑反思的心智的清水，让它陷入应该可以避免的各种混乱，只要我们能像帕斯卡说的那样，明智地待在自己的房间里，但是，个体会谴责这个观念，满怀狂热和傲慢出发，决心在伙伴迷人的伪装中自行发现，谁是上天派来的凸面体的人，他迫切想要以之和所有没有实现的季节匹配。于是，一种明确有罪的焦虑状态开始流行，人们的目光可以因为一个浪漫的陌生人经过就偏离真理，那陌生人身上的香水味就能调动各种懒惰无聊的思想的火车，谁知道它们会驶向哪里——最有可能是驶向地狱，最好也就是驶向一个空位，计划不周地休憩在洪水边上，因而，俯视它的时候，一个人再也看不见给人安慰的自己面孔的倒影，无论结果如何，这斗争是在自己胸膛的舞台上展开，知道这一点也不再让人觉得安全。真正的反思的基础已经毁于灾祸，与此同时，在许多前线上都存在着不可否认的升华的事实，一种神圣感生长起来，穿过众多种类的激情，像一棵树的枝条承载着大烛台，越来越高，直到几乎从视野中消失，和作为它们尘世替身的群星混淆在一起；进入另一个世界，又依然愉快地注视着这个尘世天堂许诺的欢乐。于是，以一种半生不熟的方式，宇宙混乱的魅力逐渐取代了真实之物，如果它要成为自己所源自的原始能量的真实反映，它就必须无色无形，那曾经是一种突出的力量，能够以任何力求完成宇宙任务的巨大冲动的形式出现，可现在，它停滞于一个单独的方面，成了有损于其他方面的东西，开始

but now bogged down in a single aspect of these to the detriment of the others, which begin to dwindle, jejeune, etiolated, as though not really essential, as though someone had devised them for the mere pleasure of complicating the already complicated texture of the byways and torments through which we have to stray, plagued by thorns, chased by wild beasts, as though it were not commonly known from the beginning that not one of these tendrils of the tree of humanity could be bruised without endangering the whole vast waving mass; that that gorgeous, motley organism would tumble or die out unless each particle of its well-being were conserved as preciously as the idea of the whole. For universal love is as special an aspect as carnal love or any of the other kinds: all forms of mental and spiritual activity must be practiced and encouraged equally if the whole affair is to prosper. There is no cutting corners where the life of the soul is concerned, even if a too modest approximation of the wish that caused it to begin to want to flower be the result—a result that could look like overpruning to the untrained eye. Thus it was that a kind of blight fell on these early forms of going forth and being together, an anarchy of the affections sprung from too much universal cohesion. Yet so blind are we to the true nature of reality at any given moment that this chaos—bathed, it is true, in the iridescent hues of the rainbow and clothed in an endless confusion of fair and variegated forms which did their best to stifle any burgeoning notions of the formlessness of the whole, the muddle really as ugly as sin, which at every moment shone through the colored masses, bringing a telltale finger squarely down on the addition line, beneath which these self-important and self-convoluted shapes added disconcertingly up to zero—this chaos began to seem like the normal way of being, so that some time later even very sensitive and perceptive souls had been taken in: it was for them life's rolling river, with its calm eddies and shallows as well as its more swiftly moving parts and ahead of these the rapids, with an awful roar somewhere in the distance; and yet, or so it seemed to

缩小，变得空洞而衰弱，仿佛真的不必要，仿佛有人设计出它们来纯粹是为了取乐，让已经很复杂的旁道的结构更加复杂，而我们的流浪不得不经历这些折磨，被荆棘困扰，被野兽追逐，仿佛通常人们并不知道，从一开始，人性之树的这些卷须中没有一个可以遭到擦伤而不危及整个巨大波动的群体；那灿烂华丽、五颜六色的有机体将会翻倒或是死掉，除非它幸福的每一个分子得以保全，和整体的思想同样珍贵。因为宇宙的爱是和肉身之爱或任何其他类型的爱同样的特殊方面；如果整个事件想要繁荣的话，所有形式的心理和精神活动都必须得到实践，同等地加以鼓励。关心灵魂生活的地方是没有切角的，即便一个促使它想要开花的近乎过谦的希望，也总归是个结果——在未经训练的眼里可能像是一个修剪过度的结果。所以，正是那种枯萎病落在这些一同出现和存在的早期形式之上，一种从过于普遍的凝聚力中生发出来的情感的无政府状态。不过，对于真实的真正本质而言，我们就是这样盲目，在任何给定的时刻，这种混乱——的确，沐浴在彩虹的虹彩之中，覆盖在美丽斑驳的形式那无尽的混乱之中，尽已所能地要扼杀任何迅速发展的有关整体无定形的观念，这种混沌状态果真和罪一样丑陋，随时闪耀着穿透彩色的群体，让搬弄是非的手指直接落在附加系上，在它下面，这些自大而费解的形状的总和令人不安地归结为零——这混沌开始显得像是存在的正常方式，以至于一段时间之后，甚至非常敏锐和有洞察力的灵魂也被吸收了：对于他们来说，生活就是翻腾的河流，有着沉静的漩涡和阴影，同样还有更为迅疾的移动的部分，而在这些前面，急流发出可怕的

these more sensible than average folk, a certain amount of hardship has to be accepted if we want the river-journey to continue; life cannot be a series of totally pleasant events, and we must accept the bad if we also wish the good; indeed a certain amount of evil is necessary to set it in the proper relief: how could we know the good without some experience of its opposite? And so these souls took over and dictated to the obscurer masses that follow in the wake of the discoverers. The way was picturesque and even came to seem carefully thought out; controls were waiting, in case things got out of hand, to restore the inevitable balance of happiness and woe; meanwhile the latter kept gradually diminishing whenever its turn came round and one really felt that one had set one's foot on the upward path, the spiral leading from the motley darkened and lightened landscape here below to the transparent veils of heaven. All that was necessary were patience and humbleness in recognizing one's errors, so as to be sure of starting out from the right place the next time, and so a sense of steady advancement came to reward one's efforts each time it seemed that one had been traveling too long without a view of the sun. And even in darkest night this sense of advancement came to whisper at one's side like a fellow traveler pointing the way.

Things had endured this way for some time, so that it began to seem as though some permanent way of life had installed itself, a stability immune to the fluctuations of other eras: the pendulum that throughout eternity has swung successively toward joy and grief had been stilled by a magic hand. Thus for the first time it seemed possible to consider ways toward a more fruitful and harmonious manner of living, without the fear of an adverse fate's coming to reduce one's efforts to nothing so soon as undertaken. And yet it seemed to those living as though even this state had endured for a considerable length of time. No one had anything against it, and most reveled in the creative possibilities its freedom offered, yet to all it seemed as though

咆哮奔腾在远处；而且，或许正是这样，对于这些比普通人更为敏锐的灵魂来说，如果我们想要河流继续前进的话，就必须接受一定数量的艰难困苦；生活不可能是一系列纯然愉悦的事件，我们必须接受坏的东西，如果我们希望得到好的东西；的确，为了正当的救济，一定量的恶是必要的：对于善的反面没有一定的经验，我们如何能够知善？于是，这些灵魂接管了，并对跟随着发现之航迹前进的更为模糊的群众发令。一路上风景如画，甚至看上去经过了深思熟虑；控制装置已经就绪，以防事物一旦失控，就可以恢复幸福和灾祸的不可避免的平衡；同时，每当轮到灾祸发生，就能使之持续减少，让人真正觉得自己走的是向上的路，从下界斑驳黑暗轻盈的风景螺旋形通向天堂透明的面纱。所需要的一切就是耐心和谦卑，承认自己的错误，以确保自己下一次能从正确的地方出发，能有一种稳固进步的感觉来回报一个人的努力，每当他似乎在不见天日的情况下走过了太长的距离。甚至在最黑暗的夜里，这种进步的感觉也会在一个人的身边低语，就像是一个旅伴在指引道路。

事物忍受这种方式已经有段时间了，以至于某种永久性的生活方式似乎已然确立，一种不受其他时代波动影响的稳定性：在快乐和悲哀之间不断摇摆的永恒的钟摆，被一只有魔力的手停住。于是，第一次，似乎有可能考虑其他的方式，追求更有成效更和谐的生活方式，而无需恐惧厄运会将一个人的努力化为虚无。甚至这种状态的生活也忍受了相当长的一段时间。没有人反对它，大多数人陶醉在它的自由所提供的创造的可能性

a major development had been holding off for quite a while and that its effects were on the verge of being felt, if only the present could give a slight push into the haphazard field of potentiality that lay stretched all around like a meadow full of wild flowers whose delightful promise lies so apparent that all question of entry into it and enjoyment is suspended for the moment. Hence certain younger spectators felt that all had already come to an end, that the progress toward infinity had crystallized in them, that they in fact were the other they had been awaiting, and that any look outward over the mild shoals of possibilities that lay strewn about as far as the eye could see was as gazing into a mirror reflecting the innermost depths of the soul.

Who has seen the wind? Yet it was precisely this that these enterprising but deluded young people were asking themselves. They were correct in assuming that the whole question of behavior in life has to be rethought each second; that not a breath can be drawn nor a footstep taken without our being forced in some way to reassess the age-old problem of what we are to do here and how did we get here, taking into account our relations with those about us and with ourselves, and the ever-present issue of our eternal salvation, which looms larger at every moment—even when forgotten it seems to grow like the outline of a mountain as one approaches it. To be always conscious of these multiple facets is to incarnate a dimensionless organism like the wind's, a living concern that can know no rest, by definition: it *is* restlessness. But this condition of eternal vigilance had been accepted with the understanding that somehow it would also mirror the peace that all awaited so impatiently: it could not proceed unless the generalized shape of this nirvana-like state could impose its form on the continually active atoms of the moving forward which was the price it exacted: hence a dilemma for any but the unrepentant hedonists or on the contrary those who chose to remain all day on the

当中，而对所有人来说，仿佛一个重要的发展已经拖延了相当长的时间，它的效果几乎已经能够感觉得到了，只要现在能轻轻推它一下，进入可能性的偶然领域，它在周围延伸开去，像一片满是野花的草地，它怡人的许诺如此明显地存在着，所有相关问题和享受都被暂时中止。于是，某些更年轻的观众觉得一切都已到了终点，朝向无限的进步已经在他们心中结晶，瞭望任何散落在周围的眼睛能看到的可能性的浅滩，都像是凝视一面反映着灵魂秘密深渊的镜子。

谁看见过风？这恰恰是这些有魄力的轻信的年轻人在问他们自己。他们正确地设想，生活中的整个行为问题必须每秒钟都重新思考一遍；我们在这里要做什么和我们如何抵达这里，没有被迫以某种方式重新考虑这些古老的问题，我们就不会喘上一口，也不会迈出一步，考虑到我们与周围人和我们自身的关系，我们永恒救赎的始终存在的问题，每一个时刻都在逼近——甚至在把它忘记的时候，它也像一个人在靠近时，山的轮廓不停变大一样。始终意识到这些多重方面就是使一个无边无际的有机体具体化，就像风一样，显然是一种不懂得休息的活跃的关切：它是躁动不安。但是这种永远警醒的状态被充满理解地接受了，某种程度上它也会反映出耐心等待的和平：它无法继续进行，除非这种涅槃状态的普遍形式能够为前进着的不断活跃的原子赋予形式，那就是它索取的代价：于是，所有人都陷入一种进退两难的困境，除了那些顽固不化的享乐主义者或是相反的人，他们选择整天留在粪堆上，扯着他们的头发

dung-heap, rending their hair and clothing and speaking of sackcloth and ashes: these, by far the noisiest group, made the least impression as usual, yet the very fact that they existed pointed to what seemed to be a tragic flaw in the system's structure; for among penance or perpetual feasting or the draconian requirements of a conscience eternally mobilized against itself, feeding on itself in order to recreate itself in a shape that the next instant would destroy, how was one to choose? So that those who assumed that they had reached the end of an elaborate but basically simple progression, the logical last step of history, came more and more to be the dominant party: a motley group but with many level heads among them, whose voices chanting the wise maxims of regular power gradually approached the point of submerging the other cacophony of tinkling cymbals and wailing and individual voices raised in solemn but unreal debate. This was the logical cutting-off place, then: ahead might lie new forms of life, some of them beautiful perhaps, but the point was that the effort of establishing them or anything else that was to come had ended here: a permanent now had taken over and was free to recast the old forms, riddles that had been expected to last until the Day of Judgment, as it saw fit, in whatever shape seemed expedient for living the next few crucial moments into a future without controls.

It seemed, just for a moment, that a new point had now been reached. It was not the time for digressions yet it made them inevitable, like a curtain at the end of an act. It brought you to a pass where turning back was unthinkable, and where further progress was possible only after it had been discussed at length, but which also outlawed discussion. Life became a pregnant silence, but it was understood that the silence was to lead nowhere. It became impossible to breathe easily in this constricted atmosphere. We ate little, for it seemed that in this way we could produce the inner emptiness from which alone understanding can spring up,

和衣服，诉说着自己的懊悔：这些人，迄今为止是最吵闹的群体，像通常那样毫无效果，他们存在的这个事实表明，系统结构中似乎有着一个严重的缺陷；因为在忏悔、永久的盛宴、苛刻的要求之中，良知始终在动员反抗自己，以自身为食，以便在下一个时刻就会毁灭的形式中重新创造出自身，那么，一个人要如何选择呢？以为自己已经抵达了看似复杂、本质上却非常简单的进程终点，完成了历史那合乎逻辑的最后一步，这样的人越来越多地成了执政党：五花八门的一群人，其中有众多高低不等的脑袋，念诵着有关常规性权力的智慧格言，他们的声音逐渐升高，淹没了其他的不谐之音，叮叮当当的铙钹、哀号和在庄严而不真实的辩论中抬高的个体的声音。那么，这就是逻辑上的断点：前面也许存在着生活的新形式，它们也许很美，可是关键在于，确立它们的努力或其他一切都已在此结束：一个永久性的现在已经接管，并随意改动旧有的形式，期待能持续到审判日的谜，根据自己的想法，采取任何似乎有利的形式，只为了活过后面少数决定性的时刻，进入一个失控的未来。

现在，仅仅一瞬间，就似乎抵达了一个新的目的。现在还不是离题的时机，尽管离题不可避免，就像一场戏结束时降下的大幕。它把你带到一个关口，转身回去是不可想象的，继续向何处前进，只有最后经过讨论才有可能，可那又是禁止讨论的。生活成了一种意味深长的寂静，但是人们懂得，这寂静不通向任何地方。我们吃得很少，因为似乎这样我们就能产生出内在的空虚，从中只有理解力能够萌芽，那矛盾之树，快乐而鲜活，用它复杂的物质自我覆盖着那片空洞。这时，我们被古

the tree of contradictions, joyous and living, investing that hollow void with its complicated material self. At this time we were surrounded by old things, such as need not be questioned but which distill the meek information that is within them like a perfume on the air, to be used and disposed of; and also by certain new things which wear their newness like a quality, perhaps as an endorsement of the present, in all events as a vote of confidence in the currency of the just-created as a common language available to all men of good will, however disturbing the times themselves might turn out to be. Gradually one grew less aware of the idea of not turning back imposed as a condition for progress, as one imbibed the magic present that drew everything—the old and the new— along in the net of its infectious charm. Surely it would be possible to profit from the options of this cooperative new climate as though they were a charter instead of a vague sense of wellbeing, like a mild day in early spring, ready to be dashed to pieces by the first seasonable drop in temperature. And meanwhile there was a great sense of each one's going about his business, quiet in the elation of that accomplishment, as though it were enough to set one's foot on a certain path to be guaranteed of arriving at some destination. Yet the destinations were few. What actually was *wanted* from this constructive feeling? A "house by the side of the road" in which one could stay indefinitely, arranging new opportunities and fixing up old ones so that they mingled in a harmonious mass that could be called living with a sense of purpose? No, what was wanted and was precisely lacking in this gay and salubrious desert was an end to the "end" theory whereby each man was both an idol and the humblest of idolaters, in other words the antipodes of his own universe, his own redemption or his own damnation, with the rest of the world as a painted backdrop to his own monodrama of becoming of which he was the lone impassioned spectator. But the world avenges itself on those who would lose it by skipping over the due process of elimination, from whatever

老的事物所包围，比如不需要被质疑的事物，从它们内部提取出谦恭的信息，像空气中的一阵芳香，得到利用和处置；同样还会凭借某些新事物，它们穿着自己的新像一种品质，也许，作为一种对现在的支持，在所有事件中如同信任的选举那样，在刚刚造出来的货币中，作为一种通用的语言可以为所有有信誉的人所用，无论他们自己最后会面对怎样困扰的时刻。一个人越来越意识不到往回走的念头，那是进步强加给他的条件，因为那吸收一切的有魔力的现在——无论新旧——将他一同吸入具有传染性的魅力之网。选择这种有合作精神的新气候也许能够受益，仿佛它们是一份执照，而不是一种模糊的幸福感，就像早春一个温煦的日子，准备让最初的季节的温度骤降冲击成碎片。与此同时，有一种很强烈的感觉，每个人都在干着这件事情，悄悄地为自己的成就而洋洋自得，仿佛它足以让一个人踏上一条有把握的道路，保证能抵达某个目的地。不过，目的地本就很少。从这种建设性的感觉中我们到底想要什么？"路边的一座房子"，一个人可以无限期地在里面停留，安排新的时机，改进旧的时机，以便带着一种目的感融进一个可以称作生活的和谐的群体？不，真正需要的，而在这快乐清爽的荒漠中又恰恰缺乏的，是对"终点"理论的终结，这个终点使得每个人都成了偶像，同时又是最为谦卑的偶像崇拜者，换句话说，他自己的宇宙的对映体，他自己的救赎或是他自己的诅咒，世界上其他一切都是他独角戏的彩绘背景，他自己是唯一充满激情的观众。但是，世界本身会报复那些出于无私动机而越过正常淘汰过程、从而失去它的人，在这些自我更新的努力中给自

altruistic motive, by incrusting itself so thoroughly in these efforts at self-renewal that no amount of wriggling can dislodge its positive or negative image from all that is contemplated of present potentialities or the great sane simplifications to come. So that it was all lost, or rather all in the shade that instills weariness and sickness into the limbs under the guise of enraptured satiety. There was, again, no place to go, that is, no place that would not make a mockery of the place already left, casting all progress forward into the confusion of an eternally misapplied present. This was the stage to which reason and intuition working so well together had brought us, but it was scarcely their fault if now fear at the longest shadows of approaching darkness began to prompt thoughts of stopping somewhere for the night, as well as a serious doubt that any such place existed on the face of the earth.

On this Sunday which is also the last day of January let us pause for a moment to take note of where we are. A new year has just begun and now a new month is coming up, charged with its weight of promise and probable disappointments, standing in the wings like an actor who is conscious of nothing but the anticipated cue, totally absorbed, a pillar of waiting. And now there is no help for it but to be cast adrift in the new month. One is plucked from one month to the next; the year is like a fast-moving Ferris wheel; tomorrow all the riders will be under the sign of February and there is no appeal, one will have to get used to living with its qualities and perhaps one will even adjust to them successfully before the next month arrives with a whole string of new implications in its wake. Just to live this way is impossibly difficult, but the strange thing is that no one seems to notice it; people sail along quite comfortably and actually seem to enjoy the way the year progresses, and they manage to fill its widening space with multiple activities which apparently mean a lot to them. Of course some are sadder than the others but it doesn't seem to be because of

己彻底包上硬壳，即便再多的扭动挣扎也无法从一切当中驱逐它或积极或消极的形象，那是对当下潜力的预期，或是将未来的强大理智简单化。所以，它完全或几乎完全地迷失在阴影中，在狂喜的满足感的伪装之下，将疲惫和病态慢慢灌输到四肢之中。而且，也没有任何地方可去，亦即，没有什么地方不会嘲弄那留在后面的地方，将所有进展向前投进混乱的永远被误用的现在。这是理智和直觉通力合作才使我们抵达的阶段，可那几乎并不是它们的错，如果我们现在就恐惧黑暗那正在逼近的最长的阴影，就开始打起在某处停下过夜的主意，而且还严重怀疑这样的地方在地球表面是否存在。

这个星期天也是一月的最后一天，让我们停上片刻，看看我们置身于何处。新的一年刚刚开始，一个新的月份正在走近，承载着它许诺的重量和很有可能的失望，站在侧厅里，像一个演员，什么都意识不到，除了他所预期的提示，完全沉浸其中，一个等待的柱子。对此，现在无计可施，只能任其漂泊在新的月份之中。一个人从一个月份被拽向下一个月份；一年就像一个快速运转的摩天轮；明天，所有的骑手都将服从于一月的指示，没有诉诸裁判的机会，一个人不得不习惯于忍受它的质量，也许还会成功地适应它们，当下一个月在尾迹中带着一整串新的暗示到来之前。这样生活恰恰有着不可克服的困难，可奇怪的是，似乎没人注意到这一点；人们十分舒适地继续航行，实际上很是享受岁月前进的方式，他们设法用多种多样明显对他们意义重大的活动填补日益扩大的空间。当然，有些人比别人

the dictatorship of the months and years, and it goes away after a while. But the few who want order in their lives and a sense of growing and progression toward a fixed end suffer terribly. Sometimes they try to dope their consciousness of the shifting but ineluctable grid of time that has been arbitrarily imposed on them with alcohol or drugs, but these lead merely to mornings after whose waking is ten times more painful than before, bringing with it a new and more terrible realization of the impossibility of reconciling their own ends with those of the cosmos. If by chance you should be diverted or distracted for a moment from awareness of your imprisonment by some pleasant or interesting occurrence, there is always the shape of the individual day to remind you. It is a microcosm of man's life as it gently wanes, its long morning shadows getting shorter with the approach of noon, the high point of the day which could be likened to that sudden tremendous moment of intuition that comes only once in a lifetime, and then the fuller, more rounded shapes of early afternoon as the sun imperceptibly sinks in the sky and the shadows start to lengthen, until all are blotted in the stealthy coming of twilight, merciful in one sense that it hides the differences, blemishes as well as beauty marks, that gave the day its character and in so doing caused it to be another day in our limited span of days, the reminder that time is moving on and we are getting older, not older enough to make any difference on this particular occasion, but older all the same. Even now the sun is dropping below the horizon; a few moments ago it was still light enough to read but now it is no more, the printed characters swarm over the page to create an impressionistic blur. Soon the page itself will be invisible. Yet one has no urge to get up and put on a light; it is enough to be sitting here, grateful for the reminder that yet another day has come and gone, and you have done nothing about it. What about the morning resolutions to convert all the confused details in the air about you into a column of

要悲哀一些，可那似乎并不是因为月份和年度的独裁，并且，这种悲哀也会在片刻之后消散。但是有少数人需要自己的生活富有秩序，需要一种成长的感觉，和朝向一个固定终点前进的感觉，这样的人苦难深重。有时他们试图专横地用酒精或毒品来麻痹自己对移动着又躲不开的时间格栅的意识，但这只能让他们苏醒后的早晨比以前还要痛苦十倍，带给他们一种新的更为可怕的认识，他们自己的目的不可能和宇宙的目的调和一致。如果你偶然有片刻时间的转移或分心，不再意识到你被某种愉快或有趣的事件囚禁，却又始终有独特的日子的形式来提醒你。这是人类生活的小天地，它悄悄衰落，早晨长长的阴影随着正午临近而缩短，这一天的高潮类似于一生中只出现一次的那种突如其来的惊人的顿悟时刻，然后，下午的形式随着太阳在天空中觉察不到的沉降和开始加长的阴影，变得更为丰满圆润，直到一切都在薄暮的秘密降临中变得脏污，在一种慈悲的感觉中隐藏起差异，涂掉美人痣，为这一天赋予个性，同时在我们有限的时日中，使它成为另一个日子，提醒我们时间在推移，我们在变老，不是老得足以让这个特定情况变得有所不同，而是老得和从前一样。甚至此刻太阳也在落向地平线下面；片刻之前它还亮得足够用来阅读，但现在已好景不再，印刷字符拥挤在书页上，造成一片印象派一般的模糊。不久，书页本身就看不见了。但是，一个人没有起身开灯的迫切欲望；坐在这里就够了，对这提醒心存感激，又一天来了又去，你对它什么都没做。想要把周围空气中所有混淆的细节都转变成一列明了的图形，这早晨的决心又怎么样了呢？起草一个资产负债表

311

intelligible figures? To draw up a balance sheet? This naturally went undone, and you are perhaps grateful also for your laziness, glad that it has brought you to this pass where you must now face up to the day's inexorable end as indeed we must all face up to death some day, and put our faith in some superior power which will carry us beyond into a region of light and timelessness. Even if we had done the things we ought to have done it probably wouldn't have mattered anyway as everyone always leaves something undone and this can be just as ruinous as a whole life of crime or dissipation. Yes, in the long run there is something to be said for these shiftless days, each distilling its drop of poison until the cup is full; there is something to be said for them because there is no escaping them.

On the streets, in private places, they have no idea of the importance of these things. This exists only in our own minds, that is not in any place, nowhere. Possibly then it does not exist. Even its details are hazardous to consider. Most people would not consider it in its details, because (a) they would argue that details, no matter how complete, can give no adequate idea of the whole, and (b), because the details can too easily become fetishes, i. e., become prized for themselves, with no notion of the whole of which they were a part, with only an idolatrous understanding of the qualities of the particular detail. Certainly even this limited understanding can lead to a conception of beauty, insofar as any detail is a microcosm of the whole, as is so often the case. Thus you find people whose perfect understanding of love is deduced from lust, as the description of a flower can generate an idea of what it looks like. It is even possible that this irregular but satisfying understanding is the only one really allotted to us; that knowledge of the whole is impossible or at least so impractical as to be rarely or never feasible; that as we are born among imperfections we are indeed obligated to use

吗？这当然不成，你也许还要感谢你的懒惰，欣然于它把你带到这个关口，现在你必须面对日子无情的终结，如同我们某一天都要面对死亡，信任某种超然力量会将我们带入一个光明永恒的领域。即便我们完成了我们应该完成的事情，那也许同样无关紧要，因为每个人都经常留下一些未竟之事，这可能与罪恶累累、虚掷光阴的一生具有同样的毁灭性。是的，在这长跑中，对于这些偷懒的日子的确有话要说，它们每一个都滴下毒素，直到把杯子充满；对于它们有话要说，因为没有人能逃开它们。

在街上，在隐秘之处，他们全然想不到这些事物的重要性。它只存在于我们自己的思想中，它不在任何地方，它无处存在。也许它根本就不存在。甚至思考它的细节也是有风险的，因为他们会争辩说，首先，细节无论多么完整，都不能提供有关整体的恰当概念，其次，细节可以很轻易地变成偶像，例如，变成对自身的奖赏，对它们作为部分的整体毫无概念，仅仅对特定细节的质量具有一种偶像崇拜式的理解。当然，甚至这种有限的理解也有可能导向一种美的观念，因为任何细节都是整体的一个小宇宙，情况往往如此。于是，你发现人们对爱的理解完全是从性欲中推断出来的，正如对一朵花的描述可以使人对它的模样产生想法。甚至有可能这不规则但又令人满意的理解真的是唯一一种分派给我们的理解；了解整体是不可能的，至少是不切实际，很少或永远不具备可行性；我们生来就不完美，我们确有义务利用这些不完美来同化我们现在的不完美和

them toward an assimilation of the imperfections that we are and the greater ones that we are to become; that not to do so would be to sin against nature, that is to end up with nothing, not even the reassuring knowledge that we have sinned to some purpose, but are instead empty and blameless as an inanimate object. Yet we know not what we are to become, therefore we can never completely rule out the possibility of intellectual understanding, even though it seems nothing but a snare and a delusion; we might miss out on everything by ignoring its call to order, which is in fact audible to each of us; therefore how can we decide? It is no solution either to combine the two approaches, to borrow from right reason or sensory data as the case seems to warrant, for an amalgam is not completeness either, and indeed is far less likely to be so through an error in dosage. So of the three methods: reason, sense, or a knowing combination of both, the last seems the least like a winner, the second problematic; only the first has some slim chance of succeeding through sheer perversity, which is possibly the only way to succeed at all. Thus we may be spared at least the agonizing wading through a slew of details of theories of action at the risk of getting hopelessly bogged down in them: better the erratic approach, which wins all or at least loses nothing, than the cautious semi-failure; better Don Quixote and his windmills than all the Sancho Panzas in the world; and may it not eventually turn out that to risk all is to win all, even at the expense of intimate, visceral knowledge of the truth, of its graininess and contours, even though this approach leads despite its physicality to no practical understanding of the truth, no grasp of how to use it toward ends it never dreams of? . This, then, is surely the way; but discovery of where it begins is another matter.

  The great careers are like that: a slow burst that narrows to a final release, pointed but not acute, a life of suffering redeemed and

将来更大的不完美；不这样做就是违反我们的本性，就是最终一无所获，甚至连我们为了某个目的而违反的可靠的知识都得不到，而是成为无机物那样空虚而无可指责的东西。不过，我们不知道我们会变成什么，所以我们永远也无法完全排除知识上理解的可能性，即便它似乎什么都不是，只是一个陷阱和骗局；我们可能会错失一切，忽略它们对秩序的呼唤，实际上我们每个人都能听到这呼唤；所以，我们怎么能决定呢？将两种途径结合起来也同样不是办法，在情况似乎允许的时候，借用正确的理智或感觉经验，因为混合物并不完整，事实上远远不能以这样的剂量来纠正一个错误。三种途径都是如此：理智，感觉，或者两者心照不宣的结合，最后一种似乎最不容易成功，第二种途径疑问重重；只有第一种有点渺茫的机会成功通过纯粹邪恶的考验，那也许是唯一最后取得胜利的途径。因而，我们至少可以免于在理论细节的沼泽中，冒着泥足深陷的风险绝望而苦恼地跋涉；不规则的途径更胜过谨慎的不输不赢，它将赢得一切，至少什么都不会丧失；堂吉诃德和他的风车更胜过世界上所有的桑丘；也许最后的结果不是为赢得一切而豁出一切，甚至以亲切的、发自肺腑的有关真理的知识为代价，以它的颗粒度和轮廓为代价，即便这种途径不顾它的物质性而导向对真理的不切实际的理解，不明白如何将它用于从未梦想到的目标？那么，无疑这就是道路；但是，发现它从何处开始就是另一码事儿了。

伟大的生涯是那样的：缓慢的爆发逐渐缩减成最后的释放，

annihilated at the end, and for what? For a casual moment of knowing that is here one minute and gone the next, almost before you were aware of it? Whole tribes of seekers of phenomena who mattered very much to themselves have gone up in smoke in the space of a few seconds, with less fuss than a shooting star. Is it then that our bodies combined in such a way as to show others that we really mean it to each other—is this really all we ever intended to do? Having been born with knowledge or at least with the capacity to judge, to spend all our time working toward a way to show off that knowledge, so as to be able to return to it at the end for what it is? Besides the obvious question of who knows whether it will still be there, there is the even more urgent one of whose life are we taking into our hands? Is there no way in which these things may be done for themselves, so that others may enjoy them? Already we have wandered far from the track and, as always happens in such cases, darkness has fallen and it would be impossible to find one's way back without getting lost. Is this a reason to stay where we are, on the false assumption that we are less lost right here, and thus to complete the cycle of inertia that we began wrongly supposing that it would lead to knowledge? No, it is far better to continue on our way, even at the risk of getting more lost (an impossibility, of course). We might at least wind up with a knowledge of who *they* are, with whom we began, and at the very least with a new respect toward the others, reached through a more perfect understanding of ourselves and the true way. But still the "career" notion intervenes. It is impossible for us at the present time not to think of these people as separate entities, each with his development and aim to be achieved, careers which will "peak" after a while and then go back to being ordinary lives that fade quite naturally into air as they are used up, and are as though they never were, except for the "lesson" which has added an iota to the sum of

尖锐但不锋利，痛苦的一生最后得到了救赎和胜利，为了什么？为了偶然的一瞬间，知道这里的一刻接下来便会消失，几乎在你意识到它之前？对自己颇为看重的整个探求现象的族类几秒钟后便在烟雾中消失，比一颗流星更不值得大惊小怪。正是在那时，我们的身体以这种方式结合起来，向其他人表明，我们真的彼此在意——这真的就是我们想要做的全部吗？先天具有知识，或至少具有判断的能力，把我们所有的时间都用于开辟一条道路，去炫耀那知识，以便能够在最后为了那知识本身而向它回归？除了何人知道它是否仍会在那里这个显而易见的问题，甚至还有一个更为迫切的问题，我们手里掌握着的到底是谁的生活？难道没有任何方法，让这些事物可以为其自身而完成，让其他人能够享受它们？我们已经漫游得太远，远离了轨道，就像这种情况下经常发生的那样，黑暗已经降临，不可能找到回去的路而又不至于迷失。这是一个在我们现在之处停留的理由吗，错误地假设我们在这里没有迷失，于是，为了完成惯性的循环，我们开始错误地认为它会通往知识？不，它要远远好过继续我们的路程，甚至冒着更多迷失的风险（当然，这是不可能的）。我们最后至少会获得这样一种知识，与我们一同开始的他们是谁，至少会对他人获得一种崭新的敬意，更为完善地理解我们自身和真正的道路。但是，"生涯"观念依然在起干预作用。我们现在不可能不把这些人当作独立的实体，每一个都有自己的发展和要实现的目标，片刻之后达到"高峰"的生涯，随后便恢复成平凡的生活，非常自然地消退在空气中，当它们被耗尽，仿佛从未存在过一般，只留下给人类理解的总

all human understanding. And this way of speaking has trapped each one of us.

An alternative way would be the "life-as-ritual"concept. According to this theory no looking back is possible, in itself a considerable advantage, and the stages of the ritual are each considered in themselves, for themselves, but here no danger of fetichism is possible because all contact with the past has been severed. Fetichism comes into being only when there is a past that may seem more or less attractive when compared with the present; the resulting inequality causes a rush toward the immediate object of contemplation, hardens it into a husk around its own being, which promptly ceases. But the ritual approach provides some bad moments too. All its links severed with the worldly matrix from which it sprang, the soul feels that it is propelling itself forward at an ever-increasing speed. This very speed becomes a source of intoxication and of more gradually accruing speed; in the end the soul cannot recognize itself and is as one lost, though it imagines it has found eternal rest. But the true harmony which would render this peace interesting is lacking. There is only a cold knowledge of goodness and nakedness radiating out in every direction like the spines of the horse chestnut; mere knowledge and experience without the visual irregularities, those celestial motes in the eye that alone can transform ecstasy into a particular state beyond the dearly won generality. Here again, if backward looks were possible, not nostalgia but a series of carefully selected views, hieratic as icons, the difficulty would be eased and self could merge with selflessness, in a true appreciation of the tremendous volumes of eternity. But this is impossible because the ritual is by definition something impersonal, and can only move further in that direction. It was born without a knowledge of the past. And any attempt to hybridize it can only result in destruction

和增加一粒芥子的"教训"。此处谈论的这条道路困住了我们每一个人。

一条可供选择的道路是"作为圣礼的生活"观念。遵照这种理论，没有任何回顾是可能的，它本身具备可观的优势，圣礼的各个阶段都从其自身出发、为了自身考虑，这里没有任何拜物教的危险，也许是因为所有与过去的接触都被割断了。只有当存在着一种与现在相比似乎多少有点吸引力的过去，拜物教才存在；由此产生的不平等导致人们匆忙奔向意图的直接对象，将它硬化成一个围绕其本身存在的外壳，并迅速终结。但是，仪式化的途径同样带来了糟糕的时刻。它与它从中萌芽的尘世母体的关联全都被割断了，灵魂觉得它在驱使自身以日益增长的速度前进。正是这速度成了中毒的原因，使它的速度自然递增；到最后，灵魂无法识别自身，像一个迷失的人，尽管它想象自己已经找到了永恒的安息。但是，能使这份和平变得有趣的那种真正的和谐，始终是付诸阙如的。关于善和赤裸，只有一种冷酷的知识，在各个方向发散，就像七叶树的树干一样；纯粹的知识和经验没有视觉上的不规则性，眼睛看到的那些天上的微粒单独就能把狂喜变成一种独特状态，超越来之不易的普遍性。这里重申一下，如果回顾是可能的，不是怀旧的回顾，而是一系列谨慎选择的视野，如圣像一般神圣，那样，困难便会减轻，自我便可以和忘我融为一体，便可以真正欣赏永恒那巨大的体积。但这是不可能的，因为圣礼显然是非个人化的，只能沿着那个方向前进。它天生就不具备有关过去的知

and even death.

In addition to these twin notions of growth, two kinds of happiness are possible: the frontal and the latent. The first occurs naturally throughout life; it is experienced as a kind of sense of immediacy, even urgency; often we first become aware of it at a moment when we feel we need outside help. Its sudden balm suffuses the soul without warning, as a kind of bloom or grace. We suppose that souls "in glory" feel this way permanently, as a day-to-day condition of being: yes, as a condition, for it is both more and less than a state; it exacts certain prerequisites and then it builds on these, but the foundation is never forgotten; it is the foundation that is happiness. And as it exacts, so it bestows. There is not the mindlessness, no idea of eternal lassitude permeated with the light of the firmament or whatever; there are only the value judgments of truth, exposed one after another like colored slides on the white wall that is the naked soul, or a kind of hard glaze that definitively transforms the ordinary clay of the soul into an object of beauty by obliterating the knowledge of what lies underneath. This is what we are all hoping for, yet we know that very few among us will ever achieve it; those who do will succeed less through their own efforts than through the obscure workings of grace as chance, so that although we would be very glad to have the experience of this sudden opening up, this inundation which shall last an eternity, we do not bother our heads too much about it, so distant and far away it seems, like those beautiful mosaic ceilings representing heaven which we crane up at from below, knowing that we cannot get near enough for it to be legible but liking all the same the vastness and aura of the conception, glad to have seen it and to know it's there but nevertheless firmly passing outward into the sunlight after two or three turns around the majestic dim interior. This kind of beauty

识。任何使之杂交的企图都只能导致破坏，甚至是死亡。

除了这一对有关生长的观念之外，有两种幸福是可能的：正面的和潜在的。前者在一生中会自然发生；它被体验成一种及时性的感觉，甚至是紧迫性的感觉；我们往往首先意识到它，当我们觉得我们需要外在帮助的时刻。它的抚慰突然弥漫在灵魂之中，没有警告，像一种花的盛开或者是恩典。我们假设灵魂"于荣耀中"能永久保有这样的感觉，作为存在的一个日常条件；是的，作为一个条件，因为它与一个状态相比，可谓不多不少；它急需某些先决条件，然后在上面进行建设，但是基础从来没有遭到遗忘；它的基础便是幸福。它怎样强求，便怎样赐予。没有漫不经心，不知道永恒的疲倦随着天空的光芒或是任何东西而弥漫；只有对真理的价值判断，一个接一个暴露，像白墙上彩色的幻灯片，那白墙是赤裸的灵魂，或者一种硬釉，抹掉了有关下面存在的一切的知识，决定性地将灵魂的普通黏土转变成美的物体。这是我们全都希望得到的东西，我们也知道很少有人能够得到它；那些确会成功的人不是通过他们的努力，而是通过恩典运气一般费解的做工，因而，尽管我们很乐意体验这种突然的暴露，这股将要持续到永世的洪水，我们却并不怎么为之操心，它显得如此冷漠而遥远，像那些代表天堂的美丽的马赛克天花板，我们从下面把它们吊起来，知道我们靠得足够近，无法让它们变得清晰，而是希望它们完全像观念那样巨大，光环闪耀，我们乐于看见这观念，知道它在那里，然而却围绕那庄严暗淡的内部转上两三圈，便坚决地走进

is almost too abstract to be experienced as beauty, and yet we must realize that it is not an abstract notion, that it really can happen at times and that life at these times seems marvelous. Indeed this is truly what we were brought into creation for, if not to experience it, at least to have the knowledge of it as an ideal toward which the whole universe tends and which therefore confers a shape on the random movements outside us—these are all straining in the same direction, toward the same goal, though it is certain that few if any of those we see now will attain it.

The second kind, the latent or dormant kind, is harder to understand. We all know those periods of balmy weather in early spring, sometimes even before spring has officially begun: days or even a few hours when the air seems suffused with an unearthly tenderness, as though love were about to start, now, at this moment, on an endless journey put off since the beginning of time. Just to walk a few steps in this romantic atmosphere is to experience a magical but quiescent bliss, as though the torch of life were about to be placed in one's hands: after having anticipated it for so long, what is one now to do? And so the happiness withholds itself, perhaps even indefinitely; it realizes that the vessel has not yet been fully prepared to receive it; it is afraid it will destroy the order of things by precipitating itself too soon. But this in turn quickens the dismay of the vessel or recipient; it, or we, have been waiting all our lives for this sign of fulfillment, now to be abruptly snatched away so soon as barely perceived. And a kind of panic develops, which for many becomes a permanent state of being, with all the appearances of a calm, purposeful, reflective life. These people are awaiting the sign of their felicity without hope; its *nearness* is there, tingeing the air around them, in suspension, in escrow as it were, but they cannot get at it. Yet so great is their eagerness that they believe that they have already absorbed it, that they have attained that plane of final

阳光之中。这种美几乎过于抽象了，无法像美那样被体验，我们还要认识到它并非一个抽象观念，它可以时时发生，在这些时刻，生活显得神奇起来。的确，我们受造的目的就是它，即便不是为了体验它，至少也是要拥有关于它的知识，作为一个理想，整个宇宙都趋向于它，它由此为我们外面的随机运动赋予形式——这一切都在同一方向上努力，朝向同一目标，尽管我们现在看见的人中肯定很少有人会得到它。

第二种，潜在的幸福，更难理解。我们全都知道早春那些温和的天气，有时甚至在春天正式开始之前：连续几天抑或是几个小时，空气中似乎弥漫着一种神秘的温柔，仿佛爱，就是现在，此时此刻，即将开始一次自时间开始以来就被推迟的无尽旅程。在这浪漫气氛中只是走上几步，就能体验到一种神奇又静止的狂喜，仿佛生活的触摸即将落在一个人的手上：经过这么漫长的期待，一个人现在要做什么呢？于是，幸福就这样克制住自己，甚或无限期地克制下去；它认识到，承载它的容器还没有完全准备停当；它担心自己过快地陷身其中会毁灭事物的秩序。但是，这反过来又加剧了对容器或是接受者的失望；它，或者是我们，终其一生都在等待这个圆满的迹象，现在刚觉察就被猛然攫走。一种恐慌显露出来，在许多人那里变成了存在的永恒状态，连同沉静、自觉、沉思的生活的全部表象。这些人在无希望地等待他们幸福的迹象；它很近，就在那里，给他们周围的空气着上淡色，悬浮着，像过去那样由第三方托管，但是他们够不到它。然而，他们的渴望如此巨大，他

realization which we are all striving for, that they have achieved a state of permanent grace. Hence the air of joyful resignation, the beatific upturned eyelids, the paralyzed stance of these castaways of the eternal voyage, who imagine they have reached the promised land when in reality the ship is sinking under them. The great fright has turned their gaze upward, to the stars, to the heavens; they see nothing of the disarray around them, their ears are closed to the cries of their fellow passengers; they can think only of themselves when all the time they believe that they are thinking of nothing but God. Yet in their innermost minds they know too that all is not well; that if it were there would not be this rigidity, with the eye and the mind focused on a nonexistent center, a fixed point, when the common sense of even an idiot would be enough to make him realize that nothing has stopped, that we and everything around us are moving forward continually, and that we are being modified constantly by the speed at which we travel and the regions through which we pass, so that merely to think of ourselves as having arrived at some final resting place is a contradiction of fundamental logic, since even the dullest of us knows enough to realize that he is ignorant of everything, including the basic issue of whether we are really moving at all or whether the concept of motion is something that can even be spoken of in connection with such ignorant beings as we, for whom the term ignorant is indeed perhaps an overstatement, implying as it does that something is known somewhere, whereas in reality we are not even sure of this: we in fact cannot aver with any degree of certainty that we *are* ignorant. Yet this is not so bad; we have at any rate kept our open-mindedness—*that*, at least, we may be sure that we have—and are not in any danger, or so it seems, of freezing into the pious attitudes of those true spiritual bigots whose faces are turned toward eternity and who therefore can see nothing. We know that we are en route in a certain sense, and also that there has been a

们相信自己已经吸收了它，已经达到了那个我们都在为之奋斗的最终实现的层次，已经进入了一种永恒恩典的状态。这些永恒航行中的遇难者，他们摆出欢乐顺从的模样，幸福上翻的眼睑和瘫痪的姿势，他们想象自己已经抵达了应许之地，而实际上船只正在他们脚下沉没。巨大的惊恐让他们向上仰望群星和苍天；他们看不到周围任何的混乱，他们充耳不闻同伴的哭喊；他们只能想起自己，而他们始终相信自己，除了上帝什么都不想。然而，他们内心深处也知道大事不妙；如果一切不是这般僵硬，眼睛和思想不是集中在一个不存在的中心，那固定的点上，那么，甚至一个白痴的常识也足以让他认识到一切都没有停止，我们和周围的一切都在继续向前运动，我们旅行的速度和经过的地区在不断地改变着我们，以至于单单以为我们已经抵达了某个最后的休憩之所，就是不符合基本逻辑的矛盾，既然我们当中最为沉闷的人也足以认识到他对一切都是无知的，包括下面的基本问题，我们是否真的在运动，或者，运动的概念是否可以由我们这样无知的生命来谈论，对于我们来说，无知这个术语也许的确是个言过其词的说法，实际上暗示着某处存在着某种已知的东西，然而，我们甚至确定不了这一点：事实上我们无法以任何程度的确定性断言我们的无知。不过，情况并不是如此糟糕；无论如何，我们保持住了开放的心胸——这一点，至少我们可以确定——而且根本或大概没有僵化成那些真正的精神盲信者的虔诚姿势的危险，他们的面孔朝向永恒，因而看不见任何东西。我们知道在某种意义上我们尚在途中，在某处一直存在着一个故障：我们像过去那样登上火车，但出

hitch somewhere: we have as it were boarded the train but for some unexplained reason it has not yet started. But there is in this as yet only slight delay matter for concern even for the likes of us, intelligent and only modestly expectant as we are, patient, meek without any overtones of ironic resignation before a situation we are powerless to change and secretly believe is likely to go from bad to worse. There is nothing of that in us, we are not bigots and we have kept an open mind, we have all our mobility in a word, yet we too sense a danger and we do not quite know how we are going to react. Those first few steps, in the prematurely mild air that a blizzard is surely destined to dash from living memory before tomorrow comes—aren't we in danger of accepting these only for what they are, of being thankful for them and letting our gratitude take the place of further inquiry into what they were like, of letting it stand both for our attitude as eternity will view it and also for the fulfillment of which this was just the promise? That surely is the danger we run in our state of sophisticated but innocent enlightenment: that of not *demanding* and getting a hearing, of not finding out where these steps were leading even in the teeth of an almost dead certainty that it was nowhere, even of doubting that they ever took place, that any kind of structure or fabric in which they would assume being could ever have existed. So that in our way we are worse off or at least in worse danger than those others who imagine themselves already delivered from the chain of rebirth. *They* have their illusions to sustain them, even though these are full of holes and sometimes don't prevent their possessors from feeling the chilly drafts of doubt, while we can be brought to doubt that any of this, which we know in our heart of hearts to be a real thing, an event of the highest spiritual magnitude, ever happened. Here it is that our sensuality can save us in extremis: the atmosphere of the day that event took place, the way the trees and buildings looked, what we said to the person who was both the bearer and fellow recipient of that message

于某种不明原因，火车还没有启动。不过，这还只是事关稍微的延误，甚至和我们相似的人也为此担心，他们和我们一样聪明，一样心怀谦卑的期待，耐心而温顺，没有任何带有讽刺意味的放弃的弦外之音，面对我们无力改变的处境，背地里相信它很可能会变得恶化。我们心里没有任何那样的东西，我们不是盲信者，我们保持住了开放的心胸，总之，我们全都具有机动性，我们也感觉到了一种危险，我们还不太清楚自己要做出怎样的反应。最初的那几步，早熟的温和空气中的一场暴风雪，注定要在明天降临之前冲出活的记忆——难道我们没有面临危险吗？只为了他们本身才接受这些，对他们心存感激，让我们的感激之情取代了对他们本来面目的深入探究，让它既代表我们的态度，就像永恒看待它那样，又让它恰好代表这永恒承诺的履行？在我们复杂又无辜的启蒙状态中，我们遭遇的肯定是这种危险：不要求为人所闻，也无人听闻，不去发现这些步骤通往何处，哪怕置身于几乎致命的确定性的利齿之中，它也不存在，哪怕怀疑它们曾经发生过，在任何种类的结构或组织中，它们都会承担能够始终存在的存在。因而，在我们的路上，我们的情况在恶化，或至少存在恶化的危险，超过了那些想象自己业已摆脱再生之锁链的人。他们用幻觉支撑自己，即便这些幻觉满是漏洞，有时无法阻止他们感受怀疑的冷风，却能引发我们怀疑任何这样的事情，我们在内心深处知道它是真实的东西，是一个具有最高精神量级的事件，确曾发生过。就在这里，我们的感官享受能够拯救我们于危难之中：事件发生那天的气氛，树木和建筑物的模样，我们对别人说的话，他既

and what that person replied, words that were not words but sounds out of time, taken out of any eternal context in which their content would be recognizable—these facts have entered our consciousness once and for all, have spread through us even into our pores like a marvelous antidote to the cup that the next moment had already prepared and which, whether hemlock or nectar, could only have proved fatal because it *was* the next, bringing with it the unspoken message that motion could be accomplished only in time, that is in a preordained succession of moments which must carry us far from here, far from this impassive but real moment of understanding which may be the only one we shall ever know, even if it is merely the first of an implied infinite series. But what if this were all? What if it were true that "once is enough"? That all consequences, all resonances of this singular event were to be cut off by virtue of its very singularity; nay, that even for memory, insofar as it can profit anyone, this instant were to be as though it had never existed, expunged from the chronicles of recorded time, fallen lower than the last circle of hell into a pit of total negation, and all this in our own best interests, so that we might not be led astray into imagining its goodness infinitely extendible, a thing that could never happen given the absolute and all-pervading nature of that goodness, destined to occur only once in the not-to-be-repeated cycle of eternity? Yet this seems not quite right, a little too pat perhaps, and here again it is our senses that are of some use to us in distinguishing verity from falsehood. For they never would have been able to capture the emanations from that special point of life if they were not meant to do something with them, weave them into the pattern of the days that come after, sunlit or plunged in shadow as they may be, but each with the identifying scarlet thread that runs through the whole warp and woof of the design, sometimes almost disappearing in its dark accretions, but at others emerging as the full inspiration of the plan of the whole, grandly organizing its repeated vibrations and imposing its

是信息的携带者，又是同等的收信人，以及那人的回答，那些词语不是词语，而是不合时宜的声音，从永恒的语境中取出来，它们的内容将无法辨认——这些事实一劳永逸地进入我们的意识，穿过我们展开，甚至进入我们的毛孔，如同神奇的解毒剂落进杯中，下一个瞬间已经在等待，无论它是毒芹还是花蜜，都只能证明是致命的，因为它就是下一个瞬间，携带着无言的信息，运动只能在时间中，亦即预先注定的一连串瞬间中完成。这些瞬间必定带我们远离此地，远离这冷漠而真实的理解的时刻，这也许是我们唯一要知道的瞬间，即便它仅仅是一个暗示出的无尽系列的开端。可万一这就是全部呢？万一真的"一次就够了"呢？这个单一事件的所有结果、所有反响，正是由于它的单一性而被全部切断；不，甚至对于记忆来说，迄今它也能使每个人受益，这个瞬间仿佛从未存在过，从有记载的时间编年史中被抹去了，坠落到比地狱最后一圈还低的全然否定的深坑中，这一切都符合我们的最大利益，这样我们便不会被引入歧途，想象它的善可以无限延伸，这样一件由于那善的无所不在的本质而永远不可能发生的事，注定只在不会重复的永恒循环中出现一次吗？不过，这似乎并不太对，也许有点不太合适了，这里，又是我们的感官对我们起了作用，让我们将事实与虚假分开。因为它们永远无法捕获从生活的那个特殊时刻发散出来的东西，如果它们想要用这些发散物做些什么，把它们编织成后续日子的图案，被阳光照亮或是投入阴影，每一个都以可供识别的红色线头贯穿整个设计的经纬线，有时几乎消失在它黑暗的累积物中，但是在另外的时刻又会浮现出来，当整

stamp on these until the meaning of it all suddenly flashes out of the shimmering pools of scarlet like a vast and diaphanous though indestructible framework, not to be lost sight of again? And here we may say that even if the uniqueness were meant to last only the duration of its unique instant, which I don't for a moment believe, but let us assume so for the sake of argument—even if this were the case, its aura would still be meant to linger on in our days, informing us of and gently prodding us toward the right path, even though we might correctly consider ourselves shut off from the main source, never to be in a position to contemplate its rightness again, yet despite this able to consider its traces in the memory as a supreme good, as a god come down to earth to instruct us in the ways of the other kingdom, for he sees that we have not progressed very far on our own—no farther than those first few steps in the suddenly mild open air. And we are lucky that he chooses so to deal with us, for as of this moment our worries are over, we have only to step forward to be in the right path, we are all walking in it and we always have been, only we never knew it. The end is still shrouded in mystery, but the mystery diminishes without, exactly becoming clearer the more we advance, like a city whose plan begins to take shape on the horizon as we approach it, yet that is not precisely the case here because we certainly perceive no more of the divine enigma as we progress, it is just that its mystery lessens and comes to seem, whenever we stop to think of it which is not very often, the least important feature of the whole. What does matter is our growing sense of certainty, whether deduced by the intellect or the sensual intelligence (this is immaterial): it is there, and this is all we need bother about, just as there is no need to examine a man's ancestry or antecedents in evaluating his personal qualities. But, after the question of how did it get there, which we now perceive to be futile, another question remains: how are we to use it? Not only by what means, which is an important enough

体计划的完整灵感，宏伟地组织起它反复的振动，在上面强行盖上印记，直到它的全部意义突然从波光粼粼的红色池塘中闪射出来，如同一个巨大、精致但不可摧毁的框架，再也不会消失不见？这里，我们可以说，即便这唯一性意味着仅仅持续它唯一的瞬间，这一点我片刻都不会相信，但是让我们为了讨论的方便，假设就是这样——即便情况的确如此，它的气氛仍会刻意流连在我们的日子里，通知我们，轻轻地刺激我们走向正确的道路，即便我们会正确地考虑切断主要来源，永远不要再次处于沉思它的正确性的状态，然而，尽管如此，我们依然能在记忆中考虑它的轨迹，如同至高的善，如同一个神，降到世间，以另一王国的方式指导我们，因为他看见，我们靠自己还没有取得很大的进展——在突然变得温和的户外，还没有超过最初的几步。我们的幸运在于，他选择这样与我们打交道，因为这时我们的忧虑已经过去，我们只需走上正确的路径，我们全都走在上面，我们始终如此，只是我们从来不知道这一点。终点依然隐藏在神秘中，但是这神秘在削弱，恰恰没有因我们的前进而变得清晰，就像一座城市，随着我们的靠近，它的计划开始在地平线上成形，然而，这里的情况恰恰不是这样，因为随着我们的进步，我们自然不再能感知到神圣之谜，正是如此，它的神秘逐渐削弱，每当我们停下来思考它的时候，这样的时候不是很多，似乎它就成了整体最不重要的特征。关键的是我们日益增长的对确定性的感觉，无论它是凭智性还是凭感性（这是无形的）推断出来的：它就在那里，这就是我们需要操心的一切，就像估价一个男人的个人品质时无需检查他的血

consideration, but toward what end? Toward our own betterment and by extension that of the world around us or conversely toward the improvement of the world, which we might believe would incidentally render us as its citizens better people, even though this were just a side effect? The answer is in our morning waking. For just as we begin our lives as mere babes with the imprint of nothing in our heads, except lingering traces of a previous existence which grow fainter and fainter as we progress until we have forgotten them entirely, only by this time other notions have imposed themselves so that our infant minds are never a complete *tabula rasa*, but there is always something fading out or just coming into focus, and this whatever-it-is is always projecting itself on us, escalating its troops, prying open the shut gates of our sensibility and pouring in to augment its forces that have begun to take over our naked consciousness and driving away those shreds of another consciousness (although not, perhaps, forever—nothing is permanent—but perhaps until our last days when their forces shall again mass on the borders of our field of perception to remind us of that other old existence which we are now called to rejoin) so that for a moment, between the fleeing and the pursuing armies there is almost a moment of peace, of purity in which what we are meant to perceive could almost take shape in the empty air, if only there were time enough, and yet in the time it takes to perceive the dimness of its outline we can if we are quick enough seize the meaning of that assurance, before returning to the business at hand—just, I say, as we begin each day in this state of threatened blankness which is wiped away so soon, but which leaves certain illegible traces, like chalk dust on a blackboard after it has been erased, so we must learn to recognize it as the form—the only one—in which such fragments of the true learning as we are destined to receive will be vouchsafed to us, if at all. The unsatisfactoriness, the frowns and squinting, the itching and scratching as you listen without taking in what

统或祖先。但是，它是如何抵达那里的，在我们现在认为无用的这个问题之后，还有另一个问题：我们要怎样利用它？不仅在于用什么方法，这是一个足够重要的考虑，而且在于为了什么目的？为了我们自身的改善，扩展我们周围的世界，或者相反，为了改善世界，我们相信世界会附带地把作为它的公民的我们变成更好的人，即便这仅仅是一个附带效果？答案在于我们早晨的苏醒。正如我们作为纯粹的婴儿开始生活，头脑中没有任何的印记，随着我们的进展，只有前世徘徊不去的轨迹变得越来越模糊，直到我们完全把它们忘记，只有到了这个时候，其他观念才会发挥影响，我们婴儿的头脑从来就不是一个完全的白板，而是始终存在着某个东西，逐渐淡出，或是变得清晰，无论它是什么，它总是将自身投射在我们身上，逐步扩大它的军队，撬开我们感受力那封闭的门户，蜂拥而入，增强它的力量，开始接管我们赤裸的意识，赶走另一种意识的那些残余（尽管，也许不是永远驱逐——无物永恒——但也许直到我们最后的时日，它们的力量还会集结在我们知觉的战场边缘，提醒我们另一种古老的存在在呼唤我们重新加入），以至于在一瞬间，在奔逃和追击的军队之间，便几乎出现了一个和平与纯净的瞬间，其中，我们想要感知的一切几乎都能在空虚的空气中显形，只要时间充足，而且，到那时，我们便可以感知到它暗淡的轮廓，如果我们足够快地捕捉住那个保证的含意，在返回手边的事务之前——我敢说，那恰如我们在这受到威胁的茫然状态中开始每一天一样，这种茫然很快就被抹掉了，但是它留下了某些难以辨认的轨迹，就像黑板上擦掉的粉笔灰，所以，

is being said to you, or only in part, so that you cannot piece the argument together, should not be dismissed as signs of our chronic all-too-human weakness but welcomed and examined as signs of life in which part of the whole truth lies buried. And as the discourse continues and you think you are not getting anything out of it, as you yawn and rub your eyes and pick your nose or scratch your head, or nudge your neighbor on the hard wooden bench, this knowledge is getting through to you, and taking just the forms it needs to impress itself upon you, the forms of your inattention and incapacity or unwillingness to understand. For it is certain that you will rise from the bench a new person, and even before you have emerged into the full daylight of the street you will feel that a change has begun to operate in you, within your very fibers and sinews, and when the light of the street floods over you it will have become real at last, all traces of doubt will have been pulverized by the influx of light slowly mounting to bury those crass seamarks of egocentricity and warped self-esteem you were able to navigate by but which you no longer need now that the rudder has been swept out of your hands, and this whole surface of daylight has become one with that other remembered picture of light, when you were setting out, and which you feared would disappear because of its uniqueness, only now realizing that this singleness was the other side of the coin of its many-faceted diversity and interest, and that it may be simultaneously cherished for the former and lived in thanks to the versatility of the latter. It may be eaten, and breathed, and it would indeed have no reason to exist if this were not the case. So I think that the question of how we are going to use the reality of our revelation, as well as to what end, has now been resolved. First of all we see that these two aspects of our question are actually one and the same, that there is only one aspect as well as only one question, that to wonder how is the same as beginning to know why. For no choice is possible. In the early moments of

我们必须学会把它当作形式来辨认——唯一的形式——果真如此的话，我们注定要接受的真知的片段将会被赐予我们。不满，皱眉和斜视，发痒和抓搔，当你听不进任何说给你的东西，或者只是听进去一部分，以至于你无法把论据拼在一起，不应该把它们当作我们习惯性的人之常情的软弱标志而打发掉，而是欢迎它们，把它们当作埋藏真理的一部分的生活标志来予以考察。而且，随着谈话的继续，你认为你从中得不到任何东西，当你打呵欠、揉眼睛、挖鼻孔、挠脑袋，或是在硬邦邦的木头长凳上，用肘轻推你旁边的人，这知识正在向你传递，为了给你留下印象，它正在取得它所需要的形式，你的疏忽、无能和不情愿理解的形式。可以肯定，你将作为一个新人从长凳上起身，甚至在你之前就已经融入街头充沛的阳光之中，你将感觉到一种变化已经在你内部开始起作用，就在你的纤维和肌腱中，而当街头的光把你淹没，它最后将变得真实，所有怀疑的痕迹都将被光的洪流所粉碎，这光缓慢升起，埋葬自我中心的那些愚钝的航标和反常的自尊，你能够用它们来导航，但是你现在已不再需要，船舵已经从你的手中被卷走了，这阳光的整个表面已经与另一幅记忆中的光的图画合为一体，你当初出发的时候曾担心这幅图画会消失，因为它独一无二，现在你才认识到，这种独特性是它那多面的多样性和利益之硬币的反面，你可以珍惜其独特性，同时又充满感激地生活在其多功能性之中。它可以被吃掉，被呼吸掉，如果情况不是这样，它真的就没有理由存在了。所以，我认为，我们要如何利用我们启示的真实性，以及用于什么目的，这个问题现在已经得到解决。最重要的是，

wondering after the revelation had been received it could have been that this way of doing seemed to promise more, that that one had already realized its potential, that therefore there was matter for hesitation and the possibility of loss between a way that had already proved itself and another, less sure one that could lead to greener pastures, to cloud-cuckoo land and even farther, just because the implied risk seemed to posit a greater virtue in the acceptance. But it is certain now that these two ways are the same, that we *have* them both, the risk and the security, merely through being human creatures subject to the vicissitudes of time, our earthly lot. So that this second kind of happiness is merely a fleshed-out, realized version of that ideal first kind, and more to be prized because its now ripe contours enfold both the promise and the shame of our human state, which they therefore proceed to transmute into something that is an amalgam of both, the faithful reflection of the idealistic concept that got us started along this path, but a reflection which is truer than the original because more suited to us, and whose shining perspectives we can feel and hold, clenching the journey to us like the bread and meat left by the wayside for the fatigued traveler by an anonymous Good Samaritan—ourselves, perhaps, just as Hop-o'-My-Thumb distributed crumbs along the way to guide him back in the dark, only these the birds have miraculously spared: they are ours. To know this is to be able to relax without any danger of becoming stagnant. Thus the difficulty of living with the unfolding of the year is erased, the preparing for spring and then for the elusive peace of summer, followed by the invigorating readjustments of autumn and the difficult and never very successful business of adapting to winter and the approach of another year. This way we are automatically attuned to these progressions and can forget about them; what matters is us and not what time makes of us, or rather it is what we make of ourselves that matters. What is this? Just the absorption of ourselves seen from the outside,

我们看见我们问题的这两个方面实际上是一体的，是一回事，只有一个方面，也只有一个问题，想知道"如何"就和想知道"为何"一样是一回事。因为没有任何选择的可能。在收到启示之后，在疑惑的初期阶段，这样做似乎更有希望，一个人已经认识到它的潜力，因而，在已经得到证明的路，和另一条没有把握的路之间，存在着让人犹豫的事和丧失的可能性，后一条路可以通向更加翠绿的草场，通向幻境，甚至更远，恰恰是因为暗含的风险似乎能给接受者带来更大的益处。但是，可以肯定，既然这两条道路是一样的，我们就同时拥有它们，拥有风险和安全，只需作为人类顺服于时间的无常变迁，我们尘世的命运。这样一来，这第二种幸福就仅仅是那理想的第一种幸福的一个有血有肉、实现了的版本，更其珍贵，因为它现在成熟的轮廓同时包裹着许诺和我们人类的羞愧处境，它们会进而嬗变成两者的混合物，促使我们沿着这条路开始的理想观念的可信倒影，可是这倒影永远也没有原型真实，因为原型更适合我们，我们可以感受和拥有它闪光的远景，牢牢把握住我们的旅程，就像一个匿名的乐善好施的人为疲惫的旅行者留在路边的面包和肉——也许，我们自己，恰恰像小矮人一样沿途撒下面包屑，以便引导自己在黑暗中返回，鸟儿神奇地放过了这些面包屑：它们是我们的。知道这一点就可以放松下来，又不会有任何停滞的危险。于是，度过这一年的演变的困难便被消除了，为春天和随后夏天那难以捉摸的和平做准备，接着是秋天精力充沛的调整，困难和从来不很成功的对冬天的适应，以及又一年的临近。在这方面，我们能自动习惯于这些进步，可以把它

when it is really what is going on inside us—all this overheard chatter and speculation and the noises of the day as it wears on into the calm of night, joyful or abysmal as it may be: this doesn't matter once we have accepted it and taken it inside us to be the interior walls of our chamber, the place where we live. And so all these conflicting meaningless details are transformed into something peaceful that surrounds, like wallpaper that could be decorated with scenes of shipwrecks or military attributes or yawning crevasses in the earth and which doesn't matter, which indeed can paradoxically heighten the feeling of a peaceful domestic interior. Yet this space wasn't made just for the uses of peace, but also for action, for planned assaults on the iniquity and terror outside, though this doesn't mean either that we shall have at some point to go outside or on the contrary that our plans will remain at the stage of dreams or armies in the fire: we carry both inside and outside around with us as we move purposefully toward an operation that is going to change us on every level, and is also going to alter the balance of power of happiness in the world in our favor and that of all the human beings in the world. And how is this to become possible? Let us assume for the sake of argument that the blizzard I spoke of earlier has occurred, shattering the frail décor of your happiness like a straw house, replunging you and your world into the gray oblivion you had been floundering in all your life until the day your happiness was given to you as a gift, a reward or so it seemed for the stale unprofitable journey you called your life, only now it seemed that it was just beginning, and at the same moment you had an impression of stopping or ending. Apparently then happiness was to be a fixed state, but then you perceived that it was both fixed and mobile at the same time, like a fixed source of light with rays running out from and connecting back to it. This suited you very well, because it replied to your twin urges to act and to remain at peace with yourself and with the warring elements outside. And now these have again taken over and

们忘掉；重要的是我们本身，而不是时间让我们成了什么，更确切地说，我们让自己成了什么才是重要的。这是什么？仅仅是专注于从外部看见的我们自己，当它真的就是在我们内部持续的东西——当这全部偷听到的闲聊、推测和日子的噪音逐渐消逝在夜晚的沉静之中，它终归是快乐的，或是深不可测的：这无关紧要，一旦我们接受了它，吸收到我们内部，成为我们房间的内墙，成为我们生活的地方。所有这些矛盾的无意义细节就这样被转变成周遭的宁静，就如同墙纸可以装饰以船难、军事题材或是地上的裂缝这样的风景，这都不要紧，它们反倒能够悖谬地强化家居内部的和平宁静之感。不过，这个空间并不仅仅是为和平而创造的，也是为了行动，为了抵御外部邪恶和恐怖有计划的攻击，尽管这并不意味着我们在某一时刻会到外面去，或者相反，我们的计划将停留在梦境或火中军队的阶段：我们同时将内在和外在携带在我们周围，当我们自觉地展开一个行动，那就是要在各个层面上改变我们自己，也是要改变世界上幸福力量的平衡，使我们和世上所有人都受益。这又怎么可能呢？为了便于讨论，让我们假设我早先提到的暴风雪已经发生了，粉碎了你的幸福那脆弱的装饰，像一座茅草屋，重新把你和你的世界抛进灰色的遗忘中，你整整一生都在里面挣扎辗转，直到幸福像一件礼物、一份回报之类的东西，被赐予你的那天，为了你称之为生活的这沉闷而无利可图的旅程，只是现在它似乎才刚刚开始，而在同一时刻，你有了一种停顿或是结束的印象。显然，那时的幸福是一种固定状态，但是你随后意识到，它同时既是固定的又是机动的，像一个固定光源，

crushed your fragile dream of happiness, so that it all seems meaningless. Gazing out at the distraught but inanimate world you feel that you have lapsed back into the normal way things are, that what you were feeling just now was a novelty and hence destined to disappear quickly, its sole purpose if any being to light up the gloom around you sufficiently for you to become aware of its awesome extent, more than the eye and the mind can take in. The temptation here is to resume the stoic pose, tinged with irony and self-mockery, of times before. There was no point in arriving at this place, but neither, you suppose, would there have been any in avoiding it. It is all the same to you. And you turn away from the window almost with a sense of relief, to bury yourself again in the task of sorting out the jumbled scrap basket of your recent days, without any hope of completing it or even caring whether it gets done or not. But you find that you are unable to pick up the threads where you left off; the details of things shift and their edges swim before your tired eyes; it is impossible to make even the rudimentary sense of them that you once could. You see that you cannot do without it, that singular isolated moment that has now already slipped so far into the past that it seems a mere spark. You cannot do without it and you cannot have it. At this point a drowsiness overtakes you as of total fatigue and indifference; in this unnatural, dreamy state the objects you have been contemplating take on a life of their own, in and for themselves. It seems to you that you are eavesdropping and can understand their private language. They are not talking about you at all, but are telling each other curious private stories about things you can only half comprehend, and other things that have a meaning only for themselves and are beyond any kind of understanding. And these in turn would know other sets of objects, limited to their own perceptions and at the limit of the scope of visibility of those that discuss them and dream about them. It could be that time and space are filled up with these to infinity and beyond; that there is no

光线流出来，同时又与光源相连。这非常适合于你，因为它对应着你的双重需求，行动的同时又与你自己及外部互相冲突的元素保持和平。而现在，这些又再次接管了，碾碎了你脆弱的幸福之梦，让它显得毫无意义。凝视着发狂的、了无生气的世界，你觉得你又回到了事物的正常状态，你此刻感受的一切仅仅是一种新奇，因此注定要迅速消失，它唯一可能的目的是照亮你周围的阴暗，足以让你意识到眼睛和大脑无法接受的它那可怕的广度。这里的诱惑在于恢复斯多葛派的姿势，用过去时代的讽刺和自嘲染上淡彩。抵达这个地方没有任何意义，但是你推测，逃避它同样也没有意义。对你都是一回事。你带着一种几乎是解脱的感觉从窗边转身，重新埋头忙碌，整理你那最近几天一篮子乱七八糟的零碎，没有任何完成这项任务的希望，甚至也不在乎是否能完成。可你发现你无法拾起你留下的线索；事物的细节在变，它们的边缘在你疲惫的双眼前漂浮，不可能像曾经那样搞清它们基本的意义。你明白你没有它不行，那个独一的孤立瞬间现已远远溜进了过去，似乎成了一个火花。没有它你不行，而你又无法拥有它。这时，一阵睡意袭来，你变得极其疲惫而冷漠；在这不自然的、梦一般的状态中，你一直在思考的对象获得了它们自己的生命。在你看来，你似乎在偷听，你能理解它们秘密的语言。它们根本不是在谈论你，而是在彼此讲述奇怪的秘密故事，你只能一知半解的事物，以及其他只对它们自己有意义且超乎任何理解的事物。而这些事物反过来又会知道其他的对象群，限于它们自己的知觉力，以及那些讨论和梦见它们的人的能见度范围。也许时间和空间能够被

such thing as a void, only endless lists of things that may or may not be aware of one another, the "sad variety of woe." And this pointless diversity plunges you into a numbing despair and blankness. The whole world seems dyed the same melancholy hue. Nothing in it can arouse your feelings. Even the sun seems dead. And all because you succumbed to what seemed an innocent and perfectly natural craving, to have your cake and eat it too, forgetting that, widespread as it is, it cannot be excused on any human grounds because it cannot be realized. Therefore even to contemplate it is a sin. But, you say, in those first moments… Never mind that now. You must forget them. The dream that was fleetingly revealed to you was a paradox, and for this reason must be forgotten as quickly as possible. But, you continue to argue, it mattered precisely because it was a paradox and about to be realized here on earth, in human terms; otherwise one would have forgotten it as quickly as any morning dream that clings to you in the first few waking moments, until its incongruities become blatant in the reasonable daylight that seeps back into your consciousness. It was not a case of a spoiled child asking its mother for something for the nth time or of wishing on a star; it was a *new arrangement* that existed and was on the point of working. And now it is all the same; any miracles, if there ever are any again, will be partial ones, mere virtuosic exhibitions beside the incontrovertible reality of that other, as amazingly real as a new element or a new dimension. And so it goes. But if it was indeed as real as all that, then it *was* real, and therefore it *is* real. Just as matter cannot be added to or subtracted from the universe, or energy destroyed, so with something real, that is, real in the sense you understood it and understand it. When will you realize that your dreams have eternal life? I of course don't mean that you are a moonstruck dreamer, but that they do exist, outside of you, without your having to do anything about it. Even if you do something it won't matter. And it is possible that you will always remain unaware of their

这些事物填满，直到无限；不存在无效又无尽的事物清单这样的东西，其中的事物也许能意识到彼此的存在，"各种各样悲哀的灾难"。而这无意义的多样性将你投进麻木的绝望和茫然。整个世界似乎染上了同样忧郁的色调。没有任何东西能激发你的感情。甚至太阳似乎也死掉了。这一切都是因为你屈服于一种看似无辜又完全自然的渴望，想要鱼和熊掌兼得，忘记了它的广泛性，无法以任何人类的理由为借口，因为它是不能实现的。所以，甚至把它思考一番都是罪。但是，你说，在那些最初的时刻……现在不要再提那个了。你必须忘掉它们。向你飞快显现的梦是个悖论，因为这个原因必须尽快忘掉。但是，你继续争辩说，就人类而言，它恰恰因为是悖论才重要，它即将在地球上实现；否则一个人就会尽快忘掉它，就像早晨的梦，在你最初苏醒的瞬间还依附着你，直到它的不协调在渗透你意识的理智之光中变得明目张胆。这情况不是一个被宠坏的孩子在向母亲 N 次要东西，或者是在向星星许愿；它是一种新的安排，它存在，并即将发挥作用。而现在它完全是一回事；任何奇迹，如果再有的话，都将是局部的奇迹，仅仅是与另一种无可争议的真实并排展示的艺术品，真实得让人吃惊，如同一个新元素或是一个新维度。就这么回事。但是，如果它真的那么真实，那么它过去就是真实的，因而现在也是真实的。正如宇宙中的物质不增不减，或者说能量不灭，真实的事物也是如此，亦即，它的真实在于你过去和现在都理解它。你何时才会认识到你的梦拥有永恒的生命？我当然不是指你是个耽于幻想的梦想家，而是指它们确实存在，在你外面，与你没有一点关系。即便你

existence; this won't matter either, to them, that is. But you must try to seize the truth of this: whatever was, is, and must be. The darkness that surrounds you now does not exist, because it never had any independent existence: you created it out of the spleen and torment you felt. It looks real enough to hide you from the light of the sun, but its reality is as specious as that of a mirage. The clouds are dispersing. And nothing comes to take their place, to interpose itself between you and the reality which you dreamed and which is therefore real. This new arrangement is already guiding your steps and indicating the direction you should take without your realizing it, for it is invisible now; it still seems that it is lost for there is of course no tangible evidence of it: *that* happens only once, it is true. But now to have absorbed the lesson, to have recovered from the shock of not being able to remember it, to again be setting out from the beginning—is this not something good to you? You no longer have to remember the principles, they seem to come to you like fragments of a buried language you once knew. You are like the prince in the fairy tale before whom the impenetrable forest opened and then the gates of the castle, without his knowing why. The one thing you want is to pause so as to puzzle all this out, but that is impossible; you are moving much too quickly for your momentum to be halted. How will it all turn out? What will the end be? But these are questions of the ignorant novice which you have forgotten about already. You think now only in terms of the speed with which you advance, and which you drink in like oxygen; it has become the element in which you live and which is you. Nothing else matters.

And so, not bothering about anything, you again took things into your own hands. You were a little incredulous as to the outcome, but you decided to try it anyway. Who could tell what would happen? It didn't do to dwell too much on those ideal forms of happiness that had haunted you ever since the cradle and had now defined themselves

做了什么，那也不要紧。有可能你经常会意识不到它们的存在；也就是说，这对于它们也不要紧。可是你必须试着抓住这个真理：无论过去、现在还是未来。现在围绕你的黑暗并不存在，因为它从来没有任何独立的存在：它是你从你感受到的怨气和折磨中创造出来的。它看起来真实得足以把你藏起来，远离阳光，但是它的真实性和海市蜃楼一样似是而非。云彩在散开。没有什么来取代它们的位置，插在你和你梦见的并因此成真的真实之间。这个新的安排在引导你的脚步，指示你应该接受但又没有认识到的方向，因为它现在是无形的；但是它似乎失踪了，自然是因为没有相关的任何切实证据：那只发生过一次，这是真的。但是，现在要吸取教训，从无法回忆起它的震惊中恢复过来，再次从头开始——这对你难道不是一件好事吗？你不再需要记得那些原则，它们似乎像你曾经懂得但业已埋葬的语言的片段，来到你身边。你像童话里的王子，在他面前，无法通过的森林敞开了，然后是城堡的大门，他不知道是为什么。你唯一想要的是停下来，以便把这一切苦苦思索个明白，可那是不可能的；你运动得太快，你的势头停顿了。它最后的结果会是什么？目的是什么？可这些是无知新手的问题，你已经忘了。你现在只想着你前进的速度，你像氧气一样吸收它；它已经变成了你活在其中的元素，它就是你。其他一切都无关紧要。

于是，你不再操心任何事，你再次将事物握在掌中。你对结果有一点怀疑，但是你决定无论如何也要尝试一番。谁能说清会发生什么呢？不要过度沉迷于幸福的那些理想形式，它们

almost in a paroxysm; they could be assigned to the corners and cubbyholes of your mind since it didn't matter whether they were in evidence as long as you never actually lost sight of them. What did matter now was getting down to business, or back to the business of day-to-day living with all the tiresome mechanical problems that this implies. And it was just here that philosophy broke down completely and was of no use. How to deal with the new situations that arise each day in bunches or clusters, and which resist categorization to the point where any rational attempt to deal with them is doomed from the start? And in particular how to deal with this one that faces you now, which has probably been with you always; now it has a different name and a different curriculum vitae; its qualities are combined in such a way as to seem different from all that has gone before, but actually it is the same old surprise that you have always lived with. Forget about the details of name and place, forget also the concepts and archetypes that haunt you and which are as much a part of the typical earthbound situation you find yourself in as those others: neither the concept nor the state of affairs logically deduced from it is going to be of much help to you now. What is required is the ability to enter into the complexities of the situation as though it really weren't new at all, which it isn't, as one takes the first few steps into a labyrinth. Here one abruptly finds one's intuition tailored to the needs of the new demanding syndrome; each test is passed flawlessly, as though in a dream, and the complex climate that is formed by the vacillating wills and energies of the many who surround you becomes as easy as pie for you. You take on all comers but you do not advertise your presence. Right now it is important to slip as quickly as possible into the Gordian contours of the dank, barren morass (or so it seems at present) without uttering so much as a syllable; to live in that labyrinth that seems to be directing your steps but in reality it

从摇篮起就纠缠着你，现在几乎在一阵发作中确立了自己；可以把它们安置在你头脑的角落里和文件架上，既然是否看得见它们并不重要，只要你事实上从未忘记它们就可以了。现在重要的是着手处理业务，或者回到日常生活上来，连同它所意味着的所有厌倦而机械的问题。恰恰在这里，哲学完全崩溃了，一无用处。如何应对每天成捆成串出现的新状况，它们抗拒分类的程度达到让任何应对它们的合理企图从一开始就注定失败？尤其是如何处理你目前面临的这个情况，它也许一直与你相伴；现在它有了另一个名字和另一份简历；它的品质以这样的方式结合起来，显得不同于以往一切，可实际上它还是那同一个你一直忍受的古老的意外。忘记有关名称和地点的细节，也忘记那纠缠着你的观念和原型，它们和其他的一样，都是你置身其中的典型世俗情况的一部分：逻辑上从它演绎出来的观念和情势对现在的你都不会有什么大的帮助。当一个人向迷宫迈出最初的几步，需要的是深入情况复杂性之中的能力，仿佛那情况过去和现在都根本不是新的。在这里，一个人突然发现自己的直觉根据新的紧迫的综合征的需要进行了调整；每次测试都完美无瑕地通过了，仿佛在梦中，由围绕着你的众人的优柔寡断的意志和能量形成的复杂气候，对于你变得易如反掌。你来者不拒，但是你不声张。现在重要的是尽快溜进潮湿贫瘠的沼泽（或许它现在正是这样）那难解的轮廓，不发出一个音节；生活在那似乎指引着你的脚步的迷宫里，可实际上是你创造了它的图案，实施一个困难得难以置信的新策略，不过，它的成功是有保证的。你知道这点。但是，在你目前所处的奇怪

is you who are creating its pattern, embarked on a new, fantastically difficult tactic whose success is nevertheless guaranteed. You know this. But it will be a long time before the ordinary assurances will be able to make themselves felt in the strange, closed-off state you are in now. You may as well forget them and abandon yourself to the secret growing that has taken over. Nothing can stop it, so there is no point in worrying about it or even thinking about it.

How we move around in our little ventilated situation, how roomy it seems! There is so much to do after all, so many people to be with, and we like them all. But meanwhile it seems as if our little space were moving counter to us, dragging us backward. We have reached this far point of where we are by following someone's advice, and at times it seems as though it might have been the wrong advice. If this were the case, to become aware of it would be no help because we have refined the baser elements out of our present situation and are technically on the same footing with others of different origins who meet and socialize with us. One sign of this is that no one remarks on the lateness of the hour, for we all believe we have reached a point where such details no longer count; we believe that we are immune to time because we are "out of" it. Yet we know dimly that the stillness we have attained is racing forward faster than ever toward its rendezvous with the encroaching past; we know this and we turn from it, to take refuge in dreams where all is not exactly well either, in which we reach the summit of our aspirations to find the mass below riddled and honeycombed with vacancy, yet there is room on the crest to move around in; it might almost qualify as an oasis. But as we all know, the thing about an oasis is that the whole desert has to become one before its exotic theories can benefit us, and even that would not be enough because then there would be too much of a contrast with the ordinary temperate climate leading up to it.

封闭的状态中,在能够感觉到这些普通的保证之前,还有一段很长的时间。你同样会忘记它们,沉湎于那已经接管一切的秘密的生长。没有什么能阻止它,所以,为之焦虑,甚至想着它,都是毫无意义的。

我们怎样在我们很少通风的处境中绕来绕去,它显得有多么宽敞!毕竟还有这么多事情要做,这么多人要相处,而且我们喜欢他们所有人。但与此同时,似乎我们的小空间在与我们背道而驰,拖着我们向后去。我们根据某人的建议,来到这个遥远的所在,那建议有时似乎是错误的。如果情况果真如此,意识到这点也无济于事,因为我们已经改良了目前处境中不纯正的元素,在技术基础上,我们与我们遇见并与之交往的其他出身不同的人是一样的。这方面的一个标志是,没人注意到时间已经很晚,因为我们全都相信在我们抵达的地方,这样的细节不再有价值;我们相信我们对时间是免疫的,因为我们在它"之外"。不过,我们模糊地知道,我们达到的静止是在比以往更快地奔向被过去渐渐侵蚀的集结地;我们知道这点,我们转身置之于不顾,逃避到梦中,而梦中的一切也同样糟糕,我们在梦中抵达了我们渴望的山顶,发现下面人群泛滥,满是蜂窝状的空缺,不过,山顶上尚有余地可以走动;它几乎可以充当绿洲了。关于绿洲这件事我们全都知道,在有关绿洲的外来理论能够让我们受益之前,整个沙漠必须变成一个绿洲,甚至那样还不够,因为那时就会造成一个与普通的温和气候相比反差太大的情况。然而,一个人来到这个可能是世界尽头的地方,

Yet one can very well live and enjoy the fruits of one's considerable labors in arriving at this place which could be the end of the world in no unfavorable sense; there are the same things to look at and be surrounded by although in lesser numbers; what it is is quality as opposed to quantity. But can the one exist without the other? These thoughts oppress one in the social world one has built around oneself, especially the thought of those other infinite worlds upon worlds; and when one really examines one's own world in the harsher light of its happiness-potential one sees that it is a shambles indeed. Yet there is air to breathe. One may at least stay here a while hoping for more and better things to come.

That's the way it goes. For many weeks you have been exploring what seemed to be a profitable way of doing. You discovered that there was a fork in the road, so first you followed what seemed to be the less promising, or at any rate the more obvious, of the two branches until you felt you had a good idea of where it led. Then you returned to investigate the more tangled way, and for a time its intricacies seemed to promise a more complex and therefore a more practical goal for you, one that could be picked up in any number of ways so that all its faces or applications could be thoroughly scrutinized. And in so doing you began to realize that the two branches were joined together again, farther ahead; that this place of joining was indeed the end, and that it was the very place you set out from, whose intolerable mixture of reality and fantasy had started you on the road which has now come full circle. It has been an absorbing puzzle, but in the end all the pieces fit together like a ghost story that turns out to have a perfectly rational explanation. Nothing remains but to begin living with this discovery, that is, without the hope mentioned above. Even this is not so easy, for the reduced mode or scope must itself be nourished by a form of hope, or hope that

没有任何不利的感觉，他能活得非常好，享受自己可观的劳动果实；有同样的事物可以看，可以为其所环绕，尽管数量要少一些；重要的是质量而不是数量。但是，没有他者，一个人能存在吗？在一个人围绕自己建设起来的社会世界中，这些思想会让他感到压抑，尤其是有关其他那些无穷的多重世界的思想；当一个人在更为刺眼的光线下，真正考察过自己世界的幸福潜力之后，他看到的实际是一片废墟。不过，还有空气可以呼吸。一个人至少可以在这里待上一会儿，盼望有更多更好的东西出现。

它就是那么回事。有很多个星期，你一直在探索看似有益的行为方式。你发现路上有个分岔口，于是，再来那条岔道上，你先是沿着似乎希望不大的一条走，或至少是比较平常的那条，直到你觉得自己对这条路通向哪里已经心里有数了。然后你回去研究那条更为复杂的路，有一段时间，它的错综复杂似乎许诺给你一个更为复杂并因此更为现实的目标，这个目标可经由众多路径抵达，它的所有方面或是用途都可以进行彻底的检查。在这么做的过程中你开始认识到，这两条岔路在很远的前方又汇合在一起了；汇合之处实际上就是终点，那正是你出发的地方，它无法忍受地将真实与幻想混合起来，让你出发上路，现在兜了个圈又回到原地。它一直是个有趣的谜，可到最后，所有片段都组合起来，像一个鬼故事，结果有了一个完全合理的解释。没有什么留下来，开始忍受这个发现，亦即，没有上面提到的希望。即使这样也不是很容易，因为简化过的模式或是

doesn't take itself seriously. One must move very fast in order to stay in the same place, as the Red Queen said, the reason being that once you have decided there is no alternative to remaining motionless you must still learn to cope with the onrushing tide of time and all the confusing phenomena it bears in its wake, some of which perfectly resemble the unfinished but seemingly salvageable states of reality at cross-purposes with itself that first caused you to grow restless, to begin fidgeting with various impractical schemes that were in the end, we have seen, finally reduced to zero. Yet they cannot be banished from the system any more than physical matter can, and their nature, which is part and parcel of their existence, is to remain incomplete, clamoring for wholeness. So that now two quite other and grimmer alternatives present themselves: that of staying where you are and risking eventual destruction at the hands of those dishonest counselors of many aspects, or of being swept back by them into a past drenched in nostalgia whose sweetness burns like gall. And it is a choice that we have to make.

As a lost dog on the edge of a sidewalk timidly approaches first one passerby and then another, uncertain of what to ask for, taking a few embarrassed steps in one direction and then suddenly veering to another before being able to ascertain what reception his mute entreaty might have met with, lost, puzzled, ashamed, ready to slink back into his inner confusion at the first brush with the outside world, so your aspirations, my soul, on this busy thoroughfare that is the great highway of life. What do you think to gain from merely standing there looking worried, while the tide of humanity sweeps ever onward, toward some goal it gives every sign of being as intimately acquainted with as you are with the sharp-edged problems that beset you from every angle? Do you really think that if you succeed in looking pathetic enough some kindly stranger will

范围必须以一种希望的形式，或是不再严肃对待自己的希望来滋养自身。一个人必须很快地移动，以便停留在同一个地方，就像红皇后说的，理由在于一旦你判断没有保持静止的选择，你就必须学会应付时间汹涌的浪潮，及其尾波中携带的所有乱象，其中有些现象完全类似于未完成的但显然可以挽救的真实状态，它们与自身相抵牾，最初正是它们让你变得不安，开始摆弄各种不切实际的计划，到头来我们看到，一切终归化为乌有。然而，无法将它们像具体物质那样从系统里驱逐，它们的本质，作为它们存在的重要部分，仍然是不完善的，仍然在为整体呼吁。所以，现在有其他两种严酷的选择摆在它们面前：停留在你现在所在之处，在那些不忠的各种顾问手里，冒最后毁灭的风险，或者是被它们扫回过去，浸透在甜蜜如胆汁一般灼人的乡愁之中。这是一个我们不得不做的选择。

像一条迷路的狗，在人行道的边上，胆怯地靠近第一个经过的人，然后是另一个，确定不了自己想要什么，在一个方向迈出尴尬的几步，然后又突然转到另一个方向，在能够确定自己沉默的恳求会遇到怎样的反应之前，他迷失，困惑，羞愧，外界最初的轻轻一碰，便准备溜回自己内心的混乱之中，我的灵魂，你的渴望也是如此，在这繁忙的大街上，那就是生活的康庄大道。你想得到什么，你只是站在那里焦虑地观望，当人群如潮水滚滚向前，涌向某个目标，它发出的每一个信号你都很熟悉，就像从各个角度围攻你的锋利的难题？你真的以为，如果你设法显得足够可怜，就会有好心的陌生人停下来，询问

stop to ask your name and address and then steer you safely to your very door? No, I do not think you are afflicted with that kind of presumption, and yet your pitiable waif's stance, that inquiring look that darts uneasily from side to side as though to ward off a blow—these do not argue in your favor, even though we both know you to be a strong upright character, far above such cheap attempts to play on the emotions of others. And there is no use trying to tell them that the touching melancholy of your stare is the product not of self-pity but of a lucid attempt to find out just where you stand in the fast-moving stream of traffic that flows endlessly from horizon to horizon like a dark river. *We* know that the pose you happen to be striking for the world to see matters nothing to you, it could just as easily be some other one, joyous-looking or haughty and overbearing, or whatever. It is only that you happened to be wearing this look as you arrived at the end of your perusal of the way left open to you, and it "froze" on you, just as your mother warned you it would when you were little. And now it is the face you show to the world, the face of expectancy, strange as it seems. Perhaps Childe Roland wore such a look as he drew nearer to the Dark Tower, every energy concentrated toward the encounter with the King of Elfland, reasonably certain of the victorious outcome, yet not so much as to erase the premature lines of care from his pale and tear-stained face. Maybe it is just that you don't want to outrage anyone, especially now that the moment of your own encounter seems to be getting closer. You can feel it in every pore, in the sudden hush that falls over the din of the busy street and the unusual darkness in the sky even though no clouds are apparent. Your miserable premature spring has finally turned into the real thing, confirmed by the calendar, but what a sad look it wears, especially after its promising beginnings that now seem so far back in the past. The air is moist and almost black, and sharp with

你的姓名和地址，然后安全地开车把你送回家？不，我不认为你会受到那种假设的折磨，你可怜的流浪儿姿态，仿佛要避开打击一般不安地投向两边的探询的目光——这些都对你不利，即便我们都知道你是一个坚强正直的人，远非要小气地玩弄别人的感情。告诉他们你那动人的忧郁目光并非自怜的产物，而只是要在黑色河流一般不息地从地平线涌向地平线的迅疾车流中弄清你的位置，这样做毫无用处。我们知道，你偶然摆出的姿势，在世界看来是惊人的，但在你看来却不值一提，它可能和另一个姿势一样简单，开心观望的，傲慢专横的，或随便什么姿势。只不过你碰巧这么一副表情，当你读到这条向你敞开的路的尽头，它就把你"冻住"了，就像你的母亲在你小时候警告过的你那样。现在，你向世界露出的正是这样一副面孔，期待的面孔，它显得很陌生。也许恰尔德·罗兰靠近黑暗塔的时候就是带着这么一副表情，打点起所有精神，准备与仙境之王相遇，在理性上确信最后胜利的结果，可还不足以从他沾染泪水的苍白的脸上擦去早生的忧虑的皱纹。也许正是这样，你不想对任何人发怒，尤其是既然你与仙境之王遭遇的时刻已在靠近。你每个毛孔都能感觉到，在突然落在繁忙街道的喧嚣之上的寂静中，在即便万里无云时天空那非同寻常的黑暗中。你可怜的早熟的春天最终成了一件真实之物，由日历确定下来，但是它带着怎样一副悲哀的表情啊，尤其是它充满希望的开始如今已远远成为过去。风是潮湿的，几乎发黑，因寒意而锐利；木兰花瓣耷拉下来，一片片落在地上半结冻的烂泥里，只有几棵病恹恹的绿草勉强昂起头来。这一切的出现都毫无意外，甚

the chill; the magnolia petals flatten and fall off one after the other onto the half-frozen mud of the ground where only a few spears of sickly green grass have managed to lift their heads. All this comes as no surprise, it is even somewhat of a relief, and better than the dire sequel that those precocious moments seemed to promise, cataclysms instead of the ominous hush that now lies over everything. And who is to say whether or not this silence isn't the very one you requested so as to be able to speak? Perhaps it seems ominous only because it is concentrating so intensely on you and what you have to say.

"Whatever was, is, and must be"—these words occur again to you now, though in a different register, transposed from a major into a minor key. Yet they are the same words as before. Their meaning is the same, only you have changed: you are viewing it all from a different angle, perhaps not more nor less accurate than the previous one, but in any case a necessary one no doubt for the in-the-round effect to be achieved. We see it all now. The thing that our actions have accomplished, and its results for us. And it is no longer a nameless thing, but something colorful and full of interest, a chronicle play of our lives, with the last act still in the dim future, so that we can't tell yet whether it is a comedy or a tragedy, all we know is that it is crammed with action and the substance of life. Surely all this living that has gone on that is ours is good in some way, though we cannot tell why: we know only that our sympathy has deepened, quickened by the onrushing spectacle, to the point where we are like spectators swarming up onto the stage to be absorbed into the play, though always aware that this is an impossibility, and that the actors continue to recite their lines as if we weren't there. Yet in the end, we think, this may become possible; that is the time when audience and actor and writer and director all mingle joyously together as one, as the curtain descends a last time to separate them from the half-empty theater.

至是某种解脱，胜过了那些早熟的时刻所许诺的可怕续集，不祥的寂静取代了大洪水笼罩着万物。谁能说这寂静不正是你为了能够说话而竭力以求的？也许它的不祥仅仅是因为它如此强烈地集中在你身上，和你必须说的东西上面。

"无论过去、现在，还是将来"——这些词语再次出现在你脑海，以一种不同的音区，从大调降到小调。它们仍是和以前一样的词。它们的意义是同样的，只是你变了：你从一个完全不同的角度观察这意义，也许多少比不上以前那么精确，但是无疑，为了达到全面的效果，它终归是必要的。我们现在看到了它的全部。我们为之行动的事物已经完成，它的结果是为了我们。它不再是一件无名之物，而是充满色彩和趣味，我们生活的一出历史剧，最后一幕仍在模糊的未来之中，所以我们说不清它究竟是喜剧还是悲剧，只知道它充满了行动和生活的实质。可以肯定，这业已消逝的生活属于我们，在某些方面是好的，尽管我们无法说清原因：我们只知道我们的同情被汹涌的奇观加深加快了，以至于我们就像观众一样蜂拥到舞台上，沉浸在剧情之中，尽管始终明白这不可能，而演员们继续背台词，仿佛我们并不存在。到最后，我们以为，这也许会成为可能；到那时，观众、演员、作者和导演全都快乐地混在一起，成为一体，帷幕最后一次降下，将他们与半空的剧场隔开。这样的事何时发生——不过，盼望它发生是毫无意义的。典范从来也吸引不了你，只有倒数第二幕中那些稀少的时刻，那时，一切都突然暂时变得清晰了，在最后的光辉面前再次沉入半明半暗

When this happens—yet there is no point in looking to that either. The apotheosis never attracted you, only those few moments in the next-to-last act where everything suddenly becomes momentarily clear, to sink again into semi-obscurity before the final blaze which merely confirms the truth of what had been succinctly stated long before. But there does not seem to be any indication that this moment is approaching.

Except that the silence continues to focus on you. Who am I after all, you say despairingly once again, to have merited so much attention on the part of the universe; what does it think to get from me that it doesn't have already? I know too that my solipsistic approach is totally wrongheaded and foolish, that the universe isn't listening to me any more than the sea can be heard inside conch shells. But I'm just a mute observer—it isn't my fault that I can really notice how everything around me is waiting just for me to get up and say the word, whatever that is. And surely even the eyes of the beloved are fixed on you as though wondering, "What is he going to do *this* time? " And those eyes as well as the trees and skies that surround you are full of apprehension, waiting for this word that must come from you and that you have not in you. "What am I going to say? " But as you continue gazing embarrassedly into the eyes of the beloved, talking about extraneous matters, you become aware of an invisible web that connects those eyes to you, and both of you to the atmosphere of this room which is leading up to you after the vagaries of the space outside. Suddenly you realize that you have been talking for a long time without listening to yourself; you must have said *it* a long way back without knowing it, for everything in the room has fallen back into its familiar place, only this time organized according to the invisible guidelines that radiate out from both of you like the laws that govern a kingdom. Now there is so much to talk about that it seems neither of you will ever get done talking. And the word that everything hinged on is

之中，只不过证实了很久以前简单陈述过的真理。但是，似乎还没有任何这个时刻即将临近的迹象。

只有寂静还继续集中在你身上。我究竟是谁，你再次绝望地说，值得宇宙付出这么大的关注；它想从我这里得到它还没有的什么东西呢？我同样知道，我的唯我论的方法完全是错误和愚蠢的，宇宙并没有在倾听我，就像在海螺壳里听不见大海一样。可我仅仅是一个沉默的观察者——这并不是我的错，我的确能注意到周围的一切在怎样等着我起来说话，无论说些什么。甚至你钟爱的人的眼睛也盯着你，仿佛在疑惑，"这次他要做什么呢？"那些眼睛，还有你周围的树木和天空，都充满了忧惧，等待你必须说出的这句话，以及你心里没有的话。"我要说什么呢？"但是，当你继续尴尬地凝视恋人的眼睛，谈论着无关紧要的琐事，你意识到一张无形的网将那些眼睛与你联系在一起，又将你俩与这个房间的气氛联系在一起，继变化无常的外在空间之后，将你引向此处。突然，你认识到你已经说了很长时间，很长时间没有倾听你自己了；你一定在很久很久以前说过它，你自己不知道，因为房间里的一切都已重新回到自己熟悉的位置，只在这时才根据从你们两那里传播出来的、像统治一个王国的法律那样无形的指导方针组织起来。现在有这么多的事情要谈，你们俩似乎都不会结束谈话。万物作为枢纽的词语被埋在后面；因为互相赞同，当这个词语被说出来，冲向它最后的安息之所，你们俩都没有检查它。在它进行组织的过程中，指导方针从它的控制中传播出来；因此，不知道它是什

buried back there; by mutual consent neither of you examined it when it was pronounced and rushed to its final resting place. It is doing the organizing, the guidelines radiate from its control; therefore it is good not to know what it is since its results can be known so intimately, appreciated for what they are; it is best then that the buried word remain buried for we were intended to appreciate only its fruits and not the secret principle activating them—to know this would be to know too much. Meanwhile it is possible to know just enough, and this is all we were supposed to know, toward which we have been straining all our lives. We are to read this in outward things: the spoons and greasy tables in this room, the wooden shelves, the flyspecked ceiling merging into gloom—good and happy things, nevertheless, that tell us little of themselves and more about ourselves than we had ever imagined it was possible to know. They have become the fabric of life.

Until, accustomed to disappointments, you can let yourself rule and be ruled by these strings or emanations that connect everything together, you haven't fully exorcised the demon of doubt that sets you in motion like a rocking horse that cannot stop rocking. You may have scored a few points there where you first took those few steps (no more than three, in all likelihood) when you first realized the enormity of the choice between two kinds of mutually exclusive universal happiness. And you also realized the error of forever ruminating on and repeating those fatal steps, like a broken movie projector that keeps showing the same strip of film—you realized this when you were already far from that experience which had indeed begun to take on the unearthly weirdness of an old photograph. You cried out in the desert and you collapsed into yourself, indifferent to the progress of the seasons and the planets in their orbits, and you died for the first time. And now that you have been raised from the tomb like Lazarus by obscure miraculous forces you are surprised

么为好，既然可以如此清楚地认识到它的结果，因其本身而得到欣赏；那么，最好让那被埋葬的词语继续埋葬，我们只想欣赏它的成果，而不是激活它的秘密原则——知道这一点就是知道得太多了。与此同时，知道得刚刚好是有可能的，那就是我们想知道的一切，我们毕生为之努力的就是这个。我们要在外在事物中读懂这个：这房间里的汤匙和油腻的桌子，木头架子，有蝇粪留下污点的没入阴暗的天花板——然而，美好而幸福的事物，很少向我们谈论它们自己，它们对我们的了解超乎我们的想象。它们已经成了生活的织物。

直到习惯了失望，你才能让自己支配这些将一切联系起来的线索或发散物，也被它们所支配，你还没有完全驱除怀疑的恶魔，它促使你行动，像一匹摇晃的马无法停止摇晃。你也许能得上几分，在你迈出最初几步的地方（十有八九不超过三步），当你最初认识到在两种互相排斥的普遍幸福之间做出选择的艰巨性。你也同样认识到永远反刍下去是错误的，重复那些重大步骤，像一架坏掉的电影放映机一直在投放同一个片段——你认识到这一点，当你已经远离那种经验，实际上，它开始显出一张老照片那样神秘的怪异之感。你在沙漠中哭喊，你的内心崩溃了，对季节的进程和行星的运行漠不关心，你第一次死掉了。既然现在你已经像拉撒路那样被一股模糊神奇的力量拔出坟墓，你吃惊于地球并没有好过你留在后面的那个地球，万物并没有像你相信的那样完善自身，你已经凭借自己的死亡做到了，早春这个日子的无常的荣耀已经将你复活。你不

that the earth isn't better than the one you left behind, that all things haven't yet perfected themselves as you believe you have done by dying and being resuscitated to the uncertain glory of this day in early spring. You can't get over the fact that conversations still sound the same, that clouds of unhappiness still persist in the unseen mesh that draws around everything, uniting it in a firm purpose as it causes each individual thing to bulge more brightly and more darkly at the same time, drawing out the nature of its real being. But that is the wonder of it: that you have returned not to the supernatural glow of heaven but to the ordinary daylight you knew so well before it passed from your view, and which continues to enrich you as it steeps you and your ageless chattels of mind, imagination, timid first love and quiet acceptance of experience in its revitalizing tide. And the miracle is not that you have returned—you always knew you would—but that things have remained the same. The day is not far advanced: it still half-seriously offers with one hand the promise that it pockets with the other, and it is still up to you to seize the occasion, jump into the fray, not be ruled by its cruel if only human whims. The person sitting opposite you who asked you a question is still waiting for the answer; he has not yet found your hesitation unusual, but it is up to you to grasp it with both hands, wrenching it from the web of connectives to rub off the grime that has obscured its brilliance so as to restore it to him, that pause which is the answer you have both been expecting. When it was new everybody could tell this, but years of inactivity and your own inattention have tarnished it beyond recognition. It needs a new voice to tell it, otherwise it will seem just another awkward pause in a conversation largely made up of similar ones, and will never be able to realize its potential as a catalyst, turning you both in on yourself and outward to that crystalline gaze that has been the backing of your days and nights for so long

能原谅这样的事实，交谈听起来还是一样的老套，不幸的云彩依然留在围住万物的无形网眼中，这罗网以坚定的意志把万物联合起来，促使每一个个体事物都膨胀起来，变得更为明亮，同时也更为暗淡，取出自己真实存在的本质。但是，那正是它的神奇之处：你没有回到超自然的绚烂天堂，而是回到你如此熟悉的普通阳光之中，它从你眼前经过，在它复活的潮汐中，继续丰富你，浸透你和你思想的永恒财产，想象，羞怯的初恋，悄悄接受的经验。奇迹不在于你已经回来了——你始终知道你会回来——而是在于事物依然如故。日子远远没有什么进展，依然半真半假地将许诺用一只手藏起来，用另一只手给你，依然要靠你来抓住机会，加入竞争，不受它的残忍的支配，即便只是人类的突发奇想。坐在对面问了你一个问题的人依然在等待答案；他还没有发现你不同寻常的犹豫，但是那要靠你用双手抓住这答案，把它从关联物的网中拽出来，擦掉使它的光辉晦暗的污点，以便把它还给他，那个停顿便是你们俩都在期待的答案。当它是新的时候，每个人都能辨别，但是，经年累月的静止和你自己的疏忽，已经让它失去光泽，难以辨认。它需要一个新的声音来把它说出来，否则它就仅仅是主要由熟悉的人构成的交谈中的又一个尴尬的停顿，永远无法认识到它作为催化剂的潜能，让你们闭关自守，同时又朝向外面迄今一直支持着你们日日夜夜的透明目光。因为这时只有你知道它是什么，但是，当你继续抓住它，其他人开始认识到它真正的本质，直到它终于作为最短的距离横在你和你恋人的目标之间，唯一能够滋养你的希望和恐惧长成大树的人类大地，大得像宇宙一样，

now. For the time being only you know it for what it is, but as you continue to hold on to it others will begin to realize its true nature, until finally it stands as the shortest distance between your aims and those of the beloved, the only human ground that can nurture your hopes and fears into the tree of life that is as big as the universe and entirely fills it up with its positive idea of growth and gaining control. So it is permissible to rest here awhile in this pause you alone discovered: a little repose can do no harm at this stage; meanwhile do not fear that when you next speak the whole scene will come to life again, as though triggered by invisible machines. There is not much for you to do except wait in the anticipation of your inevitable reply.

Inevitable, but so often postponed. Whole eras of history have sprung up in the gaps left by these pauses, dynasties, barbarian invasions and so on until the grass and shards stage, and still the answer is temporarily delayed. During these periods one thought enclosed everything like the blue sky of history: that it really was this one and no other. As long as this is the case everything else can take its course, time can flow into eternity leaving a huge deltalike deposit whose fan broadens and broadens and is my life, the time I am taking; we get up in the morning and blow on some half-dead coals, maybe for the last time; my hair is white and straggly and I hardly recognize my face any more, yet none of this matters so long as your reply twists it all together, the transparent axle of this particular chapter in history. It seems that the blue of the sky is a little paler each morning, as happens toward the end of each epoch, yet one doesn't want to move hastily, but to continue at this half-savage, half-pastoral existence, until one day the unmistakable dry but deep accent is heard:

"You waited too long. And now you are going to be rewarded by my attention. Make no mistake: it will probably seem to you as though nothing has changed; nothing will show in the outward details of

充满了有关成长的积极思想并正在取得控制权。于是，可以允许在这里休息一会儿，在这停顿中你独自发现：稍微休息一会儿无害于当下；同时也不要害怕，当你接着说的时候，整个场景会再次复活，仿佛被无形的机器所触发。你没有太多的事情可做，除了在期望中等待你不可避免的回答。

不可避免，但又经常推迟。所有历史时期在这些停顿留下的空隙中萌发出来，历代王朝、蛮族入侵等等，直到青草和瓦砾阶段，答案依然被暂时推迟。在这些阶段中，一个思想包裹万物，像历史的蓝天：它真的是这一个，而非其他。只要是这种情况，其他一切就能按照正常程序进行，时间就能流进永恒，留下一个巨大的三角洲一样的沉积物，其扇形变得越来越宽，越来越宽，我的生活和我耗费的时间也是如此；我们早上起来，吹起半明半灭的木炭，也许这是最后一次了；我的头发白了，乱蓬蓬，我几乎认不出自己的面孔了，这也无关紧要，只要你的回答把它们编织在一起，那是历史中这特殊一章的透明车轴。似乎天空的蓝色每天早晨都在变浅，就像每个纪元趋向终结时那样，不过，一个人不想匆忙离开，而是想继续这种半野蛮半田园的存在，直到有一天听到那不会弄错的枯燥而深沉的口音：

"你等待得太久了。现在你将得到我的关注作为报偿。不要搞错：也许在你看来，一切都没有变；没有什么会在外在细节中显示你的生活，每天晚上你会疲倦而愤怒地爬上床。可你要

your life and each night you will creep tired and enraged into bed. Know however that I am listening. From now on the invisible bounty of my concern will be there to keep you company, and as you mature it will unlock more of the same space for you so that eventually all your territory will have become rightfully yours again."

I know now that I am no longer waiting, and that the previous part of my life in which I thought I was waiting and therefore only half-alive was not waiting, although it was tinged with expectancy, but living under and into this reply which has suddenly caused everything in my world to take on new meaning. It is as though I had picked up a thread which I had merely mislaid but which for a long time seemed lost. And all because I am certain now, albeit for no very good reason, that it was this one and no other. The sadness that infected us as children and stayed on through adulthood has healed, and there can be no other way except this way of health we are taking, silent as it is. But it lets us look back on those other, seemingly spoiled days and re-evaluate them: actually they were too well-rounded, each bore its share of happiness and grief and finished its tale just as twilight was descending; those days are now an inseparable part of our story despite their air of immaturity and tentativeness; they have the freshness of early works which may be wrongly discarded later. Nor is today really any different: we are as childish as ever, it turns out, only perhaps a little better at disguising it, but we still want what we want when we want it and no power on earth is strong enough to deny it to us. But at least we see now that this is how things are, and so we have the sense to stop insisting every so often under the guise of some apparently unrelated activity, because we think we shall be better satisfied this way; underneath the discreet behavior the desire is as imperious as ever, but after so many postponements we now realize that a little delay won't hurt

知道我在倾听。从现在起，我无形的慷慨的关切将与你同在，随着你的成熟，它将为你开启更多同样的空间，这样，最终你所有的领土当然都会重新归你所有。"

我知道既然我不会再等待，我先前那部分我以为我在等待并因而只是半死不活地活过的生活便不是等待，尽管它染上了期望的色彩，但是，在这个答案的统治下生活突然使得我世界中的一切具有了新的意义。这就好像是我捡起了一个线头，我只是放错了地方，可是很长时间它似乎丢失了。全都是因为我现在确信，虽然没有非常好的理由，它就是这一个，而非其他。我们孩提时染上的、整个成年时期一直存在的悲哀，已经治愈了，除了我们正在采取的这个疗法，没有任何方法能这样安静。但是它让我们回顾其他那些显然变质了的日子，重新估价它们：实际上它们都过于丰满了，每一个都拥有自己的那份幸福和悲哀，都完成了自己的故事，如同薄暮正在降临；那些日子成了我们故事不可分割的部分，尽管它们显得幼稚，带有尝试性；它们具有早期作品的清新，这一点可能在后来被错误地抛弃了。今天实际上没有任何不同：我们和以前一样孩子气，结果，也许只是稍微擅长了一点伪装，我们还是想要我们想要的东西，当我们想要它的时候，世界上没有任何力量强大到足以拒绝我们。可至少我们现在看到了，事物就是这样，于是，我们觉得需要停止自己的坚持，我们时常以显然无关的一些活动作为伪装，认为自己最好是满足于这种方式；在谨慎的行为下面，欲望依然和以往一样迫切，但在这么多次的推迟之后，我们如今

and we can relax in the assurance of eventual satisfaction. This was the message of that day in the street, when you first perceived that conventional happiness would not do for you and decided to opt for the erratic kind despite the dangers that its need for continual growth and expansion exposed it to. This started you on your way, although it often seemed as though your feet had struck roots into the ground and you were doomed to grow and decay like a tree. Nevertheless you were aware of moving, whether it was you who were moving or the landscape moving forward toward you, and you could remain patient with the idea of growth as long as the concept of uniqueness—that one and no other—shone like a star in the sky above you.

Today your wanderings have come full circle. Having begun by rejecting the idea of oneness in favor of a plurality of experiences, earthly and spiritual, in fact a plurality of different lives that you lived out to your liking while time proceeded at another, imperturbable rate, you gradually became aware that the very diversity of these experiences was endangered by its own inner nature, for variety implies parallelism, and all these highly individualistic ways of thinking and doing were actually moving in the same direction and constantly threatening to merge with one another in a single one-way motion toward that invisible goal of concrete diversity. For just as all kinds of people spring up on earth and imagine themselves very different from each other though they are basically the same, so all these ideas had arisen in the same head and were merely aspects of a single organism: yourself, or perhaps your desire to be different. So that now in order to avoid extinction it again became necessary to invoke the idea of oneness, only this time if possible on a higher plane, in order for the similarities in your various lives to cancel each other out and the differences to remain, but under the aegis of singleness, separateness, so that each difference might be taken as

认识到，一次小小的拖延没有什么害处，我们可以在最终会得到满足的保证中放松下来。这就是那一天的信息，在街上，当你最初感知到惯例的幸福不会再对你起作用，你决定选择那种不稳定的幸福，尽管它持续生长与扩张的需要让它暴露在危险之中。这促使你走上自己的路，尽管你的脚往往显得好像是在地上扎了根，你注定像一棵树那样生长和腐烂。然而，你意识到了运动，无论是你在运动还是风景在朝你运动，你可以对有关成长的思想保持耐心，只要独一性的观念——那一个，而非其他——像你头顶天空中的星星一样闪耀。

今天你的漫游已经兜了一个完整的圈。从拒绝一元性思想开始，以支持经验的多元性，亦即尘世和精神两方面的经验，事实上，你依据自己喜好所过的不同生活的多元性，随着时间以另一种冷静的速度前进，你逐渐意识到这些经验的多样性受到它固有性质的威胁，因为多样化隐含着类似，所有这些高度个人化的思考和行为方式实际上在同一方向运动，并一直威胁着要彼此混合，以唯一单向的运动趋向具体多元的无形目标。正如所有类型的人在大地上出现，想象自己彼此颇为不同，尽管他们基本上是一样的，所有这些思想也是在同样的头脑中产生的，仅仅是一个有机体的众多方面；是你自己，或许是你的欲望，想要与众不同。所以，为了避免灭绝，现在有必要再次激活一元性的思想，只是这一次是否有可能达到一个更高的水平，以便让你多样化生活中的相似性彼此消除，把差异留下来，但又处于唯一性和独立性的庇护之下，这样一来，每个差异都

the type of all the others and yet remain intrinsically itself, unlike anything in the world. Which brings us to you and the scene in the little restaurant. You are still there, far above me like the polestar and enclosing me like the dome of the heavens; your singularity has become oneness, that is your various traits and distinguishing marks have flattened out into a cloudlike protective covering whose irregularities are all functions of its uniformity, and which constitutes an arbitrary but definitive boundary line between the new informal, almost haphazard way of life that is to be mine permanently and the monolithic samenesses of the world that exists to be shut out. For it has been measured once and for all. It would be wrong to look back at it, and luckily we are so constructed that the urge to do so can never waken in us. We are both alive and free.

If you could see a movie of yourself you would realize that this is true. Movies show us ourselves as we had not yet learned to recognize us—something in the nature of daily being or happening that quickly gets folded over into ancient history like yesterday's newspaper, but in so doing a new face has been revealed, a surface on which a new phrase may be written before it rejoins history, or it may remain blank and do so anyway: it doesn't matter because each thing is coming up in its time and receding into the past, and this is what we all expect and want. What does matter is what becomes of it once it has entered the past's sacred precincts; when, bending under the weight of an all-powerful nostalgia, its every contour is at last revealed for what it was, but this can be known only in the past. It isn't wrong to look at things in this way—how else could we live in the present knowing it was the present except in the context of the important things that have already happened? No, one must treasure each moment of the past, get the same thrill from it that one gets from watching each moment of an old movie. These windows

会被当作所有其他差异的代表，但又保持自身的固有本质，不同于世上任何事物。它们把我们带到你和这小餐馆里的景象面前。你仍在那里，像北极星一样远在我之上，像天空的穹庐覆盖着我；你的唯一性已成了一元性，你多样化的品质和独特标志已经变平，成了一种云彩般保护性的覆盖物，其一致性的所有功能便是它的不规则性，在我即将永久采用的新的非正式的、几乎随意的生活方式，与即将被排除的世界的完全统一的同一性之间，构成一个武断又明确的边界线。它已经一劳永逸地测量过了。回顾它将是错误的，很幸运，我们生来如此，这种回顾的冲动永远不会在我们心中苏醒。我们都活着而且自由。

如果你能看一部关于你自己的电影，你就会认识到这是真的。电影向我们显示我们自身，我们还没有学会认识自己——具有日常性质的东西或事件迅速被折叠进古老的历史，就像是昨天的报纸，但在这么做的过程中，一个新面孔显露出来，一个表面，可以在上面写下一个新的短语，在它重新加入历史之前，或许它会保持空白并这样继续下去：这无关紧要，因为每件事物的出现都有定时，并在历史中消退，这正是我们全都期待和需要的。要紧的是它一旦进入过去的神圣领域，它会变成什么；什么时候，屈服于全能乡愁的重压，它的每一个轮廓线最终显示出它过去的本质，但是这一点在过去之中才能知道。以这种方式看待事物并没错——此外我们如何能够生活在现在，知道它是现在，除了置身于重要的事情已经发生的语境之中？不，一个人必须珍惜过去的每一个瞬间，从中得到同样的激动，

on the past enable us to see enough to stay on an even keel in the razor's-edge present which is really a no-time, continually straying over the border into the positive past and the negative future whose movements alone define it. Unfortunately we have to live in it. We are appalled at this. Because its no-time, no-space dimensions offer us no signposts, nothing to be guided by. In this dimensionless area a single step can be leagues or inches; the flame of a match can seem like an explosion on the sun or it can make no dent in the matte-gray, uniform night. The jolting and loss of gravity produce a permanent condition of nausea, always buzzing faintly at the blurred edge where life is hinged to the future and to the past. But only focus on the past through the clear movie-theater dark and you are a changed person, and can begin to live again. That is why we, snatched from sudden freedom, are able to communicate only through this celluloid vehicle that has immortalized and given a definitive shape to our formless gestures; we can live as though we had caught up with time and avoid the sickness of the present, a shapeless blur as meaningless as a carelessly exposed roll of film. There is hardness and density now, and our story takes on the clear, compact shape of the plot of a novel, with all its edges and inner passages laid bare for the reader, to be resumed and resumed over and over, that is taken up and put aside and taken up again.

What place is there in the continuing story for all the adventures, the wayward pleasures, the medium-size experiences that somehow don't fit in but which loom larger and more interesting as they begin to retreat into the past? There were so many things held back, kept back, because they didn't fit into the plot or because their tone wasn't in keeping with the whole. So many of these things have been discarded, and they now tower on the brink of the continuity, hemming it in like dark crags above a valley stream. One sometimes

就像观看一部老电影的每一个瞬间那般。这些关于过去的窗口能让我们看个够，在剃刀边缘般的现在之中保持平衡，现在实际上是无时间的持续流浪，越过只有它的运动才能定义的边界，进入肯定的过去和否定的未来。很不幸，我们不得不生活在其中。我们为此而惊骇。因为它无时间、无空间的尺度没有为我们提供路标，没有可做引导的东西。在这没有尺度的领域，每一步都可能是数里格或是数英寸；一根火柴的火焰可能像太阳上的一次爆炸，也可能在晦暗均匀的夜色中都弄不出个凹痕来。重力的震动和缺失将导致一种永恒的恶心，始终微弱地在模糊的边缘喻营，在那里，生活取决于未来和过去。但是，通过电影院清澈的黑暗，仅仅专注于过去，你就会变了一个人，你就能重新开始生活。那就是为什么，从突然的自由中被抢夺出来的我们，仅仅通过这赛璐珞设备就能交流，它为我们无定形的姿势赋予了明确的形式，使之永恒；我们可以生活得好像已经赶上了时间，避免了现在的病态，一种不定型的模糊污迹，和不小心曝光的胶卷一样没有意义。现在，我们的故事有了一种硬度和密度，获得了一部小说情节那样清晰紧实的形式，它所有的边缘和内部走廊都向读者敞开，可以一遍又一遍地重新开始，拿起又放下，然后再拿起来。

那是什么地方，在不断持续的故事中，不知怎么，所有那些不适合的冒险、任性的欢乐、中等大小的经验，却在它们开始退回过去的时候，变得更大也更有趣？有这么多妨碍和阻止的东西，因为它们与情节不相适应，或是因为它们的调子与整

forgets that to be all one way may be preferable to eclectic diversity in the interests of verisimilitude, even for those of the opposite persuasion; the most powerful preachers are those persuaded in advance and their unalterable lessons are deeply moving just because of this rigidity, having none of the tepidness of the meandering stream of our narration with its well-chosen and typical episodes, which now seems to be trying to bury itself in the landscape. The rejected chapters have taken over. For a long time it was as though only the most patient scholar or the recording angel himself would ever interest himself in them. Now it seems as though that angel had begun to dominate the whole story: he who was supposed only to copy it all down has joined forces with the misshapen, misfit pieces that were never meant to go into it but at best to stay on the sidelines so as to point up how everything else belonged together, and the resulting mountain of data threatens us; one can almost hear the beginning of the lyric crash in which everything will be lost and pulverized, changed back into atoms ready to resume new combinations and shapes again, new wilder tendencies, as foreign to what we have carefully put in and kept out as a new chart of elements or another planet—unimaginable, in a word. And would you believe that this word could possibly be our salvation? For we are rescued by what we cannot imagine: it is what finally takes us up and shuts our story, replacing it among the millions of similar volumes that by no means menace its uniqueness but on the contrary situate it in the proper depth and perspective. At last we have that rightness that is rightfully ours. But we do not know what brought it about.

It could be anything, you say. But it could not have been an exercise in defining the present when our position, our very lives depend on those fixed loci of past and future that leave no room for the nominal existence of anything else. But it turns out you have

体不够和谐。这些东西中有很多被抛弃了,它们现在耸立在连续性的边缘,包围着它,如同峡谷激流之上的黑色峭壁。一个人有时会忘记,为了保持逼真,始终如一比折中的多样性更为可取,甚至对于那些持相反信念的人也是如此;最有力的鼓吹者是那些预先被说服的人,他们不变的教训感人至深,恰恰是因为这种坚硬,没有任何的温热,不像我们的故事那蜿蜒的激流,带有精挑细选的典型的插曲,它现在似乎想把自己埋葬在风景中。被拒绝的章节已经取得了控制权。有很长时间,仿佛只有最具耐心的学者或是记录天使本人才对它们有兴趣。现在那天使仿佛已经开始主宰整个故事:我们以为他只是照盘抄录,他却与那些畸形的、不和谐的片段联合起来,这些片段从来没有打算进入故事之中,而是至多停留在边线上,以便强调其他一切如何合成整体,作为结果的数据的大山如何威胁着我们;一个人几乎可以听到抒情诗的崩溃,其中一切都将丧失,碎成齑粉,还原成原子,准备再次采取新的组合和形状,新的更为荒凉的倾向,对于我们小心放进去的和排除在外的东西都非常陌生,就像一张新的元素表或是另一个行星——一句话,不可想象。你相信这个词语有可能拯救我们吗?因为我们被自己不能想象的事物所拯救:正是这些事物最后接受我们,结束我们的故事,把它放回无数相似的书卷当中,那丝毫无损于它的独特性,反而让它处于合适的深度和透视之中。我们终于获得了那本该属于我们的公正。但是我们不知道它是怎么来的。

它可以是任何东西,你说。但是它不可能是定义现在的一

been pursuing the discussion in a leisurely way throughout January and February and now to a point farther into the wilderness of this new year which makes such a commotion and goes by so quickly. These ample digressions of yours have carried you ahead to a distant and seemingly remote place, and it is here that you stop to give emphasis to all the way you have traveled and to your present silence. And it is here that I am quite ready to admit that I am alone, that the film I have been watching all this time may be only a mirror, with all the characters including that of the old aunt played by me in different disguises. If you need a certain vitality you can only supply it yourself, or there comes a point, anyway, when no one's actions but your own seem dramatically convincing and justifiable in the plot that the number of your days concocts. I have been watching this film, therefore, and now I have seen enough; as I leave the theater I am surprised to find that it is still daylight outside (the darkness of the film as well as its specks of light were so intense); I am forced to squint; in this way I gradually get an idea of where I am. Only this world is not as light as the other one; it is made gray with shadows like cobwebs that deepen as the memory of the film begins to fade. This is the way all movies are meant to end, but how is it possible to go on living just now except by plunging into the middle of some other one that you have doubtless seen before? It seems truly impossible, but invariably at this point we are walking together along a street in some well-known city. The allegory is ended, its coils absorbed into the past, and this afternoon is as wide as an ocean. It is the time we have now, and all our wasted time sinks into the sea and is swallowed up without a trace. The past is dust and ashes, and this incommensurably wide way leads to the pragmatic and kinetic future.

个练习，当我们的位置、我们的生活恰好依赖于过去与未来的那些固定轨迹，它们没有为任何其他事物名义上的存在留下空间。但事实证明，你一直在以一种从容的方式进行讨论，贯穿整个一月和二月，现在已远远进入这个新年的荒原，造成这般的骚动，并很快就过去了。你的这些丰富的离题之举将你带到了一个似乎遥不可及的地方，正是在这里，你停下，强调你走过的这一路，和你现在的寂静。正是在这里，我准备承认我的孤独，我这段时间一直在看的电影也许仅仅是一面镜子，具备所有的角色，包括由我以不同伪装扮演的老姑妈。如果你需要某种活力，你只能由自己提供，或者有一个临界点，到了那时，除了你自己，没有任何人的行为是明显令人信服的，在你众多日子所捏造的情节中是合理的。所以，我一直在看这部电影，现在我已经看够了；当我离开影院，我吃惊地发现，外面还是白天（胶卷上的黑暗和光点如此强烈）；我被迫眯起眼睛；这样，我逐渐知道了我在哪里。只是这个世界不像另一个那么亮；蛛网一般的阴影让它变得灰暗，随着对电影的记忆开始消退而逐渐加深。所有电影到最后都注定如此，但是，现在如何能够继续生活，除了投入另一部你以前无疑看过的电影之中？这似乎真的是不可能的，但我们总是在这时走在一起，沿着一条街道，在某座熟悉的城市。寓言结束了，它的喧闹吸进了过去，这个下午宽阔得有如海洋。这正是我们现在拥有的时间，所有我们浪费的时间沉入了海底，被吞没了，了无痕迹。过去是尘土和灰烬，而这宽得无法测量的道路将通向务实而活跃的未来。

From
SELF-PORTRAIT IN A CONVEX MIRROR
凸面镜中的自画像
(1975)

As One Put Drunk into the Packet-boat

I tried each thing, only some were immortal and free.

Elsewhere we are as sitting in a place where sunlight

Filters down, a little at a time,

Waiting for someone to come. Harsh words are spoken,

As the sun yellows the green of the maple tree. . .

So this was all, but obscurely

I felt the stirrings of new breath in the pages

Which all winter long had smelled like an old catalogue.

New sentences were starting up. But the summer

Was well along, not yet past the mid-point

But full and dark with the promise of that fullness,

That time when one can no longer wander away

And even the least attentive fall silent

To watch the thing that is prepared to happen.

A look of glass stops you

And you walk on shaken: was I the perceived?

Did they notice me, this time, as I am,

Or is it postponed again? The children

Still at their games, clouds that arise with a swift

当一个人把醉鬼放入邮船

每件事我都试过,只有一部分永恒而自由。
我们像在别处那样坐在一个地方
阳光滤下来,每次一小点,
等待某人出现。说出严厉的话,
当阳光使枫树的绿色变黄……

一切就是这样,但很费解
我感到新的呼吸在书页中搅动
整个漫长的冬天散发出一份旧目录的气息。
新的句子正在开始。但是夏天
还很漫长,还没有越过中点
却因那圆满的许诺充实而黑暗,
那时一个人再也无法走失
甚至最不细心的人也静下来
观察那准备发生的事。

玻璃的注视让你停下来
你摇摆而行:感知到的是我吗?
这次,他们注意到我了吗,像我一样,
或是它再次被推迟?孩子们
仍在游戏,云彩在午后的天空

Impatience in the afternoon sky, then dissipate

As limpid, dense twilight comes.

Only in that tooting of a horn

Down there, for a moment, I thought

The great, formal affair was beginning, orchestrated,

Its colors concentrated in a glance, a ballade

That takes in the whole world, now, but lightly,

Still lightly, but with wide authority and tact.

The prevalence of those gray flakes falling?

They are sun motes. You have slept in the sun

Longer than the sphinx, and are none the wiser for it.

Come in. And I thought a shadow fell across the door

But it was only her come to ask once more

If I was coming in, and not to hurry in case I wasn't.

The night sheen takes over. A moon of cistercian pallor

Has climbed to the center of heaven, installed,

Finally involved with the business of darkness.

And a sigh heaves from all the small things on earth,

The books, the papers, the old garters and union-suit buttons

Kept in a white cardboard box somewhere, and all the lower

Versions of cities flattened under the equalizing night.

The summer demands and takes away too much,

But night, the reserved, the reticent, gives more than it takes.

迅速而急躁地升起，然后消散
当透明、密集的微光出现。
仅仅在一只喇叭的嘟嘟声中
在那儿，有片刻，我才想起
那伟大的、正式的事件正在开始，精心安排，
将它的色彩集中在一瞥之中，一首叙事曲
欺骗了整个世界，现在，却轻柔地，
依然轻柔地，带有广泛的权威和机智。

那些灰色斑点到处在坠落吗？
它们是太阳耀斑。你在阳光中
睡得比斯芬克斯还久，可并没有因此变得聪明。
进来。我以为是一个影子从门上投射进来
却只是她又来询问
是否我要进来，如果不，就不要着急了。

夜晚的光辉接管。西多会修士般苍白的月亮
攀上天穹中央，安顿下来，
最后卷入了黑暗的交易。
大地上所有渺小的事物都发出叹息，
书籍、纸张、旧吊袜带和连衫裤的纽扣
保存在某处的一个白色纸箱中，众城
所有较低的版本都在平等的夜幕下变平了。
夏天需要带走的东西太多，
可是夜晚，保守而沉默，它的给予多过索取。

Worsening Situation

Like a rainstorm, he said, the braided colors
Wash over me and are no help. Or like one
At a feast who eats not, for he cannot choose
From among the smoking dishes. This severed hand
Stands for life, and wander as it will,
East or west, north or south, it is ever
A stranger who walks beside me. O seasons,
Booths, chaleur, dark-hatted charlatans
On the outskirts of some rural fete,
The name you drop and never say is mine, mine!
Some day I'll claim to you how all used up
I am because of you but in the meantime the ride
Continues. Everyone is along for the ride,
It seems. Besides, what else is there?
The annual games? True, there are occasions
For white uniforms and a special language
Kept secret from the others. The limes
Are duly sliced. I know all this
But can't seem to keep it from affecting me,
Every day, all day. I've tried recreation,
Reading until late at night, train rides

恶化的事态

像一场暴雨,他说,那混在一起的色彩
冲刷在我身上没一点儿用处。或者像一个
宴会上不吃东西的人,因为他不能
从那些冒烟的盘子中选择。这只割下的手
代表生活,随意漫游,
东西,南北,它曾是一个走在我旁边的
陌生人。哦!季节
展台,炎热,黑帽子的江湖郎中
在某个郊区游乐会的外围,
你扔下并从未说过的名字是我的,我的!
某一天我会要求你承认一切是怎样用光的
我是因为你,可这时赛马
仍在继续。似乎,每个人都在逢场作戏,
此外,那里还有什么?
一年一度的游戏?的确,在某些情况下
白制服和一种特殊语言
对其他人保守秘密。酸橙子
按时切开。这些我都知道
却似乎无法避免它的影响,
每一天,所有的日子。我试图消遣,
阅读到深夜,乘火车

And romance.

                    One day a man called while I was out
And left this message: "You got the whole thing wrong
From start to finish. Luckily, there's still time
To correct the situation, but you must act fast.
See me at your earliest convenience. And please,
Tell no one of this. Much besides your life depends on it."
I thought nothing of it at the time. Lately
I've been looking at old-fashioned plaids, fingering
Starched white collars, wondering whether there's a way
To get them really white again. My wife
Thinks I'm in Oslo—Oslo, France, that is.

还有风流韵事。
     有一天一个男人在我出去时打来电话
并留下这样的信息:"你把整件事都弄错了
从开始到结束。所幸仍有时间
去改正事态,但是你必须迅速行动。
得便时就尽早去看我。请不要
告诉任何人这个。另外你的生活极大地依赖于它。"
当时我什么都没想。后来
我一直在看老式的格子布,用手指摸着
浆挺的白领,奇怪是否有一种方法
让它们真的再度变白。我的妻子
以为我在奥斯陆——奥斯陆,那是,法兰西。

387

Forties Flick

The shadow of the Venetian blind on the painted wall,
Shadows of the snake-plant and cacti, the plaster animals,
Focus the tragic melancholy of the bright stare
Into nowhere, a hole like the black holes in space.
In bra and panties she sidles to the window:
Zip! Up with the blind. A fragile street scene offers itself,
With wafer-thin pedestrians who know where they are going.
The blind comes down slowly, the slats are slowly tilted up.

Why must it always end this way?
A dais with woman reading, with the ruckus of her hair
And all that is unsaid about her pulling us back to her, with her
Into the silence that night alone can't explain,
Silence of the library, of the telephone with its pad,
But we didn't have to reinvent these either:
They had gone away into the plot of a story,
The "art" part—knowing what important details to leave out
And the way character is developed. Things too real
To be of much concern, hence artificial, yet now all over the page,
The indoors with the outside becoming part of you
As you find you had never left off laughing at death,
The background, dark vine at the edge of the porch.

四十年代的电影

油漆过的墙上软百叶帘的影子,
虎尾兰,仙人掌,石膏动物的影子,
把明亮目光的悲惨忧郁聚焦到
虚空,一个像宇宙黑洞的洞。
穿着乳罩和内裤她挨近窗边:
嗖!百叶帘拉起。一幅易碎的街景呈现
有着知道自己在去向哪里的极薄的行人,
百叶帘慢慢落下,板条缓缓倾斜。

为什么总是要这样结束?
有妇女在讲台上朗读,用她头发的骚动
和未说出的关于她的一切把我们拖回,和她一起
进入夜晚单独无法解释的寂静。
图书馆的寂静,电话和通讯簿的寂静,
可我们没有必要重新发明这些:
它们已经进入了一个故事中的情节,
那"人工的"部分——知道要忽略哪些重要的细节
以及性格的发展方式。事物太真实
以致不能有太多关联,因此人工之物,仍布满纸页,
室内和室外变成你的一部分
当你发现你从未停止过嘲笑死亡,
背景,门廊边黑色的藤蔓。

As You Came from the Holy Land

of western New York state

were the graves all right in their bushings

was there a note of panic in the late August air

because the old man had peed in his pants again

was there turning away from the late afternoon glare

as though it too could be wished away

was any of this present

and how could this be

the magic solution to what you are in now

whatever has held you motionless

like this so long through the dark season

until now the women come out in navy blue

and the worms come out of the compost to die

it is the end of any season

you reading there so accurately

sitting not wanting to be disturbed

as you came from that holy land

what other signs of earth's dependency were upon you

what fixed sign at the crossroads

what lethargy in the avenues

因为你来自圣地

纽约州西部

灌木丛中都是坟墓

八月下旬的空气中有一种恐慌的信号

因为老人又尿裤子了

并从下午晚些时候的强光转身

仿佛能够期望它离开

这些现在存在吗

这些如何能成为

你目前状况魔术般的解决

无论什么都这样抓住你一动不动

如此长久地穿过黑暗的季节

直到现在,女人们穿着海军蓝出现

蠕虫从肥堆里爬出,死掉

这是任何季节的终结

你在那里如此谨慎地阅读

坐着,不想被打扰

因为你来自那块圣地

什么大地依赖的信号依赖于你

什么指示牌固定在十字路口

什么昏睡在林荫道上

where all is said in a whisper

what tone of voice among the hedges

what tone under the apple trees

the numbered land stretches away

and your house is built in tomorrow

but surely not before the examination

of what is right and will befall

not before the census

and the writing down of names

remember you are free to wander away

as from other times other scenes that were taking place

the history of someone who came too late

the time is ripe now and the adage

is hatching as the seasons change and tremble

it is finally as though that thing of monstrous interest were
     happening in the sky

but the sun is setting and prevents you from seeing it

out of night the token emerges

its leaves like birds alighting all at once under a tree

taken up and shaken again

put down in weak rage

knowing as the brain does it can never come about

那里的一切以低语说出

什么树篱间的声调

什么苹果树下的声调

那标上数字的土地延伸开去

而你的房子建在明天

但肯定不是在检验

什么是正确的、会遭遇什么之前

不是在人口统计

和写下名字之前

记住你可以自由地走开

仿佛离开其他曾经有过的时代和场景

来得太迟的某人的历史

现在时间成熟了，格言

正在孵化，当季节转变、颤抖

最后好像那庞大有趣的事物

正在天空出现

但太阳西沉，使你看不见它

那些记号涌出夜晚

它的树叶像鸟群同时降落在树下

升高，又再次颤抖

在虚弱的愤怒中迫降

像大脑一样知道，它永远无法出现

not here not yesterday in the past

only in the gap of today filling itself

as emptiness is distributed

in the idea of what time it is

when that time is already past

不是这里，不是过去的昨天
只是把自己填满今天的缝隙
像虚无被填入
关于时间的思想
当那时间已经过去

Scheherazade

Unsupported by reason's enigma

Water collects in squared stone catch basins.

The land is dry. Under it moves

The water. Fish live in the wells. The leaves,

A concerned green, are scrawled on the light. Bad

Bindweed and rank ragweed somehow forget to flourish here.

An inexhaustible wardrobe has been placed at the disposal

Of each new occurrence. It can be itself now.

Day is almost reluctant to decline

And slowing down opens out new avenues

That don't infringe on space but are living here with us.

Other dreams came and left while the bank

Of colored verbs and adjectives was shrinking from the light

To nurse in shade their want of a method

But most of all she loved the particles

That transform objects of the same category

Into particular ones, each distinct

Within and apart from its own class.

In all this springing up was no hint

Of a tide, only a pleasant wavering of the air

In which all things seemed present, whether

山鲁佐德

不被季节之谜所支持的水
积存在方形的石头滤污器中。
土地干燥。在它下面水在
移动。鱼住在井里。树叶,
一种相关的绿,被潦草地涂在光上。糟糕的
旋花植物和丛生的荒草不知怎么忘了在此繁衍。
安置一个取之不竭的衣橱,为每一件新事物
随意使用。现在它能做它自己了。
白昼几乎不情愿衰落
慢慢落下新林荫道之外的旷野
不侵占空间而是和我们一起在此生活。
其他的梦来了又去,当着彩色的
动词和形容词的银行因为光而萎缩
在阴影中培养它们对一种方法的需求
但是最主要的是她爱这些虚词
将同一范畴的事物转换成
独特之物,每一个都清晰
区别于它所属的种类。
在这整个涌现中没有任何潮汐的暗示,
只有空气的一阵愉快的波动
其中一切似乎都存在,无论是

Just past or soon to come. It was all invitation.
So much the flowers outlined along the night
Alleys when few were visible, yet
Their story sounded louder than the hum
Of bug and stick noises that brought up the rear,
Trundling it along into a new fact of day.
These were meant to be read as any
Salutation before getting down to business,
But they stuck to their guns, and so much
Was their obstinacy in keeping with the rest
(Like long flashes of white birds that refuse to die
When day does) that none knew the warp
Which presented this major movement as a firm
Digression, a plain that slowly becomes a mountain.

So each found himself caught in a net
As a fashion, and all efforts to wriggle free
involved him further, inexorably, since all
Existed there to be told, shot through
From border to border. Here were stones
That read as patches of sunlight, there was the story
Of the grandparents, of the vigorous young champion
(The lines once given to another, now
Restored to the new speaker), dinners and assemblies,

刚刚过去的还是即将到来的。那是全部邀请。

这么多的花映衬出夜晚小巷的轮廓

它们很少可以看见,它们的故事

依然比臭虫的哼声和拐杖

落在后面的噪音响亮,

沿它移动,进入日子的一个新事实中。

这些被刻意读成

坐下来交易之前的问候,

可是他们坚守立场,如此固执

和其他人保持一致

(像白昼死去时拒绝去死的白鸟

那长长的闪光)无人知道

偏见把这主要的运动描述成一种坚定的

偏离,一片在慢慢变成山的平原。

于是每个人发现自己落入了一张网中

作为一种时髦,所有想要挣脱的扭动

都使他被无情地裹得更紧,既然

那里的所有人都被告知,射穿

从边界到边界。这里的石头

被读作阳光的补丁,有一个关于祖父们的

故事,关于强壮的年轻冠军

(这故事曾给过另一个人,现在

还给了新的讲述者),午餐和集会,

The light in the old home, the secret way

The rooms fed into each other, but all

Was wariness of time watching itself

For nothing in the complex story grew outside:

The greatness in the moment of telling stayed unresolved

Until its wealth of incident, pain mixed with pleasure,

Faded in the precise moment of bursting

Into bloom, its growth a static lament.

Some stories survived the dynasty of the builders

But their echo was itself locked in, became

Anticipation that was only memory after all,

For the possibilities are limited. It is seen

At the end that the kind and good are rewarded,

That the unjust one is doomed to burn forever

Around his error, sadder and wiser anyway.

Between these extremes the others muddle through

Like us, uncertain but wearing artlessly

Their function of minor characters who must

Be kept in mind. It is we who make this

Jungle and call it space, naming each root,

Each serpent, for the sound of the name

As it clinks dully against our pleasure,

Indifference that is pleasure. And what would they be

老房子中的光,秘密的路径

彼此进入的房间,但是一切

都在小心着时间,观察它自己

因为在这复杂的故事里没有生长出什么:

它的美妙在讲述时没有得到证明

直到它的大量细节,与快乐混在一起的痛苦,

消失在绽放的精确瞬间,

它的成长是一个静止的哀悼。

有些故事拯救了建设者的王朝

它们的回声被锁在自身当中,变成了

预期,可那毕竟只是回忆,

因为可能性是有限的。在最后

看到善良和美好得到奖赏,

不义之人被判决永远焚烧

围绕他的错误,至少更为悲哀和明智。

其他人从这些极限中间混过去

如同我们,不可靠却拙劣地承担起

他们必须牢记的小角色的作用。

是我们造了这片丛林

并称之为宇宙,命名每棵树根,

每一条蛇,因为当名字

向我们的快乐发出单调的叮铃声,

冷淡就是快乐。他们会怎么样

Without an audience to restrict the innumerable

Passes and swipes, restored to good humor as it issues

Into the impervious evening air? So in some way

Although the arithmetic is incorrect

The balance is restored because it

Balances, knowing it prevails,

And the man who made the same mistake twice is exonerated.

如果没有一个成人来约束这些数不清的
关口与啤酒，恢复善意的幽默当它流入
傍晚无动于衷的空气？于是在某些方面
虽然计算是错误的
平衡仍然恢复了因为它
就是平衡，知道它占了上风，
而那两次犯下同样错误的人被免除了罪责。

Grand Galop

All things seem mention of themselves

And the names which stem from them branch out to other referents.

Hugely, spring exists again. The weigela does its dusty thing

In fire-hammered air. And garbage cans are heaved against

The railing as the tulips yawn and crack open and fall apart.

And today is Monday. Today's lunch is: Spanish omelet, lettuce and
    tomato salad,

Jello, milk and cookies. Tomorrow's: sloppy joe on bun,

Scalloped corn, stewed tomatoes, rice pudding and milk.

The names we stole don't remove us:

We have moved on a little ahead of them

And now it is time to wait again.

Only waiting, the waiting: what fills up the time between?

It is another kind of wait, waiting for the wait to be ended.

Nothing takes up its fair share of time,

The wait is built into the things just coming into their own.

Nothing is partially incomplete, but the wait

Invests everything like a climate.

What time of day is it?

Does anything matter?

Yes, for you must wait to see what it is really like,

This event rounding the corner

大加洛普舞曲

所有事物似乎都提到它们自己

从它们起源的名字向其他所指物扩展。

巨大的春天再度存在。锦带花在火焰捶打的天空

干着它灰扑扑的事儿。垃圾桶顶着栅栏

当郁金香打着呵欠,裂开,碎落。

今天是星期一。午餐是:西班牙煎蛋卷,莴苣番茄沙拉,

冻子,牛奶和小甜饼。明天是:小圆面包和淡咖啡

烤玉米,炖土豆,大米布丁和牛奶。

我们偷来的名字不能移动我们:

我们走在了它们前面一点

现在是再次等待的时间了。

只是等待,等待:有什么来填满时间?

那是另一种等待,等待着等待结束。

没有什么占有它公平分配的时间,

筑入事物的等待正在发挥作用。

一切都是半完成的,可是等待

像一种气候包围一切。

现在几点?

有任何要紧的事吗?

是的,因为你必须等着看它真正像什么,

角落附近的这个事件

Which will be unlike anything else and really

Cause no surprise: it's too ample.

Water

Drops from an air conditioner

On those who pass underneath. It's one of the sights of our town.

Puaagh. Vomit. Puaaaaagh. More vomit. One who comes

Walking dog on leash is distant to say how all this

Changes the minute to an hour, the hour

To the times of day, days to months, those easy-to-grasp entities,

And the months to seasons, which are far other, foreign

To our concept of time. Better the months—

They are almost persons—than these abstractions

That sift like marble dust across the unfinished works of the studio

Aging everything into a characterization of itself.

Better the cleanup committee concern itself with

Some item that is now little more than a feature

Of some obsolete style—cornice or spandrel

Out of the dimly remembered whole

Which probably lacks true distinction. But if one may pick it up,

Carry it over there, set it down,

Then the work is redeemed at the end

Under the smiling expanse of the sky

That plays no favorites but in the same way

将与不同于任何其他事物

真的是因为没啥好惊奇的：它太丰富了。

水

从一台空调滴落在

下面经过的行人身上。这是我们城市的一项名胜。

哇。呕吐。哇哇。更多的呕吐。来了一个

用皮带遛狗的人，远得说不出这一切

如何将分钟变成了小时，小时

变成了天，天变成了月，那些容易把握的实体，

月份变成季度，其他更远的，对于我们的时间概念

陌生的东西。月份优于——

它们几乎是人——这些抽象

纷落如大理石粉穿过未完成的雕塑

使每件事物变旧，变成自己的一个特征。

整顿委员会最好把它自己和某个条款相联

那只不过是某种过时风格的一个特征

——飞檐或拱肩

超出也许缺乏真正特色的

暗淡的记忆整体。可一旦能拾起它，

把它带到那里，放下，

那么这件艺术品最后就能得救

在广袤微笑的天空下

没有任何益处，只在某个方面

Is honor only to those who have sought it.

The dog barks, the caravan passes on.

The words had a sort of bloom on them

But were weightless, carrying past what was being said.

"A nice time," you think, "to go out:

The early night is cool, but not

Too anything. People parading with their pets

Past lawns and vacant lots, as though these too were somehow imponderables

Before going home to the decency of one's private life

Shut up behind doors, which is nobody's business.

It does matter a little to the others

But only because it makes them realize how far their respect

Has brought them. No one would dare to intrude.

It is a night like many another

With the sky now a bit impatient for today to be over

Like a bored salesgirl shifting from foot to stockinged foot."

These khaki undershorts hung out on lines,

The wind billowing among them, are we never to make a statement?

And certain buildings we always pass which are never mentioned—

It's getting out of hand.

As long as one has some sense that each thing knows its place

All is well, but with the arrival and departure

Of each new one overlapping so intensely in the semi-darkness

是对那些寻觅它的人的奖赏。

狗在吠叫,大篷车经过。

词语上面有一种花

却没有重量,将正在说的传送过去。

"一个美好的时刻,"你想,"到外面去:

入夜是凉爽的,可也不是

所有东西。人们带着宠物游行

经过草坪和空地,仿佛这些也是无法衡量的

在回家回到一个人正当的私生活之前

关在门后,与任何人都无关。

它与其他人的确有点关系

但只是因为它使他们认识到自己的敬意

已把他们带出了多远。无人敢去侵犯。

这是一个和许多其他夜晚一样的夜,此刻

天空对即将结束的白昼有些不耐

像一个厌倦的卖货女从赤裸的脚移向穿袜子的脚。"

这些卡其布短内衣成排挂着,

风在它们中间汹涌,我们永远也不做出声明吗?

我们经常路过的建筑物也从未提到——

它正逃出掌握。

只要一个人有某种万物都清楚自己位置的感觉

一切就好办了,可当每个新事物来来去去

在半明半暗中如此热切地重叠

It's a bit mad. Too bad, I mean, that getting to know each just for a
    fleeting second
Must be replaced by imperfect knowledge of the featureless whole,
Like some pocket history of the world, so general
As to constitute a sob or wail unrelated
To any attempt at definition. And the minor eras
Take on an importance out of all proportion to the story
For it can no longer unwind, but must be kept on hand
Indefinitely, like a first-aid kit no one ever uses
Or a word in the dictionary that no one will ever look up.
The custard is setting; meanwhile
I not only have my own history to worry about
But am forced to fret over insufficient details related to large
Unfinished concepts that can never bring themselves to the point
Of being, with or without my help, if any were forthcoming.

It is just the movement of the caravan away
Into an abstract night, with no
Precise goal in view, and indeed not caring,
That distributes this pause. Why be in a hurry
To speed away in the opposite direction, toward the other end of infinity?
For things can harden meaningfully in the moment of indecision.
I cannot decide in which direction to walk
But this doesn't matter to me, and I might as well

那就有点糟了。太糟了，我指的是，对每一个只有转瞬即逝的
　　一秒钟的了解

必须被无特征的整体那不完善的知识所代替，

仿佛世界的某种袖珍历史，如此一般

仅仅组成了一声呜咽或哭泣

无关于任何定义的企图。而次要的时代

获得了与故事不相称的某种重要性

因为它不再能够展开，而是被留在手里

不确定，像没人使过的急救包

或者没人会查的词典中的一个词。

蛋奶糕正在准备；与此同时

我不仅要操心我自己的历史

也要被迫为不充分的细节而烦恼，它们关系到

如果有什么发生，有没有我的帮助

都不能实现自我表述的未完成的大概念。

那运动只是大篷车在离开

进入一个抽象的夜，视野中

没有任何明确的目的，真的不在意，

这次暂停。为什么要匆忙地

在相反的方向加速离去，朝向无限的另一端？

因为事物在犹豫的瞬间能意味深长地变硬。

我决定不了向哪个方向走

但这对我无所谓，我不妨

Decide to climb a mountain (it looks almost flat)

As decide to go home

Or to a bar or restaurant or to the home

Of some friend as charming and ineffectual as I am

Because these pauses are supposed to be life

And they sink steel needles deep into the pores, as though to say

There is no use trying to escape

And it is all here anyway. And their steep, slippery sides defy

Any notion of continuity. It is this

That takes us back into what really is, it seems, history—

The lackluster, disorganized kind without dates

That speaks out of the hollow trunk of a tree

To warn away the merely polite, or those whose destiny

Leaves them no time to quibble about the means,

Which are not ends, and yet . . . What precisely is it

About the time of day it is, the weather, that causes people to note it
    painstakingly in their diaries

For them to read who shall come after?

Surely it is because the ray of light

Or gloom striking you this moment is hope

In all its mature, matronly form, taking all things into account

And reapportioning them according to size

So that if one can't say that this is the natural way

It should have happened, at least one can have no cause for complaint

Which is the same as having reached the end, wise

决定去爬山（它看上去几乎是平的）

和决定回家一样好

或者去酒吧、饭店，某个和我一样

迷人而无用的朋友家

因为这些暂停被假想为生活

他们把钢针深深沉入针眼，仿佛是说

企图逃跑没一点用处

无论如何都在这里。他们陡峭、光滑的侧面否定

任何继续的意见。是这个

带我们返回它真正的本质，那似乎是，历史——

无光泽无组织的种类，没有日期

在一棵空心树干里说话

警告有教养的离开，或者那些其命运

不给他们时间去挑剔手段的人，

手段不是目的，不过……到底是什么时候了，

是天气，促使人们在日记中小心地记下它

让随后到来的人去读？

的确是因为，这一刻撞击你的

光线或者幽暗便是希望

以它全然成熟而庄重的形式，将一切计算在内

并根据大小重新分配

这样一来，即便人们不能说这是自然的方式

早该如此，也至少没有理由抱怨

到达终点时还是一个样，聪明

In that expectation and enhanced by its fulfillment, or the absence of it.
But we say, it cannot come to any such end
As long as we are left around with no place to go.
And yet it has ended, and the thing we have fulfilled we have become.

Now it is the impulse of morning that makes
My watch tick. As one who pokes his head
Out from under a pile of blankets, the good and bad together,
So this tangle of impossible resolutions and irresolutions:
The desire to have fun, to make noise, and so to
Add to the already all-but-illegible scrub forest of graffiti on the shithouse wall.
Someone is coming to get you:
The mailman, or a butler enters with a letter on a tray
Whose message is to change everything, but in the meantime
One is to worry about one's smell or dandruff or lost glasses—
If only the curtain-raiser would end, but it is interminable.
But there is this consolation:
If it turns out to be not worth doing, I haven't done it;
If the sight appalls me, I have seen nothing;
If the victory is pyrrhic, I haven't won it.
And so from a day replete with rumors
Of things being done on the other side of the mountains
A nucleus remains, a still-perfect possibility

在于那个期望,被它的充盈或匮乏所加强。
可是我们说,它不可能达到这样的终点
只要我们被留在周围无处可去。
然而它已经结束了,我们已经变成了我们完成的东西。

现在是早晨的脉搏使我的表
走动。像一个人把脑袋
从一叠好的坏的撂一起的毯子下面,拱出来,
这就是乱作一团的不可能的解决和犹豫不决:
想要寻欢作乐,弄出噪音,甚至增加
茅厕墙上几乎无法辨认的涂鸦的矮树丛。
有人要来找你:
邮差,或一个男管家用托盘端着一封信进来
其信息将改变一切,可这时
一个人在为他的气味、皮屑或丢失的眼镜烦恼——
要是开台戏结束就好了,可它却无休无止。
然而有这样的安慰:
如果它证明是不值得做的,我还没有做;
如果这景象让我惊骇,我还什么都没看见;
如果这胜利代价太大,我还没有获胜。
于是,一个在山那边结束的
充满谣传的日子
留下了一个原子核,一个依然完美的
可以无限期保留的可能性。然而

That can be kept indefinitely. And yet

The groans of labor pains are deafening; one must

Get up, get out and be on with it. Morning is for sissies like you

But the real trials, the ones that separate the men from the boys, come later.

Oregon was kinder to us. The streets

Offered a variety of directions to the foot

And bookstores where pornography is sold. But then

One whiffs just a slight odor of madness in the air.

They all got into their cars and drove away

As in the end of a movie. So that it finally made no difference

Whether this were the end or it was somewhere else:

If it had to be somewhere it might as well be

Here, on top of one. Here, as elsewhere,

April advances new suggestions, and one may as well

Move along with them, especially in view of

The midnight-blue light that in turning itself inside out

Offers something strange to the attention, a thing

That is not itself, gnat whirling before my eyes

At an incredible, tame velocity. Too pronounced after all

To be that meaningless. And so on to afternoon

On the desert, with oneself cleaned up, and the location

Almost brand-new what with the removal of gum wrappers, etc.

But I was trying to tell you about a strange thing

产痛的呻吟依旧震耳欲聋；你必须起床，

出去和它同在。早晨就是为你这样的懦夫准备的

而那使男孩变成男人的真实的考验，却来得太迟了。

俄勒冈对我们更友好。街道

为脚提供许许多多的方向

书店在卖色情画。随后

一个人向空气中喷出一股淡淡的疯狂气味。

他们全都上了自己的汽车开走了

就像一部影片的结尾。这就是结尾，还是在其他地方结束

最终没有造成任何差别：

如果它必须在某处，那在这里

也是一样，在一个上面。这里，和别处一样，

四月提出了新的建议，一个人同样可以

随它们移动，尤其看到

由内向外翻转的午夜蓝光

为注意力提供某种陌生的东西，一件

不是其本身的东西，叮人小虫在我眼前旋转

以难以置信、无精打采的速度。毕竟过于确切

以至于不能毫无意义。如此等等直到下午

在废墟上，一个人独自清理，一个几乎全新的地点

清走了橡胶包装的东西，等等。

可我正试图告诉你一件

发生在我身上的怪事，可让它真的发生，

That happened to me, but this is no way to tell about it,

By making it truly happen. It drifts away in fragments.

And one is left sitting in the yard

To try to write poetry

Using what Wyatt and Surrey left around,

Took up and put down again

Like so much gorgeous raw material,

As though it would always happen in some way

And meanwhile since we are all advancing

It is sure to come about in spite of everything

On a Sunday, where you are left sitting

In the shade that, as always, is just a little too cool.

So there is whirling out at you from the not deep

Emptiness the word "cock" or some other, brother and sister words

With not much to be expected from them, though these

Are the ones that waited so long for you and finally left, having given up hope.

There is a note of desperation in one's voice, pleading for them,

And meanwhile the intensity thins and sharpens

Its point, that is the thing it was going to ask.

One has been waiting around all evening for it

Before sleep had stopped definitively the eyes and ears

Of all those who came as an audience.

Still, that poetry does sometimes occur

If only in creases in forgotten letters

绝不是讲述它的办法。它零零碎碎地飘走了。

一个人被留下坐在院子里

试图写诗

使用瓦特和索尼留在附近的东西,

拿起又放下

令人满意的原始材料,

仿佛它经常会以某种方式发生

与此同时,既然我们都在进步

无论怎样它肯定会出现

尽管在一个星期天,你留下坐在

影子里,和往常一样,一切只稍微凉了一点。

于是从那并不太深的空虚中"公鸡"这个词

向你回旋而来,或另一个词,兄妹们的词

不要对它们有太多期待,尽管这些词

等了你那么长时间,最终离开了,放弃了希望。

在一个人的声音中有一种失望的音调,在为它们辩护,

与此同时,豁然开朗,那就是它的要求。

一个人整个傍晚都在等它

在睡眠永远关闭了那些作为听众

出现的人的耳目之前。

确实,那首诗仍时有出现

但仅是在摺痕中在忘记了的书信中

装在阁楼的衣箱中——你忘记的你曾拥有的东西

无论它如何至关重要,

Packed away in trunks in the attic—things you forgot you had

And what would it matter anyway,

That recompense so precisely dosed

As to seem the falling true of a perverse judgment.

You forget how there could be a gasp of a new air

Hidden in that jumble. And of course your forgetting

Is a sign of just how much it matters to you:

"It must have been important."

The lies fall like flaxen threads from the skies

All over America, and the fact that some of them are true of course

Doesn't so much not matter as serve to justify

The whole mad organizing force under the billows of correct delight.

Surrey, your lute is getting an attack of nervous paralysis

But there are, again, things to be sung of

And this is one of them, only I would not dream of intruding on

The frantic completeness, the all-purpose benevolence

Of that still-moist garden where the tooting originates:

Between intervals of clenched teeth, your venomous rondelay.

Ask a hog what is happening. Go on. Ask him.

The road just seems to vanish

And not that far in the distance, either. The horizon must have been moved up.

So it is that by limping carefully

From one day to the next, one approaches a worn, round stone tower

那回报如此精确

像一个荒谬的审判果真降临了。

你忘了怎么能渴望一种新空气

藏在那一堆杂碎中。当然你的遗忘

正是它对你多么重要的一个信号：

"它一定很重要。"

谎言从天而降像淡黄色的纤维

落在全美国，它们之中有些是真的这一事实

当然也并非不那么要紧，在用来为正当嗜好的波浪下面

那整个疯狂的组织力量辩护的时候。

索尼，你的诗琴在遭受神经麻痹的攻击

可仍然有要唱的东西

这是其中一个，只是我不愿意梦想着去侵扰

它疯狂的完美，发出嘟嘟声的依然湿润的花园

完全有意的善行：

在咬紧的齿缝间，你充满毒液的回旋曲。

问一个贪婪的人出了什么事。继续。问他。

道路似乎就要消失了

不是远方的那条。地平线一定上升了。

于是从一个日子到另一个日子

一个人小心跛行，接近一座圆形的旧石塔

它低低地蹲在一个空空的小溪谷中

没有门窗，只有许多旧牌照

Crouching low in the hollow of a gully

With no door or window but a lot of old license plates

Tacked up over a slit too narrow for a wrist to pass through

And a sign: "Van Camp's Pork and Beans."

From then on in: *angst*-colored skies, emotional withdrawals

As the whole business starts to frighten even you,

Its originator and promoter. The horizon returns

As a smile of recognition this time, polite, unquestioning.

How long ago high school graduation seems

Yet it cannot have been so very long:

One has traveled such a short distance.

The styles haven't changed much,

And I still have a sweater and one or two other things I had then.

It seems only yesterday that we saw

The movie with the cows in it

And turned to one at your side, who burped

As morning saw a new garnet-and-pea-green order propose

Itself out of the endless bathos, like science-fiction lumps.

Impossible not to be moved by the tiny number

Those people wore, indicating they should be raised to this or that power.

But now we are at Cape Fear and the overland trail

Is impassable, and a dense curtain of mist hangs over the sea.

钉在一个手腕都不能穿过的窄缝上

还有一个告示:"梵·康珀的猪肉和豆子。"

从那时起:不安的彩色天空,情绪崩溃

当整个交易甚至开始让你

这个发起人和促进者惊骇。地平线返回

这次像一个赞成的微笑,礼貌,没有异议。

很久以前的中学教育

似乎不是这么漫长:

一个人度过了这么短的旅途。

风格没有多大的变化,

我依然拥有一件汗衫和一两件那时就有的东西。

似乎就在昨天我们看了一部

里面有公牛的电影

转向你旁边的一个打嗝的人

如同早晨看见一个深红色和豌豆绿的新秩序

计划脱出无尽的陈腐,像科幻小说中的大块头。

不可能不被微小的数字所感动

那些人厌倦了,暗示着应被赋予这种或那种权利。

但现在我们是在恐惧海角,陆路小道

无法穿越,一面浓雾的帘子悬挂在海上。

Hop O' My Thumb

The grand hotels, dancing girls

Urge forward under a veil of "lost illusion"

The deed to this day or some other day.

There is no day in the calendar

The dairy company sent out

That lets you possess it wildly like

The body of a dreaming woman in a dream:

All flop over at the top when seized,

The stem too slender, the top too loose and heavy,

Blushing with fine foliage of dreams.

The motor cars, tinsel hats,

Supper of cakes, the amorous children

Take the solitary downward path of dreams

And are not seen again.

What is it, Undine?

The notes now can scarcely be heard

In the hubbub of the flattening storm,

With the third wish unspoken.

I remember meeting you in a dark dream

Of April, you or some girl,

小矮人

大饭店，正在跳舞的女孩们
在"失去的幻象"的面纱下推进
今天或某天的行为。
乳品公司派送的日历
里面没有日子
那让你狂野占有的
如一个梦着的妇女梦中的身体：
在攫取时笨拙地从顶端落下
茎太纤弱了，顶端太松太沉了，
因梦的美好的叶子而羞赧。
汽车，金属片装饰的帽子，
晚餐糕饼，多情的孩子们
选择偏僻的梦的小径
再也无人看见。
它是什么，女水妖？
现在勉强能听见那些音符
在风暴逐渐平息的喧嚣之中，
带着未说出的第三个愿望。

我记起在四月一个黑暗的梦中
遇见你，你或某个姑娘，

The necklace of wishes alive and breathing around your throat.

In the blindness of that dark whose

Brightness turned to sand salt-glazed in noon sun

We could not know each other or know which part

Belonged to the other, pelted in an electric storm of rain.

Only gradually the mounds that meant our bodies

That wore ourselves concaved into view

But intermittently as through dark mist

Smeared against fog. No worse time to have come,

Yet all was desiring though already desired and past,

The moment a monument to itself

No one would ever see or know was there.

That time faded too and the night

Softened to smooth spirals or foliage at night.

There were sleeping cabins near by, blind lanterns,

Nocturnal friendliness of the plate of milk left for the fairies

Who otherwise might be less well disposed:

Friendship of white sheets patched with milk.

And always an open darkness in which one name

Cries over and over again: Ariane! Ariane!

Was it for this you led your sisters back from sleep

And now he of the blue beard has outmaneuvered you?

But for the best perhaps: let

愿望的活项链,绕你的喉咙呼吸。

在那盲目的黑暗中谁的明亮

在正午的阳光中转变成覆有盐渍的沙子

我们不可能彼此了解或者了解哪一部分

属于对方,在一场雨的电子风暴中骤降。

只有那意味着我们尸体的土堆

带着我们的自我逐渐凹进视野

但是断断续续,如同黑色雾气

把烟雾涂脏。艰难时刻还没有到来,

一切仍在渴望尽管已经渴望过并已成过去,

此刻是它自身的纪念碑

没人看见也没人知道它曾经存在。

那个时刻也消逝了

夜软化成光滑的螺旋或夜晚的植物。

附近有卧舱,盲目的灯笼,

留给小精灵的牛奶碟的夜的友善

否则他们就不会有什么好感:

用牛奶弥补白床单的友谊。

一个名字总是在开阔的黑暗中

一次次哭喊:艾丽安!艾丽安!

就为了这个你把妹妹们从睡眠中领回来

现在他这个蓝胡子已经用计谋胜过了你?

最好的可能:让

Those sisters slink into the sapphire

Hair that is mounting day.

There are still other made-up countries

Where we can hide forever,

Wasted with eternal desire and sadness,

Sucking the sherbets, crooning the tunes, naming the names.

那些妹妹溜进宝蓝色

头发那是进攻的日子。

还有其他虚构的国家

我们能永远藏在那里,

消磨于永恒的欲望和悲哀,

吮着冰冻果子露,哼着小调,取着名字。

Mixed Feelings

A pleasant smell of frying sausages
Attacks the sense, along with an old, mostly invisible
Photograph of what seems to be girls lounging around
An old fighter bomber, circa 1942 vintage.
How to explain to these girls, if indeed that's what they are,
These Ruths, Lindas, Pats and Sheilas
About the vast change that's taken place
In the fabric of our society, altering the texture
Of all things in it? And yet
They somehow look as if they knew, except
That it's so hard to see them, it's hard to figure out
Exactly what kind of expressions they're wearing.
What are your hobbies, girls? Aw nerts,
One of them might say, this guy's too much for me.
Let's go on and out, somewhere
Through the canyons of the garment center
To a small café and have a cup of coffee.
I am not offended that these creatures (that's the word)
Of my imagination seem to hold me in such light esteem,
Pay so little heed to me. It's part of a complicated
Flirtation routine, anyhow, no doubt. But this talk of

混杂的情感

一股烤香肠的诱人气味

侵入感觉,沿着一张,大部已看不清的

旧照片,似乎是一群少女懒洋洋倚在

一架老式战斗轰炸机周围,大约在一九四二年的葡萄收获季。

如何对这些姑娘解释,如果那确实是她们,

这些露丝们,琳达们,帕特们和希拉们

我们社会结构中发生的

沧桑巨变,改变着其中

所有事物的质地?并且

不知怎么她们看上去似乎都知道,除了

太难看见她们,很难准确断定

她们正带着何种表情。

你们有什么嗜好,姑娘们?哦,呸,

其中一个会说,这家伙对我太过分。

让我们继续,去外面

穿过服装中心的峡谷

去一个小咖啡馆喝杯咖啡。

我没有遭到冒犯,我想象的创造物

(那是词语)似乎对我很不尊重,

很少对我留意。毫无疑问,这是一个

复杂调情惯例的一部分。可这是在

The garment center? Surely that's California sunlight

Belaboring them and the old crate on which they

Have draped themselves, fading its Donald Duck insignia

To the extreme point of legibility.

Maybe they were lying but more likely their

Tiny intelligences cannot retain much information.

Not even one fact, perhaps. That's why

They think they're in New York. I like the way

They look and act and feel. I wonder

How they got that way, but am not going to

Waste any more time thinking about them.

I have already forgotten them

Until some day in the not too distant future

When we meet possibly in the lounge of a modern airport,

They looking as astonishingly young and fresh as when this picture was made

But full of contradictory ideas, stupid ones as well as

Worthwhile ones, but all flooding the surface of our minds

As we babble about the sky and the weather and the forests of change.

服装中心的谈话吗?那的确是加利福尼亚的阳光
在痛打她们和她们松弛地靠在上面的
旧飞机,让它的唐老鸭徽章褪色
到了几乎无法分辨的程度。
也许她们正在撒谎,但更有可能她们的
小聪明也保留不了多少信息。
甚或一个事实。那就是为什么
她们认为自己是在纽约。我喜欢
她们注视、行动和抚摸的样子。我惊奇
她们怎么变成了那个样子,但我不打算
再浪费时间想着她们了。
我已经忘记了她们
直到在不远的将来有一天
我们也许在一个现代机场的休息室里相遇,
她们令人吃惊,和照片上一样青春年少
满是互相矛盾的想法,有的愚蠢
有的有价值,全都泛滥在我们心灵的表面上
当我们唠叨起天空、气候和森林的变化。

Märchenbilder

Es war einrnal... No, it's too heavy

To be said. Besides, you aren't paying attention any more.

How shall I put it?

"The rain thundered on the uneven red flagstones.

The steadfast tin soldier gazed beyond the drops

Remembering the hat-shaped paper boat, that soon..."

That's not it either.

Think about the long summer evenings of the past, the queen anne's lace.

Sometimes a musical phrase would perfectly sum up

The mood of a moment. One of those lovelorn sonatas

For wind instruments was riding past on a solemn white horse.

Everybody wondered who the new arrival was.

Pomp of flowers, decorations

Junked next day. Now look out of the window.

The sky is clear and bland. The wrong kind of day

For business or games, or betting on a sure thing.

The trees weep drops

童话场景

从前……不，它太沉重了
没法说。另外，你也不再注意。
我该怎么说呢?
"雷雨倾注在粗糙的红色铺路石上。

坚定的锡兵凝视雨珠之外
回忆着帽形纸船，不久便……"
那也不是它。
想想过去那漫长的夏日黄昏，安妮女王的花边。

有时一个乐句就能完美地聚集起
瞬间的情绪。一支管乐演奏的失恋奏鸣曲
正骑着一匹庄严的白马驰过。
每个人都想知道新来的是谁。

花事盛大，奖章
第二天的废铜烂铁。现在看看窗子外面。
天空清澈怡人。这个日子不适合交易
和游戏，或是为一件确定的事打赌。

夜晚，树的眼泪

Into the water at night. Slowly couples gather.

She looks into his eyes. "It would not be good

To be left alone." He: "I'll stay

As long as the night allows." This was one of those night rainbows

In negative color. As we advance, it retreats; we see

We are now far into a cave, must be. Yet there seem to be

Trees all around, and a wind lifts their leaves, slightly.

I want to go back, out of the bad stories,

But there's always the possibility that the next one. . .

No, It's another almond tree, or a ring-swallowing frog. . .

Yet they are beautiful as we people them

With ourselves. They are empty as cupboards.

To spend whole days drenched in them, waiting for the next whisper,

For the word in the next room. This is how the princes must have behaved,

Lying down in the frugality of sleep.

落到水里。夫妇们慢慢聚到一起。
她凝视他的眼睛。"一个人留下
可不是件好事。"他说:"夜晚允许多久

我便留多久。"这是一道夜虹的
彩色负片。我们前进,它便后撤;我们看见
我们现在已深入一个洞穴,一定如此。但那里似乎
到处都是树,一阵风轻柔地,掀起它们的叶子。

我要回去,摆脱这糟糕的故事,
可是总有可能那下一个……
不,那是另一棵扁桃树,或者一只吞指环的青蛙……
它们仍然很美,当我们居住在

它们中间。它们空如食橱。
浸在里面度过所有的日子,等待下一声低语,
等待隔壁房间里的话语。王子们必须做的,
就是躺下睡上简单的一觉。

Oleum Misericordiae

To rub it out, make it less virulent
And a stab too at rearranging
The whole thing from the ground up.
Yes we were waiting just now
Yes we are no longer waiting.

Afterwards when I tell you
It's as though it all only happened
As siding of my story

I beg you to listen
You are already listening

It has shut itself out
And in doing so shut us accidentally in

And meanwhile my story goes well
The first chapter
    Endeth

But the real story, the one

慈悲之油

把它擦掉，让它少一点毒性
并试试重新安排
这来自土地的整件东西。
是的我们现在正在等待
是的我们已不再等待。

后来我告诉你
仿佛它的出现只是
为了支持我的故事

我恳求你听
你已经在听

它已经把自己关在外面
而这样做时偶然把我们关在了里面

此时我的故事仍在继续
第一章
    结束

可他们讲给我们的

They tell us we shall probably never know

Drifts back in bits and pieces

All of them, it turns out

So lucky

Now we really know

It all happened by chance:

A chance encounter

The dwarf led you to the end of a street

And pointed flapping his arms in two directions

You forgot to misprize him

But after a series of interludes

In furnished rooms (describe wallpaper)

Transient hotels (mention sink and cockroaches)

And spending the night with a beautiful married woman

Whose husband was away in Centerville on business

(Mention this wallpaper: the purest roses

Though the creamiest and how

Her smile lightens the ordeal

Of the last 500 pages

Though you never knew her last name

Only her first: Dorothy)

You got hold of the water of life

真正的故事,我们也许永远不能知道

它们全都零零碎碎地

漂回来,结果

如此幸运

现在我们真的知道了

它的发生完全是偶然:

一次偶然的邂逅

那小矮人把你领向一条街的尽头

拍动他的双臂指向两个方向

你忘了嘲笑他

在一系列插曲之后

在有家具的屋子里(描述一下墙纸)

在寄宿旅馆(提一提洗涤槽和蟑螂)

和一个美丽的已婚妇女过夜

她的丈夫去森特维尔做生意去了

(提一提这墙纸:最纯粹的玫瑰

滑腻如脂,还有她的微笑

怎样照亮了最后

五百页的严酷考验

尽管你从不知道她的姓

只知她的名:多萝西)

你得到了生命之水

Rescued your two wicked brothers Cash and Jethro

Who promptly stole the water of life

After which you got it back, got safely home,

Saved the old man's life

And inherited the kingdom.

But this was a moment

Under the most cheerful sun.

in poorer lands

No one touches the water of life.

It has no taste

And though it refreshes absolutely

It is a cup that must also pass

Until everybody

Gets some advantage, big or little

Some reason for having come

So far

Without dog or woman

So far alone, unasked.

救了你的两个坏哥哥卡什和杰斯罗
他们在你取到生命之水，安全回家以后
马上把它偷走，
救了那老人的命
并继承了王位。

可这只是一瞬
在最悦人的阳光下
在更贫穷的土地
无人接触到这生命之水。

它没有味道
但它绝对能让人恢复精神
它是必须传下去的一杯

直到每个人
都得到某种或大或小的好处，
某种延续至今的
理由
没有狗或女人
孤独至今，无人过问。

Self-Portrait in a Convex Mirror

As Parmigianino did it, the right hand

Bigger than the head, thrust at the viewer

And swerving easily away, as though to protect

What it advertises. A few leaded panes, old beams,

Fur, pleated muslin, a coral ring run together

In a movement supporting the face, which swims

Toward and away like the hand

Except that it is in repose. It is what is

Sequestered. Vasari says, "Francesco one day set himself

To take his own portrait, looking at himself for that purpose

In a convex mirror, such as is used by barbers...

He accordingly caused a ball of wood to be made

By a turner, and having divided it in half and

Brought it to the size of the mirror, he set himself

With great art to copy all that he saw in the glass,"

Chiefly his reflection, of which the portrait

Is the reflection once removed.

The glass chose to reflect only what he saw

Which was enough for his purpose: his image

Glazed, embalmed, projected at a 180-degree angle.

The time of day or the density of the light

凸面镜中的自画像

正如帕米加尼诺所做的,右手

比头还大,插向观察者

并轻松地偏斜,像是要去保护

它所宣告的。一些铅灰色的窗格,旧横梁

毛皮,打褶的细棉布,一个珊瑚指环一起奔跑

以运动支撑着那张脸,那脸向前

游动,又像那只手一样离开

只可惜它在休憩。它是被隐藏的

东西。瓦萨利说,"有一天弗朗西斯科

开始画他的自画像,为此他在一个凸面镜中

看着他自己,就像理发师用的那种……

他随后让一个镟工做了一个

木球,把它分成两半

使之和镜子同样大小,他开始

以杰出的技艺复制他在镜中看到的一切,"

主要是他的映像,那自画像

作为其映像的映像曾经被去除过。

玻璃选择反射的只是他所看到的

那对他的目的已经够了:他的形象

上釉,敷香,以一百八十度角投射。

那一天的时辰或光的密度

Adhering to the face keeps it
Lively and intact in a recurring wave
Of arrival. The soul establishes itself.
But how far can it swim out through the eyes
And still return safely to its nest? The surface
Of the mirror being convex, the distance increases
Significantly; that is, enough to make the point
That the soul is a captive, treated humanely, kept
In suspension, unable to advance much farther
Than your look as it intercepts the picture.
Pope Clement and his court were "stupefied"
By it, according to Vasari, and promised a commission
That never materialized. The soul has to stay where it is,
Even though restless, hearing raindrops at the pane,
The sighing of autumn leaves thrashed by the wind,
Longing to be free, outside, but it must stay
Posing in this place. It must move
As little as possible. This is what the portrait says.
But there is in that gaze a combination
Of tenderness, amusement and regret, so powerful
In its restraint that one cannot look for long.
The secret is too plain. The pity of it smarts,
Makes hot tears spurt: that the soul is not a soul,
Has no secret, is small, and it fits
Its hollow perfectly: its room, our moment of attention.

附在脸上使它在不断循环而来的波浪中

保持生动和完整。灵魂确立它自己。

可是它能穿过眼睛游出多远

并能平安地返回它的巢穴？镜子的表面

凸起，距离意味深长地

增加；那就足以证明

灵魂已被捕获，受到人道的对待，保持

悬浮，无法比你的目光进展得

更远，因为它中途截住了画面。

教皇克莱门特和他的教廷被它

"惊呆了"，据瓦萨利说，还许诺了一笔

从未兑现的酬金。灵魂不得不停在它的所在之处，

即使不安地，倾听着窗上的雨滴，

被风鞭打的秋叶的叹息，

渴望，外面的自由，可它必须继续

在这儿摆着姿式。它必须尽可能

少移动。这就是自画像所讲的。

然而在那凝视中混合了

敏感，愉悦和懊悔，在它的克制中

那么有力，让人不能看得过久。

这秘密过于清楚。它的怜悯让人刺痛，

使热泪涌出：灵魂不是一个灵魂，

它没有秘密，很小，完全适合

它的空洞：它的房间，我们关注的瞬间。

That is the tune but there are no words.

The words are only speculation

(From the Latin *speculum*, mirror):

They seek and cannot find the meaning of the music.

We see only postures of the dream,

Riders of the motion that swings the face

Into view under evening skies, with no

False disarray as proof of authenticity.

But it is life englobed.

One would like to stick one's hand

Out of the globe, but its dimension,

What carries it, will not allow it.

No doubt it is this, not the reflex

To hide something, which makes the hand loom large

As it retreats slightly. There is no way

To build it flat like a section of wall:

It must join the segment of a circle,

Roving back to the body of which it seems

So unlikely a part, to fence in and shore up the face

On which the effort of this condition reads

Like a pinpoint of a smile, a spark

Or star one is not sure of having seen

As darkness resumes. A perverse light whose

Imperative of subtlety dooms in advance its

那是曲调却没有词语。

词语只是推测

（来自拉丁语 speculum，镜子）：

他们寻找但无法找到音乐的含意。

我们只看见梦的姿势。

移动的骑手摇摆着脸孔

在黄昏的天空下进入视野，没有任何

人为的紊乱作为真实性的证明。

可它是包入球体中的生命。

一个人想要把自己的手

穿出球体，可那承载它的

维度，不会允许。

无疑是这个，而不是反射

要藏起什么，让手隐约变大

当它微微后移。没有任何办法

把它造得像墙一样平坦：

它必须加入一段圆弧，

游回它似乎不像是其一部分的

躯体，围起并将这面孔撑起来

这种情况下的努力看起来

就像一个微笑的针尖，一个火花

或当黑暗重临，一个人不能肯定

曾经见过的星。一束反常的光

它微妙的需要注定要强化

Conceit to light up: unimportant but meant.

Francesco, your hand is big enough

To wreck the sphere, and too big,

One would think, to weave delicate meshes

That only argue its further detention.

(Big, but not coarse, merely on another scale,

Like a dozing whale on the sea bottom

In relation to the tiny, self-important ship

On the surface.) But your eyes proclaim

That everything is surface. The surface is what's there

And nothing can exist except what's there.

There are no recesses in the room, only alcoves,

And the window doesn't matter much, or that

Sliver of window or mirror on the right, even

As a gauge of the weather, which in French is

Le temps, the word for time, and which

Follows a course wherein changes are merely

Features of the whole. The whole is stable within

Instability, a globe like ours, resting

On a pedestal of vacuum, a ping-pong ball

Secure on its jet of water.

And just as there are no words for the surface, that is,

No words to say what it really is, that it is not

Superficial but a visible core, then there is

它要去照明的自负：不重要但有意味。

弗朗西斯科，你的手大得足以

毁坏这球体，而且太大了，

一个人会想，要编织柔软的网

那只是主张将它更长地拖延。

（大，却并不粗糙，只是在另一种尺度中

像海底一条假寐的鲸

和水面自大的小船

之间的关系。）可你的眼睛宣告

一切都是表面。表面是那里的一切

除了那里的一切其他都不能存在。

屋子里没有隐蔽处，只有壁龛，

窗户也不太要紧，或者

那窗子的木条或右边的镜子，即便

作为天气计量器，在法语中是

le temps，关于时间的词，它

遵循一个其中的种种变化仅仅是

整体特征的过程。整体是不稳定中的

稳定，一个同我们星球一样的球，停歇在

一个真空的垫座上，一个乒乓球

安稳于它喷射的水上。

而且正如对表面无话可说，亦即

没有词语去说出它真的是什么，它不是

表面的而是一个可见的核，那么

No way out of the problem of pathos vs. experience.
You will stay on, restive, serene in
Your gesture which is neither embrace nor warning
But which holds something of both in pure
Affirmation that doesn't affirm anything.

The balloon pops, the attention
Turns dully away. Clouds
In the puddle stir up into sawtoothed fragments.
I think of the friends
Who came to see me, of what yesterday
Was like. A peculiar slant
Of memory that intrudes on the dreaming model
In the silence of the studio as he considers
Lifting the pencil to the self-portrait.
How many people came and stayed a certain time,
Uttered light or dark speech that became part of you
Like light behind windblown fog and sand,
Filtered and influenced by it, until no part
Remains that is surely you. Those voices in the dusk
Have told you all and still the tale goes on
In the form of memories deposited in irregular
Clumps of crystals. Whose curved hand controls,
Francesco, the turning seasons and the thoughts

就没有办法摆脱激情对经验这个问题。
你将不安地停留,沉静在
你既非拥抱又非警告的姿势中
却抓住两者中的某个东西
在那不肯定任何东西的纯粹肯定中。

气球砰砰响着,注意力
迟钝地转移。云朵
在小水潭中搅成锯齿形碎片。
我想起来看我的
朋友们,想着昨天
像什么。记忆独有的一个倾向
是侵扰在画室的寂静中
做梦的模特,当他思忖着
把铅笔伸向自画像。
多少人来了,停留一段时间,
发出成为你一部分的或明或暗的话语
像风吹的雾和沙子后面的光,
被它过滤和影响,直到没有留下
任何肯定是你的部分。黄昏那些声音
已告诉你一切而故事仍在继续
以记忆的形式沉淀在
不规则的水晶中。弗朗西斯科,
谁弯曲的手控制着,季节的转变和思想

That peel off and fly away at breathless speeds

Like the last stubborn leaves ripped

From wet branches? I see in this only the chaos

Of your round mirror which organizes everything

Around the polestar of your eyes which are empty,

Know nothing, dream but reveal nothing.

I feel the carousel starting slowly

And going faster and faster: desk, papers, books,

Photographs of friends, the window and the trees

Merging in one neutral band that surrounds

Me on all sides, everywhere I look.

And I cannot explain the action of leveling,

Why it should all boil down to one

Uniform substance, a magma of interiors.

My guide in these matters is your self,

Firm, oblique, accepting everything with the same

Wraith of a smile, and as time speeds up so that it is soon

Much later, I can know only the straight way out,

The distance between us. Long ago

The strewn evidence meant something,

The small accidents and pleasures

Of the day as it moved gracelessly on,

A housewife doing chores. Impossible now

To restore those properties in the silver blur that is

它们剥离并以无声无息的速度飞走

像最后的顽固的叶子从潮湿的树上

扯掉？我看见只有你圆镜的纷乱

在这之中将一切围绕你

眼睛的北极星组织起来，它们空空如也

一无所知，梦着但却一无所示。

我感到旋转木马正在慢慢启动

越来越快：桌子，纸张，书本，

朋友们的照片，窗子和树

联合成一个中立组织，从各个侧面

我看到的每个地方，围绕我。

我无法解释这拉平的行为，

为什么一切都要缩减成一种

统一的物质，一种内部的岩浆。

在这些事情上我的向导是你的自我，

坚定，含蓄，用同样微笑的鬼魂

接受每一件事，而当时间加速以至于不久

天就很晚了，我只能认得出去的直路，

我们之间的距离。很久以前

散落的事件意味着什么，

当日子粗野地向前

它那小小的事故和乐趣，

一个家庭主妇在做家务。现在不可能

在银色的污迹中恢复那些财产

The record of what you accomplished by sitting down

"With great art to copy all that you saw in the glass"

So as to perfect and rule out the extraneous

Forever. In the circle of your intentions certain spars

Remain that perpetuate the enchantment of self with self:

Eyebeams, muslin, coral. It doesn't matter

Because these are things as they are today

Before one's shadow ever grew

Out of the field into thoughts of tomorrow.

Tomorrow is easy, but today is uncharted,

Desolate, reluctant as any landscape

To yield what are laws of perspective

After all only to the painter's deep

Mistrust, a weak instrument though

Necessary. Of course some things

Are possible, it knows, but it doesn't know

Which ones. Some day we will try

To do as many things as are possible

And perhaps we shall succeed at a handful

Of them, but this will not have anything

To do with what is promised today, our

Landscape sweeping out from us to disappear

On the horizon. Today enough of a cover burnishes

那是你坐下来完成的记录

"用伟大的技艺复制你在玻璃中看见的一切"

为了完善而永远拒绝外来的事物。

在你意图的圈子里某些争论留了下来

用自我使自我的魅力不朽:

眼光,细棉布,珊瑚。无关紧要

因为这些东西还是和今天一样

在一个人的影子之前日益生长

超出这个领域进入明天的思想。

明天容易,可今天却未经探测,

荒芜,同所有风景一样

勉强产生出透视法则

毕竟只有对画家怀有深深的

怀疑,一个无力的工具

才成其为必要。当然它知道

有些事情是可能的,可它不知道

是哪些。有一天我们会尝试

尽可能多做点事

也许我们会成功完成

少许,但这与今天许诺的东西

毫无关系,我们的

风景从我们这里席卷而去,消失在

地平线上。今天一个擦亮的封面足以

To keep the supposition of promises together

In one piece of surface, letting one ramble

Back home from them so that these

Even stronger possibilities can remain

Whole without being tested. Actually

The skin of the bubble-chamber's as tough as

Reptile eggs; everything gets "programmed" there

In due course: more keeps getting included

Without adding to the sum, and just as one

Gets accustomed to a noise that

Kept one awake but now no longer does,

So the room contains this flow like an hourglass

Without varying in climate or quality

(Except perhaps to brighten bleakly and almost

Invisibly, in a focus of sharpening toward death—more

Of this later). What should be the vacuum of a dream

Becomes continually replete as the source of dreams

Is being tapped so that this one dream

May wax, flourish like a cabbage rose,

Defying sumptuary laws, leaving us

To awake and try to begin living in what

Has now become a slum. Sydney Freedberg in his

Parmigianino says of it: "Realism in this portrait

No longer produces an objective truth, but a *bizarria*...

However its distortion does not create

A feeling of disharmony.... The forms retain

让许诺的臆测一起留在一个表面上，

让一个人从它们那里漫步回家

以便那些更强的可能性能够

不被测试地完整保留。实际上

气泡室的皮肤坚韧得

像爬虫类的卵；每件事物在那里以正当的程序

被"程序化"：持续囊括进更多的

但总数并不增加，如同一个人

习惯了使他不眠而现在却失效了的噪音，

于是这房间包含了这种流动像一个沙漏

在气候或质量上没有变化

（除了也许冷冷地并几乎看不见地

发亮，尖锐地向死亡聚焦——以后

更是如此）。应该是这个梦的真空的东西

不断地变得充盈，因为众梦之源泉

被分流以便让这个梦

能够圆满，茂盛如百叶蔷薇，

抗拒禁奢令，让我们

醒过来并尝试在已变成贫民窟的一切中

开始生活。西德尼·弗瑞德伯格在他的

《帕米加尼诺》中谈到它："这幅肖像画中的现实性

不再产生一个客观真理，而是一种怪异……

然而它的变形没有造成

一种不和谐之感……形式保留了

A strong measure of ideal beauty," because
Fed by our dreams, so inconsequential until one day
We notice the hole they left. Now their importance
If not their meaning is plain. They were to nourish
A dream which includes them all, as they are
Finally reversed in the accumulating mirror.
They seemed strange because we couldn't actually see them.
And we realize this only at a point where they lapse
Like a wave breaking on a rock, giving up
Its shape in a gesture which expresses that shape.
The forms retain a strong measure of ideal beauty
As they forage in secret on our idea of distortion.
Why be unhappy with this arrangement, since
Dreams prolong us as they are absorbed?
Something like living occurs, a movement
Out of the dream into its codification.

As I start to forget it
It presents its stereotype again
But it is an unfamiliar stereotype, the face
Riding at anchor, issued from hazards, soon
To accost others, "rather angel than man" (Vasari).
Perhaps an angel looks like everything
We have forgotten, I mean forgotten

理想美的有力尺度,"因为
被我们的梦所喂养,如此无关紧要,直到有一天
我们注意到它们留下的洞。现在它们的重要性
显然不在于它们的意义。它们要去滋养
一个囊括它们全部的梦,当最终
它们在积聚着的镜子里被颠倒。
它们显得陌生因为我们实际上看不到它们。
我们只是在它们堕落的一个点上认识到这个
像一个波浪打碎在岩石上,
以表达那形式的姿式放弃它的形式。
形式保留了理想美的一个有力尺度
当它们秘密地搜寻我们有关变形的思想。
为什么要因这种安排而不快,既然
梦拖延我们而它们也被吸引?
某种像生命的东西出现,一个出自
梦的运动进入了它的法典编纂。

当我开始忘记它的时候
它再次表现出它的陈腐
可那是一种陌生的陈腐,面孔
起锚,脱出危险,很快
就去勾引他人,"与其是天使不如是人"(瓦萨利)。
也许天使看上去像我们遗忘的
任何东西,我指的遗忘的东西是

Things that don't seem familiar when

We meet them again, lost beyond telling

Which were ours once. This would be the point

Of invading the privacy of this man who

"Dabbled in alchemy, but whose wish

Here was not to examine the subtleties of art

In a detached, scientific spirit: he wished through them

To impart the sense of novelty and amazement to the spectator"

(Freedberg). Later portraits such as the Uffizi

"Gentleman," the Borghese "Young Prelate" and

The Naples "Antea" issue from Mannerist

Tensions, but here, as Freedberg points out,

The surprise, the tension are in the concept

Rather than its realization.

The consonance of the High Renaissance

Is present, though distorted by the mirror.

What is novel is the extreme care in rendering

The velleities of the rounded reflecting surface

(It is the first mirror portrait),

So that you could be fooled for a moment

Before you realize the reflection

Isn't yours. You feel then like one of those

Hoffmann characters who have been deprived

Of a reflection, except that the whole of me

我们再次遇见时显得

陌生的东西,无从讲述,

那曾经是我们的。这可能就是

侵入这个男人的隐私的关键

他"涉猎炼金术,可他此处的愿望

不是以一种超然的、科学的精神

去检验艺术的微妙;他希望透过它们

传达给观者新奇和愉悦的感觉"

(弗雷德伯格)。后来的肖像画比如

乌菲兹的"绅士",博格斯的"青年主教"

和那不勒斯的"安蒂"源自风格主义者的

张力,可是这里,正如弗雷德伯格所指,

惊奇,张力在于观念

而不在于它的实现。

文艺复兴盛期的和谐

得以表现,尽管被镜子变形了。

新奇的是,最终的用心在于如何表现

圆形反射面微弱的愿望

(它是最初的镜像)。

以至于你会被愚弄上片刻

在你认出这个影像

不是你的之前。于是你感觉就像

霍夫曼那些人物当中的一个,被剥夺了

影像,除了看见全部的我

Is seen to be supplanted by the strict
Otherness of the painter in his
Other room. We have surprised him
At work, but no, he has surprised us
As he works. The picture is almost finished,
The surprise almost over, as when one looks out,
Startled by a snowfall which even now is
Ending in specks and sparkles of snow.
It happened while you were inside, asleep,
And there is no reason why you should have
Been awake for it, except that the day
Is ending and it will be hard for you
To get to sleep tonight, at least until late.

The shadow of the city injects its own
Urgency: Rome where Francesco
Was at work during the Sack: his inventions
Amazed the soldiers who burst in on him;
They decided to spare his life, but he left soon after;
Vienna where the painting is today, where
I saw it with Pierre in the summer of 1959; New York
Where I am now, which is a logarithm
Of other cities. Our landscape
Is alive with filiations, shuttlings;
Business is carried on by look, gesture,

被另一个房间里的画家

用严格的他性取代。我们惊动了

工作中的他,不,在他工作时

他震惊了我们。画几乎要完成了,

惊奇也几乎过去了,仿佛一个人向外望去,

惊讶于一场甚至现在仍在

雪的星斑闪耀中结束着的降雪。

它发生时你在里面,正在睡着,

没有任何理由你该

为它醒着,除非白昼

在结束,它将使你

今夜难眠,至少会很晚。

城市的影子注满它自己的

紧急需要:罗马被洗劫时

弗朗西斯科正在那里工作,他的发明

让冲进来的士兵惊奇;

他们决定饶了他,但他后来很快离开了;

那幅画现今在维也纳,在那儿

一九五九年夏天我和皮埃尔一块看到了它;现在

我在纽约,它是其他城市的

对数。我们的风景

因血统和往返运动而充满活力;

用目光、手势、谣传

Hearsay. It is another life to the city,

The backing of the looking glass of the

Unidentified but precisely sketched studio. It wants

to siphon off the life of the studio, deflate

Its mapped space to enactments, island it.

That operation has been temporarily stalled

But something new is on the way, a new preciosity

In the wind. Can you stand it,

Francesco? Are you strong enough for it?

This wind brings what it knows not, is

Self-propelled, blind, has no notion

Of itself. It is inertia that once

Acknowledged saps all activity, secret or public:

Whispers of the word that can't be understood

But can be felt, a chili, a blight

Moving outward along the capes and peninsulas

Of your nervures and so to the archipelagoes

And to the bathed, aired secrecy of the open sea.

This is its negative side. Its positive side is

Making you notice life and the stresses

That only seemed to go away, but now,

As this new mode questions, are seen to be

Hastening out of style. If they are to become classics

They must decide which side they are on.

进行交易。对城市来说那是另一种生活，

未经确认但却精确描绘过的

画室的镜子背面。它要

用虹吸管吸走画室的生命，将它

绘制的空间缩减成条令，成为孤岛。

那操作暂时停顿

可有什么新东西正在路上，风中

一种新的矫揉造作。你能抗得住吗，

弗朗西斯科？对它你足够强大吗？

这风带来了它不了解的东西，

自我驱动，盲目，没有任何

自己的见解。是曾经承认的惯性

耗尽了所有的活动，或秘密或公开：

不能理解但能感觉的

词的低语，一阵寒意，一种枯萎

沿着你叶脉的海角和半岛

向外移，就这样去往群岛

直到开阔的海洋，那风吹日晒的秘密。

这是它消极的一面。它积极的一面

提醒你注意生活和那

似乎只是要离开的压力，可是现在，

就像这新方式的问题，被发现

匆匆走出风格。如果它们要变成经典

就必须决定自己站在哪一边。

Their reticence has undermined

The urban scenery, made its ambiguities

Look willful and tired, the games of an old man.

What we need now is this unlikely

Challenger pounding on the gates of an amazed

Castle. Your argument, Francesco,

Had begun to grow stale as no answer

Or answers were forthcoming. If it dissolves now

Into dust, that only means its time had come

Some time ago, but look now, and listen:

It may be that another life is stocked there

In recesses no one knew of; that it,

Not we, are the change; that we are in fact it

If we could get back to it, relive some of the way

It looked, turn our faces to the globe as it sets

And still be coming out all right:

Nerves normal, breath normal. Since it is a metaphor

Made to include us, we are a part of it and

Can live in it as in fact we have done,

Only leaving our minds bare for questioning

We now see will not take place at random

But in an orderly way that means to menace

Nobody—the normal way things are done,

Like the concentric growing up of days

它们的沉默已经逐渐损坏

都市的风景，使它的含混

显得任性而疲倦，一个老人的游戏。

我们现在需要的是这无希望的

挑战者砰砰敲打惊愕城堡的

大门。你的理由，弗朗西斯科，

已经开始变得过时，因为没有

现成的答案。如果它现在融为

尘土，那只意味着一段时间以前

它的时辰已到，可是现在你看，你听：

它可能是另一种生活存在那里

在无人知道的隐蔽之处；是它，

不是我们，在变化；我们实际上是它

如果我们能回到它，复活它的某种

观看方式，把我们的脸转向事先放置的

球体，并仍然一切完好：

神经正常，呼吸正常。既然它是一个隐喻

为包括我们而造，我们是它的一部分

并且能生活在里面就像我们实际做到的一样，

只把我们的思想赤裸地留给疑问

我们现在看见的不会随机发生

而是采取一种有序的方式，那意味着

不去威胁任何人——正常的处事方式，

就像日子围绕着一生

Around a life: correctly, if you think about it.

A breeze like the turning of a page

Brings back your face: the moment

Takes such a big bite out of the haze

Of pleasant intuition it comes after.

The locking into place is "death itself,"

As Berg said of a phrase in Mahler's Ninth;

Or, to quote Imogen in *Cymbeline*, "There cannot

Be a pinch in death more sharp than this," for,

Though only exercise or tactic, it carries

The momentum of a conviction that had been building.

Mere forgetfulness cannot remove it

Nor wishing bring it back, as long as it remains

The white precipitate of its dream

In the climate of sighs flung across our world,

A cloth over a birdcage. But it is certain that

What is beautiful seems so only in relation to a specific

Life, experienced or not, channeled into some form

Steeped in the nostalgia of a collective past.

The light sinks today with an enthusiasm

I have known elsewhere, and known why

It seemed meaningful, that others felt this way

Years ago. I go on consulting

同轴心的生长:如果你想的没错。

一阵微风像翻开一页书
把你的脸带回:这一刻
从随后出现的愉快的直觉的
薄雾中大大咬了一口。
锁在某处的是"死亡本身",
像贝格说起"马勒第九"中的一个乐句;
或者,引用《辛白林》中伊摩琴的话,"在死亡中
不可能有比这更锐利的一招了",因为,
尽管只是练习或策略,它携带着
业已确立的信仰的冲力。
仅靠健忘不能去除它
也没有希望带它回来,只要它留下
它梦的白色沉淀物
在飞越我们世界的叹息的气候中,
鸟笼上的一件衣服。可的确
那美的东西似乎仅仅与一种特殊的生活
相关联,无论是否经历过,导向某种形式
沉浸在对一个共同过往的怀旧中。
今天带着一种热爱沉落的光
我在别处已经认识了,并且知道为什么
它显得意味深长,许多年以前
其他人也有这样的感觉。我继续求教

This mirror that is no longer mine

For as much brisk vacancy as is to be

My portion this time. And the vase is always full

Because there is only just so much room

And it accommodates everything. The sample

One sees is not to be taken as

Merely that, but as everything as it

May be imagined outside time—not as a gesture

But as all, in the refined, assimilable state.

But what is this universe the porch of

As it veers in and out, back and forth,

Refusing to surround us and still the only

Thing we can see? Love once

Tipped the scales but now is shadowed, invisible,

Though mysteriously present, around somewhere.

But we know it cannot be sandwiched

Between two adjacent moments, that its windings

Lead nowhere except to further tributaries

And that these empty themselves into a vague

Sense of something that can never be known

Even though it seems likely that each of us

Knows what it is and is capable of

Communicating it to the other. But the look

Some wear as a sign makes one want to

这面已不再是我的镜子

因为这次和空虚一样轻快的

是成为我的一部分。花瓶总是满的

因为只有这么多空间

容纳了每一件事物。一个人

看见的样本不会仅仅被当作

样本，而是作为一切能在时间之外

被想象的事物——不是作为一个手势

而是作为全部，在净化过的、可同化的状态之中。

可是这门廊是什么样的宇宙

当它里里外外，前前后后地转来转去，

拒绝围绕我们却仍是

我们唯一能看见的东西？爱曾是

决定性因素可现在被遮蔽了，看不见了，

尽管奇迹般地存在于周围某处。

可是我们知道它不能夹入

两个相邻的时刻中间，它的蜿蜒曲折

除了更远的支流，不导向任何地方

这一切使它们自身变得空虚

模糊地感觉某种事物永远不能了解

即使我们每个人似乎都有可能

知道它是什么并能够

把它传达给别人。可某些人

作为信号的表情使人想要向前推进

Push forward ignoring the apparent

Naïveté of the attempt, not caring

That no one is listening, since the light

Has been lit once and for all in their eyes

And is present, unimpaired, a permanent anomaly,

Awake and silent. On the surface of it

There seems no special reason why that light

Should be focused by love, or why

The city falling with its beautiful suburbs

Into space always less clear, less defined,

Should read as the support of its progress,

The easel upon which the drama unfolded

To its own satisfaction and to the end

Of our dreaming, as we had never imagined

It would end, in worn daylight with the painted

Promise showing through as a gage, a bond.

This nondescript, never-to-be defined daytime is

The secret of where it takes place

And we can no longer return to the various

Conflicting statements gathered, lapses of memory

Of the principal witnesses. All we know

Is that we are a little early, that

Today has that special, lapidary

Todayness that the sunlight reproduces

忽略明显天真的企图，不在乎

没人倾听，既然光

已在他们眼中永远点燃

并且存在，没有变弱，一个永恒的特例，

苏醒而沉静。在它的表面上

似乎没有什么特殊的原因为什么

那光应该被爱聚焦，或者为什么

带着它美丽的郊区坠入宇宙的城市

始终不太清晰，不太分明，

应该读作它进步的支撑，

戏剧在上面展开的画架

为了它自己的满足，为了我们梦着的

终结，因为我们从未想象到

它会终结，在磨损的日光中随画出的许诺

作为一个抵押物，一个契约展出。

这难以归类，永不能定义的白昼时光

是它在何处发生的秘密

我们再不能返回那种种

聚到一起的矛盾陈述，主要目击者的

记忆差错。我们知道的全部

是我们早了一点，今天

有着特殊的，确凿的今天性，

它以阳光投射在漫不经心的

人行道上的细细树影忠实地复制而出。

Faithfully in casting twig-shadows on blithe

Sidewalks. No previous day would have been like this.

I used to think they were all alike,

That the present always looked the same to everybody

But this confusion drains away as one

Is always cresting into one's present.

Yet the "poetic," straw-colored space

Of the long corridor that leads back to the painting,

Its darkening opposite—is this

Some figment of "art," not to be imagined

As real, let alone special? Hasn't it too its lair

In the present we are always escaping from

And falling back into, as the waterwheel of days

Pursues its uneventful, even serene course?

I think it is trying to say it is today

And we must get out of it even as the public

Is pushing through the museum now so as to

Be out by closing time. You can't live there.

The gray glaze of the past attacks all know-how:

Secrets of wash and finish that took a lifetime

To learn and are reduced to the status of

Black-and-white illustrations in a book where colorplates

Are rare. That is, all time

Reduces to no special time. No one

没有任何以往的日子会与此相似。
我曾经认为它们全都是相似的，
现在对每个人看来都是一样的
可是这混乱正在排干，因为每个人
总是会登顶，到达自己的现在。
这"诗意的"，返回绘画的
漫长走廊的稻草色空间，
它黑下来的背面——就是
"艺术"的某种虚构，不可被想象成
真实，更不必说特殊？它也没有自己的巢穴吗
在我们总是从中逃离又不断
跌回的现在，当日子的水轮
追逐着它常规，甚至平静的过程？
我认为它在试图说它就是今天
而我们必须摆脱它就像公众
现在正挤过博物馆为了
在闭馆时出去。你不能在那里生活。
过去的灰釉袭击所有的技巧：
需要一生去学习刷洗和完成的秘密
被降到一本彩版寥寥的书里
黑白插图的地位。亦即，所有时间
简化为毫无特殊性的时间。无人
提及变化，这样做可能会
将注意力引向自身

Alludes to the change; to do so might

Involve calling attention to oneself

Which would augment the dread of not getting out

Before having seen the whole collection

(Except for the sculptures in the basement:

They are where they belong).

Our time gets to be veiled, compromised

By the portrait's will to endure. It hints at

Our own, which we were hoping to keep hidden.

We don't need paintings or

Doggerel written by mature poets when

The explosion is so precise, so fine.

Is there any point even in acknowledging

The existence of all that? Does it

Exist? Certainly the leisure to

Indulge stately pastimes doesn't,

Any more. Today has no margins, the event arrives

Flush with its edges, is of the same substance,

Indistinguishable. "Play" is something else;

It exists, in a society specifically

Organized as a demonstration of itself.

There is no other way, and those assholes

Who would confuse everything with their mirror games

Which seem to multiply stakes and possibilities, or

会在见到全部收藏品之前

增加摆脱不了的恐惧

(地下室中的雕塑除外:

它们在它们的所属之处)。

我们的时间被遮上面纱,

被这肖像画想要忍受的愿望所牵累。它暗示

我们自己的,我们希望隐藏的愿望。

我们不需要绘画或者

成年诗人写的打油诗

当爆破是如此精确,如此成功。

有意义吗,即便承认

那一切的存在?它

存在吗?当然,那堂皇地

纵情娱乐的闲暇,

再也没有了。今天没有边缘,事件到达

和它的边缘齐平,是同样的物质,

不能分辨。"游戏"是另外一回事;

它,在一个经过特殊组织的社会中

作为它自己的一个演示而存在。

没有任何其他的办法,那些蠢驴

用他们的镜子游戏弄混了一切

似乎是要增加赌注和可能性,或至少

以一种会腐蚀全部建筑的

投资气氛来混淆问题

At least confuse issues by means of an investing
Aura that would corrode the architecture
Of the whole in a haze of suppressed mockery,
Are beside the point. They are out of the game,
Which doesn't exist until they are out of it.
It seems like a very hostile universe
But as the principle of each individual thing is
Hostile to, exists at the expense of all the others
As philosophers have often pointed out, at least
This thing, the mute, undivided present,
Has the justification of logic, which
In this instance isn't a bad thing
Or wouldn't be, if the way of telling
Didn't somehow intrude, twisting the end result
Into a caricature of itself. This always
Happens, as in the game where
A whispered phrase passed around the room
Ends up as something completely different.
It is the principle that makes works of art so unlike
What the artist intended. Often he finds
He has omitted the thing he started out to say
In the first place. Seduced by flowers,
Explicit pleasures, he blames himself (though
Secretly satisfied with the result), imagining

在一阵压抑的嘲笑的薄雾中
他们离题了。他们出局了,
这游戏直到他们出局才存在。
它像一个怀有强烈敌意的宇宙
可正如每一单独物的原则
都怀有敌意,以所有他者为代价来存在
就像哲学家们经常指出的,至少
这个东西,这哑巴,混沌未分的现在,
拥有逻辑的理由,
在这种情况下不是件坏事
或者不应该是,如果讲述的方式
不知怎么强行侵入,将最后的结果拧成
它自己的一幅漫画。这经常
发生,就像在游戏中
一个低声说出的短语传过房间各处
作为某种完全不同的东西结束了。
就是这原理使得艺术品如此不同于
艺术家设想的模样。他经常发现
在最初的地方,他就已经忽略了
他开始时要说的东西。被花引诱,
明显的乐趣,他责备自己(尽管
对结果感到隐秘的满足),想象着
他在这件事上有着发言权并实践了
一次他简直没有意识到的选择

He had a say in the matter and exercised

An option of which he was hardly conscious,

Unaware that necessity circumvents such resolutions

So as to create something new

For itself, that there is no other way,

That the history of creation proceeds according to

Stringent laws, and that things

Do get done in this way, but never the things

We set out to accomplish and wanted so desperately

To see come into being. Parmigianino

Must have realized this as he worked at his

Life-obstructing task. One is forced to read

The perfectly plausible accomplishment of a purpose

Into the smooth, perhaps even bland (but so

Enigmatic) finish. Is there anything

To be serious about beyond this otherness

That gets included in the most ordinary

Forms of daily activity, changing everything

Slightly and profoundly, and tearing the matter

Of creation, any creation, not just artistic creation

Out of our hands, to install it on some monstrous, near

Peak, too close to ignore, too far

For one to intervene? This otherness, this

"Not-being-us" is all there is to look at

没有注意那必然性阻碍了结果的实现。
于是，为了给它自己创造某种
新东西，没有任何其他方法，
创造的历史遵照严峻的规律
发展，而事物
确实是以这种方式完成，可是
我们开始去完成并亟待看见的事物
却从未出现。帕米加尼诺
一定已经认识到了这点，当他埋头于
他妨碍生命的工作时。一个人被迫
将一个计划完全合乎情理的完成
读成平淡，甚或乏味的（但如此
令人迷惑）结局。除了这种他性
还有什么需要认真考虑
它包括在日常活动
最普通的形式中，轻微而深刻地
改变着一切，从我们手中
撕去创造物，任何创造，不只是
艺术的创造，把它安置在附近
某座很高的山峰上，近得不能忽略，又远得
无法使人干预？这种他性
这"不存在的我们"是要在镜中看见的
一切，尽管没有人能够说出
它是如何变成这样的。一艘船

In the mirror, though no one can say

How it came to be this way. A ship

Flying unknown colors has entered the harbor.

You are allowing extraneous matters

To break up your day, cloud the focus

Of the crystal ball. Its scene drifts away

Like vapor scattered on the wind. The fertile

Thought-associations that until now came

So easily, appear no more, or rarely. Their

Colorings are less intense, washed out

By autumn rains and winds, spoiled, muddied,

Given back to you because they are worthless.

Yet we are such creatures of habit that their

Implications are still around *en permanence*, confusing

Issues. To be serious only about sex

Is perhaps one way, but the sands are hissing

As they approach the beginning of the big slide

Into what happened. This past

Is now here: the painter's

Reflected face, in which we linger, receiving

Dreams and inspirations on an unassigned

Frequency, but the hues have turned metallic,

The curves, and edges are not so rich. Each person

Has one big theory to explain the universe

But it doesn't tell the whole story

飞舞着不明国籍的旗帜进入港口。

你允许与本题无关的事情

打碎你的日子，用云遮住

水晶球的焦点。它的风景飘走了

像烟雾被风驱散。丰富的

直到现在仍这么容易出现的

思想的结合，不再出现，或很少出现。

它们不再强烈的色调，被秋天的

风雨冲淡，损坏，沾上了泥，

还给你，因为已经毫无价值。

我们依然是这种习性的生物

他们的暗示依然伴随左右，混淆着

问题。只严肃地对待性

也许是个办法，可是沙子在嘶嘶作响

当它们接近那大滑坡的开始

进入发生的一切。这个过去

现在在这儿：画家

反射的面孔，我们在其中徘徊，接收着

梦和灵感，以一个未指定的

频率，可色调已变成金属一般，

曲线和边缘已不是那么丰富。每一个人

都有一套大理论来解释宇宙

可是它说不出整个故事

到最后是他之外的东西

And in the end it is what is outside him

That matters, to him and especially to us

Who have been given no help whatever

In decoding our own man-size quotient and must rely

On second-hand knowledge. Yet I know

That no one else's taste is going to be

Any help, and might as well be ignored.

Once it seemed so perfect—gloss on the fine

Freckled skin, lips moistened as though about to part

Releasing speech, and the familiar look

Of clothes and furniture that one forgets.

This could have been our paradise: exotic

Refuge within an exhausted world, but that wasn't

In the cards, because it couldn't have been

The point. Aping naturalness may be the first step

Toward achieving an inner calm

But it is the first step only, and often

Remains a frozen gesture of welcome etched

On the air materializing behind it,

A convention. And we have really

No time for these, except to use them

For kindling. The sooner they are burnt up

The better for the roles we have to play.

Therefore I beseech you, withdraw that hand,

Offer it no longer as shield or greeting,

The shield of a greeting, Francesco:

才举足轻重，对于他尤其对于
在译解我们自己真人大小的商数时
一直没有得到任何帮助而必须
依赖于二手知识的我们。我还知道
没有任何一个人的口味
可以有所助益，同样也应该忽略。
它曾经显得如此完美——有雀斑的
细腻皮肤上的光泽，湿润的嘴唇仿佛要
发表演说，熟悉的衣服式样
和一个人忘记了的家具。
这可能一直是我们的乐园：
一个耗尽了的世界中的外来避难所，
可那不是命中注定，因为它不可能是
关键。模仿自然可能是
通向内在平静的第一步
可它仅仅只是第一步，并且总是
留下一个刻板的欢迎的手势
蚀刻在它后面实体化的空气上，
一个惯例。而我们真的
没有为这些准备的时间，除了将它们
用做引火物。它们烧得越快
对我们扮演的角色就越有好处。
因此我恳求你，收回那只手，
别再为了防卫或欢迎伸出它来，
一个欢迎的防卫，弗朗西斯科：

There is room for one bullet in the chamber:
Our looking through the wrong end
Of the telescope as you fall back at a speed
Faster than that of light to flatten ultimately
Among the features of the room, an invitation
Never mailed, the "it was all a dream"
Syndrome, though the "all" tells tersely
Enough how it wasn't. Its existence
Was real, though troubled, and the ache
Of this waking dream can never drown out
The diagram still sketched on the wind,
Chosen, meant for me and materialized
In the disguising radiance of my room.
We have seen the city; it is the gibbous
Mirrored eye of an insect. All things happen
On its balcony and are resumed within,
But the action is the cold, syrupy flow
Of a pageant. One feels too confined,
Sifting the April sunlight for clues,
In the mere stillness of the ease of its
Parameter. The hand holds no chalk
And each part of the whole falls off
And cannot know it knew, except
Here and there, in cold pockets
Of remembrance, whispers out of time.

室内有给一颗子弹的空间：
我们从望远镜颠倒的一端
望出去，当你以超光速的速度
坠回来，最后在房间的特点中
变得扁平，一个从未寄出的
邀请，"它完全是一个梦"
虽然这"完全"足够简洁地
说明它如何不是并发症。它的存在
曾是真实的，尽管受到了打扰，
而这梦醒的疼痛永不能淹没
依然勾画在风上的图表
被选择，对我富有意味
并在我房间伪装的闪烁中具体化。
我们已看见这城市；它是一只昆虫
圆凸如镜的眼睛。一切都在
它的阳台上发生并在里面得到恢复，
可是这行动是寒冷的，一次游行
糖浆似的流动。一个人感到过于局限，
为寻找线索而过滤四月的阳光，
在它决定性因素仅有的
安逸的静止中。手里不握粉笔
整体的每一部分都在脱落
且无法知道它已知道，除了
这里和那里，在记忆
寒冷的口袋里，在时间之外低语。

From
HOUSEBOAT DAYS
船屋的日子
(1977)

Street Musicians

One died, and the soul was wrenched out

Of the other in life, who, walking the streets

Wrapped in an identity like a coat, sees on and on

The same corners, volumetrics, shadows

Under trees. Farther than anyone was ever

Called, through increasingly suburban airs

And ways, with autumn falling over everything:

The plush leaves the chattels in barrels

Of an obscure family being evicted

Into the way it was, and is. The other beached

Glimpses of what the other was up to:

Revelations at last. So they grew to hate and forget each other.

So I cradle this average violin that knows

Only forgotten showtunes, but argues

The possibility of free declamation anchored

To a dull refrain, the year turning over on itself

In November, with the spaces among the days

More literal, the meat more visible on the bone.

Our question of a place of origin hangs

Like smoke: how we picnicked in pine forests,

街头音乐家

一个死了,另一个活着

灵魂被拽走,行走在街道上

像外衣裹着一个身份,继续不停地看见

同样的角落,容量计,树下的

阴影。被唤向比任何人都远的

地方,穿过日益增长的郊区的风气

和道路,秋天落在万物之上:

豪华的落叶,成桶的杂物

属于一个无名的家庭,被逼成

过去和现在的模样。一个身无分文

瞧着另一个要干什么:

终于露了馅。于是他们彼此憎恨,又互相遗忘。

所以,我轻柔地抱着这只普通的提琴

它只知道那些已被遗忘的流行曲调,

但坚持认为,它可以自如地演绎

一段沉闷的叠句,一年交出自身

在十一月,日子之间的空隙

更实在了,骨头上的肉更明显。

我们关于起源之处的问题

像烟雾悬挂:我们如何在松林里野餐,

In coves with the water always seeping up, and left

Our trash, sperm and excrement everywhere, smeared

On the landscape, to make of us what we could.

洞里一直在渗水,到处留下
我们的垃圾、精液和粪便,弄脏了
风景,使我们成为可能的样子。

The Other Tradition

They all came, some wore sentiments

Emblazoned on T-shirts, proclaiming the lateness

Of the hour, and indeed the sun slanted its rays

Through branches of Norfolk Island pine as though

Politely clearing its throat, and all ideas settled

In a fuzz of dust under trees when it's drizzling:

The endless games of Scrabble, the boosters,

The celebrated omelette au Cantal, and through it

The roar of time plunging unchecked through the sluices

Of the days, dragging every sexual moment of it

Past the lenses: the end of something.

Only then did you glance up from your book,

Unable to comprehend what had been taking place, or

Say what you had been reading. More chairs

Were brought, and lamps were lit, but it tells

Nothing of how all this proceeded to materialize

Before you and the people waiting outside and in the next

Street, repeating its name over and over, until silence

Moved halfway up the darkened trunks,

And the meeting was called to order.

                                          I still remember

另外的传统

他们都来了,有的带着温情
T恤上装饰着纹章,宣布时辰
已晚;阳光的确已经倾斜
穿过诺福克岛的松枝,仿佛
在优雅地清理喉咙,所有思想都安顿在
树下绒毛般的灰尘中,当下起毛毛细雨:
无止尽的拼字游戏,啦啦队,
著名的坎特尔煎蛋卷,通过它
时间的轰鸣不羁地跃入日子的
水闸,拖曳它每一个性感的时刻
经过镜头;某个事物的终结。
那时你才从书中抬头向上一瞥,
弄不懂正在发生什么,或者
说出你正在读什么。更多的椅子
搬来了,灯火点燃,可这说明不了
一切是如何发生的,在你和等待在
外面的人面前成为现实,在下一条
街上,一遍遍重复它的名字,直到寂静
半路上把发黑的运动短裤往上挪,
并召集了会议发号施令。
　　　　　我还记得

How they found you, after a dream, in your thimble hat,
Studious as a butterfly in a parking lot.
The road home was nicer then. Dispersing, each of the
Troubadours had something to say about how charity
Had run its race and won, leaving you the ex-president
Of the event, and how, though many of those present
Had wished something to come of it, if only a distant
Wisp of smoke, yet none was so deceived as to hanker
After that cool non-being of just a few minutes before,
Now that the idea of a forest had clamped itself
Over the minutiae of the scene. You found this
Charming, but turned your face fully toward night,
Speaking into it like a megaphone, not hearing
Or caring, although these still live and are generous
And all ways contained, allowed to come and go
Indefinitely in and out of the stockade
They have so much trouble remembering, when your forgetting
Rescues them at last, as a star absorbs the night.

他们如何找到你,在一场梦后,戴着你的顶针,
像停车场上的一只蝴蝶那样专心。
回家的路从此更顺了。行吟诗人各自散开,
每个都有事情要讲,关于慈善团体
如何跑完了比赛,获胜了,把前任总统的事件
留给你,如何如何,尽管现在有许多人
希望出点事儿,哪怕只是一阵
遥远的烟雾,但也没有人上当
追求那几分钟前的寒冷的非存在,
既然一片树林的思想自行强加在
风景的细节上。你发现
这很迷人,但你把脸彻底转向夜晚,
像对着一个扩音器说话,既听不见
也不关心,这一切依然生动而慷慨
囊括了所有道路,允许自由来去
无限期地从栅栏进进出出
他们的记忆有这么多的麻烦,你的遗忘
最终拯救了他们,像一颗星星吸收着夜晚。

Variant

Sometimes a word will start it, like

Hands and feet, sun and gloves. The way

Is fraught with danger, you say, and I

Notice the word "fraught" as you are telling

Me about huge secret valleys some distance from

The mired fighting—"but always, lightly wooded

As they are, more deeply involved with the outcome

That will someday paste a black, bleeding label

In the sky, but until then

The echo, flowing freely in corridors, alleys,

And tame, surprised places far from anywhere,

Will be automatically locked out— *vox*

Clamans—do you see? End of tomorrow.

Don't try to start the car or look deeper

Into the eternal wimpling of the sky: luster

On luster, transparency floated onto the topmost layer

Until the whole thing overflows like a silver

Wedding cake or Christmas tree, in a cascade of tears."

变　量

有时一个词就能启动它，就像

手和脚，太阳和手套。道路

充满了危险，你说，而我

注意到"充满"这个词，当你向我说起

离鏖战之处有一定距离的

巨大的秘密峡谷——"但树木始终稀少

像现在一样，更深地关系到结果

终有一天会把一个黑色的、流血的标签

贴在天空上，但在那之前

回声，在远离任何地方的走廊、小巷

和顺从而出乎意料的所在，自由流淌，

它会自动关闭——喧嚷声

你看见了吗？明天的终结。

不要试图启动汽车，或是更深地

注视天空的永恒涟漪：光彩重叠，

透明漂浮在最上一层

直到整件事情溢出，像一个银婚蛋糕，

或者圣诞树，在眼泪的小瀑布中。"

Wooden Buildings

The tests are good. You need a million of them.

You'd die laughing as I write to you

Through leaves and articulations, yes, laughing

Myself silly too. The funniest little thing...

That's how it all began. Looking back on it,

I wonder now if it could have been on some day

Findable in an old calendar? But no,

It wasn't out of history, but inside it.

That's the thing. On whatever day we came

To a small house built just above the water,

You had to stoop over to see inside the attic window.

Someone had judged the height to be just right

The way the light came in, and they are

Giving that party, to turn on that dishwasher

And we may be led, then, upward through more

Powerful forms of poetry, past columns

With peeling posters on them, to the country of indifference.

Meanwhile if the swell diapasons, blooms

Unhappily and too soon, the little people are nonetheless real.

木　楼

那些测试不错。你需要测一百万次。
你会笑死，因为我写信给你
通过树叶和关节，是的，笑我自己
也一样蠢。最可笑的小事情……

一切就是那样开始的。回头看看，
我现在奇怪是否有一天
能在旧日历中找到它？但是不，
它没有超越历史，而是在历史里面。
事情就是那样。无论哪天我们
去建在水上的一座小房子那里，
你都得弯腰才能看见阁楼窗户里面。
有人判断房子的高度刚好
能让阳光透进来，他们正在
开派对，要打开那台洗碗机
那时，我们会被领着，向上穿过更多
强有力的诗歌形式，经过一根根圆柱
上面有剥落的海报，来到冷漠的国度。
这时，如果膨胀的和音，不幸地
过早激增，不过那些小人倒是真的。

Pyrography

Out here on Cottage Grove it matters. The galloping

Wind balks at its shadow. The carriages

Are drawn forward under a sky of fumed oak.

This is America calling:

The mirroring of state to state,

Of voice to voice on the wires,

The force of colloquial greetings like golden

Pollen sinking on the afternoon breeze.

In service stairs the sweet corruption thrives;

The page of dusk turns like a creaking revolving stage in Warren, Ohio.

If this is the way it is let's leave,

They agree, and soon the slow boxcar journey begins,

Gradually accelerating until the gyrating fans of suburbs

Enfolding the darkness of cities are remembered

Only as a recurring tic. And midway

We meet the disappointed, returning ones, without its

Being able to stop us in the headlong night

Toward the nothing of the coast. At Bolinas

The houses doze and seem to wonder why through the

Pacific haze, and the dreams alternately glow and grow dull.

烙　画

在外面这里的"茅屋树丛"它很重要。
奔驰的风回避着它的影子。马车
在冒烟橡树的天空下被拖向前方。
这是美国在呼唤：
州和州在互相反射，
线路上的声音和声音，
口头欢迎的力量像金色的花粉
随着午后的微风下沉。
旁门楼梯上甜蜜的腐败旺盛发达；
黄昏的书页翻动如同俄亥俄的沃伦嘎吱作响的旋梯。

如果它就这样让我们离开，
他们同意，乘货车的缓慢旅行很快开始，
逐渐加速，直到郊区不停旋转的扇子
展开众城的黑暗，在记忆中
只是一次复发的痉挛。中途
我们遇见了失望而返的人们，
无法组织我们在轻率的夜晚
奔向海岸的虚无。在波利纳斯
房屋在打瞌睡，似乎在奇怪为什么
透过太平洋的薄雾，梦境交替闪亮并变得沉闷。

Why be hanging on here? Like kites, circling,

Slipping on a ramp of air, but always circling?

But the variable cloudiness is pouring it on,

Flooding back to you like the meaning of a joke.

The land wasn't immediately appealing; we built it

Partly over with fake ruins, in the image of ourselves:

An arch that terminates in mid-keystone, a crumbling stone pier

For laundresses, an open-air theater, never completed

And only partially designed. How are we to inhabit

This space from which the fourth wall is invariably missing,

As in a stage-set or dollhouse, except by staying as we are,

In lost profile, facing the stars, with dozens of as yet

Unrealized projects, and a strict sense

Of time running out, of evening presenting

The tactfully folded-over bill? And we fit

Rather too easily into it, become transparent,

Almost ghosts. One day

The birds and animals in the pasture have absorbed

The color, the density of the surroundings,

The leaves are alive, and too heavy with life.

A long period of adjustment followed.

In the cities at the turn of the century they knew about it

为什么要在此逗留?像风筝,盘旋着,
在空气的斜坡上滑动,始终在盘旋?

但是变幻的云彩倾泻在它上面,
向你涌回来,仿佛一个玩笑的含意。
陆地并不直接呼吁;我们把它部分地
建在伪装的废墟上,我们自己的形象中:
一个在拱心石中间到头了的拱形,一个适合洗衣女工的
崩塌的石墩,一个露天剧场,始终没有完成
并且只设计了一部分。我们如何继承
这个空间,它总是缺少第四堵墙,
就像舞台背景或玩具屋,除了继续逗留
在丢失的轮廓中,面对群星,带着几十个
尚未实现的计划,和一种严酷的感觉
时间即将耗尽,黄昏正拿出一张
得体地折叠起来的账单?我们
很容易就适应了它,变得透明,
几乎成了幽灵。有一天
草原上的鸟群和动物吸收了
色彩,周围事物的密度,
树叶还活着,因生命而过于沉重。

随后是长时间的调整。
在世纪之交的城市,他们了解它的情况

But were careful not to let on as the iceman and the milkman

Disappeared down the block and the postman shouted

His daily rounds. The children under the trees knew it

But all the fathers returning home

On streetcars after a satisfying day at the office undid it:

The climate was still floral and all the wallpaper

In a million homes all over the land conspired to hide it.

One day we thought of painted furniture, of how

It just slightly changes everything in the room

And in the yard outside, and how, if we were going

To be able to write the history of our time, starting with today,

It would be necessary to model all these unimportant details

So as to be able to include them; otherwise the narrative

Would have that flat, sandpapered look the sky gets

Out in the middle west toward the end of summer,

The look of wanting to back out before the argument

Has been resolved, and at the same time to save appearances

So that tomorrow will be pure. Therefore, since we have to do our business

In spite of things, why not make it in spite of everything?

That way, maybe the feeble lakes and swamps

Of the back country will get plugged into the circuit

And not just the major events but the whole incredible

Mass of everything happening simultaneously and pairing off,

Channeling itself into history, will unroll

但却小心地不去泄露,当送冰人和送奶人

消失在街区中,当邮差按惯例

每天喊圈。树下的儿童知道它

但是在办公室度过满足的一天后

所有乘街车回家的父亲都不管它:

天气仍然像花一样,整片大陆

一百万户人家的墙纸都合谋要藏起它。

有一天我们想起油漆过的家具,

它怎样微微改变着房间中

和院子里的一切,如果我们

能够写下我们时代的历史,从今天开始,

模仿所有这些琐碎的细节有多么必要

以便能够包括它们;否则这叙述

就会拥有接近夏末的中西部天空的

那种平坦的、砂纸般的表情,

在争论解决以前想要退出

同时还想保全面子的表情

这样明天就是清白的了。所以,既然我们必须继续

无论发生什么,为何不抛开一切?

那条路,也许偏僻乡村

无力的湖泊和沼泽,将被插入电路

不只是主要事件,而是难以置信的

所有事件,同时发生,成双成对,

把自己导入历史,将会展开

As carefully and as casually as a conversation in the next room,

And the purity of today will invest us like a breeze,

Only be hard, spare, ironical: something one can

Tip one's hat to and still get some use out of.

The parade is turning into our street.

My stars, the burnished uniforms and prismatic

Features of this instant belong here. The land

Is pulling away from the magic, glittering coastal towns

To an aforementioned rendezvous with August and December.

The hunch is it will always be this way,

The look, the way things first scared you

In the night light, and later turned out to be,

Yet still capable, all the same, of a narrow fidelity

To what you and they wanted to become:

No sighs like Russian music, only a vast unravelling

Out toward the junctions and to the darkness beyond

To these bare fields, built at today's expense.

小心而随意，像隔壁房间的一场谈话，
今天的纯净将像一阵微风包围我们，
只是坚硬，多余，充满讽刺：某种仍能
对之脱帽和加以利用的东西。

游行队伍转进我们这条街了。
我的星星，擦亮的制服和这一刻
五光十色的特征属于这里。陆地
脱离神奇、闪光的沿岸城镇
撤向上述八月和十二月的汇合之地。
预感将始终是这个样子，
表情，夜晚的光中
事物起初让你害怕的习惯，后来证明，
对于你和他们想要变成的东西
是依然胜任的一种狭隘的忠诚：
没有俄罗斯音乐似的叹息，只有广阔的空虚
向汇合处敞开，漫向黑暗之外
漫向这些光秃的田野，以今天的代价确立。

The Gazing Grain

The tires slowly came to a rubbery stop.

Alliterative festoons in the sky noted

That this branchy birthplace of presidents was also

The big frigidaire-cum-cowbarn where mendicant

And margrave alike waited out the results

Of the natural elections. So any openness of song

Was the plainer way. O take me to the banks

Of your Mississippi over there, etc. Like a plant

Rooted in parched earth I am

A stranger myself in the dramatic lighting,

The result of war. That which is given to see

At any moment is the residue, shadowed

In gold or emerging into the clear bluish haze

Of uncertainty. We come back to ourselves

Through the rubbish of cloud and tree-spattered pavement.

These days stand like vapor under the trees.

注目的谷物

轮胎缓慢地滚向一个橡皮止挡。
头韵般的花彩在天空中注意到
总统们这个枝繁叶茂的出生地
也是有大冰箱的牛棚,在那里

乞丐和侯爵同样在等待
自然选择的结果。所以,歌曲的率真
在于更为朴实的方式。啊,带我去到
你密西西比的河岸,等等。像一棵植物

扎根在干透的大地上,我本身
是舞台灯光中的一个陌生人,
战争的结果。任何时候
只让我们看见残渣,遮掩在金色中

或是融进不确定性那清澈发蓝的
薄雾。我们返回自身
穿过云彩的垃圾和树木点缀的人行道。
这些日子如同蒸汽立在树下。

Unctuous Platitudes

There is no reason for the surcharge to bother you.
Living in a city one is nonplussed by some

Of the inhabitants. The weather has grown gray with age.
Poltergeists go about their business, sometimes

Demanding a sweeping revision. The breath of the air
Is invisible. People stay

Next to the edges of fields, hoping that out of nothing
Something will come, and it does, but what? Embers

Of the rain tamp down the shitty darkness that issues
From nowhere. A man in her room, you say.

I like the really wonderful way you express things
So that it might be said, that of all the ways in which to

Emphasize a posture or a particular mental climate
Like this gray-violet one with a thin white irregular line

虚情假意的陈词滥调

没有理由让这超载来打扰你。
住在一个城市里,一些居民

让你为难。天气随着年龄变灰。
吵闹鬼继续捣乱,有时

需要一次彻底的修正。风
是无形的。人们停留在

田野边上,盼望从虚无中
出现点什么,出现了,可它是什么?

雨的灰烬夯实倒霉的不知来自何处的
黑暗。一个男人在她的房间里,你说。

我喜欢你表达事情的的确奇妙的方式
以至于可以说,所有的方式

都强调一个姿势或特殊的精神气候
像灰紫色的这个,有一道不规则的白色细线

Descending the two vertical sides, these are those which

Can also unsay an infinite number of pauses

In the ceramic day. Every invitation

To every stranger is met at the station.

降下垂直的两侧,这些
也能取消一个无穷大的停顿

在陶制的日子。对于陌生人
每一次邀请都是在车站会面。

The Couple in the Next Room

She liked the blue drapes. They made a star

At the angle. A boy in leather moved in.

Later they found names from the turn of the century

Coming home one evening. The whole of being

Unknown absorbed into the stalk. A free

Bride on the rails warning to notice other

Hers and the great graves that outwore them

Like faces on a building, the lightning rod

Of a name calibrated all their musing differences.

Another day. Deliberations are recessed

In an iron-blue chamber of that afternoon

On which we wore things and looked well at

A slab of business rising behind the stars.

隔壁的夫妻

她喜欢蓝窗帘。他们在一角
做了颗星星。一个穿皮衣的男孩搬进来。
后来他们发现来自世纪之交的一些名字
有天傍晚回家了。整件事
默默无闻地吸到茎秆里。一个免费新娘
在铁轨上警告人们注意她其他的
东西和比她们耐久的大坟墓
像一座建筑上的面孔,一个名字的避雷针
调整所有她们正在沉思的差别。

另一天。协商暂停了
在下午的一个钢蓝色房间
我们穿戴东西,好好看着
一桩买卖在群星后升起。

Business Personals

The disquieting muses again: what are "leftovers"?

Perhaps they have names for it all, who come bearing

Worn signs of privilege whose authority

Speaks out of the accumulation of age and faded colors

To the center of today. Floating heart, why

Wander on senselessly? The tall guardians

Of yesterday are steep as cliff shadows;

Whatever path you take abounds in their sense.

All presently lead downward, to the harbor view.

Therefore do your knees need to be made strong, by running.

We have places for the training and a special on equipment:

Knee-pads, balancing poles and the rest. It works

In the sense of aging: you come out always a little ahead

And not so far as to lose a sense of the crowd

Of disciples. That were tyranny,

Outrage, hubris. Meanwhile this tent is silence

Itself. Its walls are opaque, so as not to see

The road; a pleasant, half-heard melody climbs to its ceiling—

Not peace, but rest the doctor ordered. Tomorrow. . .

And songs climb out of the flames of the near campfires,

商业人事广告

令人不安的缪斯们又问：何谓"残留物"？
也许她们为它命名了，她们带着
磨损的特权标志，其权威性
来自岁月的累积和消褪的色彩
来到今天的中心。漂浮的心，为何
无意识地漫游？昨天高大的警卫
陡峭得如同悬崖的阴影；
你选择的任何道路都充满她们的感觉。
现在全都向下，通往港口的风景。

所以，你的双膝需要通过奔跑来强化。
我们有训练场所和一种特殊设备：
护膝，平衡杆及其他。它有助于
衰老：你总是提前一点出来
还不至于对拥挤的门徒失去
感觉。那曾是暴政，
侮辱，傲慢。此时这顶帐篷便是寂静
本身。篷壁不透明，这样就看不见
路了；一支愉快、隐约的旋律攀向篷顶——
不是和平，而是约好的医生休息了。明天……
歌曲从附近的篝火中爬出来，

Pale, pastel things exquisite in their frailness
With a note or two to indicate it isn't lost,
On them at least. The songs decorate our notion of the world
And mark its limits, like a frieze of soap-bubbles.

What caused us to start caring?
In the beginning was only sedge, a field of water
Wrinkled by the wind. Slowly
The trees increased the novelty of always being alone,
The rest began to be sketched in, and then... silence,
Or blankness, for a number of years. Could one return
To the idea of nature summed up ill these pastoral images?
Yet the present has done its work of building
A rampart against the past, not a rampart,
A barbed-wire fence. So now we know
What occupations to stick to (scrimshaw, spinning tall tales)
By the way the songs deepen the color of the shadow
Impregnating your hobby as you bend over it,
Squinting. I could make a list
Of each one of my possessions and the direction it
Pointed in, how much each thing cost, how much for wood, string,
    colored ink, etc.

The song makes no mention of directions.
At most it twists the longitude lines overhead

苍白柔和的东西因脆弱而精美
用一两个便条表明这优美没有失去,
至少还在。歌曲装饰我们的世界观
标出其界限,像一条肥皂泡组成的饰带。

是什么促使我们关心起来?
一开始只是莎草,一片水域
被风吹皱。慢慢地
树木因为一直孤独而变得新奇,
其他的开始被勾勒下来,然后是……寂静,
或者是茫然,持续了很多年。一个人能够返回
累积在这些田园意象中的自然的理念吗?
不过,现在已经完成了它的工作
建造了一座对抗过去的壁垒,不是壁垒,
是一座铁丝网栅栏。于是我们现在知道
要坚持什么样的消遣(解闷的手工活,编织荒诞故事)
顺便说一下,歌曲加深了阴影的颜色
培养你的嗜好,当你俯身其上,
眯着眼看。我可以列个清单
所有令我着迷的东西及其所指的方向,
每件东西有多贵,需要多少木头,绳子,彩色墨水等等。

歌曲没有提到任何方向。
它顶多在头顶上编织经线

Like twigs to form a crude shelter. (The ship
Hasn't arrived, it was only a dream. It's somewhere near
Cape Horn, despite all the efforts of Boreas to puff out
Those drooping sails.) The idea of great distance
Is permitted, even implicit in the slow dripping
Of a lute. How to get out?
This giant will never let us out unless we blind him.

And that's how, one day, I got home.
Don't be shocked that the old walls
Hang in rags now, that the rainbow has hardened
Into a permanent late afternoon that elicits too-long
Shadows and indiscretions from the bottom
Of the soul. Such simple things,
And we make of them something so complex it defeats us,
Almost. Why can't everything be simple again,
Like the first words of the first song as they occurred
To one who, rapt, wrote them down and later sang them:
"Only danger deflects
The arrow from the center of the persimmon disc,
its final resting place. And should you be addressing yourself
To danger? When it takes the form of bleachers
Sparsely occupied by an audience which has
Already witnessed the events of which you write,

像嫩枝形成一个粗糙的遮蔽物。(船

还没到,它只是一个梦。它在合恩角

附近,尽管北风之神竭力要鼓起那些

松垂的船帆。)有关远方的想法

得到了允许,甚至暗含在一把诗琴

缓慢的滴水中。如何出去?

这巨人永远不会放我们出去,除非我们弄瞎他。

就是那样,有一天,我回到了家。

参差不齐的旧城墙

没有让我吃惊,彩虹已经硬化成

一个永恒的傍晚,从灵魂深处

引出过长的阴影,触发

轻率的行为。如此单纯的事物,

我们把它们变得如此复杂,它几乎

挫败了我们。为什么一切不能重新变得单纯,

就像最初那首歌曲最初的歌词,当它们出现

一个人狂喜地,把它们写下来,然后唱出来:

"只有危险

能让箭矢偏离箭靶中心,

它最终的休止之地。你应该让自己

面对危险吗?当它采取露天看台的形式

被一群观众稀稀落落地占据着,

他们目睹过你在自己日志中

Tellingly, in your log? Properly acknowledged

It will dissipate like the pale pink and blue handkerchiefs

That vanished centuries ago into the blue dome

That surrounds us, but which are, some maintain, still here."

生动记录过的事件?加以恰当的领会
它就会消散,如同淡粉色和蓝色的手绢
几世纪以前便消失在围绕着我们的蓝色圆顶
之中,但有人坚持认为,它还在这里。"

Crazy Weather

It's this crazy weather we've been having:

Falling forward one minute, lying down the next

Among the loose grasses and soft, white, nameless flowers.

People have been making a garment out of it,

Stitching the white of lilacs together with lightning

At some anonymous crossroads. The sky calls

To the deaf earth. The proverbial disarray

Of morning corrects itself as you stand up.

You are wearing a text. The lines

Droop to your shoelaces and I shall never want or need

Any other literature than this poetry of mud

And ambitious reminiscences of times when it came easily

Through the then woods and ploughed fields and had

A simple unconscious dignity we can never hope to

Approximate now except in narrow ravines nobody

Will inspect where some late sample of the rare,

Uninteresting specimen might still be putting out shoots, for all we know.

疯狂的天气

我们正在经历的是这疯狂的天气:
一时向前跌倒,一时又躺下
在松弛的草间和柔软、白色、无名的花朵中。
人们一直在用它做衣服,
用闪电把丁香花的白缝在一起
在某些无名的十字路口。天空召唤着
失聪的大地。当你站起身
早晨众所周知的混乱纠正了自己。
你厌倦了一个文本。句子
凋萎成你的鞋带,而我永远不需要
其他的文学,除了这泥浆的诗
和时间野心勃勃的回忆录,当它轻松地
穿过那时的树林和犁过的田野
有着一种单纯的无意识的高贵
我们现在永远没有希望接近
除了在无人检查的狭窄的沟壑中
在那里,某个令人厌倦的稀有物种
那最后残余的样本可能仍在被猎杀,我们全都知道。

On the Townpath

At the sign "Fred Muffin's Antiques" they turned off the road into a
 narrow lane lined with shabby houses.

If the thirst would subside just for awhile
It would be a little bit, enough.
This has happened.
The insipid chiming of the seconds
Has given way to an arc of silence
So old it had never ceased to exist
On the roofs of buildings, in the sky.

The ground is tentative.
The pygmies and jacaranda that were here yesterday
Are back today, only less so.
It is a barrier of fact
Shielding the sky from the earth.

On the earth a many-colored tower of longing rises.
There are many ads (to help pay for all this).
Something interesting is happening on every landing.
Ladies of the Second Empire gotten up as characters from Perrault:

牵 道

在"弗瑞德·穆非的古董"的标记前
他们拐下道路,进入一条排满破房子的窄巷。

如果渴意能消退片刻
那一小点,就够了。
这已经发生。
时间平淡的滴答声
已经让位于一段寂静的弧
古老得永远不会消亡
在建筑物的屋顶,在天空。

土地是暂时的。
昨天还在这里的俾格米人和紫薇花
今天回来了,只是少了很多。
是事实的一道屏障
把天空和大地隔开。

大地上升起一座五彩缤纷的希望之塔。
有许多广告(为了帮助支付这堆费用)。
每次着陆都有一件有趣的事发生。
第二帝国的女士们像佩罗童话中的人物一样站起来:

Red Riding Hood, Cinderella, the Sleeping Beauty,

Are silhouetted against the stained-glass windows.

A white figure runs to the edge of some rampart

In a hurry only to observe the distance,

And having done so, drops back into the mass

Of clock-faces, spires, stalactite machicolations.

It was the walking sideways, visible from far away,

That told what it was to be known

And kept, as a secret is known and kept.

The sun fades like the spreading

Of a peacock's tail, as though twilight

Might be read as a warning to those desperate

For easy solutions. This scalp of night

Doesn't continue or break off the vacuous chatter

That went on, off and on, all day:

That there could be rain, and

That it could be like lines, ruled lines scored

Across the garden of violet cabbages,

That these and other things could stay on

Longer, though not forever of course;

That other commensals might replace them

And leave in their turn. No,

小红帽,灰姑娘,睡美人
都在彩色玻璃窗上映出剪影。
一个白影奔向壁垒边缘
急匆匆只为了观察一下远方,
然后,又跌回到一大堆
钟面、尖顶、钟乳石堞口中。
很远就能看见的人行道
泄露了将要知道和保守的东西,
像一个为人所知并被保守的秘密。

太阳暗淡下去,像孔雀
展开的尾巴,仿佛微光
可以读成是对那些渴望简单的
解决办法的人的警告。这剥头皮的夜
没有继续,也没有打断空虚的唠叨
它还在继续,整日,时断时续:
可能会有雨,
它可能像线条,平行线
穿过紫甘蓝的花园,
这些和其他东西能够保持得
更长久,当然,也不会永远;
其他的共生体会取代它们
并在时辰到来时离去。

We aren't meaning that any more.

The question has been asked

As though an immense natural bridge had been

Strung across the landscape to any point you wanted.

The ellipse is as aimless as that,

Stretching invisibly into the future so as to reappear

In our present. Its flexing is its account,

Return to the point of no return.

不，我们不再是那个意思。

问题已经提过了

仿佛一座巨大的天然桥梁

横跨整个风景，通向你想去的任何地点。

和它一样没有目标的椭圆，

无形地伸入未来，为了重现于

我们的现在。弯曲就是它的理由，

返回一去不回的地点。

Bird's-Eye View of the Tool and Die Co.

For a long time I used to get up early.
20—30 vision, hemorrhoids intact, he checks into the
Enclosure of time familiarizing dreams
For better or worse. The edges rub off,
The slant gets lost. Whatever the villagers
Are celebrating with less conviction is
The less you. Index of own organ-music playing,
Machinations over the architecture (too
Light to make much of a dent) against meditated
Gang-wars, ice cream, loss, palm terrain.

Under and around the quick background,
Surface is improvisation. The force of
Living hopelessly backward into a past of striped
Conversations. As long as none of them ends this side
Of the mirrored desert in terrorist chorales.
The finest car is as the simplest home off the coast
Of all small cliffs too short to be haze. You turn
To speak to someone beside the dock and the lighthouse
Shines like garnets. It has become a stricture.

鸟瞰工具及冲模公司

有很长时间我习惯早起。
视力20—30，痔疮完好，他检查
时间的围墙熟悉那些
或好或坏的梦境。棱角磨没了，
偏见消除了。无论村民们
在庆祝什么，他们越不信
你就越不信。我们风琴演奏的索引，
建筑上的阴谋诡计（轻得
弄不出多大的凹痕）抵抗精心计划的
群殴，冰淇淋，损失，棕榈带。

短暂的背景下面和周围，
表面是即兴创作。生存的力量
无望地退回一个满是醉话的过去。
只要没有人终止于镜子般的沙漠
这一侧恐怖分子的合唱队。
最精致的汽车就像海岸边最简单的家
所有的小悬崖都矮得无法起雾。你转身
对码头边的某人说话，灯塔闪耀
如同石榴石。它已变成了一种约束。

Wet Casements

> When Eduard Raban, coming along the passage,
> walked into the open doorway, he saw that it was
> raining. It was not raining much.
>
>   KAFKA, *Wedding Preparations in the Country*

The concept is interesting: to see, as though reflected
In streaming windowpanes, the look of others through
Their own eyes. A digest of their correct impressions of
Their self-analytical attitudes overlaid by your
Ghostly transparent face. You in falbalas
Of some distant but not too distant era, the cosmetics,
The shoes perfectly pointed, drifting (how long you
Have been drifting; how long I have too for that matter)
Like a bottle-imp toward a surface which can never be approached,
Never pierced through into the timeless energy of a present
Which would have its own opinions on these matters,
Are an epistemological snapshot of the processes
That first mentioned your name at some crowded cocktail
Party long ago, and someone (not the person addressed)
Overheard it and carried that name around in his wallet
For years as the wallet crumbled and bills slid in

潮湿的地下室

爱德华·拉班穿过走廊,
来到门口时,他看到
天正在下雨。雨下得不大。
　　　　——卡夫卡,《乡村婚事》

概念是有趣的:就像从淌水的窗户
去看别人映在里面的表情
通过他们自己的眼睛。他们自我分析的态度
给你留下的准确印象,被你
幽灵般透明的面孔覆盖。你置身于
某个遥远又不太遥远的时代的荷叶边、化妆品、
溜尖的鞋子中间,漂移着(你漂了
多久;我渴望那件事就有多久)
像浮沉子朝向一个永远抵达不了的表面,
永远不能穿透此刻那永恒的能量
它对这些事情会有自己的观点,
那是对过程的一个认识论快照
最初提到你的名字是在很久以前
一个拥挤的鸡尾酒会上,有人(不是讲话的那个)
偷听到了,他把那名字装在钱夹中
到处转,许多年钱夹破了,账单

And out of it. I want that information very much today,

Can't have it, and this makes me angry.

I shall use my anger to build a bridge like that

Of Avignon, on which people may dance for the feeling

Of dancing on a bridge. I shall at last see my complete face

Reflected not in the water but in the worn stone floor of my bridge.

I shall keep to myself.

I shall not repeat others' comments about me.

滑进滑出。我今天非常需要那信息,

无法拥有它,这让我愤怒。
我要用我的愤怒建一座
阿维尼翁那样的桥,人可以在上面跳舞
感受在桥上跳舞的滋味。我终会看见我完整的脸
不是投影在水中,而是在我这磨损的石头桥面上。

我将保守秘密。
我不会重复别人对我的评论。

Saying It to Keep It from Happening

Some departure from the norm

Will occur as time grows more open about it.

The consensus gradually changed; nobody

Lies about it any more. Rust dark pouring

Over the body, changing it without decay—

People with too many things on their minds, but we live

In the interstices, between a vacant stare and the ceiling,

Our lives remind us. Finally this is consciousness

And the other livers of it get off at the same stop.

How careless. Yet in the end each of us

Is seen to have traveled the same distance—it's time

That counts, and how deeply you have invested in it,

Crossing the street of an event, as though coming out of it were

The same as making it happen. You're not sorry,

Of course, especially if this was the way it had to happen,

Yet would like an exacter share, something about time

That only a clock can tell you: how it feels, not what it means.

It is a long field, and we know only the far end of it,

Not the part we presumably had to go through to get there.

If it isn't enough, take the idea

Inherent in the day, armloads of wheat and flowers

说它是为了阻止它发生

对规范的某种偏离将要发生

因为时代在这方面日益开放。

舆论逐渐改变:没有人

再就此撒谎。铁锈色的黑暗倾泻在

尸体上,改变着它,但没有腐烂——

人们的头脑里有太多的事情,可我们

生活在空隙中,在茫然的目光和天花板之间,

我们的生活提醒我们。最后这就是意识

而它的其他居民在同一车站离开。

多么粗心。不过,最后我们每个人

都被人看见旅行了同样的距离——是时间

在计数,你多么深地陷在里面,

穿过一个事件的街道,仿佛从它里面出来

就是使它发生。你没有歉意,

当然,尤其是,如果它只能这样发生,

那就像是勒索者的一个份额,关于时间的事

只有一只表能告诉你:它是什么感觉,而非它是什么意思。

它是一片漫长的田野,我们只知道它遥远的尽头,

而不是我们为了去那边而假定要穿过的部分。

如果这还不够,就请接受

日子固有的思想,一捆捆小麦和鲜花

Lying around flat on handtrucks, if maybe it means more

In pertaining to you, yet what is is what happens in the end

As though you cared. The event combined with

Beams leading up to it for the look of force adapted to the wiser

Usages of age, but it's both there

And not there, like washing or sawdust in the sunlight,

At the back of the mind, where we live now.

平躺在手推车上,也许在属于你的时候
它更有意义,仿佛你很关心
最后发生的是什么。事件和光束结合起来
通向它,为了寻找适合更聪明的
时代用语的力量,可是它既在那里
又不在那里,像阳光中洗好的衣服和锯屑,
在心灵的背面,我们现在就生活在那里。

Daffy Duck in Hollywood

Something strange is creeping across me.
La Celestina has only to warble the first few bars
Of "I Thought about You" or something mellow from
Amadigi di Gaula for everything—a mint-condition can
Of Rumford's Baking Powder, a celluloid earring, Speedy
Gonzales, the latest from Helen Topping Miller's fertile
Escritoire, a sheaf of suggestive pix on greige, deckle-edged
Stock—to come clattering through the rainbow trellis
Where Pistachio Avenue rams the 2300 block of Highland
Fling Terrace. He promised he'd get me out of this one,
That mean old cartoonist, but just look what he's
Done to me now! I scarce dare approach me mug's attenuated
Reflection in yon hubcap, so jaundiced, so *déconfit*
Are its lineaments fun, no doubt, for some quack phrenologist's
Fern-clogged waiting room, but hardly what you'd call
Companionable. But everything is getting choked to the point of
Silence. Just now a magnetic storm hung in the swatch of sky
Over the Fudds' garage, reducing it—drastically—
To the aura of a plumbago-blue log cabin on
A Gadsden Purchase commemorative cover. Suddenly all is
Loathing. I don't want to go back inside any more. You meet

达菲鸭在好莱坞

某个陌生的东西正在爬着穿过我。
塞莱斯蒂娜只需用颤音唱出"我想你"的
最初几个小节,或是圆润地唱完
"高卢的阿马迪吉"——一个崭新的拉姆福德
发酵粉罐头,一只赛璐珞耳环,飞毛腿冈萨雷斯,
最后这个来自海伦·托平·米勒多产的写字台,
一捆用灰褐色毛边纸印的有启发性的照片
——哗啦啦穿过彩虹的棚架
那里,开心果大道充塞着两千三百个苏格兰
高地舞露台。他许诺他会把我从这里弄出去,
那指的是老漫画家,可是只要看看他现在
都对我做了什么!我几乎不敢靠近那边轮毂盖中
伦敦人衰减的影像,它的轮廓满怀偏见,
如此沮丧——对于某个冒牌骨相学家塞满蕨类植物的
候诊室,无疑是个玩笑,但几乎不像你所说的
那么友善。一切都窒息到寂静的程度。
就是现在,一场磁暴悬挂在天空的色卡里
在福兹车库上方,把它彻底缩小成——
加兹登购地纪念封上的一个
石墨蓝的小木屋。突然,一切都让人
厌恶。我再也不想回到里面了。你在这翡翠色的

Enough vague people on this emerald traffic-island—no,

Not people, comings and goings, more: mutterings, splatterings,

The bizarrely but effectively equipped infantries of happy-go-nutty

Vegetal jacqueries, plumed, pointed at the little

White cardboard castle over the mill run. "Up

The lazy river, how happy we could be? "

How will it end? That geranium glow

Over Anaheim's had the riot act read to it by the

Etna-size firecracker that exploded last minute into

A *carte du Tendre* in whose lower right-hand corner

(Hard by the jock-itch sand-trap that skirts

The asparagus patch of algolagnic *nuits blanches*) Amadis

Is cozening the Princesse de Clèves into a midnight micturition spree

On the Tamigi with the Wallets (Walt, Blossom, and little

Skeezix) on a lamé barge "borrowed" from Ollie

Of the Movie's dread mistress of the robes. Wait!

I have an announcement! This wide, tepidly meandering,

Civilized Lethe (one can barely make out the maypoles

And *châlets de nécessité* on its sedgy shore) leads to Tophet, that

Landfill-haunted, not-so-residential resort from which

Some travellers return! This whole moment is the groin

Of a borborygmic giant who even now

Is rolling over on us in his sleep. Farewell bocages,

Tanneries, water-meadows. The allegory comes unsnarled

.

交通岛上遇见了足够多的暧昧之人——不，

不再是人，来来去去：嘟嘟囔囔，结结巴巴，

怪诞而有效率地武装起采野果的步兵

植物的农民起义，插着羽毛，指向磨坊水车

动力水流上方小小的白纸板城堡。

"在懒散的河上，我们该多么幸福？"

它将怎样结束？在阿纳海姆闪耀的天竺葵

有埃特纳火山那般大的鞭炮

向它解释暴动行为，最后一刻爆炸成

爱情国地图，在它的右下角

（因性虐待不眠夜的芦笋片周围

股癣的沙坑而变硬）阿玛迪斯

正哄骗克利夫斯的公主加入午夜的排尿热潮

在泰晤士河上和瓦莱特一家（瓦尔特、布鲁索姆和小斯科吉科斯）

在一艘蹩脚驳船上向电影中的奥利

"借来"可怕主妇的长袍。等一下！

我有个声明！这宽阔、微温、曲折

文明的忘川（勉强可以在它莎草茂密的岸上

辨认出五朔节花柱和路边厕所）通向地狱，

垃圾填埋场一般闹鬼的、不宜居住的度假胜地

正有一些旅客从那里归来！这瞬间整个是一个

有腹鸣症的巨人的腹股沟，他甚至此刻

就在我们头上打滚，睡觉。再见了森林，

制革厂，淹水草甸。来得太早的

Too soon; a shower of pecky acajou harpoons is
About all there is to be noted between tornadoes. I have
Only my intermittent life in your thoughts to live
Which is like thinking in another language. Everything
Depends on whether somebody reminds you of me.
That this is a fabulation, and that those "other times"
Are in fact the silences of the soul, picked out in
Diamonds on stygian velvet, matters less than it should.
Prodigies of timing may be arranged to convince them
We live in one dimension, they in ours. While I
Abroad through all the coasts of dark destruction seek
Deliverance for us all, think in that language: its
Grammar, though tortured, offers pavilions
At each new parting of the ways. Pastel
Ambulances scoop up the quick and hie them to hospitals.
"It's all bits and pieces, spangles, patches, really; nothing
Stands alone. What happened to creative evolution? "
Sighed Aglavaine. Then to her Sélysette: "If his
Achievement is only to end up less boring than the others,
What's keeping us here? Why not leave at once?
I have to stay here while they sit in there,
Laugh, drink, have fine time. In my day
One lay under the tough green leaves,
Pretending not to notice how they bled into

未解决的寓言；一阵有霉斑的桃花心木捕鲸叉
大概是龙卷风之间可以注意到的全部。我
只是断断续续地活在你的思想里
像是用另一种语言思考。每件事物
都依赖于是否有人让你想起我。
这是一个虚构的情节，那些"其他时刻"
事实上是灵魂的寂静，从幽暗的天鹅绒上的
宝石里面挑选出来，应该不那么要紧。
可以安排定时的奇迹来证明它们
我们生活在一个维度，它们在我们里面。
当我穿过所有暗黑破坏的海岸，为我们所有人
寻求解放，以那种语言思考：它的
语法，尽管折磨人，却在道路的
每一处新的分岔口提供了凉亭。蜡笔画的
救护车舀出伤口的嫩肉，催促它们去医院。
"它全都是碎片和片段，亮片和斑点，真的；
没有什么能独自挺立。创造进化论怎么了？"
阿吉丽凡妮叹息。然后对她的西拉西特说：
"如果他的成就仅仅是不像别人那样厌倦而死，
是什么让我们留在这里？为什么不马上离开？
我不得不留在这儿，因为他们坐在那儿，
欢笑，喝酒，消磨好时光。在我的时代
一个人躺在结实的绿叶下面，
装作没有注意到它们如何渗进

The sky's aqua, the wafted-away no-color of regions supposed
Not to concern us. And so we too
Came where the others came: nights of physical endurance,
Or if, by day, our behavior was anarchically
Correct, at least by New Brutalism standards, all then
Grew taciturn by previous agreement. We were spirited
Away *en bateau*, under cover of fudge dark.
It's not the incomplete importunes, but the spookiness
Of the finished product. True, to ask less were folly, yet
If he is the result of himself, how much the better
For him we ought to be! And how little, finally,
We take this into account! Is the puckered garance satin
Of a case that once held a brace of dueling pistols our
Only acknowledging of that color? I like not this,
Methinks, yet this disappointing sequel to ourselves
Has been applauded in London and St. Petersburg. Somewhere
Ravens pray for us."

                        The storm finished brewing. And thus
She questioned all who came in at the great gate, but none
She found who ever heard of Amadis,
Nor of stern Aureng-Zebe, his first love. Some
There were to whom this mattered not a jot: since all
By definition is completeness (so
In utter darkness they reasoned), why not

天空的浅绿色，假设飘走的无色部分
与我们无关。于是我们也同样来到
其他人到过的地方：生理忍耐力的夜晚，
或者，白天，如果我们的无政府行为
是正确的，至少以新野兽派标准来看
一切就会因之前的协议而沉默无言。我们
被用小船偷偷带走，在黑暗谎言的掩护下。
它不是未完成的要求，而是令人毛骨悚然的
成品。的确，不提问是愚蠢的，但是
如果他就是他自身的结果，我们应该为他存在
这要好得多！而最后，我们对这点
考虑的又是多么少！一箱起皱的暗红色缎子
曾经保存过一对儿决斗用的手枪
我们只认识那种颜色吗？我不喜欢这个，
不过，我想，这让人失望的续集
我们已经在伦敦和圣彼得堡喝过彩了。在某处
群鸦在为我们祈祷。"
　　　　　　　风暴酝酿完毕。于是
她询问所有从大门进来的人，但是她
没有发现谁曾听说过阿玛迪斯，
也不知道严厉的奥朗则布，他的初恋。
对于某人来说，这一点也不重要：既然
显然一切都是圆满（他们
在彻底的黑暗中这样推断），为何不

Accept it as it pleases to reveal itself? As when
Low skyscrapers from lower-hanging clouds reveal
A turret there, an art-deco escarpment here, and last perhaps
The pattern that may carry the sense, but
Stays hidden in the mysteries of pagination.
Not what we see but how we see it matters; all's
Alike, the same, and we greet him who announces
The change as we would greet the change itself.
All life is but a figment; conversely, the tiny
Tome that slips from your hand is not perhaps the
Missing link in this invisible picnic whose leverage
Shrouds our sense of it. Therefore bivouac we
On this great, blond highway, unimpeded by
Veiled scruples, worn conundrums. Morning is
Impermanent. Grab sex things, swing up
Over the horizon like a boy
On a fishing expedition. No one really knows
Or cares whether this is the whole of which parts
Were vouchsafed—once—but to be ambling on's
The tradition more than the safekeeping of it. This mulch for
Play keeps them interested and busy while the big,
Vaguer stuff can decide what it wants—what maps, what
Model cities, how much waste space. Life, our
Life anyway, is between. We don't mind

接受它，既然它乐于揭示自身？

就像当低矮的摩天大楼从更低的悬云中显露出来

那里一个小塔，这里一个装饰艺术的陡崖，最后，

也许把图案能够带出感觉，

却一直隐藏在页码的秘密之中。

重要的不是我们看见的，而是我们如何看；

一切都是类似，相同，我们欢迎他这宣布

变化的人就像我们欢迎变化本身。

整个生活不过是一个虚构；相反，

从你手里滑落的小册子也许不是

这无形野餐中失落的环节，它的影响力

遮蔽着我们对它的感觉。因此，我们

在这金光大道上露营，不受

隐藏的顾虑、过时的难题的干扰。早晨

是短暂的。被性事霸占，在地平线上

荡秋千，像一个男孩

试探一下。没有人真的知道

或是在乎这是不是其所有部分

都已被赐予的整体——而是继续漫步

传统更胜于对传统的保护。这护根物

保持他们对游戏的兴趣，让他们忙碌，这时，

更加暧昧的大人物可以决定它需要什么——什么样的地图，

什么样的模范城市，多少浪费的空间。生活，

我们的生活，终归介于其间。我们不再介意

Or notice any more that the sky *is* green, a parrot

One, but have our earnest where it chances on us,

Disingenuous, intrigued, inviting more,

Always invoking the echo, a summer's day.

也不再注意天空是绿色的，一只鹦鹉
一只，而是在有机会的时候拿到我们的定金，
虚伪，好奇，更有魅力，
总是在激起回声，夏季的一天。

Houseboat Days

"The skin is broken. The hotel breakfast china
Poking ahead to the last week in August, not really
Very much at all, found the land where you began..."
The hills smouldered up blue that day, again
You walk five feet along the shore, and you duck
As a common heresy sweeps over. We can botanize
About this for centuries, and the little dazey
Blooms again in the cities. The mind
Is so hospitable, taking in everything
Like boarders, and you don't see until
It's all over how little there was to learn
Once the stench of knowledge has dissipated, and the trouvailles
Of every one of the senses fallen back. Really, he
Said, that insincerity of reasoning on behalf of one's
Sincere convictions, true or false in themselves
As the case may be, to which, if we are unwise enough
To argue at all with each other, we must be tempted
At times—do you see where it leads? To pain,
And the triumph over pain, still hidden
In these low-lying hills which rob us
Of all privacy, as though one were always about to meet

船屋的日子

"爆皮了。旅馆早餐的瓷器
指向八月的最后一周,并不是真的
很在意,发现你开始的土地……"
那天,群山冒着蓝火,
你再次沿岸走了五英尺,你闪避开
一个掠过的常见异端。我们能够
几世纪地采集植物,城市里
再次开满了炫目的小花。心灵
如此好客,吸收着一切
像寄宿生,直到一切结束
你也不明白可学的有多么少
一旦知识的恶臭消散,每种感官的
意外收获都将退却。真的,他说,
对一个人真诚信念的不真诚的推断,
无论本身是真是假
情况都可能是,如果我们不够聪明地
彼此说服,我们必定时时
受其诱惑——你看见它通往何处吗?通往痛苦,
克服痛苦的凯旋,仍然隐藏在
这些低低的山中,它们掠走我们
所有的秘密,仿佛一个人一直打算

One's double through the chain of cigar smoke

And then it... happens, like an explosion in the brain,

Only it's a catastrophe on another planet to which

One has been invited, and as surely cannot refuse:

Pain in the cistern, in the gutters, and if we merely

Wait awhile, that denial, as though a universe of pain

Had been created just so as to deny its own existence.

But I don't set much stock in things

Beyond the weather and the certainties of living and dying:

The rest is optional. To praise this, blame that,

Leads one subtly away from the beginning, where

We must stay, in motion. To flash light

Into the house within, its many chambers,

Its memories and associations, upon its inscribed

And pictured walls, argues enough that life is various.

Life is beautiful. He who reads that

As in the window of some distant, speeding train

Knows what he wants, and what will befall.

Pinpricks of rain fall again.

And from across the quite wide median with its

Little white flowers, a reply is broadcast:

"Dissolve parliament. Hold new elections."

It would be deplorable if the rain also washed away

在雪茄的烟圈中遇见自己的替身
然后它……发生了,像脑袋里的一次爆炸,
在另一个行星上它仅仅对于那受到邀请
又肯定无法拒绝的人,才是场大灾难:
痛苦在水塔里,在排水沟里,只要我们
等上片刻,那拒绝,就像一个痛苦的宇宙
被创造出来只是为了否定它自己的存在。
但是我不太相信这些事
除了天气和生与死的确定性:
其他都是选择。赞美这个,诋毁那个,
会微妙地使你偏离开端,
我们必须留在那里,在运动中。
把灯照进房子,它的许多房间,
它的记忆和联想,在它有题字
和图画的墙上,足以证明生活是多样化的。
生活是美的。读到这一切的他
就像在远处加速的火车车窗中,
知道他需要什么,以及什么会降临。

一簇簇的雨再次落下。
穿过很宽的中间地带
带着它的小白花,播送一个答复:
"解散议会。举行新选举。"
那将令人遗憾,如果雨也洗去了

This profile at the window that moves, and moves on,

Knowing that it moves, and knows nothing else. It is the light

At the end of the tunnel as it might be seen

By him looking out somberly at the shower,

The picture of hope a dying man might turn away from,

Realizing that hope is something else, something concrete

You can't have. So, winding past certain pillars

Until you get to evening's malachite one, it becomes a vast dream

Of having that can topple governments, level towns and cities

With the pressure of sleep building up behind it.

The surge creates its own edge

And you must proceed this way: mornings of assent,

Indifferent noons leading to the ripple of the question

Of late afternoon projected into evening.

Arabesques and runnels are the result

Over the public address system, on the seismograph at Berkeley.

A little simple arithmetic tells you that to be with you

in this passage, this movement, is what the instance costs:

A sail out of some afternoon, beyond amazement, astonished,

Apparently not tampered with. As the rain gathers and protects

Its own darkness, the place in the slipcover is noticed

For the first and last time, fading like the spine

Of an adventure novel behind glass, behind the teacups.

一直在不停运动的窗上的侧影,
知道它在运动,此外一无所知。
那是隧道尽头的光,如果他忧郁地
望着外面的阵雨,他应该能看见,
一个垂死之人会转身离开一幅希望的图画,
认识到希望是别的东西,你不能拥有的
具体的东西。于是,曲折穿过一些柱子
直到你靠近黄昏的孔雀石柱,它在变成一个巨大的梦
可以推翻政府,夷平村镇和城市
用它后面积聚的睡眠的压力。
巨浪创造着它自己的边界
你必须这样继续:赞同的早晨,
冷漠的中午导向下午晚些时候
投射进黄昏的问题的涟漪。
阿拉伯式花纹和细流便是结果
在公共广播系统上,在伯克利的地震仪上。
一个简单的小算术就能告诉你,为了和你一起
在这个段落中,在这个运动里,需要怎样的代价:
驶出某个下午的帆,不只是惊奇,而是震惊,
明显没有受到损害。当雨水聚集起来
保护它自己的黑暗,覆盖物里的空间
被最初和最后一次注意到,像玻璃后面
一本冒险小说的书脊,在茶杯后消失。

The Lament Upon the Waters

For the disciple nothing had changed. The mood was still
Gray tolerance, as the road marched along
Singing its little song of despair. Once, a cry
Started up out of the hills. That old, puzzling persuasion

Again. Sex was part of this,
And the shock of day turning into night.
Though we always found something delicate (too delicate
For some tastes, perhaps) to touch, to desire.

And we made much of this sort of materiality
That clogged the weight of starlight, made it seem
Fibrous, yet there was a chance in this
To see the present as it never had existed,

Clear and shapeless, in an atmosphere like cut glass.
At Latour-Maubourg you said this was a good thing, and on the steps
Of Métro Jasmin the couriers nodded to us correctly, and the
Pact was sealed in the sky. But now moments surround us

Like a crowd, some inquisitive faces, some hostile ones,

水上的哀悼

对信徒来说一切都没变。情绪仍是
灰色的忍耐,就像道路延伸
唱着它绝望的小曲。曾经,有一声哭叫
从群山中响起。又是那古老,迷惑的

信念。性是它的一部分,
白昼的震惊正在转变成夜晚。
尽管我们总能发现某种精美的东西(也许
精美得不能品尝),去触摸,去渴望。

我们大大利用了这种物质性
以妨碍星光的重量,使它呈
纤维状,这里仍有一个机会
把现在看作从未存在一般,

清晰而无形,在刻花玻璃一样的大气中。
在劳图尔-毛博格你说这是好事,
在素馨花地铁站的台阶上导游向我们告诫地点头,
合同密封在天空中。但现在,时辰环绕我们

像一群人,一些脸好奇,一些脸带有敌意,

Some enigmatic or turned away to an anterior form of time
Given once and for all. The jetstream inscribes a final flourish
That melts as it stays. The problem isn't how to proceed

But is one of being: whether this ever was, and whose
It shall be. To be starting out, just one step
Off the sidewalk, and as such pulled back into the glittering
Snowstorm of stinging tentacles of how that would be worked out

If we ever work it out. And the voice came back at him
Across the water, rubbing it the wrong way: "Thou
Canst but undo the wrong thou hast done." The sackbuts
Embellish it, and we are never any closer to the collision

Of the waters, the peace of light drowning light,
Grabbing it, holding it up streaming. It is all one. It lies
All around, its new message, guilt, the admission
Of guilt, your new act. Time buys

The receiver, the onlooker of the earlier system, but cannot
Buy back the rest. It is night that fell
At the edge of your footsteps as the music stopped.
And we heard the bells for the first time. It is your chapter, I said

一些脸莫测高深,或者转向时间一劳永逸
赋予的先前的形式。喷气流铭刻最后的繁荣
一边延续一边融化。问题不在于如何前进

而是如何存在:是否曾经是这样,以及
它将属于谁。开始出发,只是离开人行道
迈出一步,就这样被拖回闪光的暴风雪
刺人的触须中,那怎么能够实现

如果我们想要实现它。声音向他返回
穿过水面,激怒了它:"你
不能只解决你已经犯下的错误。"长号
为它润色,我们永远不能进一步靠近

碰撞的水了,光的宁静淹没着光,
抓住它,抱着它喷涌。它是完整的。它躺在
附近,它的新信息,罪,认罪,
你的新法令。时间收买了

接收器,更早的系统的旁观者,但不能
买回其他的。是夜晚
落在你脚步旁边,当音乐停歇。
而我们第一次听到钟声。是你那章,我说。

And Ut Pictura Poesis Is Her Name

You can't say it that way any more.

Bothered about beauty you have to

Come out into the open, into a clearing,

And rest. Certainly whatever funny happens to you

Is OK. To demand more than this would be strange

Of you, you who have so many lovers,

People who look up to you and are willing

To do things for you, but you think

It's not right, that if they really knew you. . .

So much for self-analysis. Now,

About what to put in your poem-painting:

Flowers are always nice, particularly delphinium.

Names of boys you once knew and their sleds,

Skyrockets are good—do they still exist?

There are a lot of other things of the same quality

As those I've mentioned. Now one must

Find a few important words, and a lot of low-keyed,

Dull-sounding ones. She approached me

About buying her desk. Suddenly the street was

Bananas and the clangor of Japanese instruments.

Humdrum testaments were scattered around. His head

而诗如画是她的名字

你不能再那样说它。

为美操心,你不得不

来到开阔地,进入一片空地,

然后歇下来。当然,任何趣事发生在你身上

都是正常。比这更多的要求在你将是

奇怪的,你这情人众多的人,

仰望你的和愿意

为你做事的人,但是你认为

这是不对的,如果他们真的了解你……

自我分析到此为止。现在,

说说要在你的诗—画中放些什么:

鲜花总是好的,尤其是飞燕草。

你曾经认识的男孩们的名字和他们的雪橇,

焰火是好的——它们还存在吗?

还有许多其他东西和我提到的那些

具有同样的品质。好了,一个人必须

发现一些重要的词语,和大量低调的,

听着没趣的词语。她和我商量

给买她桌子的事儿。突然,街道上满是

香蕉和日本乐器的丁当声。

单调的自白播散在周围。他的头

Locked into mine. We were a seesaw. Something

Ought to be written about how this affects

You when you write poetry:

The extreme austerity of an almost empty mind

Colliding with the lush, Rousseau-like foliage of its desire to communicate

Something between breaths, if only for the sake

Of others and their desire to understand you and desert you

For other centers of communication, so that understanding

May begin, and in doing so be undone.

与我的头连锁起来。我们是一副跷跷板。
关于你在写诗时，这一切如何影响你
应该写点东西：
一副几近空洞的大脑的极端苦行
与它要在呼吸之间传达某种东西的欲望
那繁茂的、卢梭风格的叶子相悖，如果只是为了
别人和他们想要理解你并抛弃你的欲望
为了其他的通讯中心，以便可以
开始理解，并在这样做的同时遭到毁灭。

What Is Poetry

The medieval town, with frieze
Of boy scouts from Nagoya? The snow

That came when we wanted it to snow?
Beautiful images? Trying to avoid

Ideas, as in this poem? But we
Go back to them as to a wife, leaving

The mistress we desire? Now they
Will have to believe it

As we believe it. In school
All the thought got combed out:

What was left was like a field.
Shut your eyes, and you can feel it for miles around.

Now open them on a thin vertical path.
It might give us—what? —some flowers soon?

什么是诗歌

中世纪的城镇，有着来自
名古屋的童子军中楣？我们

想要它下时就下的雪？
美丽的意象？试着避开

思想，就像在这首诗中？可我们
回到思想就像回到妻子身边，离开

我们渴望的情妇？现在他们
将不得不相信它

就像我们相信它。在学校
所有思想都被去除：

剩下的像一片田野。
闭上眼睛，你能感觉到它漫延数里。

现在睁开眼看一条垂直的狭径。
不久它能给我们——什么？——一些花吗？

And Others, Vaguer Presences

Are built out of the meshing of life and space
At the point where we are wholly revealed
In the lozenge-shaped openings. Because
It is argued that these structures address themselves
To exclusively aesthetic concerns, like windmills
On a vast plain. To which it is answered
That there are no other questions than these,
Half squashed in mud, emerging out of the moment
We all live, learning to like it. No sonnet
On this furthest strip of land, no pebbles,

No plants. To extend one's life
All day on the dirty stone of some plaza,
Unaware among the pretty lunging of the wind,
Light and shade, is like coming out of
A coma that is a white, interesting country,
Prepared to lose the main memory in a meeting
By torchlight under the twisted end of the stairs.

而其他人,模糊的存在

从生命和空间的交织中建立
在我们被完整发现的地点
在菱形的林间空地。因为
它表明这些结构在面向
唯一的审美对象说话,就像风车
在一片广阔的平原上。它得到的回答是
除了这些,再没有别的问题了,
一半压扁在烂泥里,从瞬间出现
我们全都活着,学着喜欢它。没有十四行
这片遥远至极的土地上,没有鹅卵石,

没有植物。整天把一个人的生活
铺展在广场肮脏的石头上,
觉察不到风的优美扑刺,
光与影,仿佛正在从昏迷
那有趣的白色国度苏醒,
准备在一次会议上失去主要的记忆
借着扭曲的楼梯尽头下的火炬。

The Wrong Kind of Insurance

I teach in a high school

And see the nurses in some of the hospitals,

And if all teachers are like that

Maybe I can give you a buzz some day,

Maybe we can get together for lunch or coffee or something.

The white marble statues in the auditorium

Are colder to the touch than the rain that falls

Past the post-office inscription about rain or snow

Or gloom of night. I think

About what these archaic meanings mean,

That unfurl like a rope ladder down through history,

To fall at our feet like crocuses.

All of our lives is a rebus

Of little wooden animals painted shy,

Terrific colors, magnificent and horrible,

Close together. The message is learned

The way light at the edge of a beach in autumn is learned.

The seasons are superimposed.

In New York we have winter in August

投错的保险

我在一所中学教书
见过一些医院的护士,
如果所有的教师都那个样
也许有一天我能给你一阵嗡嗡声,
也许我们能一起吃午饭,或者喝咖啡什么的。

礼堂里白色的大理石雕像
摸起来比雨还冷
那雨飘过邮局有关雨雪的铭文
或者夜的阴暗。我想着
这些陈旧字句的意义,
像一架绳梯从历史中降落
像番红花落在我们脚边。

我们全部的生活是一个有关
小木头动物的画谜,涂着羞怯
而可怕的颜色,华丽而恐怖,
紧紧靠在一起。信息收到了
秋天熟悉了海滩边缘的路灯。
季节重叠。
在纽约我们八月份就是冬天了

As they do in Argentina and Australia.

Spring is leafy and cold, autumn pale and dry.

And changes build up

Forever, like birds released into the light

Of an August sky, falling away forever

To define the handful of things we know for sure,

Followed by musical evenings.

Yes, friends, these clouds pulled along on invisible ropes

Are, as you have guessed, merely stage machinery,

And the funny thing is it knows we know

About it and still wants us to go on believing

In what it so unskillfully imitates, and wants

To be loved not for that but for itself:

The murky atmosphere of a park, tattered

Foliage, wise old treetrunks, rainbow tissue-paper wadded

Clouds down near where the perspective

Intersects the sunset, so we may know

We too are somehow impossible, formed of so many different things,

Too many to make sense to anybody.

We straggle on as quotients, hard-to-combine

Ingredients, and what continues

Does so with our participation and consent.

就像他们在阿根廷和澳大利亚。
春天树叶茂盛，寒冷，秋天苍白而干燥。
变化积聚起来，
不断地，像鸟儿释放在八月
天空的光中，不断地消失着
去定义我们确实了解的少数事物，
随后是音乐的傍晚。

是的，朋友们，这些云彩被无形的绳索牵动
就像你猜的那样，只不过是舞台机械，
有趣之处在于它知道我们知道
它的情况但仍想要我们继续相信
它如此笨拙地模仿的东西，仍想
为人所爱，不是为了那个而是凭其本身：
一座公园的阴沉气氛，褴褛的植物，
聪明的老树干，彩虹棉纸填絮的
云彩低垂，靠近远景
与日落交叉之处，这样我们就能知道
我们同样不可能，由如此多不同的事物组成，
多得对任何人都没有意义。
我们像商数一样散乱，
难以结合的材料，继续
与我们的参与和许诺一同存在。

Try milk of tears, but it is not the same.

The dandelions will have to know why, and your comic

Dirge routine will be lost on the unfolding sheaves

Of the wind, a lucky one, though it will carry you

Too far, to some manageable, cold, open

Shore of sorrows you expected to reach,

Then leave behind.
               Thus, friend, this distilled,

Dispersed musk of moving around, the product

Of leaf after transparent leaf, of too many

Comings and goings, visitors at all hours.

                                      Each night

Is trifoliate, strange to the touch.

试试眼泪的牛奶，可是它不一样。
蒲公英将不得不知道为什么，你滑稽的
挽歌将迷失在展开的风的
禾捆上，一个幸运儿，尽管它会把你带到
远得无人管理的地方，寒冷，开阔
你期望抵达的悲哀之岸，
然后把你留下。
　　因而，朋友，这提纯过的，
四散的麝香在周围环绕，这产品
来自透明的叶子后面的叶子，太多的
来来去去，每时每刻的访问者。
　　　　　　　每一夜
都是三片叶子，摸上去有点奇怪。

Friends

I like to speak in rhymes,

because I am a rhyme myself.

NIJINSKY

I saw a cottage in the sky.

I saw a balloon made of lead.

I cannot restrain my tears, and they fall

On my left hand and on my silken tie,

But I cannot and do not want to hold them back.

One day the neighbors complain about an unpleasant odor

Coming from his room. *I went for a walk*

But met no friends. Another time I go outside

Into the world. It rocks on and on.

It was rocking before I saw it

And is presumably doing so still.

The banker lays his hand on mine.

His face is as clean as a white handkerchief.

We talk nonsense as usual.

I trace little circles on the light that comes in

朋友们

我喜欢用韵律说话，
因为我自己就是韵律
　　——尼金斯基

我看见天空中有一座小屋。
我看见一只铅做的气球。
我控制不住自己的眼泪，它们掉落
在我的左手和丝领带上，
但是我不能也不想忍住眼泪。

有一天邻居们抱怨他的房间
发出一股讨厌的气味。我去散步
但没有遇见朋友。另一次我出门
进入世界。它在不断地摇啊摇。
我看见它之前它就在摇
估计还在摇。

银行家把他的手放在我手上。
他的脸干净得像一块白手帕。
我们像往常一样胡说。
我的目光追踪透过窗户

Through the window on saw-horse legs.

Afterwards I see that we are three.

Someone had entered the room while I was discussing my money problems.

I wish God would put a stop to this. I

Turn and see the new moon through glass. I am yanked away

So fast I lose my breath, a not unpleasant feeling.

I feel as though I had been carrying the message for years

On my shoulders like Atlas, never feeling it

Because of never having known anything else. In another way

I am involved with the message. I want to put it down

(In two senses of "put it down") so that you

May understand the agreeable destiny that awaits us.

You sigh. Your sighs will admit of no impatience,

Only a vast crater lake, vast as the sea,

In which the sky, smaller than that, is reflected.

I reach for my hat

And am bound to repeat with tact

The formal greeting I am charged with.

No one makes mistakes. No one runs away

Any more. I bite my lip and

Turn to you. Maybe now you understand.

The feeling is a jewel like a pearl.

落在锯木架腿上的小光圈。
后来我看见我们是三个。
有人进了房间,在我讨论我钱的问题时。
我希望上帝能阻止这个。我
转身透过窗户看见新月。我被拖走
这么快我就没气了,一种并非不快的感觉。

我觉得好像我多年来始终携带着这个信息
像阿特拉斯扛在肩上,从来没有感觉到它
因为从来不知道别的东西。以另一种方式
我与这信息纠缠在一起。我想把它放下
(以"放下"的两种含义)以便你
可以理解那等待我们的愉快的命运。
你叹息。你的叹息不会容忍任何的不耐烦,
除了一个巨大的火山湖,海一样辽阔,
将比它小的天空映照。

我去够我的帽子
我一定要老练地重复
委托给我的正式问候。
没人犯错误。没人
再跑开。我咬着嘴唇
转向你。也许现在你能理解。

这感觉是一颗珍珠般的宝石。

The Ice-Cream Wars

Although I mean it, and project the meaning
As hard as I can into its brushed-metal surface,
It cannot, in this deteriorating climate, pick up
Where I leave off. It sees the Japanese text
(About two men making love on a foam-rubber bed)
As among the most massive secretions of the human spirit.
Its part is in the shade, beyond the iron spikes of the fence,
Mixing red with blue. As the day wears on
Those who come to seem reasonable are shouted down
(*Why you old goat*! Look who's talkin'. Let's see you
Climb off that tower—the waterworks architecture, both stupid and
Grandly humorous at the same time, is a kind of mask for him,
Like a seal's face. Time and the weather
Don't always go hand in hand, as here: sometimes
One is slanted sideways, disappears for awhile.
Then later it's forget-me-not time, and rapturous
Clouds appear above the lawn, and the rose tells
The old old story, the pearl of the orient, occluded
And still apt to rise at times.)
                    A few black smudges
On the outer boulevards, like squashed midges

冰淇淋战争

虽然我有意,并尽力把意义
投射到它擦拭过的金属表面,
在这恶化的气候中,它不能
在我离开的地方恢复。它把日文文本
(有关两个男人在海绵乳胶床上做爱)
看作人类灵魂最大的分泌物之一。
它的一部分在阴影中,超出篱笆的铁尖,
把红和蓝混在一切。随着白昼磨损
那些看上去通情达理的人被大声喝止
(为什么你这老山羊!看是谁在讲话。让我们看你
爬上那座塔——水厂的建筑,愚蠢
同时又极其幽默,那是一种适合他的面具,
像一张海豹的脸。时间和天气
并不总是像在这里,携手同行:有时
一个会向路边倾斜,消失上一会儿。
后来到了勿忘我的时间,欢天喜地的云朵
出现在草坪上空,玫瑰在讲述
古老又古老的故事,东方的珍珠,被禁锢着
但仍有不时升起的倾向。)
　　　　　一些黑色的污迹
在外面的林荫大道上,像压扁的蚊子

And the truth becomes a hole, something one has always known,

A heaviness in the tree, and no one can say

Where it comes from, or how long it will stay—

A randomness, a darkness of one's own.

真理变成了一个洞，一个人始终知道的东西，
树林里的沉重，无人能说出
它来自何处，或者它会停留多久——

一种随机性，一个人自己的黑暗。

Blue Sonata

Long ago was the then beginning to seem like now

As now is but the setting out on a new but still

Undefined way. That now, the one once

Seen from far away, is our destiny

No matter what else may happen to us. It is

The present past of which our features,

Our opinions are made. We are half it and we

Care nothing about the rest of it. We

Can see far enough ahead for the rest of us to be

Implicit in the surroundings that twilight is.

We know that this part of the day comes every day

And we feel that, as it has its rights, so

We have our right to be ourselves in the measure

That we are in it and not some other day, or in

Some other place. The time suits us

Just as it fancies itself, but just so far

As we not give up that inch, breath

Of becoming before becoming may be seen,

Or come to seem all that it seems to mean now.

The things that were coming to be talked about

蓝色奏鸣曲

很久以前曾是那时的开始，似乎就像现在
因为现在不过是在一条新的但还不确定的
路上出发。那个现在，曾经从远处
看见过的现在，是我们的命运
无论在我们身上还会发生什么。
是在现在的过去中，我们形成了
我们的特征，我们的观念。我们是它的一半
我们对它剩余的部分毫不关心。我们
能提前看得足够远，因为我们剩下的人
将盲从于那微明的周遭。
我们知道日子的这个部分天天会来
我们觉得，就像它有它的权利，所以
我们也有权以我们置身其中的尺度
做我们自己，而不是在另外一天，
或是另外一个地方。时间适合我们
刚好和它设想的那样，但是迄今
我们没有放弃那尺度，在能够
看见变化之前的变化的瞬息，
或是似乎看见那似乎意味着现在的一切。

即将被谈论的事物

Have come and gone and are still remembered
As being recent. There is a grain of curiosity
At the base of some new thing, that unrolls
Its question mark like a new wave on the shore.
In coming to give, to give up what we had,
We have, we understand, gained or been gained
By what was passing through, bright with the sheen
Of things recently forgotten and revived.
Each image fits into place, with the calm
Of not having too many, of having just enough.
We live in the sigh of our present.

If that was all there was to have
We could re-imagine the other half, deducing it
From the shape of what is seen, thus
Being inserted into its idea of how we
Ought to proceed. It would be tragic to fit
Into the space created by our not having arrived yet,
To utter the speech that belongs there,
For progress occurs through re-inventing
These words from a dim recollection of them,
In violating that space in such a way as
To leave it intact. Yet we do after all
Belong here, and have moved a considerable
Distance; our passing is a facade.
But our understanding of it is justified.

来了又去，仍被当作最近的事
被记忆。有一点好奇心
在某个新事物的根基处，打开
它的问号，像岸上的一朵新浪。
逐渐放弃，放弃我们曾经的所有，
我们明白，我们已经得到了，或是
被穿过的一切得到，被近来遗忘
又复活的事物的光辉所照亮。
每个形象都适合它的位置，带着
不求太多，只求足够的那种镇静。
我们生活在我们现在的叹息中。
如果这就是那里的所有
我们能重新想象那另外一半，推论它
从它所显现的形状，然后
被插入到它有关我们应该如何
前进的思想中。适应由我们所创造
但尚未达到的空间，那将是悲惨的，
去发表属于那里的演说，
因为进步的取得要通过重新发明
这些从它们的暗淡回忆而来的词语，
以保持其完整的方式
侵犯那个空间。不过，我们毕竟
属于这里，并且已经移动了相当一段
距离；我们的经过是一个表面。
但是我们对它的理解是公正的。

Syringa

Orpheus liked the glad personal quality

Of the things beneath the sky. Of course, Eurydice was a part

Of this. Then one day, everything changed. He rends

Rocks into fissures with lament. Gullies, hummocks

Can't withstand it. The sky shudders from one horizon

To the other, almost ready to give up wholeness.

Then Apollo quietly told him: "Leave it all on earth.

Your lute, what point? Why pick at a dull pavan few care to

Follow, except a few birds of dusty feather,

Not vivid performances of the past." But why not?

All other things must change too.

The seasons are no longer what they once were,

But it is the nature of things to be seen only once,

As they happen along, bumping into other things, getting along

Somehow. That's where Orpheus made his mistake.

Of course Eurydice vanished into the shade;

She would have even if he hadn't turned around.

No use standing there like a gray stone toga as the whole wheel

Of recorded history flashes past, struck dumb, unable to utter an intelligent

Comment on the most thought-provoking element in its train.

紫丁香

俄尔甫斯喜欢天空下的事物

那可爱的个人性。当然,欧律狄刻就在其中。

随后有一天,一切都变了。他用挽歌

把岩石撕裂。溪谷,山冈

无法忍受它。天空在地平线之间

颤抖,几乎准备全部放弃。

那时,阿波罗悄悄地告诉他:"把它留在地上吧。

你的竖琴,有什么要紧?为什么在一个很少有人

愿意应和的沉闷的孔雀舞会上演奏,

除了一些羽毛肮脏的鸟,

过去的表演都不生动。"可为什么不呢?

所有其他事物也必须改变。

季节不再是曾经的那样,

但是,只被看见一次是事物的本质,

当它们发生,撞击别的事物,和睦相处。

那就是俄尔甫斯出错的地方。

欧律狄刻当然消失在暗影中;

即使他没有回头,她也会这样。

像一件灰石托加袍那样站着根本没用

当历史的车轮闪过,惊呆了,说不出话来

对其中最能激发思想的因素也发不出一句机智的评论。

Only love stays on the brain, and something these people,
These other ones, call life. Singing accurately
So that the notes mount straight up out of the well of
Dim noon and rival the tiny, sparkling yellow flowers
Growing around the brink of the quarry, encapsulates
The different weights of the things.

                                        But it isn't enough
To just go on singing. Orpheus realized this
And didn't mind so much about his reward being in heaven
After the Bacchantes had torn him apart, driven
Half out of their minds by his music, what it was doing to them.
Some say it was for his treatment of Eurydice.
But probably the music had more to do with it, and
The way music passes, emblematic
Of life and how you cannot isolate a note of it
And say it is good or bad. You must
Wait till it's over. "The end crowns all,"
Meaning also that the "tableau"
Is wrong. For although memories, of a season, for example,
Melt into a single snapshot, one cannot guard, treasure
That stalled moment. It too is flowing, fleeting;
It is a picture of flowing, scenery, though living, mortal,
Over which an abstract action is laid out in blunt,
Harsh strokes. And to ask more than this

只有爱留在大脑中,这些人,

这些其他人,叫做生活的东西。准确地歌唱

以便曲调径直从暗月的井中

攀升,与闪耀的黄色小花匹敌

它们长在采石场边缘,压缩

事物不同的重量。

    但是,只是继续歌唱

这是不够的。俄尔甫斯认识到了这点

并不太在意他在天堂的回报

酒神的女祭司在把他撕碎之后,她们

被他的音乐逼得半疯,这就是他的音乐。

有人说这和他对待欧律狄刻有关。

但也许音乐与这件事的关系更大,还有

音乐进行的方式,生命的标记

你无法从中孤立出一个音符

说它是好是坏。你必须

等它结束。"结尾冠绝一切,"

同样意味着那"戏剧性局面"

是错的。因为,尽管记忆,比如对一个季节的记忆,

融入了一张快照,但那停止的瞬间

是人无法守卫和珍惜的。它也在流动,飞逝;

它是一幅流动的图画,风景,虽然生动,但终有一死,

在它上面生硬地展开一个抽象的行动,

粗糙的笔触。多过于此的要求

Is to become the tossing reeds of that slow,

Powerful stream, the trailing grasses

Playfully tugged at, but to participate in the action

No more than this. Then in the lowering gentian sky

Electric twitches are faintly apparent first, then burst forth

Into a shower of fixed, cream-colored flares. The horses

Have each seen a share of the truth, though each thinks,

"I'm a maverick. Nothing of this is happening to me,

Though I can understand the language of birds, and

The itinerary of the lights caught in the storm is fully apparent to me.

Their jousting ends in music much

As trees move more easily in the wind after a summer storm

And is happening in lacy shadows of shore-trees, now, day after day."

But how late to be regretting all this, even

Bearing in mind that regrets are always late, too late!

To which Orpheus, a bluish cloud with white contours,

Replies that these are of course not regrets at all,

Merely a careful, scholarly setting down of

Unquestioned facts, a record of pebbles along the way.

And no matter how all this disappeared,

Or got where it was going, it is no longer

Material for a poem. Its subject

Matters too much, and not enough, standing there helplessly

就是要变成摇摆的芦苇，在缓慢，
有力的激流中，这飘动的叶子
被顽皮地拖曳着，但对这个行动的参与
不过如此。然后在低低的龙胆属的天空
闪电的抽搐先是明显地变暗，然后爆发成
奶油色闪光的阵雨。每一匹马
都目睹了一份真理，尽管每一匹都认为，
"我没打烙印。这种事不会落在我头上，
虽然我可以理解鸟的语言，
我完全清楚陷入暴风雨的灯光的路线。
它们的比赛在音乐中结束了
就像夏日暴雨后风中的树木那样更轻松地移动
现在，日复一日，正在沿岸树木花边状的阴影中发生。"

可是为这一切悔恨已经太晚，甚至
心怀悔恨也总是太晚，太晚！
对此，俄尔甫斯，一朵带白边的蓝云彩，
回答说这些当然不是悔恨，
而仅仅是在谨慎、博学地记下
不成问题的事实，沿途鹅卵石的一份记录。
无论这一切如何消失，
或者抵达它要去的地方，它不再是
一首诗的材料。它的主题
过于重要，但还不足以，无助地站在那里

While the poem streaked by, its tail afire, a bad

Comet screaming hate and disaster, but so turned inward

That the meaning, good or other, can never

Become known. The singer thinks

Constructively, builds up his chant in progressive stages

Like a skyscraper: but at the last minute turns away.

The song is engulfed in an instant in blackness

Which must in turn flood the whole continent

With blackness, for it cannot see. The singer

Must then pass out of sight, not even relieved

Of the evil burthen of the words. Stellification

Is for the few, and comes about much later

When all record of these people and their lives

Has disappeared into libraries, onto microfilm.

A few are still interested in them. "But what about

So-and-so? " is still asked on occasion. But they lie

Frozen and out of touch until an arbitrary chorus

Speaks of a totally different incident with a similar name

In whose tale are hidden syllables

Of what happened so long before that

In some small town, one indifferent summer.

当诗歌飞驰而过,它的尾巴着火,一颗坏彗星
尖叫着恨和灾难,可是就此向内转
那意义,无论好坏,也永远不能
为人所知。歌手在思考,
建设性地,在进步的阶梯上建造他的圣歌
像一座摩天大楼,但在最后的时刻离开了。
歌曲马上被吞没在黑暗中
黑暗必随后泛滥整个大陆,
因为它看不见。歌手
那时必从视野中消失,甚至摆脱不了
词语罪恶的负担。能够熠熠生辉的
只是少数,而且很晚才出现
那时,这些人及其生活的所有记录
都已消失在图书馆中,成为缩微胶片。
有些人仍对它们感兴趣。"但是诸如此类
又如何呢?"偶尔还会有人这么问。但是它们
僵硬地躺着,不可企及,直到一个武断的合唱队
说起一个有类似名字的完全不同的事件
其中的故事便是隐藏的音节
关乎很久以前发生的事
在某个小镇,某个平常的夏天。

From *Fantasia on "The Nut-Brown Maid"*

Unless this is the shelf of whatever happens? The cold sunrise attacks one side of the giant capital letters, bestirs a little the landmass as it sinks, grateful but asleep. And you too are a rebus from another century, your fiction in piles like lace, in that a new way of appreciating has been invented, that tomorrow will be quantitatively and qualitatively different—young love, cheerful, insubstantial things—and that these notions have been paraded before, though never with the flashing density climbing higher with you on the beanstalk until the jewelled mosaic of hills, ploughed fields and rivers agreed to be so studied and fell away forever, a gash of laughter, a sneeze of gold dust into the prism that weeps and remains solid.

Well had she represented the patient's history to his apathetic scrutiny. Always there was something to see, something going on, *for the historical past owed it to itself, our historical present.* There were visiting firemen, rumors of chattels on a spree, old men made up to look like young women in the polygon of night from which light sometimes breaks, to be sucked back, armies of foreigners who could not understand each other, the sickening hush just before the bleachers collapse, the inevitable uninvited and only guest who writes on the wall: I choose not to believe. It became a part of oral history. Things overheard in cafes assumed an importance previously reserved for letters from the front. The past was a dream of doctors and drugs. This wasn't misspent time. Oh, sometimes it'd seem like doing the same thing over and over, until I had passed beyond whatever the sense of it had been. Besides, hadn't it all ended a long time back, on some clear, washed-out afternoon, with a stiff breeze that seemed to

有关"栗色头发的少女"的幻想曲

除非这是任何发生之事的大陆架？寒冷的日出袭击巨型大写字母的一侧，搅起一小块大陆，当它下沉，充满感激又睡意蒙眬。你也是一个画谜，来自另一个世纪，你的谎言堆积如花边，一种新的欣赏方式已经发明，明天在数量和质量上都将有所不同——年轻的爱，愉快而脆弱的东西——这些观点以前检阅过，尽管没有以闪光的密度随你在豆茎上登得更高，直到宝石镶嵌的群山，耕地与河流，同意被加以这样的研究并永远消失，笑声的一道裂缝，金色灰尘的一声喷嚏，进入哭泣但保持坚固的棱镜。

她把患者的病历交由他去冷漠地审查。总可以看见什么，正在继续的东西，因为历史的过去归于自身，我们历史的现在。有消防队员来访，狂欢之中有关垃圾的谣言，老人们化装成年轻女子的模样，置身于夜晚的多边形中，有时有光线从中迸发，又被吸回，无法彼此理解的外国军队，露天看台倒塌之前令人厌恶的寂静，不可避免的不速之客也是唯一在墙上写字的客人：我宁可不信。它成了口述历史的一部分。咖啡馆里无意中听到的事情具有以前专门属于来自前线的信件的重要性。过去是医生和药品的一个梦。这不是虚度的时间。啊，有时这就像是反反复复做同一件事，直到我超越了它过去的任何感觉。此外，很久以前它还没有完全结束，在某个晴朗褪色的下午，一阵强

shout: go back! For the moated past lives by these dreams of decorum that take into account any wisecracks made at their expense. It is not called living in a past. If history were only minding one's business, but, once under the gray shade of mist drawn across us. . . And who am I to speak this way, into a shoe? I know that evening is busy with lights, cars. . . That the curve will include me if I must stand here. My warm regards are cold, falling back to the vase again like a fountain. Responsible to whom? I have chosen this environment and it is handsome: a festive ruching of bare twigs against the sky, masks under the balconies

       that
        I sing alway

风似乎在喊：回去！因为有护城河的过去依靠这些礼仪之梦生活，任何以它们为代价的俏皮话都要予以考虑。这不是所谓的活在过去。是否历史只是当心一个人的生意，但是，一旦置身于在我们身上拉开的灰色雾影之下……我是谁，要这样对着一只鞋说话？我知道傍晚因灯光、汽车而忙乱……那曲线将包括我，如果我必须站在这里。我温暖的问候是冰冷的，像一束喷泉，再次落回花瓶。向谁负责？我已经选择了这个环境而它是可观的：光秃嫩枝的节日褶饰映衬着天空，我总是唱到的

那些
　　阳台下的面具

JOHN ASHBERY

阿什贝利自选诗集
III
（汉英对照）

马永波 译

人民文学出版社
PEOPLE'S LITERATURE PUBLISHING HOUSE

From
AS WE KNOW
正如我们所知
(1979)

From *Litany*

Some certified nut

Will try to tell you it's poetry,

(It's extraordinary, it makes a great deal of sense)

But watch out or he'll start with some

New notion or other and switch to both

Leaving you wiser and not emptier though

Standing on the edge of a hill.

We have to worry

About systems and devices there is no

Energy here no spleen either

We have to take over the sewer plans—

Otherwise the coursing clear water, planes

Upon planes of it, will have its day

And disappear. Same goes for business:

Holed up in some office skyscraper it's

Often busy to predict the future for business plans

But try doing it from down

In the street and see how far it gets you! You

Really have to sequester yourself to see

How far you have come but I'm

Not going to talk about that.

连 祷

某个有证书的狂热者
试图告诉你它是诗歌,
(它很特别,它意义重大)
但是小心,或许他会从某个新观点
或另一个观点开始,在两者间切换
留下你,更明智而不是更无知地
站在一座山的山边。
我们不得不为系统和设备
担心,这里没有能量也没有坏脾气
我们不得不接管下水道计划——
否则流淌的清水,它上面
层叠的位面,就会过时
并且消失。经商也是如此:
钻进摩天大楼的某间办公室
它经常忙着为商业计划预测未来
但是,在下面的街上试试,
看看它会把你带到多远的地方!
你真的必须自我隐退了,才能看见
你已经走出多远,但是我
不打算说那个。

I'm fairly well pleased

With the way you and I have come around the hill

Ignoring and then anointing its edge even if

We felt it keenly in the backwind.

You were a secretary at first until it

Came time to believe you and then the black man

Replaced your headlights with fuel

You seemed to grow from no place. And now,

Calmed down, like a Corinthian column

You grow and grow, scaling the high plinths

Of the sky.

Others, the tenor, the doctor,

Want us to walk about on it to see how we feel

About it before they attempt anything, yet

In whose house are we? Must we not sit

Quietly, for we would not do this at home?

A splattering of trumpets against the very high

Pockmarked wall and a forgetting of spiny

Palm trees and it is over for us all,

Not just us, and yet on the inside it was

Doomed to happen again, over and over, like a

Wave on a beach, that thinks it's had this

Tremendous idea, coming to crash on the beach

Like that, and it's true, it has, yet

我相当满意
你和我绕山边而行的方式
忽略山的边缘,又给它涂油
即便我们在逆风中觉得它很锋利。
起初你是一个秘书,一直到了
要相信你的时候,那黑人
才给你的头灯换了燃料
你似乎生自乌有乡。而现在,
镇静下来,像一根科林斯柱
你长啊长,攀登天空
高高的柱基。

其他人,男高音,医生,
想要我们在它上面走走,看看我们的感觉
在他们做出尝试之前,不过
我们是在谁的房子里呢?我们没必要安静地
坐着,因为我们在家里不会这样做?
喇叭一阵结结巴巴,对着坑坑洼洼的
高墙和一棵遗忘了的有刺的
棕榈树,对我们大家来说它完了,
不只是我们,在它的内部
这种事注定会再次发生,一遍又一遍,
如同海滩上的一头浪,以为自己有了这个
惊人的思想,便要那样撞碎在海滩上
这是真的,它已经如此,但是

Others have gone before, and still others will

Follow, and far from undermining the spiciness

Of this individual act, this knowledge plants

A seed of eternal endeavor for fear of

Happening just once, and goes on this way,

And yet the originality should not deter

Our vision from the drain

That absorbs, night and day, all our equations,

Makes us brittle, emancipated, not men in a word.

Dying of fright

In the violet night you come to understand how it

Looked to the ancestors and what there was about it

That moved them and are come no closer

To the divine riddle which is aging,

So beautiful in the eternal honey of the sun

And spurs us on to a higher pitch

Of elocution that the company

Will not buy, and so back to our grandstand

Seat with the feeling of having mended

The contrary principles with the catgut

Of abstract sleek ideas that come only once in

The night to be born and are gone forever after

Leaving their trace after the stitches have

Been removed but who is to say they are

Traces of what really went on and not

其他的浪在前面消失了,还会有其他的浪
跟上来,远远无损于这种个体行为的
痛快,这个知识种下了
一个永远在努力的种子,害怕
一旦发生,便会以这种方式继续,
不过,独创性不应该妨碍
我们来自下水道的幻象
它不分昼夜,吸收我们所有的方程式,
让我们脆弱,获得解放,不再是一个词语里的人。
死于惊吓
在紫罗兰色的夜晚,你终于明白了
它何以指望祖先们,它周围有什么
感动了他们,不再靠近
正在衰老的神圣之谜,
在太阳永恒的金蜜中如此美丽
鼓舞我们走向级别更高的
同伴得不到的雄辩术,
然后回到我们的正面看台
带着一种用抽象圆滑的
思想的肠线缝合了对立原则的
感觉,那些思想只在夜里
出现一次,出生,然后永远消失
在缝线拆除以后,留下它们的轨迹
但谁会说那些轨迹属于真实的存在

Today's palimpsest? For what

Is remarkable about our chronic reverie (a watch

That is always too slow or too fast)

Is the lively sense of accomplishment that haloes it

From afar. There is no need

To approach closely, it will be done from here

And work out better, you'll see.

So the giant slabs of material

Came to be, and precious little else, and

No information about them but that was all right

For the present century. Later on

We'd see how it might be in some other

Epoch, but for the time being it was neither

Your nor the population's concern, and may

Have glittered as it declined but for now

It would have to do, as any magic

Is the right kind at the right time.

There is no soothsaying

Yet it happens in rows, windrows

You call them in your far country.

But you are leaving:

Some months ago I got an offer

而不是今天的重写本？因为
关于我们习惯性的幻想
（一块不是太慢就是太快的手表）
最值得注意的就是生动的成就感
它从远处投射光环。没有必要
靠近，它将在这里完成
更好地实现，你会看到的。

于是，一块块巨大的材料板
形成了，还有其他珍贵的小板子
没有任何关于它们的信息，除了
当前的世纪一切顺利。以后
我们能在其他时代看见
它会怎么样，但在目前，它既不是你
也不是人民心神所系的东西，也许
它在衰落时会闪烁，但现在
它不得不如此，就像任何戏法
都是在正确的时间做正确的事。
没有任何预言
它依然发生在行列里，料堆中
你在你遥远的国度呼唤它们。

但是你要离开了：
数月之前我得到一份

From Columbia Tape Club, Terre Haute, Ind., where I could buy one Tape and get another free. I accept Ed the deal, paid for one tape and Chose a free one. But since I've been Repeatedly billed for my free tape. I've written them several times but Can't straighten it out—would you Try?

来自印第安纳州泰瑞豪特
哥伦比亚磁带俱乐部的报价,
我可以在那里买一赠一。
我接受了这笔交易,买了一盘磁带
又选了一盘免费的。可从那以后
我就一直反复地为那免费磁带付账。
我给他们写过几次信了可是
都澄清不了这件事——你愿意
试试吗?

Silhouette

Of how that current ran in, and turned

In the climate of the indecent moment

And became an act,

I may not tell. The road

Ran down there and was afterwards there

So that no further borrowing

Of criticism or the desire to add pleasure

Was ever seen that way again.

In the blank mouths

Of your oppressors, however, much

Was seen to provoke. And the way

Though discontinuous, and intermittent, sometimes

Not heard of for years at a time, did,

Nonetheless, move up, although, to his surprise

It was inside the house,

And always getting narrower.

There is no telling to what lengths,

What mannerisms and fictitious subterranean

Flowerings next to the cement he might have

剪　影

关于那股潮流如何涌进来，旋转
在不得体的时刻的气候中
变成一个行动，
我不想说。道路
通向那里，随后在那里结束了
以至于不再借助
批评或是欲望来增加乐趣
于是便又能看见那条路了。

然而，在压迫你的人
那些空空的嘴巴里，
能看见很多让人激怒的东西。道路
尽管不连贯，断断续续，有时
连续几年都没人听说，真的，
但是，却在上升，尽管，让他吃惊的是
它是在屋子里面，
并且一直在变窄。

说不清是什么长度，
什么样的怪癖和虚构的地下工作者
近乎混凝土一样盛行，他可能

Been driven. But it all turned out another way.

So cozy, so ornery, tempted always,

Yet not thinking in his 1964 Ford

Of the price of anything, the grapes, and her tantalizing touch

So near that the fish in the aquarium

Hung close to the glass, suspended, yet he never knew her

Except behind the curtain. The catastrophe

Buried in the stair carpet stayed there

And never corrupted anybody.

And one day he grew up, and the horizon

Stammered politely. The sky was like muslin.

And still in the old house no one ever answered the bell.

一直是被动的。可结果完全是另一个样子。

如此安逸，如此低劣，总是被诱惑，

在他一九六四年的福特车里不要想

任何事的代价，葡萄，和她撩人的触摸

玻璃缸里的鱼这么近

紧贴玻璃悬浮着，停顿，他从来不认识她

除了在窗帘后面。大灾难

埋在楼梯地毯里，留在那儿

从来没有让任何人堕落。

有一天他长大了，地平线

委婉地结结巴巴。天空像棉布。

而在旧房子里依然没有人回应钟声。

Many Wagons Ago

At first it was as though you had passed,
But then no, I said, he is still here,
Forehead refreshed. A light is kindled. And
Another. But no I said

Nothing in this wide berth of lights like weeds
Stays to listen. Doubled up, fun is inside,
The lair a surface compact with the night.
It needs only one intervention,

A stitch, two, three, and then you see
How it is all false equation planted with
Enchanting blue shrubbery on each terrace
That night produces, and they are backing up.

How easily we could spell if we could follow,
Like thread looped through the eye of a needle,
The grooves of light. It resists. But we stay behind, among them,
The injured, the adored.

许多马车前

起初好像你已经过去了,
但是没有,我说,他仍在这里,
前额清凉了。一盏灯燃亮。又是
一盏。但是没有我说

在这灯的宽敞停泊处没有什么像杂草
留下来倾听。对折起来,乐趣在里面,
一个表面用夜晚压成的巢穴。
它只需要一次干预。

缝一针,两针,三针,然后你看见
那全然虚假的方程式怎样把迷人的蓝灌木
种满那个夜晚造出的
每座露台,它们正在倒退。

我们多么容易就能着迷,假如我们能跟得上,
像线头循环穿过一个针眼,
光的沟槽。它抵抗着。但我们留在后面,在它们中间,
受伤的,被爱慕的。

As We Know

All that we see is penetrated by it—
The distant treetops with their steeple (so
Innocent), the stair, the windows' fixed flashing—
Pierced full of holes by the evil that is not evil,
The romance that is not mysterious, the life that is not life,
A present that is elsewhere.

And further in the small capitulations
Of the dance, you rub elbows with it,
Finger it. That day you did it
Was the day you had to stop, because the doing
Involved the whole fabric, there was no other way to appear.
You slid down on your knees
For those precious jewels of spring water
Planted on the moss, before they got soaked up
And you teetered on the edge of this
Calm street with its sidewalks, its traffic,

As though they are coming to get you.
But there was no one in the noon glare,
Only birds like secrets to find out about

正如我们所知

我们所看见的一切都被它穿透——
遥远的树顶和它们的陡峭（如此
无辜），楼梯，窗户固定的闪光——
被不是罪恶的罪恶，
并不神秘的浪漫，不是生活的生活，
一个在别处的礼物，刺满孔眼。

进而在舞步顿挫之际，
你趁机用手臂蹭它一下，
摸它一把。你那么干的那天
是你必须停止的那天，因为你的行为
涉及整个结构，别无出路。
你双膝滑倒
为春水的那些珍宝
它们种植在苔藓上，在被浸透之前
你步履蹒跚地走在这安静街道的
边缘，它的人行道，它的交通，

仿佛它们正来接你。
但是没有人在中午闪耀，
只有鸟儿像要去发现的秘密

And a home to get to, one of these days.

The light that was shadowed then

Was seen to be our lives,

Everything about us that love might wish to examine,

Then put away for a certain length of time, until

The whole is to be reviewed, and we turned

Toward each other, to each other.

The way we had come was all we could see

And it crept up on us, embarrassed

That there is so much to tell now, really now.

和一个要返回的家,这些日子中的一个。

那时被遮住的光
被视为我们的生活,
爱希望检验的关于我们的一切,
然后放弃一段时间,直到
整体受到评论,而我们彼此
转过身来,彼此面对。
我们的来路是我们能看见的全部
它在我们身上爬行,困窘于
现在有这么多的事要说,真的就是现在。

Otherwise

I'm glad it didn't offend me
Not astral rain nor the unsponsored irresponsible musings

Of the soul where it exists
To be fed and fussed over
Are really what this trial is about.

It is meant to be the beginning
Yet turns into anthems and bell ropes
Swaying from landlocked clouds
Otherwise into memories.

Which can't stand still and the progress
Is permanent like the preordained bulk
Of the First National Bank

Like fish sauce, but agreeable.

否　则

我很高兴它没有冒犯我
不是星形的雨也不是无人倡议的不可靠的

灵魂的沉思，它在那里存在
被喂养，被娇惯
的确与这次考验有关。

它有意成为开端
却将变成圣歌和钟绳
从内陆的云摇摆而来
否则便会进入记忆。

它不能静立，进步
是永恒的，就像第一国家银行
预先决定的储量

就像鱼露，却让人愉快。

Flowering Death

Ahead, starting from the far north, it wanders.
Its radish-strong gasoline fumes have probably been
Locked into your sinuses while you were away.
You will have to deliver it.
The flowers exist on the edge of breath, loose,
Having been laid there.
One gives pause to the other,
Or there will be a symmetry about their movements
Through which each is also an individual.

It is their collective blankness, however,
That betrays the notion of a thing not to be destroyed.
In this, how many facts we have fallen through
And still the old façade glimmers there,
A mirage, but permanent. We must first trick the idea
Into being, then dismantle it,
Scattering the pieces on the wind,
So that the old joy, modest as cake, as wine and friendship
Will stay with us at the last, backed by the night
Whose ruse gave it our final meaning.

开花的死亡

前面,从遥远的北方,它开始漫游。
你不在的时候,它萝卜般强烈的汽油味
也许一直被锁在你的鼻窦里。
你将不得不释放它。
花朵存在于呼吸的边缘,松弛,
一直躺在那里。
一朵花让另一朵花停顿,
或许会有一个对称关乎它们的运动
通过它,每一朵花仍是一个个体。

这是它们集体的空白,然而,
那违背一件事物不会被摧毁的观念。
在这里,我们有多少事实已经落空
陈旧的表面仍在那里闪烁着,
一个海市蜃楼,但却永恒。我们首先必须哄骗思想
让它存在,然后拆除它,
把碎片抛撒在风中,
以便古老的欢乐,谦逊得像蛋糕,像酒和友谊
最后会与我们同在,以夜为支撑
以其策略赋予它我们最后的意义。

Haunted Landscape

Something brought them here. It was an outcropping of peace
In the blurred afternoon slope on which so many picnickers
Had left no trace. The hikers then always passed through
And greeted you silently. And down in one corner

Where the sweet william grew and a few other cheap plants
The rhythm became strained, extenuated, as it petered out
Among pots and watering cans and a trowel. There were no
People now but everywhere signs of their recent audible passage.

She had preferred to sidle through the cane and he
To hoe the land in the hope that some day they would grow happy
Contemplating the result: so much fruitfulness. A legend.
He came now in the certainty of her braided greeting,

Sunlight and shadow, and a great sense of what had been cast off
Along the way, to arrive in this notch. Why were the insiders
Secretly amused at their putting up handbills at night?
By day hardly anyone came by and saw them.

They were thinking, too, that this was the right way to begin

闹鬼的风景

什么东西把他们带到这里。它是露出地面的和平
模糊的下午,这么多郊游者倚在上面
也没有留下痕迹。那时徒步旅行者总是穿过它
沉默地迎接你。在一个角落里

生长着美洲石竹,和其他一些廉价植物
节奏变得紧张,减弱,逐渐消失在
壶、水罐和一把泥铲中间。现在没有人
但到处都有他们新近经过的迹象。

她喜欢侧身穿过竹林而他
喜欢用锄头耕地,希望有一天他们能变得快活
沉思着收成:如此果实累累。一个传奇。
现在他来了,对她编织的问候确信不疑,

阳光和阴影,和一种强烈的感觉,有什么东西被放出来
沿路朝这峡谷而来。为什么知情者
偷偷地拿他们夜里贴出的传单做消遣?
白天几乎没人经过并看见它们。

他们也认为,这是开始的正确方式

A farm that would later have to be uprooted to make way

For the new plains and mountains that would follow after

To be extinguished in turn as the ocean takes over

Where the glacier leaves off and in the thundering of surf

And rock, something, some note or other, gets lost,

And we have this to look back on, not much, but a sign

Of the petty ordering of our days as it was created and led us

By the nose through itself, and now it has happened

And we have it to look at, and have to look at it

For the good it now possesses which has shrunk from the

Outline surrounding it to a little heap or handful near the center.

Others call this old age or stupidity, and we, living

In that commodity, know how only it can enchant the dear soul

Building up dreams through the night that are cast down

At the end with a graceful roar, like chimes swaying out over

The phantom village. It is our best chance of passing

Unnoticed into the dream and all that the outside said about it,

Carrying all that back to the source of so much that was precious.

At one of the later performances you asked why they called it a "miracle,"

一座以后将不得不根除的农场

为新的平原和群山让路，它们随后

将依次被海洋淹没，而海洋将占据

冰川消失的地方，在巨浪和岩石的轰鸣中

某个东西，某个记录或其他什么，丢失了，

我们可以据此回望，不过分，只是一个记号

关乎我们时日的妥善安排，它被创造出来并牵着鼻子

引领我们穿过它自身，现在它已经发生

我们要看看它，而且必须要看看它

因为它现在拥有的一切已经从围绕它的周界

收缩成靠近中间的一小堆或一小把。

别人将此称作旧时代或愚蠢，而我们，活着

在那日用品中，知道它如何只能迷惑亲爱的灵魂

通过夜晚建筑梦境，最后随着一声

优美的吼叫被推翻，像钟声摇荡在

鬼村上方。它是我们通过的最好时机

无人察觉地进入梦境，和外界相关的传言，

携带一切返回如此珍贵的源头。

后来在一次表演中你问为何他们称它为"奇迹"，

Since nothing ever happened. That, of course, was the miracle
But you wanted to know why so much action took on so much life
And still managed to remain itself, aloof, smiling and courteous.
Is that the way life is supposed to happen? We'll probably never know

Until its cover turns into us: the eglantine for duress
And long relativity, until it becomes a touch of red under the bridge
At fixed night, and the cries of the wind are viewed as happy, salient.
How could that picture come crashing off the wall when no one was
    in the room?

At least the glass isn't broken. I like the way the stars
Are painted in this one, and those which are painted out.
The door is opening. A man you have never seen enters the room.
He tells you that it is time to go, but that you may stay,

If you wish. You reply that it is one and the same to you.
It was only later, after the house had materialized elsewhere,
That you remembered you forgot to ask him what form the change
    would take.
But it is probably better that way. Now time and the land are identical,

Linked forever.

既然什么都没有发生。当然，那就是奇迹
但你想知道为何这样的情节呈现了这样的生活
却仍要设法把它自己留下，冷淡，微笑，谦恭。
那就是所设想的生活发生的方式吗？也许我们永远不知道

直到它的覆盖物变成我们：适合监禁和长期相互依存的
野蔷薇，直到它变成桥下面的一抹红色
在固定的夜晚，风的哭泣被当做明显的幸福。
那图画如何能从墙上剥落，当屋子里空无一人？

至少玻璃没碎。我喜欢群星
涂在里面的样子，还有那些被涂掉的星星。
门开着。一个你从未见过的男人进入房间。
他告诉你该走了，但是你可以留下，

如果你愿意。你回答去留对你都是一样。
只是在后来，房子在别处突然出现之后，
你才记起你忘了问他，变化会采取什么形式。
可也许那样更好。现在时间和大地合一

永远联在一起。

My Erotic Double

He says he doesn't feel like working today.

It's just as well. Here in the shade

Behind the house, protected from street noises,

One can go over all kinds of old feeling,

Throw some away, keep others.

                                      The wordplay

Between us gets very intense when there are

Fewer feelings around to confuse things.

Another go-round? No, but the last things

You always find to say are charming, and rescue me

Before the night does. We are afloat

On our dreams as on a barge made of ice,

Shot through with questions and fissures of starlight

That keep us awake, thinking about the dreams

As they are happening. Some occurrence. You said it.

I said it but I can hide it. But I choose not to.

Thank you. You are a very pleasant person.

Thank you. You are too.

我好色的替身演员

他说他今天不想工作。
这也挺好。这里,在房子后面的
阴影中,挡住街上的喧闹,
一个人可以重温各种过去的感觉,
抛掉一些,留下一些。
　　　　　我们之间的
双关语游戏变得非常紧张
当可以把事情搞乱的感觉越来越少。
再来一轮?不,但是你总是发现
最后要说的事才是迷人的,
并先于夜晚拯救我们。我们飘浮在
我们的梦境上面,就像在一艘冰驳船上,
被问题和星光的裂缝射穿
那让我们保持清醒,思考着梦境
当它们正在发生。有的出现了。你说了它。

我说了它但我可以把它藏起来。可我选择不藏。
谢谢你。你是一个非常让人愉快的人。
谢谢你。你也是。

Train Rising out of the Sea

It is written in the Book of Usable Minutes

That all things have their center in their dying,

That each is discrete and diaphanous and

Has pointed its prow away from the sand for the next trillion years.

After that we may be friends,

Recognizing in each other the precedents that make us truly social.

Do you hear the wind? It's not dying,

It's singing, weaving a song about the president saluting the trust,

The past in each of us, until so much memory becomes an institution,

Through sheer weight, the persistence of it, no,

Not the persistence: that makes it seem a deliberate act

Of duration, much too deliberate for this ingenuous being

Like an era that refuses to come to an end or be born again.

We need more night for the sky, more blue for the daylight

That inundates our remarks before we can make them

Taking away a little bit of us each time

To be deposited elsewhere

海中升起的列车

它写在"可用时刻表"中
万物在垂死之中都有自己的中心,
每一个都离散而且模糊
把它的船首偏离沙子,为了以后的万亿年。

在那以后我们可能会成为朋友,
在彼此身上辨别着使我们真正合群的先例。
你听见风了吗?它没有减弱,
它在歌唱,编织着一支总统向信任,向我们身上的过去

致敬的歌,直到如此多的记忆变成一个制度,
穿过纯粹的重量,它的坚持,不,
不是坚持:那使它显得像一个刻意持续的
行为,对于这朴实的存在过于刻意

像一个拒绝结束或再次诞生的时代。
我们需要给天空更多的夜晚,给阳光更多的蓝色
它们会淹没我们的话,在我们能够让它们
每次带走我们一小点

去储存在别处之前

In the place of our involvement

With the core that brought excessive flowering this year

Of enormous sunsets and big breezes

That left you feeling too simple

Like an island just off the shore, one of many, that no one

Notices, though it has a certain function, though an abstract one

Built to prevent you from being towed to shore.

在我们与那核心纠缠的地方
今年的花多得过分
巨大的落日和狂风

让你觉得太简单了
像岸边的一座岛,许多中的一座,没人
注意,尽管它有一定的功能,尽管有一个抽象的岛
为防止你被拖到岸上而建造。

Late Echo

Alone with our madness and favorite flower
We see that there really is nothing left to write about.
Or rather, it is necessary to write about the same old things
In the same way, repeating the same things over and over
For love to continue and be gradually different.

Beehives and ants have to be reexamined eternally
And the color of the day put in
Hundreds of times and varied from summer to winter
For it to get slowed down to the pace of an authentic
Saraband and huddle there, alive and resting.

Only then can the chronic inattention
Of our lives drape itself around us, conciliatory
And with one eye on those long tan plush shadows
That speak so deeply into our unprepared knowledge
Of ourselves, the talking engines of our day.

迟到的回声

与我们的疯狂和喜爱的花独处
我们看见真的没剩下什么可写的了。
倒不如说，有必要去写写同样的旧东西
以同样的方式，一遍遍重复同样的东西
为了让爱继续，并逐渐变得不同。

蜂箱和蚂蚁必须时时检查
日子的颜色几百次地
加进来并从夏天变到冬天
为了慢下来，慢成一种可信的萨拉邦德舞步，
并拥挤在那里，生动而静止。

只有那时，我们生命那习惯性的疏忽
才能抚慰地裹住我们，
用一只眼睛盯着那些茶色豪华的长影子
如此深刻地诉诸我们无准备的自我认知，
我们日子的谈话引擎。

And I'd Love You to Be in It

Playing alone, I found the wall.

One side was gray, the other an indelible gray.

The two sides were separated by a third,

Or spirit wall, a coarser gray. The wall

Was chipped and tarnished in places,

Polished in places.

I wanted to put it behind me

By walking beside it until it ended.

This was never done. Meanwhile

I stayed near the wall, touching the two ends.

With all of my power of living

I am forced to lie on the floor.

To have reached the cleansing end of the journey,

Appearances put off forever, in my new life

There is still no freedom, but excitement

Turns in our throats like woodsmoke.

In what skyscraper or hut

I'll finish? Today there are tendrils

而我喜欢你在它里面

独自游戏,我发现了墙。
一侧是灰,另一侧是去不掉的灰。
墙的两侧被第三面墙,
或者灵魂之墙隔开,一种更粗糙的灰。
墙有缺口,有的地方没有光泽,
有的地方磨得很亮。

我想把它放在我后面
在它旁边走,直到它的尽头。
这一点从未做到。与此同时
我留在墙边,触摸着两端。

以我全部生的力量
我被迫躺在地板上。
为了抵达旅程清洁的终点,
永远脱掉表象,在我的新生命中
仍然没有自由,只有激动
像木头的烟进入我们的喉咙。

在什么摩天大楼或者小屋中
我才会完成?今天有一些卷须

Coming through the slats, and milky, yellowy grapes,

A mild game to divert the doorperson

And we are swiftly inside, the resurrection finished.

穿过板条,还有乳白色、淡黄色的葡萄,
一个使看门人分心的适度的游戏
我们迅速进入,复活完成了。

Tapestry

It is difficult to separate the tapestry

From the room or loom which takes precedence over it.

For it must always be frontal and yet to one side.

It insists on this picture of "history"

In the making, because there is no way out of the punishment

It proposes: sight blinded by sunlight.

The seeing taken in with what is seen

In an explosion of sudden awareness of its formal splendor.

The eyesight, seen as inner,

Registers over the impact of itself

Receiving phenomena, and in so doing

Draws an outline, or a blueprint,

Of what was just there: dead on the line.

If it has the form of a blanket, that is because

We are eager, all the same, to be wound in it:

This must be the good of not experiencing it.

But in some other life, which the blanket depicts anyway,

织　锦

很难把织锦和房间
或者先于它存在的织机分开。
因为它可能始终是正面但又偏向一边。

它坚持要完成这幅正在形成中的
"历史"图画，因为没有办法逃脱惩罚
它打算：让阳光晃瞎眼睛。
看被看见的一切吸收
在一次爆炸中突然意识到它正式的光彩。

视力，被看作内在的，
记录在它自身的效果上
接受着现象，在此过程中
描绘出一个轮廓，或者一张蓝图，
有关那里的一切：死在线条上。

如果它具有一幅毯子的形式，那是因为
我们都同样渴望，被缠在里边：
这一定是不去经历它的好处。

但在别的生活中，毯子描绘的生活中，

The citizens hold sweet commerce with one another

And pinch the fruit unpestered, as they will,

As words go crying after themselves, leaving the dream

Upended in a puddle somewhere

As though "dead" were just another adjective.

公民们与别人做着美好的交易

无忧无虑地捏水果,随心所欲,

当词语哭喊着跟在他们后面,把梦

颠倒地留在一个水坑里

仿佛"死"只是另一个形容词。

A Love Poem

And they have to get it right. We just need

A little happiness, and when the clever things

Are taken up (O has the mouth shaped that letter?

What do we have bearing down on it?) as the last thin curve

("Positively the last," they say) before the dark:

(The sky is pure and faint, the pavement still wet) and

The dripping is in the walls, within sleep

Itself. I mean there is no escape

From me, from it. The night is itself sleep

And what goes on in it, the naming of the wind,

Our notes to each other, always repeated, always the same.

一首爱情诗

他们必须更正它。我们只需要
一小点幸福,当聪明的事物
被拿起来(O 有那个字母形状的嘴吗?
我们要给它施加点什么?)像最后的细弧线
("肯定是最后的",他们说)在黑暗之前:
(天空纯净而暗淡,人行道仍是湿的)而且

滴水是在墙里,它本身在睡眠
之内。我的意思是没有人逃离
我,逃离它。夜晚就是睡眠本身
而在它里面进行的一切,对风的命名,
我们给彼此的日记,总是重复,总是同样。

This Configuration

This movie deals with the epidemic of the way we live now.

What an inane cardplayer. And the age may support it.

Each time the rumble of the age

is an anthill in the distance.

As he slides the first rumpled card

Out of his dirty ruffled shirtfront the cartoon

Of the new age has begun its ascent

Around all of us like a gauze spiral staircase in which

Some stars have been imbedded.

It is the modern trumpets

Who decide the mood or tenor of this cross-section:

Of the people who get up in the morning,

Still half-asleep. That they shouldn't have fun.

But something scary will come

To get them anyway. You might as well linger

On verandas, enjoying life, knowing

The end is essentially unpredictable.

It might be soldiers

Marching all day, millions of them

结　构

这部电影涉及我们目前生活方式的传染性。
多么空虚的玩牌者。时代会支持它。
时代的每一次轰鸣
都是远处的一座蚁山。

当他从他肮脏带褶边的胸衣
滑出第一张弄皱的牌
新时代的卡通已经开始上升
围绕着我们大家,像一个薄纱制成的旋梯
镶嵌着一些星星。

是现代的喇叭
决定这个横截面的情绪或大意:
早晨起床的人,
仍在半睡半醒。他们不应该有娱乐。
但是某个吓人的东西将会
来把他们接走。你不妨逗留
在走廊上,享受着生活,知道
结局本质上是不可预料的。
它可能是士兵
整天行军,有几百万人

Past this spot, like the lozenge pattern
Of these walls, like, finally, a kind of sleep.

Or it may be that we are ordinary people
With not unreasonable desires which we can satisfy
From time to time without causing cataclysms
That keep getting louder and more forceful instead of dying away.

Or it may be that we and the other people
Confused with us on the sidewalk have entered
A moment of seeming to be natural, expected,
And we see ourselves at the moment we see them:
Figures of an afternoon, of a century they extended.

经过这个地点,像这些墙上的
菱形图案,最后,像一种睡眠。

或许我们是普通人
怀有并非不合情理的欲望
我们时刻能够满足它们而不会导致灾难
它们变得更响亮更有力,而不是消失。

或许我们和其他人
混在一起,在人行道上进入
一个似乎自然的被期待的时刻,
我们在看见他们的瞬间看见了自己:
他们延长了的一个下午,一个世纪的形象。

Their Day

Each act of criticism is general

But, in cutting itself off from all the others,

Explicit enough.

We know how the criticism must be done

On a specific day of the week. Too much matters

About this day. Another day, and the criticism is thrown down

Like trash into a dim, dusty courtyard.

It will be built again. That's all the point

There is to it. And it is built,

In sunlight, this time. All look up to it.

It has changed. It is different. It is still

Cut off from all the other acts of criticism.

From this it draws a tragic strength. Its greatness.

They are constructing pleasure simultaneously

In an adjacent chamber

That occupies the same cube of space as the critic's study.

For this to be pleasure, it must also be called criticism.

他们的日子

每一个批评行为都是抽象的
但是,在与其他所有行为的分离中,
它显得足够清楚。

我们知道批评是怎么完成的
在本周的特定一天。它对这一天
非常关键。另一天,批评垃圾
被抛进一个暗淡、满是灰尘的院子。

它将再次被造出来。对于它
那就是所有的意义。它被造了出来,
在阳光中,这次。所有人都仰望着它。
它已经变了。它不一样了。它仍然
与所有其他批评行为分开。
它从此展开一种悲剧的力量。它的伟大。

在相邻的房间
他们在同步制造快乐
占据了和批评家书房同样大的空间。
因为这么做将是快乐,它也必须被称作批评。

It is the very expensive kind

That comes sealed in a bottle. It is music of the second night

That winds up as if to say: Well, you've had it,

And in doing so, you have it.

From these boxed perimeters

We issue forth irregularly. Sometimes in fear,

But mostly with no knowledge of knowing, only a general

But selective feeling that the world had to go on being good to us.

As long as we don't know that

We can live at the square corners of the streets.

The winter does what it can for its children.

它是非常昂贵的那种

密封在一个瓶子里。它是第二夜的音乐

缠起来，仿佛要说：好吧，你已经得到它了，

而且是在这么做的过程中，你得到了它。

从这些方形的周界

我们不定期地出去。有时在恐惧中，

但大多时候一无所知，只有一种抽象

而挑剔的感觉，世界必须继续对我们好。

只要我们不知道

我们能在街道的四方角落里生活。

冬天为它的孩子们做了所能做的一切。

A Tone Poem

It is no longer night. But there is a sameness

Of intention, all the same, in the ways

We address it, rude

Color of what an amazing world,

As it goes flat, or rubs off, and this

Is a marvel, we think, and are careful not to go past it.

But it is the same thing we are all seeing,

Our world. Go after it,

Go get it boy, says the man holding the stick.

Eat, says the hunger, and we plunge blindly in again,

Into the chamber behind the thought.

We can hear it, even think it, but can't get disentangled from our brains.

Here, I am holding the winning ticket. Over here.

But it is all the same color again, as though the climate

Dyed everything the same color. It's more practical,

Yet the landscape, those billboards, age as rapidly as before.

一首音诗

它不再是夜晚。但是我们
表述它的方式,有着同样的意图
完全一致,粗鲁
一个多么令人惊异的世界的颜色,
当它变扁,或是擦掉,我们想
这是一个奇迹,并小心地别从它旁边经过。

但是我们大家看见的是同样的东西,
我们的世界。跟随它,
得到它,男孩,握着棍子的男人说。
吃吧,饥饿说,我们再次盲目地投入,
思想后面的房间。
我们可以听到它,甚至思考它,
但是不能把它从我们大脑里清除。
这里,我握着彩票。在这里。
但是它又是完全相同的颜色,仿佛气候
给一切染上了同样的色彩。它更实际,
可是风景,那些布告板,像以前一样迅速衰老。

The Other Cindy

A breeze came to the aid of that wilted day
Where we sat about fuming at projects
With the funds running out, and others
Too simple and unheard-of to create pressure that moment,

Though it was one of these, lurking in the off-guard
Secrecy of a mind like a magazine article, that kept
Proposing, slicing, disposing, a truant idea even
In that kingdom of the blind, that finally would have
Reined in the mad hunt, quietly, and kept us there,
Thinking, not especially dozing any more, until
The truth had revealed itself the way a natural-gas
Storage tank becomes very well known sometime after
Dawn has slipped in
And seems to have been visible all along
Like a canoe route across the great lake on whose shore
One is left trapped, grumbling not so much at bad luck as
Because only this one side of experience is ever revealed.
And that meant something.

Sure, there was more to it

另一个辛迪

一阵微风前来帮助那个枯萎的日子
我们袖手旁观，为这些工程发愁
资金在逐渐耗尽，还有其他人
单纯得不知道在那个时刻要制造压力，

尽管它是工程之一，潜伏在一个大脑
不设防的秘密中，像一篇杂志文章，
一直在建议，限制，处理，一个逃学的念头
甚至在那盲人的王国，那念头最终也会
在疯狂的狩猎中勒住马，悄悄地，让我们留在那里，
思考着，不怎么瞌睡了，直到
真理自行揭示出一个天然气储气柜
有时在黄昏偷偷降临之后
变得众所周知的方式
并且似乎一直是可见的
像一只独木舟航线穿过大湖，有一个人
陷在湖岸上，并不怎么抱怨自己的坏运气
因为得到揭示的只是经验的这一面。
而那意味着什么东西。

的确，事情没那么简单

And the haunted houses in those valleys wanted to congratulate

You on your immobility. Too often the adventurous acolyte

Drops permanently from sight in this beautiful country.

There is much to be said in favor of the danger of warding off danger

But if you ever want to return

Though it seems improbable on the face of it

You must master the huge retards and have faith in the slow

Blossoming of haystacks, stairways, walls of convolvulus,

Until the moon can do no more. Exhausted,

You get out of bed. Your project is completed

Though the experiment is a mess. Return the kit

In the smashed cardboard box to the bright, bland

Cities that gave rise to you, you know

The one with the big Woolworth's and postcard-blue sky.

The contest ends at midnight tonight

But you can submit again, and again.

那些峡谷中闹鬼的房子想要庆贺
你的静止不动。在这个美丽的国度
爱冒险的助手常常从视野中永远消失。
为了避开危险的危险,有很多话要说
可如果你想回来

尽管似乎不大可能与之面对
你也必须克服巨大的阻碍,相信
慢慢开花的干草堆,楼梯,有旋花植物的墙壁,
直到月亮无所施展。筋疲力尽,
你从床上起来。你的工程完成了
尽管实验是一片混乱。归还装备
用破纸箱送回让你发生变化的

明亮而乏味的城市,你知道
其中一座有伍尔沃斯大超市,天空蓝如明信片。
竞赛将在今天午夜结束
但是你可以再次提交,再一次。

The Plural of "Jack in the Box"

How quiet the diversion stands

Beside my gate, and me all eager and no grace:

Until tomorrow with sifting hands

Uncode the sea that brought me to this place,

Discover people with changing face

But the way is wide over stubble and sands,

Wider and not too wide, as a dish in space

Is excellent, conforming to demands

Not yet formulated. Let certain trends

Believe us, and that way give chase

With hounds, and with the hare erase

All knowledge of its coming here. The lands

Are fewer now under the plain blue blanket whose

Birthday keeps them outside at the end.

玩偶盒的复数

这消遣物多么安静地站在
我的门边，我急不可耐，风度全无：
直到明天用筛选的双手
替那把我带到此地的大海解码，
发现人们有着变幻的面孔
断株和沙子上的路是宽的，
更宽了，但不是太宽，像空间里的一个盘子
好极了，符合要求

还没有设计出来。让一些倾向
相信我们，那条路让猎犬
可以追逐，让野兔擦除
它来到这里的所有知识。陆地
现在更少了，在朴素的蓝毯子下面
谁的生日把它们放在外面，直到最后。

From
SHADOW TRAIN
影子列车
(1981)

The Pursuit of Happiness

It came about that there was no way of passing

Between the twin partitions that presented

A unified façade, that of a suburban shopping mall

In April. One turned, as one does, to other interests

Such as the tides in the Bay of Fundy. Meanwhile there was one

Who all unseen came creeping at this scale of visions

Like the gigantic specter of a cat towering over tiny mice

About to adjourn the town meeting due to the shadow,

An incisive shadow, too perfect in its outrageous

Regularity to be called to stand trial again,

That every blistered tongue welcomed as the first

Drops scattered by the west wind, and yet, knowing

That it would always ever afterwards be this way

Caused the eyes to faint, the ears to ignore warnings.

We knew how to get by on what comes along, but the idea

Warning, waiting there like a forest, not emptied, beckons.

对幸福的追求

它来自那根本无路可通的地方
在代表一个统一表面的
两个部分之间,那是郊区的大型购物中心
在四月。一个人如往常那样,兴趣转移了

比如"方迪湾"的潮汐。同时有一个
完全看不见的人在这幻象的梯子上爬行
像一只猫巨大的幽灵耸立在小老鼠上面
那小鼠就要因为这阴影而推迟镇上的集会了,

一个锋利的影子,它惊人的规律性过于完美
以致不能被再次召来受审,
每条起泡的舌头都表示欢迎,当最初的水滴
被西风播散,而且,知道

它以后会一直如此
致使眼睛模糊,耳朵忽略了警告。
我们知道如何应付到来的一切,可是思想
在发出警告,像树林等在那里,不是空的,召唤着。

Punishing the Myth

At first it came easily, with the knowledge of the shadow line
Picking its way through various landscapes before coming
To stand far from you, to bless you incidentally
In sorting out what was best for it, and most suitable,

Like snow having second thoughts and coming back
To be wary about this, to embellish that, as though life were a party
At which work got done. So we wiggled in our separate positions
And stayed in them for a time. After something has passed

You begin to see yourself as you would look to yourself on a stage,
Appearing to someone. But to whom? Ah, that's just it,
To have the manners, and the look that comes from having a secret
Isn't enough. But that "not enough" isn't to be worn like a livery,

To be briefly noticed, yet among whom should it be seen? I haven't
Thought about these things in years; that's my luck.
In time even the rocks will grow. And if you have curled and dandled
Your innocence once too often, what attitude isn't then really yours?

惩罚神话

起初它来得容易，随着阴影线的知识
在各种以前的风景中谨慎前行，最后
离你远远地站着，顺便祝福你
挑选出什么对它最好，什么最合适

像雪怀有第二个想法，返回
提防着这个，修饰着那个，仿佛生活是一场晚会
工作在晚会上完成。于是我们在各自的位置上踌躇
停留一段时间。在某件事过去之后

你开始像在舞台上期望的那样看见自己，
出现在某人面前。可那是谁呢？哦，那仅仅是它，
彬彬有礼，怀有一个秘密似的表情
这不够。但是那"不够"不会被穿旧，像件制服，

被暂时注意到，在什么人中间能看见它？
我很多年没有想过这些事情了；那是我的幸运。
时辰一到岩石都会生长。如果你经常蜷缩着
逗弄你的单纯，那么你真正的态度又不是什么？

Paradoxes and Oxymorons

This poem is concerned with language on a very plain level.
Look at it talking to you. You look out a window
Or pretend to fidget. You have it but you don't have it.
You miss it, it misses you. You miss each other.

The poem is sad because it wants to be yours, and cannot be.
What's a plain level? It is that and other things,
Bringing a system of them into play. Play?
Well, actually, yes, but I consider play to be

A deeper outside thing, a dreamed role-pattern,
As in the division of grace these long August days
Without proof. Open-ended. And before you know it
It gets lost in the steam and chatter of typewriters.

It has been played once more. I think you exist only
To tease me into doing it, on your level, and then you aren't there
Or have adopted a different attitude. And the poem
Has set me softly down beside you. The poem is you.

悖论与矛盾修辞

这首诗在一个非常普通的层面上与语言相关。
看它在对你讲话。你望向窗外
或是装作坐立不安。你占有它但你没有拥有它。
你错过了它,它错过了你。你们彼此错过。

这首诗是悲哀的,因为它想属于,但不能。
什么是普通的层面?就是它和其他东西,
把它们组成一套系统进行游戏。游戏?
哦,实际上,是的,但我认为游戏

是一个更深的外部事物,一个被梦见的角色模式,
就像这些漫长的八月里分配的恩典
没有证明。没有限制。在你知道它之前
它丢失在蒸汽和打字机的喧闹中。

它又被游戏了一次。我认为你的存在只是为了
挑逗我去这样做,在你的层面上,然后你就不在那儿了
或者已经采取了另一种态度。而这首诗
已把我轻柔地放在你旁边。这首诗就是你。

Another Chain Letter

He had had it told to him on the sward

Where the fat men bowl, and told so that no one—

He least of all—might be sure in the days to come

Of the exact terms. Then, each turned back

To his business, as is customary on such occasions.

Months and months went by. The green squirearchy

Of the dandelions was falling through the hoop again

And no one, it seemed, had had the presence of mind

To initiate proceedings or stop the wheel

From the number it was backing away from as it stopped:

It was performing prettily; the puncture stayed unseen;

The wilderness seemed to like the eclogue about it

You wrote and performed, but really no one now

Saw any good in the cause, or any guilt. It was a conspiracy

Of right-handed notions. Which is how we all

Became partners in the pastoral doffing, the night we now knew.

另一封连锁信

他在草地上把这件事告诉了他
胖子们在那里玩保龄球，这样就没有人——
尤其是他——将来能够确定
确切的条款。然后，各自回到

自己的事情上，像通常这种情况下一样，
几个月几个月过去。蒲公英绿色的
地主阶级又在穿过铁环坠落
似乎没有一个人，心里意识到

要启动程序或是阻止轮子
背弃它停止时想要背弃的号码：
它表演得恰如其分；刺痕始终看不见；
荒野似乎和有关它的牧歌一样

你写作，表演，但实际上现在没有一个人
在这件事中看出任何的善恶。它是右撇子观念的
一个阴谋。我们大家就这样成了伙伴
在田园脱棉中，在我们现今熟悉的夜晚。

The Ivory Tower

Another season, proposing a name and a distant resolution.
And, like the wind, all attention. Those thirsting ears,
Climbers on what rickety heights, have swept you
All alone into their confession, for it is as alone

Each of us stands and surveys this empty cell of time. Well,
What is there to do? And so a mysterious creeping motion
Quickens its demonic profile, bringing tears, to these eyes at least,
Tears of excitement. When was the last time you *knew* that?

Yet in the textbooks thereof you keep getting mired
In a backward innocence, although that too is something
That must be owned, together with the rest.
There is always some impurity. Help it along! Make room for it!

So that in the annals of this year be nothing but what is sobering:
A porch built on pilings, far out over the sand. Then it doesn't
Matter that the deaths come in the wrong order. All has been so easily
Written about. And you find the right order after all: play, the streets,
    shopping, time flying.

象牙塔

另一个季节,提出一个名字和一个遥远的决定。
而且,像风一样,全神贯注。那些渴望的耳朵,
摇晃不已的高处的攀缘者,使你独自
为他们的忏悔感动,因为仿佛我们都是

独自站着,探索着这时间空虚的细胞。那么,
那里有什么要做的呢?如此神秘的爬行
加快了它恶魔的侧影,至少,使这些眼睛落泪,
激动的泪。你最后一次知道流泪是什么时候?

但在相关的课本里你一直陷在
迟钝的无知中,尽管那也是一件
必须拥有的东西,和其他东西的一道。
总有某种杂质存在。帮帮它!给它腾地方!

于是在今年的年鉴中只有清醒:
一个门廊建在木桩上,远在沙地那边。不要紧
死亡以错误的顺序降临。写起来
一切都这么容易。你毕竟发现了正确的顺序:游戏,街道,购
　　物,时间飞逝。

At the Inn

It was me here. Though. And whether this
Be rebus or me now, the way the grass is planted—
Red stretching far out to the horizon—
Surely prevails now. I shall return in the dark and be seen,

Be led to my own room by well-intentioned hands,
Placed in a box with a lid whose underside is dark
So as to grow, and shall grow
Taller than plumes out on the ocean,

Grazing historically. And shall see
The end of much learning, and other things
Out of control and it ends too soon, before hanging up.
So, laying his cheek against the dresser's wooden one,

He died making up stories, the ones
Not every child wanted to listen to.
And for a while it seemed that the road back
Was a track bombarded by stubble like a snow.

在旅馆

是我在这里。尽管。现在无论这是
画谜还是我,草的种植方式——
红色远远延伸向地平线——
现在肯定流行了。我将返回黑暗并被看见,

被谨慎的手领到我自己的房间,
放在一个有盖的盒子里,里面是黑的
以便生长,并会长得
比外面海洋上的烟柱还高,

历史性的放牧。并会看见
非常熟悉的结局,和其他失控的事物
而它将太早地结束,在悬挂起来之前。
于是,把他的面颊靠在木头梳妆台上

他因虚构故事而死,这些故事
不是每个孩子都想听。
有片刻那返回的路
似乎是撒满庄稼茬的车辙,像一场雪。

The Absence of a Noble Presence

If it was treason it was so well handled that it
Became unimaginable. No, it was ambrosia
In the alley under the stars and not this undiagnosable
Turning, a shadow in the plant of all things

That makes us aware of certain moments,
That the end is not far off since it will occur
In the present and this is the present.
No it was something not very subtle then and yet again

You've got to remember we don't see that much.
We see a portion of eaves dripping in the pastel book
And are aware that everything doesn't count equally—
There is dreaminess and infection in the sum

And since this too is of our everydays
It matters only to the one you are next to
This time, giving you a ride to the station.
It foretells itself, not the hiccup you both notice.

一个高贵存在的缺席

如果它是通敌,它被处理得这么好
是无法想象的。不,它是神的食物
在星光下的小巷里,不是这尚未找出原因的
转折,万物工厂中的一个阴影

使我们意识到某些瞬间,
结局不会太远,既然它将发生
在现在而这就是现在。
不,它那时就不是非常微妙的东西

你再次记起我们没有看见那么多。
我们看见屋檐的一部分在蜡笔画册中滴水
并且意识到事物的价值并不相同——
总体上存在多梦和感染

既然这也是我们的每一天
这一次,它只对你邻近的人
重要,载你去车站。
它预言自己,不是你们都注意到的打嗝。

Qualm

Warren G. Harding invented the word "normalcy,"
And the lesser-known "bloviate," meaning, one imagines,
To spout, to spew aimless verbiage. He never wanted to be president.
The "Ohio Gang" made him. He died in the Palace

Hotel in San Francisco, coming back from Alaska,
As his wife was reading to him, about him,
From *The Saturday Evening Post.* Poor Warren. He wasn't a bad egg,
Just weak. He loved women and Ohio.

This protected summer of high, white clouds, a new golf star
Flashes like confetti across the intoxicating early part
Of summer, almost to the end of August. The crowd is hysterical:
Fickle as always, they follow him to the edge

Of the inferno. But the fall is, deliciously, only his.
They shall communicate this and that and compute
Fixed names like "doorstep in the wind." The agony is permanent
Rather than eternal. He'd have noticed it. Poor Warren.

疑　虑

华伦·G.哈丁发明了"常态"这个词，
还有更少人知的"发表冗长演说"，意思是，一个人想象自己，
滔滔不绝，喷出无目的的空话。他从不想当总统。
"俄亥俄帮"造就了他。他死在旧金山

皇宫酒店，从阿拉斯加回来，
当他的妻子给他读《星期六晚邮报》上
有关他的新闻时。可怜的华伦。他不是坏蛋，
只是软弱。他喜欢女人和俄亥俄。

这受保护的夏天，高高的白云，一个高尔夫新星
闪烁如五彩纸屑穿过夏天醉人的
开端，几乎来到八月的末尾。人群疯狂：
和往常一样薄情，他们尾随他来到

地狱的边缘。但是秋天是芬芳的，只属于他。
他们将交流这样那样的信息，推断
固定的名字，如"风中门阶"。苦恼
比永恒还永恒。他注意到了。可怜的华伦。

Here Everything Is Still Floating

But, it's because the liquor of summer nights
Accumulates in the bottom of the bottle.
Suspenders brought it to its, this, level, not
The tempest in a teapot of a private asylum, laughter on the back steps,

Not mine, in fine; I must concentrate on how disappointing
It all has to be while rejoicing in my singular
Un-wholeness that keeps it an event to me. These, these young guys
Taking a shower with the truth, living off the interest of their

Sublime receptivity to anything, can disentangle the whole
Lining of fabricating living from the instantaneous
Pocket it explodes in, enters the limelight of history from,
To be gilded and regilded, waning as its legend waxes,

Disproportionate and triumphant. Still I enjoy
The long sweetness of the simultaneity, yours and mine, ours and mine,
The mosquitoey summer night light. Now about your poem
Called this poem: it stays and must outshine its welcome.

这里的一切仍在漂浮

但是,这是因为夏夜的液体
积聚在瓶底上。
吊裤带把它带到它的,这个,水平,不是
私立收容所一把茶壶里的暴风雨,后门台阶上的笑声,

总而言之,不是我的;我必须集中思考它是如何
令人失望,同时又欣喜于我异常的不完整
对于我那一直是个事儿。这些,这些年轻人
用真理洗了一次淋浴,靠他们对任何事物

超群的接受能力生活,可以解开整个
创造性生活的衬里,摆脱临时的口袋
从中爆裂,进入历史形式的灰光灯,
被反复镀金,随它的传奇增大而变小,

不成比例却得意洋洋。我还是享受
同时性漫长的甜蜜,你的和我的,我们的和我的,
多蚊的夏夜之光。现在关于你的诗
称这个为诗:它停留,一定比它的款待更出色。

Some Old Tires

This was mine, and I let it slip through my fingers.
Nevertheless, I do not want, in this airy and pleasant city,
To be held back by valors that were mine
Only for the space of a dream instant, before continuing

To be someone else's. Because there's too much to
Be done that doesn't fit, and the parts that get lost
Are the reasonable ones just because they got lost
And were forced to suffer transfiguration by finding their way home

To a forgotten spot way out in the fields. To have always
Had the wind for a friend is no recommendation. Yet some
Disagree, while still others claim that signs of fatigue
And mended places are, these offshore days, open

And a symbol of what must continue
After the ring is closed on us. The furniture,
Taken out and examined under the starlight, pleads
No contest. And the backs of those who sat there before.

一些旧轮胎

这是我的,我让它滑过我的手指。
不过,我不想,在这通风而怡人的城里,
被属于我的勇猛所阻止
只为了一个瞬间的梦的空间,在接下来

属于别人之前。因为有太多的事
要做,所以那不合适,而那些丢失的部分
是合理的,只是因为它们丢失了
且被迫忍受变形,因为寻找回家的路

而返回田野中一个被遗忘的地点。
不建议始终关注一个朋友的消息。有人
不同意,其他人则声称那是疲劳的迹象
改正的地方,这些离岸的日子,敞开着

有关什么事物的一个象征必须继续
当绳套在我们头上闭合之后。家具,
搬了出去,在星光下检查,不争辩。
谁以前坐在那些家具的背后。

Something Similar

I, the city mouse, have traveled from a long ways away

To be with you with my news. Now you have my passport

With its color photo in it, to be sweet with you

As the times allow. I didn't say that because it's true,

I said it from a dim upstairs porch into the veiled

Shapely masses of this country you are the geography of

So you can put it in your wallet. That's all we can do

For the time being. Elegance has been halted for the duration

And may not be resumed again. The bare hulk tells us

Something, but mostly about what a strain it was to be brought

To such a pass, and then abandoned. So we may never

Again feel fully confident of the stratagem that bore us

And lived on a certain time after that. And it went away

Little by little, as most things do. To profit

By this mainstream is today's chore and adventure. He

Who touches base first at dusk is possessed first, then wins.

类似的事物

我,城市老鼠,走了很远的路
来和你在一起,带着我的消息。现在你有我的护照
上面有彩色照片,甜蜜地和你在一起
在时间允许的时候。我没有那么说因为它是真的,

我在楼上暗淡的走廊说话,对着这个国家
隐藏的形状美观的群众,你是它的地理学
所以你可以把它放在你的钱夹里。我们现在
只能那么做。高雅在此期间已经丧失

也许不会再恢复。光秃的废船告诉我们
什么事,但大多有关是什么样的种族把它带到
这样的关口,然后抛弃。我们也许永远不能
完全信任让我们厌烦的计谋了

并在那之后生活一段时间。它一点一点地
消失,和大多数事物一样。从这趋势中获益
是今天的杂事和冒险。黄昏时
最早探知究竟的他最早沉迷,然后获胜。

Or in My Throat

To the poet as a basement quilt, but perhaps
To some reader a latticework of regrets, through which
You can see the funny street, with the ends of cars and the dust,
The thing we always forget to put in. For him

The two ends were the same except that he was in one
Looking at the other, and all his grief stemmed from that:
There was no way of appreciating anything else, how polite
People were for instance, and the dream, reversed, became

A swift nightmare of starlight on frozen puddles in some
Dread waste. Yet you always hear
How they are coming along. Someone always has a letter
From one of them, asking to be remembered to the boys, and all.

That's why I quit and took up writing poetry instead.
It's clean, it's relaxing, it doesn't squirt juice all over
Something you were certain of a minute ago and now your own face
Is a stranger and no one can tell you it's true. Hey, stupid!

或者在我的喉咙里

对于诗人就像地下室的一床棉被,但也许
对某个读者就是一个懊悔的格子窗,通过它
你能看见有趣的街道,汽车的尾部和灰尘,
我们经常忘记放进来的东西。对于他

两端是一样的,除非他在一端
望着另一端,他所有的不幸皆源于此:
没法欣赏任何别的事物,例如
人们多么有教养,还有颠倒的梦,变成了

一个星光照耀结冻水坑的短暂的噩梦
在可怕的垃圾中。你总是听见
他们如何出现。有人总是带着一封
来自其中人的信,要他记得交给男孩们,还有所有人。

那就是为什么我退出并继续写诗。
它干净,它放松,它不把汁液喷得到处都是
喷在你一分钟前还确信的事物上,现在你自己的脸
是一个陌生人,无人能告诉你它是真的。嘿,蠢货!

Untilted

How tall the buildings were as I began
To live, and how high the rain that battered them!
Why, coming down them, as I often did at night,
Was a dream even before you reached the first gullies

And gave yourself over to thoughts of your own welfare.
It was the tilt of the wine in the cavalier's tilted glass
That documents so unerringly the faces and the mood in the room.
One slip would not be fatal, but then this is not a win or lose

Situation, so involved with living in the past on the ridge
Of the present, hearing its bells, breathing in its steam. . . .
And the shuttle never falters, but to draw an encouraging conclusion
From this would be considerable, too odd. Why not just

Breathe in with the courage of each day, recognizing yourself as one
Who must with difficulty get down from high places? Forget
The tourists—other people must travel too. It hurts now,
Cradled in the bend of your arm, the pure tear, doesn't it?

非倾斜

当我开始生活时建筑物多高啊,
打击它们的雨多大啊!
为什么,从它们上面下来,如我晚上经常做的那样,
成了一个梦,甚至在你到达最初的溪谷

沉浸在自己幸福的思想之前。
是骑士倾斜的酒杯里酒的倾斜
如此准确地记录了面孔和房间里的情绪。
一次事故不会致命,这不是输赢问题

如此沉迷于过去的生活,在现在的屋脊上,
倾听着它的钟声,呼吸着它的蒸汽……
梭子从不颤抖,而是从这里导出一个令人鼓舞的结论
这值得考虑,太古怪。为什么不仅仅

汲取每一天的勇气,把自己认做一个
来自高地的,必须克服苦难的人?忘记
旅行者——其他人也必须旅行。它现在好痛,
躺在你的臂弯中,这纯洁的泪,不是吗?

The Leasing of September

The sleeping map lay green, and we who were never much
To begin with, except for what the attractiveness of youth
Contributed, stood around in the pastures of heaped-up, thickened
White light, convinced that the story was coming to a close,

Otherwise why all these figurines, the Latin freemasonry in the corners?
You stepped into a blue taxi, and as I swear my eyes were in keeping
With the beauty of you as they saw it, so a swallow perpetuated
In dove-gray dusk can be both the end and the exaltation of a new

Beginning, yet forever remain itself, as you
Seem to run alongside me as the car picks up speed. Is it
Your hand then? Will I always then return
To the tier upon tier of cloth layered in the closet

Against what departure? Even a departure from the normal?
So we are not recognized, under the metal. But to him
The love was a solid object, like a partly unpacked trunk,
As it was then, which is different now when remembered.

九月的出租

睡着的地图碧绿地躺着,我们从来没有
太多的事情可以开始,除了青春魅力的
贡献,站在堆积着厚厚白光的牧场上,
确信故事正在结束,

否则,为什么这些小雕像,拉丁共济会会员都在角落里?
你钻进一辆蓝色出租车,我发誓我的眼睛一直保留着
他们所看见的你的美,于是,鸽灰色黄昏里
一只不朽的燕子,可以同时是结束和一个兴奋的

新开始,永远保持着自身,就像你
似乎要在和我并排跑,当汽车开始加速。那么
这是你的手吗?我始终要回到
壁橱里一层层叠放的衣物那里

抗拒分离吗?甚至正常的一次分离?
所以我们没有被认出来,在金属下面。但对于他
爱曾是一件结实之物,像揭开一部分的箱子,
像当时那样,现在回忆起来已经有所不同。

Unusual Precautions

"We, we children, why our lives are circumscribed, circumferential;
Close, too close to the center, we are haunted by perimeters
And our lives seem to go in and out, in and out all the time,
As though yours were diagonal, vertical, shallow, chopped off

At the root like the voice of the famous gadfly: 'Oh! Aho!' it
Sits in the middle of the roadway. That's it. Worry and brown desk
Stain it by infusion. There aren't enough tags at the end,
And the grove is blind, blossoming, but we are too porous to hear it.

It's like watching a movie of a nightmare, the many episodes
That defuse the thrust of what comes to us. The girl who juggled
    Indian clubs
Belongs again to the paper space that backs the black
Curtain, as though there were a reason to have paid for these seats.

Tomorrow you'll be walking in a white park. Our interests
Are too close for us to see. There seems to be no
Necessity for it, yet in walking, we too, around, and all around
We'll come to one, where the street crosses your name, and feet run up it."

不同寻常的预防措施

"我们,我们孩子,为什么我们的生活被限制在圆周中;
靠近,过于靠近中心,我们被周界迷惑
我们的生活似乎始终在进进出出,出出进进,
仿佛你的生活是斜的,垂直的,浅的,连根

砍掉了,像著名的牛蝇声:'哦!啊嚯!'
它坐在路中央。那就是它。烦恼,棕色的桌子
用浸液玷污它。最后没有足够的标签,
树丛盲目,开着花,但是我们的漏洞太多,听不见它。

这就像是看一部噩梦电影,许多情节
缓和了事物出现时的冲力。耍瓶状棒的女孩
再次属于支撑黑窗帘的纸空间,
仿佛有理由为这些座位付钱一般。

明天你将在一座白色公园里散步。我们的兴趣
接近得连我们都看不见。这似乎没有任何必要,
我们也在散步,在周围,四处,我们将来到一个地方,
那里的街道错过了你的名字,和在上面奔跑的双脚。"

We Hesitate

The days to come are a watershed.

You have to improve your portrait of God

To make it plain. It is on the list,

You and your bodies are on the line.

The new past now unfurls like a great somber hope

Above the treeline, like a giant's hand

Placed tentatively on the hurrying clouds.

The basins come to be full and complex

But it is not enough. Concern and embarrassment

Grow rank. Once they have come home there is no cursing.

Fires disturb the evening. No one can hear the story.

Or sometimes people just forget

Like a child. It took me months

To get that discipline banned, and what is the use,

To ban that? You remain a sane, yet sophisticated, person:

Rooted in twilight, dreaming, a piece of traffic.

我们在犹豫

即将到来的日子是一座分水岭。
你必须改进你有关上帝的画像
使之清晰。它在清单上,
你和你的身体们处于危险中。

新的过去现在像一个巨大忧郁的希望
展开在沿途的树上,像一只巨手
暂时放在急匆匆的云彩上。
水池逐渐充满,变得复杂

可这还不够。忧虑和困窘
繁茂生长。它们一旦回家,就没有诅咒了。
火焰扰乱了黄昏。无人能听见故事。
或者有时人们只是忘记了

像一个孩子。我花了几个月
才取消了那个惩罚,可取消它,
又有何用?你依然是个健全、世故的人:
扎根在黎明中,梦着,一桩买卖。

Frontispiece

Expecting rain, the profile of a day
Wears its soul like a hat, prow up
Against the deeply incised clouds and regions
Of abrupt skidding from cold to cold, riddles

Of climate it cannot understand.
Sometimes toward the end
A look of longing broke, taut, from those eyes
Meeting yours in final understanding, late,

And often, too, the beginnings went unnoticed
As though the story could advance its pawns
More discreetly thus, overstepping
The confines of ordinary health and reason

To introduce in another way
Its fact into the picture. It registered,
It must be there. And so we turn the page over
To think of starting. This is all there is.

卷首插图

盼望着雨,一个日子的轮廓
厌倦了它像一顶帽子的灵魂,船头昂起
面对有深深锯齿状边缘的云彩
和突然从寒冷滑向寒冷的区域,

它不能理解的气候之谜。
有时朝向终点
一种渴望的表情破碎,绷紧,来自那些眼睛
在最后的理解中遇见你的眼睛,晚了,

经常是这样,开始时没人注意
仿佛故事能增加它的抵押
更慎重地,逾越
平常的健康和理智的局限

以另一种方式
把它的事实引进图画。它登记过了,
它一定在那里。于是我们翻过这一页
想着开头。这就是那里的全部。

The Vegetarians

In front of you, long tables leading down to the sun,

A great gesture building. You accept it so as to play with it

And translate when its attention is deflated for the one second

Of eternity. Extreme patience and persistence are required,

Yet everybody succeeds at this before being handed

The surprise box lunch of the rest of his life. But what is

Truly startling is that it all happens modestly in the vein of

True living, and then that too is translated into something

Floating up from it, signals that life flashed, weak but essential

For uncorking the tone, and now lost, recently but forever.

In Zurich everything was pure and purposeful, like the red cars

Swung around the lake on wires, against the sky, then back down

Through the weather. Which resembles what you want to do

No more than black tree trunks do, though you thought of it.

Therefore our legends always come around to seeming legendary,

A path decorated with our comings and goings. Or so I've been told.

素食者

在你面前,长桌向下通往太阳,
一个巨大的姿态在确立。你接受了它,以便和它玩耍
并作出解释当它的注意力因一秒钟的永恒
而涣散。需要极大的耐心和坚持

每个人都成功地做到了这点,在意外地
接到他生活剩余的午餐盒饭之前。
可真正惊人的是,它完全是在真正的生活的
血管中谨慎地发生,同样也被解释成某种

从它里面浮起的东西,生活闪现的信号,微弱而必要
为了吐露音调,现在丢失了,最近但永远。
在苏黎世,一切都纯净而有目的,像红色的汽车
紧张地绕过湖边,对着天空,然后让步

穿过天气。哪一个和你想做的类似
不超过黑色的树干,尽管你想到它。
所以我们的传奇总是像传奇一样,
我们来来去去的一条路。或者有人这么告诉过我。

From
A WAVE
一排浪
(1984)

At North Farm

Somewhere someone is traveling furiously toward you,

At incredible speed, traveling day and night,

Through blizzards and desert heat, across torrents, through narrow passes.

But will he know where to find you,

Recognize you when he sees you,

Give you the thing he has for you?

Hardly anything grows here,

Yet the granaries are bursting with meal,

The sacks of meal piled to the rafters.

The streams run with sweetness, fattening fish;

Birds darken the sky. Is it enough

That the dish of milk is set out at night,

That we think of him sometimes,

Sometimes and always, with mixed feelings?

在北方农场

某个地方有人狂暴地向你而来,
以难以置信的速度,日夜兼程地旅行,
穿过大风雪和沙漠的炎热,越过急流,穿过狭窄的通道。
但是他知道去哪里找你吗,
他看见你时能认出你吗,
给你他为你带来的东西?

几乎没有什么能在这里生长,
但是谷仓因谷物而胀裂,
成袋的谷物一直堆到大梁。
急流流淌着甜蜜,肥美的鱼;
鸟群遮暗了天空。这样够吗
牛奶盘夜里放在外面,
我们有时想起他,
有时和始终,带着混杂的情感?

The Songs We Know Best

Just like a shadow in an empty room

Like a breeze that's pointed from beyond the tomb

Just like a project of which no one tells—

Or didja really think that I was somebody else?

Your clothes and pantlegs lookin' out of shape

Shape of the body over which they drape

Body which has acted in so many scenes

But didja ever think of what that body means?

It is an organ and a vice to some

A necessary evil which we all must shun

To others an abstraction and a piece of meat

But when you're looking out you're in the driver's seat!

No man cares little about fleshly things

They fill him with a silence that spreads in rings

We wish to know more but we are never sated

No wonder some folks think the flesh is overrated!

The things we know now all got learned in school

我们最熟悉的歌曲

就像空房间里的一个影子
像一阵指向坟墓外的微风
就像一个没人说出的计划——
或许你真的把我当成是别人?

你的衣服和裤腿看上去变形了
它们所遮盖的身体的形状
在这么多场景中活动过的身体
你可曾想过那身体意味着什么?

对某人来说它是一个器官和恶习
我们全都得避开的一个必然的罪
对他人则是一个抽象和一片肉
可当你向外看时你是在驾驶座上!

没人不会在意肉体的事情
他们以一圈圈扩大的寂静填满他
我们想要知道更多却从未满足
难怪有人认为肉体被估价过高!

我们现在懂的都是学校学的

Try to learn a new thing and you break the rule

Our knowledge isn't much it's just a small amount

But you feel it quick inside you when you're down for the count

You look at me and frown like I was out of place

I guess I never did much for the human race

Just hatched some schemes on paper that looked good at first

Sat around and watched until the bubble burst

And now you're lookin' good all up and down the line

Except for one thing you still have in mind

It's always there though often with a different face

It's the worm inside the jumping bean that makes it race

Too often when you thought you'd be showered with confetti

What they flung at you was a plate of hot spaghetti

You've put your fancy clothes and flashy gems in hock

Yet you pause before your father's door afraid to knock

Once you knew the truth it tried to set you free

And still you stood transfixed just like an apple tree

The truth it came and went and left you in the lurch

And now you think you see it from your lofty perch

试着学一个新东西，试着打破规则
我们的知识不多，它恰恰很少
可你感到它在你内部活跃，当你为此沮丧

你看着我，皱眉，好像我站错了位置
我猜我不曾为人类贡献良多
只在纸上孵化了一些起初看着不错的主题
坐在旁边观察，直到泡沫迸出

现在你看起来很好，很好
只有一件事你仍记在心里
它始终在那里，时常有另一副面孔
是跳豆里的虫子使它跳动

当你觉得你应该沐浴五彩纸屑
它们却掷向你一盘意大利细面
你把你的奇服和珍宝拿去典当
你停在父亲的门前却害怕敲门

你曾经知道真理试图把你解放
你却呆立如故，恍若一棵苹果树
真理来了又去把你留于困境
现在你以为从高位把它看见

The others come and go they're just a dime a dozen
You react to them no more than to a distant cousin
Only a few people can touch your heart
And they too it seems have all gotten a false start

In twilight the city with its hills shines serene
And lets you make of it more than anything could mean
It's the same city by day that seems so crude and calm
You'll have to get to know it not just pump its arm

Even when that bugle sounded loud and clear
You knew it put an end to all your fear
To all that lying and the senseless mistakes
And now you've got it right and you know what it takes

Someday I'll look you up when we're both old and gray
And talk about those times we had so far away
How much it mattered then and how it matters still
Only things look so different when you've got a will

It's true that out of this misunderstanding could end
And men would greet each other like they'd found a friend
With lots of friends around there's no one to entice
And don't you think seduction isn't very nice?

其他人来来去去,他们只是一角硬币

你对待他们不过像是远房表亲

只有少数人能触到你的心脏

他们从一开始似乎就是错的

黎明的城市和山冈闪耀宁静

让你了解它超乎任何事物的盼望

白天它是同一个城市,粗鲁又冷静

你必须了解它,而不仅仅是和它使劲握手

甚至当那喇叭吹起,响亮而清晰

你知道它结束了你所有的恐惧

所有的谎言和无意识的错误

现在你已改正,你知道那代价几何

有一天我会拜访你,当我们苍苍老迈

谈论那些远离我们的遥远岁月

它那时多重要,现在仍然多重要

只是事物显得如此不同,当你下了决心

超越这种误解是可能的结局

人们彼此欢迎,仿佛找到了朋友

身边友人众多,没人再去勾引

你不认为那样的事情不太妥当?

It carries in this room against the painted wall

And hangs in folds of curtains when it's not there at all

It's woven in the flowers of the patterned spread

And lies and knows not what it thinks upon the bed

I wish to come to know you get to know you all

Let your belief in me and me in you stand tall

Just like a project of which no one tells—

Or do ya still think that I'm somebody else?

它在这房间进行，对着涂抹的墙
悬于窗帘的皱褶，当它业已不在
它织入花朵舒展的图案
躺着，不知道自己对床的想法

我希望了解你，了解你的全部
让你我彼此的信任在心中高耸
就像一个没人说出的计划——
或许你依然把我当成是别人？

Landscape (After Baudelaire)

I want a bedroom near the sky, an astrologer's cave

Where I can fashion eclogues that are chaste and grave.

Dreaming, I'll hear the wind in the steeples close by

Sweep the solemn hymns away. I'll spy

On factories from my attic window, resting my chin

In both hands, drinking in the songs, the din.

I'll see chimneys and steeples, those masts of the city,

And the huge sky that makes us dream of eternity.

How sweet to watch the birth of the star in the still-blue

Sky, through mist; the lamp burning anew

At the window; rivers of coal climbing the firmament

And the moon pouring out its pale enchantment.

I'll see the spring, the summer and the fall

And when winter casts its monotonous pall

Of snow, I'll draw the blinds and curtains tight

And build my magic palaces in the night;

Then dream of gardens, of bluish horizons,

Of jets of water weeping in alabaster basins,

Of kisses, of birds singing at dawn and at nightfall,

风景
（仿波德莱尔）

我想要一张靠近天空的床，一个占星家的洞穴
我可以在那里写下朴素庄重的田园之诗。
做梦，我将听见附近尖塔上的风
吹送庄严的圣歌。我将从我的阁楼
偷窥林立的工厂，双手托着下巴，
醉于歌曲，和沸腾的喧嚣。
我将看见烟囱和尖塔，城市的桅杆，
而广阔的天空使我们梦见永恒。

多么甜蜜，观察星辰在钢蓝色的天空
透过雾霭，诞生；窗边的灯盏
重新燃起；煤炭的河流向苍穹攀登
月亮倾注出它苍白的魔法。
我将看见春天、夏天和秋天
当冬天投下它白雪单调的幕布，
我将把百叶窗和窗帘拉得紧紧
在夜晚建造我魔法的宫殿；
然后梦见花园，发蓝的地平线，
在光洁雪白的水池中哭泣的泉流，
梦见亲吻，黎明和日落时鸟的歌唱，

Of all that's most childish in our pastoral.

When the storm rattles my windowpane

I'll stay hunched at my desk, it will roar in vain

For I'll have plunged deep inside the thrill

Of conjuring spring with the force of my will,

Coaxing the sun from my heart, and building here

Out of my fiery thoughts, a tepid atmosphere.

我们田园诗中最为童贞的一切。
当风暴摇响我的窗扇
我将伏在桌前,任它徒劳地吼叫
因为我已经潜入欢乐深处
用我意志的力量召唤春天,
从我的心脏中引出太阳,用我炽热的思想
在这里创造一个温热的气候。

Just Walking Around

What name do I have for you?
Certainly there is no name for you
In the sense that the stars have names
That somehow fit them. Just walking around,

An object of curiosity to some,
But you are too preoccupied
By the secret smudge in the back of your soul
To say much, and wander around,

Smiling to yourself and others.
It gets to be kind of lonely
But at the same time off-putting,
Counterproductive, as you realize once again

That the longest way is the most efficient way,
The one that looped among islands, and
You always seemed to be traveling in a circle.
And now that the end is near

The segments of the trip swing open like an orange.

只是在周围走走

我为你准备了什么名字?
肯定没有为你准备的名字
因为群星都有名字
与之相配。只是在周围走走,

对于某些人是好奇的东西,
对于你却过于执迷
凭借你灵魂背后那秘密的污迹
说很多话,在周围漫游,

对着自己和他人微笑。
它逐渐成了一种孤独
同时也是一种困窘,
起着反作用,就像你又一次认识到

最长的路也是最有效的路,
它在岛屿之间循环不息,
而你似乎总是在一个圆圈中旅行。
现在终点近了

旅程的片段旋转着打开如一只橘子。

There is light in there, and mystery and food.

Come see it. Come not for me but it.

But if I am still there, grant that we may see each other.

里面有光，秘密和食物。

来看看它。不是来看我，是看它。

但如果我仍在那里，我们可能会彼此看见。

The Ongoing Story

I could say it's the happiest period of my life.
It hasn't got much competition! Yesterday
It seemed a flatness, hotness. As though it barely stood out
From the rocks of all the years before. Today it sheds
That old name, without assuming any new one. I think it's still there.

It was as though I'd been left with the empty street
A few seconds after the bus pulled out. A dollop of afternoon wind.
Others tell you to take your attention off it
For awhile, refocus the picture. Plan to entertain,
To get out. (Do people really talk that way?)

We could pretend that all that isn't there never existed anyway.
The great ideas? What good are they if they're misplaced,
In the wrong order, if you can't remember one
At the moment you're so to speak mounting the guillotine
Like Sydney Carton, and can't think of anything to say?
Or is this precisely material covered in a course
Called Background of the Great Ideas, and therefore it isn't necessary
To say anything or even know anything? The breath of the moment
Is breathed, we fall and still feel better. The phone rings,

正在进行的故事

我可以说那是我一生最幸福的时期。
没有什么可以匹敌!昨天
似乎单调而炎热。仿佛它勉强站出了
往昔所有岁月的岩石。今天它摆脱了
那个旧名,没有取新名。我认为它仍在那里。

仿佛我已经离开了空空的街道
在公交车开走几秒钟之后。一阵午后的风。
别人告诉你把注意力从它上面
转移片刻,重新专注于图画。计划去娱乐,
到外面去。(人们真的那样讲话吗?)

我们可以装作不在那里的一切从来就不存在。
了不起的思想?它们有什么好,如果放错了地方,
弄错了顺序,如果你一个也想不起来
在被告知要上断头台的时候
就像悉尼·卡顿,想不起任何要说的事?
或许这材料恰恰包含在一个过程当中
亦即所谓伟大的思想背景,所以没必要
说什么,甚或知道什么?此刻的气息
被呼吸到了,我们倒下,感觉更好。电话响了,

It's a wrong number, and your heart is lighter,

Not having to be faced with the same boring choices again

Which doesn't undermine a feeling for people in general and

Especially in particular: you,

In your deliberate distinctness, whom I love and gladly

Agree to walk blindly into the night with,

Your realness is real to me though I would never take any of it

Just to see how it grows. A knowledge that people live close by is,

I think, enough. And even if only first names are ever exchanged

The people who own them seem rock-true and marvelously self

    sufficient.

是个错误的号码,你的心情轻松了许多,
不用再次面对同样恼人的选择
它总体上不会破坏你对他人的感觉
尤其特殊的是:你
在你审慎的独立中,我爱你
并欣然同意盲目地与你走进夜晚,
你的真实对于我是真的,尽管我永远不会接受
只是看着它如何生长。我认为,作为一种知识,
人们足以以之为生。即便改的只是最初的名字
拥有它们的人似乎也岩石般真实,自信非凡。

Thank You for Not Cooperating

Down in the street there are ice-cream parlors to go to

And the pavement is a nice, bluish slate-gray. People laugh a lot.

Here you can see the stars. Two lovers are singing

Separately, from the same rooftop: "*Leave your change behind,*

Leave your clothes, and go. It is time now.

It was time before too, but now it is really time.

You will never have enjoyed storms so much

As on these hot sticky evenings that are more like August

Than September. Stay. A fake wind wills you to go

And out there on the stormy river witness buses bound for Connecticut,

And tree-business, and all that we think about when we stop thinking

The weather is perfect, the season unclear. Weep for your going

But also expect to meet me in the near future, when I shall disclose

New further adventures, and that you shall continue to think of me."

The wind dropped, and the lovers

Sang no more, communicating each to each in the tedium

Of self-expression, and the shore curled up and became liquid

And so the celebrated lament began. And how shall we, people

All unused to each other and to our own business, explain

It to the shore if it is given to us

谢谢你的不合作

街道上有冷饮店可去

人行道是美丽的蓝灰色。人们老是笑。

你在这里可以看见星星。两个情侣在各自唱歌

在同一个屋顶上:"把你的零钱留下,

把你的衣服留下,走开。现在时间到了。

以前时间也到了,但现在时间真的到了。

你永远不会享受这样的风暴了

这些闷热发黏的傍晚更像是八月

而不是九月。留下。一股假风希望你出去

在汹涌的河边目睹汽车颠簸地驶向康涅迪格,

树的贸易,以及所有我们停止思考时思考的事情。

天气完美,季节不分明。你为即将离开而哭泣

但也期望在不远的将来遇见我,那时我将透露

新的进一步的冒险,你也会继续想起我。"

风停了,情侣们

不再唱歌,在自我表达的厌烦中

彼此交流,河岸蜷缩起来,变成液体

著名的挽歌就这样开始。我们将会怎样,

人们全都彼此不习惯,也不习惯我们自己的业务,

向河岸解释它,如果我们需要

To circulate there "in the near future" the why of our coming

And why we were never here before? The counterproposals

Of the guest-stranger impede our construing of ourselves as

Person-objects, the ones we knew would get here

Somehow, but we can remember as easily as the day we were born

The maggots we passed on the way and how the day bled

And the night too on hearing us, though we spoke only our childish

Ideas and never tried to impress anybody even when somewhat older.

"在不远的将来"传播我们到来的原因
为什么我们以前不在这里？陌生客人的反面建议
阻止我们把自己解释成
人员对象，我们认识的人会设法来到这里，
但是我们可以像我们出生时那样轻松地回忆起
我们路上碰见的蛆，白昼如何流血
还有偷听我们的夜晚，尽管我们说的只是我们幼稚的想法
从未企图给人留下印象，甚至在年纪大些的时候。

More Pleasant Adventures

The first year was like icing.

Then the cake started to show through.

Which was fine, too, except you forget the direction you're taking.

Suddenly you are interested in some new thing

And can't tell how you got here. Then there is confusion

Even out of happiness, like a smoke—

The words get heavy, some topple over, you break others.

And outlines disappear once again.

Heck, it's anybody's story,

A sentimental journey—"gonna take a sentimental journey,"

And we do, but you wake up under the table of a dream:

You are that dream, and it is the seventh layer of you.

We haven't moved an inch, and everything has changed.

We are somewhere near a tennis court at night.

We get lost in life, but life knows where we are.

We can always be found with our associates.

Haven't you always wanted to curl up like a dog and go to sleep like a dog?

In the rash of partings and dyings (the new twist),

There's also room for breaking out of living.

更愉快的冒险

第一年像结冰。

然后蛋糕开始出现。

它也很美,除非你忘记了你目前的方向。

突然你对某件新事物发生了兴趣

你说不清自己是怎么到这儿来的。然后是混乱

甚至从幸福中溢出,像一股烟——

词语变重了,有的倒塌了,你打断了别人。

轮廓再次消失。

真见鬼,任何人的故事都是这样,

一次伤感的旅行——"去做一次伤感的旅行",

我们做了,但你在梦的桌子下醒来:

你是那梦,它是你的第七层。

我们毫无进展,一切都变了。

夜里我们在一个网球场附近。

我们在生活中迷失了,但是生活知道我们在哪儿。

我们始终能被发现和伙伴们在一起。

难不成你一直想狗一样蜷起来像狗一样入睡吗?

在匆忙的分离和死亡中(这新的转机),

依然有空间来打破生活。

Whatever happens will be quite ingenious.

No acre but will resume being disputed now,

And paintings are one thing we never seem to run out of.

无论发生什么都会非常具有独创性。
没有田亩但将马上惹起争议,
而油画是一件我们似乎永远逃不出去的东西。

Purists Will Object

We have the looks you want:

The gonzo (musculature seemingly wired to the stars);

Colors like lead, khaki and pomegranate; things you

Put in your hair, with the whole panoply of the past:

Landscape embroidery, complete sets of this and that.

It's bankruptcy, the human haul,

The shining, bulging nets lifted out of the sea, and always a few refugees

Dropping back into the no-longer-mirthful kingdom

On the day someone sells an old house

And someone else begins to add on to his: all

In the interests of this pornographic masterpiece,

Variegated, polluted skyscraper to which all gazes are drawn,

Pleasure we cannot and will not escape.

It seems we were going home.

The smell of blossoming privet blanketed the narrow avenue.

The traffic lights were green and aqueous.

So this is the subterranean life.

If it can't be conjugated onto us, what good is it?

What need for purists when the demotic is built to last,

To outlast us, and no dialect hears us?

纯粹主义者会反对

我们有你想要的外表：
怪诞（肌肉组织显然拴在星星上）；
颜色像铅，卡其布和石榴；
你放在你头发里的东西，带着过去的全副甲胄：
风景刺绣，全套的这个和那个。
它破产了，人类从大海，
拖出膨胀闪亮的网，总是有少数流亡者
坠回不再令人高兴的王国
那天有人在卖一座老房子
另一个人开始给自己的房子加价：
一切都在这幅色情杰作的利润里，
吸引所有目光的斑驳污秽的摩天大楼，
我们不能也不愿逃避的乐趣。

似乎我们正在回家。
女贞开花的气息覆盖了狭窄的林荫道。
交通灯是绿的，像水。
这就是地下的生活。
如果它不能与我们结合，它有什么好？
纯粹主义者需要什么，当通俗的得以确立和持续，
为了比我们长久，没人倾听我们的行话？

37 Haiku

Old-fashioned shadows hanging down, that difficulty in love too soon

Some star or other went out, and you, thank you for your book and year

Something happened in the garage and I owe it for the blood traffic

Too low for nettles but it is exactly the way people think and feel

And I think there's going to be even more but waist-high

Night occurs dimmer each time with the pieces of light smaller and squarer

You have original artworks hanging on the walls oh I said edit

You nearly undermined the brush I now place against the ball field arguing

That love was a round place and will still be there two years from now

And it is a dream sailing in a dark unprotected cove

Pirates imitate the ways of ordinary people myself for instance

三十七俳句

老派的影子垂下来，难在爱得太快

某颗星星熄灭了，还有你，感谢你的书和岁月

什么事发生在车库里而我把它归之为血流通

对于荨麻太矮了但这正是人们思考和感受的方式

我认为甚至会更多但只有齐腰高

夜晚每次都更暗淡地带着更小和更方正的光的碎片降临

你把艺术品原件挂在墙上啊我说编辑一下

你几乎弄坏了画笔我现在争论的是针对球场

那爱是一块圆形场地并且从现在起还会存在两个年头

它是一个梦航行在一个未设防的黑洞里

海盗模仿普通人的习惯例如我自己

Planted over and over that land has a bitter aftertaste

A blue anchor grains of grit in a tall sky sewing

He is a monster like everyone else but what do you do if you're a monster

Like him feeling him come from far away and then go down to his car

The wedding was enchanted everyone was glad to be in it

What trees, tools, why ponder socks on the premises

Come to the edge of the barn the property really begins there

In a smaller tower shuttered and put away there

You lay aside your hair like a book that is too important to read now

Why did witches pursue the beast from the eight sides of the country

A pencil on glass—shattered! The water runs down the drain

In winter sometimes you see those things and also in summer

种了一遍又一遍，土地有了苦涩的回味

一只蓝色的锚，粗砂粒在缝补高天

他和别人一样是个怪物但如果你是个怪物你怎么办

像他那样觉得自己来自远方然后走向他的汽车

婚礼被施了魔法每个人都乐在其中

什么样的树，工具，为何思考店里的袜子

到谷仓边上去，财产真的是从那里开始的

在一座有百叶窗的更小点的塔里并放在那里

你留的头发像一本重要得不能现在就读的书

为什么女巫们在田野里四面八方地追赶那野兽

一支铅笔在玻璃上——碎了！水流入下水道

冬天你有时看见那些东西，夏天也是

A child must go down it must stand and last

Too late the last express passes through the dust of gardens

A vest—there is so much to tell about even in the side rooms

Hesitantly, it built up and passed quickly without unlocking

There are some places kept from the others and are separate, they never exist

I lost my ridiculous accent without acquiring another

In Buffalo, Buffalo she was praying, the nights stick together like pages in an old book

The dreams descend like cranes on gilded, forgetful wings

What is the past, what is it all for? A mental sandwich?

Did you say, hearing the schooner overhead, we turned back to the weir?

In rags and crystals, sometimes with a shred of sense, an odd dignity

The boy must have known the particles fell through the house after him

一个孩子必须把它传下去,必须忍受和坚持

太晚了,最后的快车穿过花园的灰尘

一件背心——即便在厢房里也有这么多要说的

犹豫地,它组合起来,快速通过,不开锁

有些地方向其他人隐瞒着并且是分开的,它们从不存在

我失去了我可笑的口音却没有学会另一种

在布法罗,她在祈祷布法罗,夜晚粘在一起像一本旧书的书页

梦下降如同吊车展开镀金的健忘的翅膀

什么是过去,它到底是用来干什么的?一个精神三明治?

你是说,听见头上的纵帆船,我们转身回到堤坝那里?

在破布和水晶中,有时有一点,奇怪的尊严感

男孩一定知道微粒在他后面穿过房子落下

All in all we were taking our time, the sea returned—no more pirates

I inch and only sometimes as far as the twisted pole gone in spare
   colors

总而言之我们别着急,大海回来了——不再有海盗

我慢慢前进,只是有时远得像扭曲的极地消失在多余的色彩
之中

The Lonedale Operator

The first movie I ever saw was the Walt Disney cartoon *The Three Little Pigs*. My grandmother took me to it. It was back in the days when you went "downtown." There was a second feature, with live actors, called *Bring 'Em Back Alive*, a documentary about the explorer Frank Buck. In this film you saw a python swallow a live pig. This wasn't scary. In fact, it seemed quite normal, the sort of thing you *would* see in a movie —"reality."

A little later we went downtown again to see a movie of *Alice in Wonderland*, also with live actors. This wasn't very surprising either. I think I knew something about the story; maybe it had been read to me. That wasn't why it wasn't surprising, though. The reason was that these famous movie actors, like W. C. Fields and Gary Cooper, were playing different roles, and eventhough I didn't know who they were, they were obviously important for doing other kinds of acting, and so it didn't seem strange that they should be acting in a special way like this, pretending to be characters that people already knew about from a book. In other words, I imagined specialties for them just from having seen this one example. And l was right, too, though not about the film, which I liked. Years later I saw it when I was grown up and thought it was awful. How could I have been wrong the first time? I knew it wasn't inexperience, because somehow I was experienced the first time I saw a movie. It was as though my taste had changed, though I had not, and I still can't help feeling that I was right the first time, when I was still relatively unencumbered by my experience.

I forget what were the next movies I saw and will skip ahead

隆台尔的报务员

我看过的第一个电影是沃尔特·迪斯尼的卡通片《三只小猪》。我祖母带我去的。那是回到你去"闹市区"的日子。我看的第二个长片，有现场演员，叫做《把他们活着带回来》，一部有关探险者弗兰克·巴克的纪录片。在这部电影中你看见一条巨蟒吞一只活猪。这不可怕。事实上，这似乎很正常，这种事儿你愿意在电影里看见——"真实"。

稍后一点，我们又去了闹市区，去看一部《爱丽丝漫游奇境》的电影，也有现场演员。这一部也不是很让人吃惊。我想这故事我知道一些；也许别人曾读给我听过。不过，那不是它不让人吃惊的原因。原因在于这些著名的电影演员，比如W.C.菲尔兹和加里·库珀，扮演着不同的角色，即使我不知道他们是谁，他们显然也很重要，因为他们在扮演别人，所以，似乎并不奇怪，他们应该以这样一种特殊方式表演，装扮成人们已经从书中知道的角色。换句话说，我能想象他们的专长恰恰是因为见过这个例子。而我也是对的，尽管我喜欢的东西与电影无关。几年后我长大了，我又看了这电影，我认为它很可怕。第一次我怎么能搞错呢？我知道不是因为没有经验，因为第一次看电影的时候我已经有了一些经验。好像是我的趣味变了，尽管我没变，我依然不由自主地觉得我第一次是对的，那时相对而言我还没有受到我经验的阻碍。

我忘了接下来我都看了些什么电影，我将向前跳到我长大

to one I saw when I was grown up, *The Lonedale Operator*, a silent short by D. W. Griffith, made in 1911 and starring Blanche Sweet. Although I was in my twenties when I saw it at the Museum of Modern Art, it seems as remote from me in time as my first viewing of *Alice in Wonderland*. I can remember almost none of it, and the little I can remember may have been in another Griffith short, *The Lonely Villa*, which may have been on the same program. It seems that Blanche Sweet was a heroic telegraph operator who managed to get through to the police and foil some gangsters who were trying to rob a railroad depot, though I also see this living room—small, though it was supposed to be in a large house—with Mary Pickford running around, and this may have been a scene in *The Lonely Villa*. At that moment the memories stop, and terror, or tedium, sets in. It's hard to tell which is which in this memory, because the boredom of living in a lonely place or having a lonely job, and even of being so far in the past and having to wear those funny uncomfortable clothes and hairstyles is terrifying, more so than the intentional scariness of the plot, the criminals, whoever they were.

Imagine that innocence (Lilian Harvey) encounters romance (Willy Fritsch) in the home of experience (Albert Basserman). From there it is only a step to terror, under the dripping boughs outside. Anything can change as fast as it wants to, and in doing so may pass through a more or less terrible phase, but the true terror is in the swiftness of changing, forward or backward, slipping always just beyond our control. The actors are like people on drugs, though they aren't doing anything unusual—as a matter of fact, they are performing brilliantly.

时看的一部《隆台尔的报务员》，一个无声短片，D.W. 格里菲斯一九一一年拍摄，主演布兰奇·斯威特。尽管我在现代艺术博物馆看这部电影时才二十来岁，却仿佛遥远得像我第一次看《爱丽丝漫游奇境》的时候。这个电影我几乎什么都不记得了，我稍微记得一点的可能是格里菲斯的另一部短片《孤独别墅》，也许是在同一个节目。似乎布兰奇·斯威特是个勇敢的报务员，设法通知了警察，挫败了一伙要抢劫铁路仓库的强盗，不过，我也看见了这间起居室——小小的，被想象成一座大房子的起居室——玛丽·皮克福德跑来跑去，这可能是《孤独别墅》里的一个场景。那一瞬间，记忆停顿了，恐惧或者是乏味，出现了。在这个记忆中，很难说清哪个是哪个，因为住在一个孤独的地方或是从事一项孤独的工作，甚至置身于遥远的过去，不得不穿着那些可笑的难受的衣服，留着可怕的发型，这种厌倦更胜于情节刻意的恐怖感，还有罪犯们，无论他们是谁。

想象那个无辜的人（莉莲·哈维）在经验之家（阿尔伯特·巴塞曼）遭遇浪漫（威利·弗里奇）。那里距恐怖仅一步之遥，在外面滴水的树枝下面。任何事情都能像想要的那样迅速改变，这么做可能要经历多少有点可怕的阶段，但是真正的恐怖在于变化的迅疾性，前进或后退，总是溜出我们的掌控。演员们就像瘾君子，尽管他们的行为毫无异常——事实上，他们的表演非常出色。

Darlene's Hospital

The hospital: it wasn't her idea

That the colors should slide muddy from the brush

And spew their random evocations everywhere,

Provided that things should pick up next season.

It was a way of living, to her way of thinking.

She took a job, it wasn't odd.

But then, backing through the way many minds had been made up,

It came again, the color, always a color

Climbing the apple of the sky, often

A secret lavender place you weren't supposed to look into.

And then a sneeze would come along

Or soon we'd be too far out from shore, on a milky afternoon

Somewhere in late August with the paint flaking off,

The lines of traffic flowing like mucus,

And they won't understand its importance, it's too bad,

Not even when it's too late.

Now we're often happy. The dark car

Moves heftily away along low bluffs,

And if we don't have our feelings, what

Good are we, but whose business is it?

达莲娜医院

医院：这不是她的想法
颜料应该从刷子上泥泞地淌下来
将它们随机的召唤到处喷溅，
假如事情下个季节能够好起来。
对于她的思维方式而言，这是一种生活方式。
她选择一份工作，这不奇怪。
然后，回溯许多思想是怎么形成的，
色彩再次出现，始终是一种色彩
攀登天空的苹果，往往是
一个你不该窥视的秘密的薰衣草田。
然后会打一个喷嚏
或许我们不久就会离岸很远，在一个乳白色的下午
油漆剥落的八月末尾的某个地方，
交通路线如同黏液流淌。
他们不理解它的重要性，它太糟糕了，
即使在它太晚的时候。

现在我们经常感到幸福。黑色的汽车
沿低低的绝壁沉重地移动，
如果我们没有感情，我们
有什么好，可这与谁有关？

Beware the happy man: once she perched light

In the reading space of my room, a present joy

For all time to come, whatever happens;

And still we rotate, gathering speed until

Nothing is there but more speed in the light ahead.

Such moments as we prized in life:

The promise of a new day, living with lots of people

All headed in more or less the same direction, the sound of this

In the embracing stillness, but not the brutality,

And lists of examples of lots of things, and shit—

What more could we conceivably be satisfied with, it is

Joy, and undaunted

She leaves the earth at that point,

Intersecting all our daydreams of breakfast and lunch.

The Lady of Shalott's in hot water again.

This and the dreams of any of the young

Were not her care. The river flowed

Hard by the hospital from whose gilded

Balconies and turrets fair spirits waved,

Lonely, like us. Here be no pursuers,

Only imagined animals and cries

In the wilderness, which made it "the wilderness,"

And suddenly the lonesomeness becomes a pleasant city

注意幸福的男人：一旦她暂时栖息
在我房间中阅读，一种暂时的快乐
终究会出现，无论发生什么；
我们仍在旋转，慢慢加速，直到
那里什么都没有，只有前面光中更快的速度。
我们在生活中赞美这样的时刻：
一个新日子的许诺，与许多人一起生活
大家或多或少都去一个方向，声音响起
在拥抱的静止中，但不是残忍，
和许多事物的样板清单，还有屎——
想来还有什么能让我们满意，
是快乐，和大无畏
她在那个地方离开地球，
与我们所有早餐和午餐的白日梦交叉着。
夏洛特夫人又在热水里了。

这一切和任何年轻人的梦
都不是她所关心的。河流艰难地
流过医院旁边，从它镀金的阳台
和塔楼，美丽的灵魂挥手致意，
像我们一样孤独。这里没有追求者，
只有想象出的动物和荒野里的
哭声，使它成了"荒野"，
突然，寂寞变成了一座怡人的城

Fanning out around a lake; you get to meet

Precisely the person who would have been here now,

A dream no longer, and are polished and directed

By his deliberate grasp, back

To the reality that was always there despairing

Of your return as months and years went by,

Now silent again forever, the perfect space,

Attuned to your wristwatch

As though time would never go away again.

His dirty mind

Produced it all, an oratorio based on love letters

About our sexual habits in the early 1950s.

It wasn't that these stories weren't true,

Only that a different kind of work

Of the imagination had grown up around them, taller

Than redwoods, and not

Wanting to embarrass them, effaced itself

To the extent that a colossus could, and so you looked

And saw nothing, but suddenly felt better

Without wondering why. And the serial continues:

Pain, expiation, delight, more pain,

A frieze that lengthens continually, in the lucky way

Friezes do, and no plot is produced,

在一座湖泊周围扇形展开；你现在会遇见

的确应该在这里的人，

一个不再有的梦，被擦亮

由他从容地紧拉着，领回现实

随着岁月流逝

那一直存在的对你的回归的绝望，

此刻永远沉静下来，完美的空间，

与你的手表相合

仿佛时间再也不会流逝。

他的肮脏头脑

创造出这一切，以情书为根据的一出宗教剧

有关我们五十年代初的性习惯。

不是这些故事不真实，

只是另一类想象的作品

在它们周围生长，高过了

红杉树林，不想

让它们不安，便抹掉了自己

达到一个巨人所能的程度，你看

你什么都没看见，却突然感觉好多了

没有奇怪是为什么。连续剧在继续：

痛苦，赎罪，快乐，更多的痛苦，

一个带状物继续拉长，以带状物的

幸运方式，没有任何情节发生，

Nothing you could hang an identifying question on.

It's an imitation of pleasure; it may not work

But at least we'll know then that we'll have done

What we could, and chalk it up to virtue

Or just plain laziness. And if she glides

Backwards through us, a finger hooked

Out of death, we shall not know where the mystery began:

Inaccurate dreamers of our state,

Sodden from sitting in the rain too long.

没有什么东西可以让你发出识别性的疑问。
它是对快乐的一种模仿；它可能不起作用
但至少我们会知道，我们已经
尽己所能，并把它归之为美德
或者只是普通的懒惰。如果她向后
滑行着穿过我们，从死亡中钩出
一根手指，我们就不会知道秘密在哪里开始：
不真实地梦见我们国家的人，
在雨中坐得太久而淋得精湿。

Whatever It Is, Wherever You Are

The cross-hatching technique which allowed our ancestors to exchange certain genetic traits for others, in order to provide their offspring with a way of life at once more variegated and more secure than their own, has just about run out of steam and has left us wondering, once more, what there is about this plush solitude that makes us think we will ever get out, or even want to. The ebony hands of the clock always seem to mark the same hour. That is why it always seems the same, though it is of course changing constantly, subtly, as though fed by an underground stream. If only we could go out in back, as when we were kids, and smoke and fool around and just stay out of the way, for a little while. But that's just it— don't you see? We are "out in back." No one has ever used the front door. We have always lived in this place without a name, without shame, a place for grownups to talk and laugh, having a good time. When we were children it seemed that adulthood would be like climbing a tree, that there would be a view from there, breathtaking because slightly more elusive. But now we can see only down, first down through the branches and further down the surprisingly steep grass patch that slopes away from the base of the tree. It certainly is a different view, but not the one we expected.

What did *they* want us to do? Stand around this way, monitoring every breath, checking each impulse for the return address, wondering constantly about evil until necessarily we fall into a state of torpor that is probably the worst sin of all? To what purpose did they cross-hatch so effectively, so that the luminous surface that was underneath is transformed into another, also luminous but so shifting and so alive with suggestiveness that it is like quicksand, to take a step there would

无论它是什么，无论你在哪儿

　　杂交技术让我们的祖先得以与他人交换某些基因特性，以便为他们的后嗣马上提供一种更为富于变化更为安全的生活方式，而他们自己的生活方式则几乎已经失去势头，让我们再次疑惑，这豪华的孤独到底是什么，它让我们以为我们会离开，或是甚至想要离开。时钟的黑手似乎总是指向同一个时辰。那就是为什么它显得总是一个样，尽管它在不断微妙地变化，仿佛由一条地下河哺育着。要是我们能够从后院出去就好了，就像我们儿时那样，有一小段时间，抽烟，闲逛，置身事外。可那就是它——难道你没看见？我们"从后院出去"。没有人用前门。我们始终生活在这个地方，没有名字，没有羞耻，一个供成人谈笑、消磨好时光的地方。当我们还是孩子时，长大成人就像是爬树，树上会看见一个风景，令人激动，因为略微有点难懂。但现在我们只能看到下面，先是透过树枝，继而是陡得让人吃惊的草地，从树根下倾斜着延伸开去。这当然是别有不同的风景，但不是我们期待的那个。

　　他们想要我们做什么？就这样闲站着，监视每一次呼吸，为回信地址检查每一次脉搏，不断地对罪恶感到好奇，直到我们必然地堕入一种麻木状态，那也许是最严重的罪？出于什么意图，他们如此有效地实施杂交，以至于曾在下方的发光表面被变成了另一种，同样光灿，但如此动荡与活跃，富有启发性，像流沙一样，迈出一步就会从不确定性的脆弱之网落进确定性

be to fall through the fragile net of uncertainties into the bog of certainty, otherwise known as the Slough of Despond?

Probably they meant for us to enjoy the things they enjoyed, like late summer evenings, and hoped that we'd find others and thank them for providing us with the wherewithal to find and enjoy them. Singing the way they did, in the old time, we can sometimes see through the tissues and tracings the genetic process has laid down between us and them. The tendrils can suggest a hand, or a specific color—the yellow of the tulip, for instance—will flash for a moment in such a way that after it has been withdrawn we can be sure that there was no imagining, no auto-suggestion here, but at the same time it becomes as useless as all subtracted memories. It has brought certainty without heat or light. Yet still in the old time, in the faraway summer evenings, they must have had a word for this, or known that we would someday need one, and wished to help. Then it is that a kind of purring occurs, like the wind sneaking around the baseboards of a room: not the infamous "still, small voice" but an ancillary speech that is parallel to the slithering of our own doubt-fleshed imaginings, a visible soundtrack of the way we sound as we move from encouragement to despair to exasperation and back again, with a gesture sometimes that is like an aborted movement outward toward some cape or promontory from which the view would extend in two directions—backward and forward—but that is only a polite hope in the same vein as all the others, crumpled and put away, and almost not to be distinguished from any of them, except that *it knows we know*, and in the context of not knowing is a fluidity that flashes like silver, that seems to say a film has been exposed and an image will, most certainly will, not like the last time, come to consider itself within the frame.

It must be an old photograph of you, out in the yard, looking almost afraid in the crisp, raking light that afternoons in the city held

的沼泽，反之则被称作"失望的深渊"？

也许他们想要我们享受他们享受过的东西，如同夏末黄昏，希望我们能发现其他的东西，感谢他们为我们提供了必要的手段来发现和享受它们。以他们过去的方式歌唱，我们有时可以透过身体组织和各种迹象看见我们和他们之间设置的基因过程。卷须可以使人想起一只手，或一种特定颜色——例如，郁金香的黄色——会以这样的方式闪烁片刻，在它撤走之后，我们可以肯定这里根本不存在任何想象，任何的自我暗示，可与此同时，它像所有消除的记忆一样变得毫无用处。它带来了没有光和热的确定性。毕竟在往昔，在遥远的夏日黄昏，对此，他们一定有一个词，或是知道我们有一天会需要一个词，他们愿意帮忙。于是，那种猫叫声出现了，就像房间护壁板中偷偷摸摸的风：不是声名狼藉的"平静微弱的声音"，而是一种从属语言，类似于我们自己可疑肉身想象中的滑行，我们用以发声的一条可见声道，当我们从勇气过渡到绝望再到恼怒，然后再返回，带着一种姿态，有时像是去往某个海角或海岬的一次夭折的运动，风景在那里会向两个方向延伸——向后和向前——但那只是一个委婉的希望，在和所有人一样的血管中，弄皱了，抛弃了，几乎与别人区分不开了，除了它知道我们知道，在一无所知的环境中作为一种流质，闪烁如水银，似乎要说一卷曝光的胶卷和一个形象，无疑将不同于上次，最终认为自己是在画里面。

它一定是你的一张旧照片，在院子里，几乎显得有些害怕，在易碎的斜光中，在城市的下午，那些没有安慰的日子，不接

in those days, unappeased, not accepting anything from anybody. So what else is new? I'll tell you what is: you are accepting this now from the invisible, unknown sender, and the light that was intended, you thought, only to rake or glance is now directed full in your face, as it in fact always was, but you were squinting so hard, fearful of accepting it, that you didn't know this. Whether it warms or burns is another matter, which we will not go into here. The point is that you are accepting it and holding on to it, like love from someone you always thought you couldn't stand, and whom you now recognize as a brother, an equal. Someone whose face is the same as yours in the photograph but who is someone else, all of whose thoughts and feelings are directed at you, falling like a gentle slab of light that will ultimately loosen and dissolve the crusted suspicion, the timely self-hatred, the efficient cold directness, the horrible good manners, the sensible resolves and the senseless nights spent waiting in utter abandon, that have grown up to be you in the tree with no view; and place you firmly in the good-natured circle of your ancestors' games and entertainments.

受任何人的任何东西。此外，还有什么是新的？我会告诉你是什么：你现在将从无形的、陌生的发送者那里接受这个，你认为，那一心只要掠过或是扫过的光，现在被完全引到了你的脸上，事实上，就像过去一样，但是你紧紧地眯起眼，害怕接受它，以至于你对此一无所知。它是温暖还是灼人，这是另一回事，我们这里不予探究。关键在于你将接受它并抓住它，像某人的爱，你总是以为你无法承受，你现在承认他是一个兄弟，一个对手。照片中某人的脸和你一样，但他是另外一个人，他全部的思想和感情都指向你，像一片温和的光芒洒落，最终会疏松和融解结了硬壳的猜疑，及时的自我憎恨，有效的冷酷直率，可怕的彬彬有礼，明智的决心，消磨于等待而终至放弃的愚蠢的夜晚，这一切长成了你，在没有风景的树上；并把你牢牢置于你的祖先的游戏与消遣那善意的循环之中。

A Wave

To pass through pain and not know it,

A car door slamming in the night.

To emerge on an invisible terrain.

So the luck of speaking out

A little too late came to be worshipped in various guises:

A mute actor, a future saint intoxicated with the idea of martyrdom;

And our landscape came to be as it is today:

Partially out of focus, some of it too near, the middle distance

A haven of serenity and unreachable, with all kinds of nice

People and plants waking and stretching, calling

Attention to themselves with every artifice of which the human

Genre is capable. And they called it our home.

No one came to take advantage of these early

Reverses, no doorbell rang;

Yet each day of the week, once it had arrived, seemed the threshold

Of love and desperation again. At night it sang

In the black trees: *My mindless, oh my mindless, oh.*

And it could be that it was Tuesday, with dark, restless clouds

And puffs of white smoke against them, and below, the wet streets

波　浪

经过痛苦但对它一无所知,
汽车门在夜里砰砰作响。
出现在一个无形的地区。

于是说话的幸运
稍晚一点终会被以各种姿态膜拜：
一个哑巴演员，一个未来的圣徒因牺牲的念头而陶醉；
我们的风景逐渐变成了今天的样子：
一部分失焦，一部分过于清晰，中景
一个平静但不可抵达的港口，有各种
美好的人和植物醒着伸展着，
用各种人类所掌握的技巧，呼吁
关注他们。他们把它叫做我们的家。

没有人来利用这些早期改变的
优势，没有门铃响起；
但每周的每一天，一旦到达，似乎仍旧是
爱和绝望的开始。夜里
它在黑色的树上歌唱：我愚笨的，哦我愚笨的，哦。
那可能是星期二，动荡的乌云
对它们喷出的白烟，下面，潮湿的街道

That seem so permanent, and all of a sudden the scene changes:
It's another idea, a new conception, something submitted
A long time ago, that only now seems about to work
To destroy at last the ancient network
Of letters, diaries, ads for civilization.
It passes through you, emerges on the other side
And is now a distant city, with all
The possibilities shrouded in a narrative moratorium.
The chroniqueurs who bad-mouthed it, the honest
Citizens whose going down into the day it was,
Are part of it, though none
Stand with you as you mope and thrash your way through time,
Imagining it as it is, a kind of tragic euphoria
In which your spirit sprouted. And which is justified in you.

In the haunted house no quarter is given: in that respect
It's very much business as usual. The reductive principle
Is no longer there, or isn't enforced as much as before.
There will be no getting away from the prospector's
Hunch; past experience matters again; the tale will stretch on
For miles before it is done. There would be more concerts
From now on, and the ground on which a man and his wife could
Look at each other and laugh, remembering how love is to them,
Shrank and promoted a surreal intimacy, like jazz music

似乎如此永恒,可是突然,景色变了:
那是另一个思想,一个新概念,很久以前
提交的一件事,现在才似乎要起作用
要最终摧毁服务于文明的
信件、日记和广告的古老网络。
它穿过你,出现在另一面
现在是一座遥远的城,
所有的可能性都遮蔽在一个叙述暂停中。
苛刻批评它的编年史作者,
到今天一直诚实的公民,
都是它的一部分,虽然没有人
和你站在一起,当你闷闷不乐,逆行穿过时间,
把它想象成一种悲惨的狂喜
你的灵魂从中萌芽。它在你内部得到了证明。

闹鬼的房子不提供住处:在那方面
一切正常一如平常。还原法则
不再存在,或者不再像以前那么迫切;
那里不会有什么偏离勘探者的预感;
过去的经验重新变得重要;故事将在结束前
延伸出数里之遥。从现在起,将有更多的
音乐会,而土地,一个男人和他的妻子能够
彼此凝视和欢笑,回忆着他们爱情的土地,
将会缩小,倡导一种超现实的亲密,像爵士乐

Moving over furniture, to say how pleased it was

Or something. In the end only a handshake

Remains, something like a kiss; but fainter. Were we

Making sense? Well, that thirst will account for some

But not all of the marvelous graffiti; meanwhile

The oxygen of the days sketches the rest,

The balance. Our story is no longer alone.

There is a rumbling there

And now it ends, and in a luxurious hermitage

The straws of self-defeat are drawn. The short one wins.

One idea is enough to organize a life and project it

Into unusual but viable forms, but many ideas merely

Lead one thither into a morass of their own good intentions.

Think how many the average person has during the course of a day, or night,

So that they become a luminous backdrop to ever-repeated

Gestures, having no life of their own, but only echoing

The suspicions of their possessor. It's fun to scratch around

And maybe come up with something. But for the tender blur

Of the setting to mean something, words must be ejected bodily,

A certain crispness be avoided in favor of a density

Of strutted opinion doomed to wilt in oblivion: not too linear

Nor yet too puffed and remote. Then the advantage of

Sinking in oneself, crashing through the skylight of one's own

在家具上移动,说它自己多么愉快
或诸如此类。最后只留下握手
像一个吻,但是更为微弱。我们
有意义吗?嗯,那渴望将解释部分
而非全部的神奇涂鸦;与此同时
日子的氧气勾勒出剩余的,
余额。我们的故事不再孤独。
那边有一阵隆隆声
现在结束了,在奢侈的修道院
画下战胜自我的稻草。短的赢。

一个思想足以组织起一种生活并把它
投射在非凡但可行的形式中,但许多思想仅仅
把一个人引向它们自己良好意愿的沼泽。
想想,有多少普通人,在一天或一夜之间,
成了发光的背景幕,永远重复着
手势,没有自己的生命,只能回应着
他们主人的猜疑。在周围乱涂是一种乐趣
也许会遇见什么。但是为了让模糊的背景
有所意味,必须把词语整体驱逐,
避免某种易碎性,以有利于一种炫耀的
意见的密度,它注定在遗忘中枯萎:不再过于线性
也不再过于蓬松和遥远。那时,沉于自身的
优势,穿过一个人自己的阳光跌碎

Received opinions redirects the maze, setting up significant
Erections of its own at chosen corners, like gibbets,
And through this the mesmerizing plan of the landscape becomes,
At last, apparent. It is no more a landscape than a golf course is,
Though sensibly a few natural bonuses have been left in. And as it
Focuses itself, it is the backward part of a life that is
Partially coming into view. It's there, like a limb. And the issue
Of making sense becomes such a far-off one. Isn't this "sense"—
This little of my life that I can see—that answers me
Like a dog, and wags its tail, though excitement and fidelity are
About all that ever gets expressed? What did I ever do
To want to wander over into something else, an explanation
Of how I behaved, for instance, when knowing can have this
Sublime rind of excitement, like the shore of a lake in the desert
Blazing with the sunset? So that if it pleases all my constructions
To collapse, I shall at least have had that satisfaction, and known
That it need not be permanent in order to stay alive,
Beaming, confounding with the spell of its good manners.

As with rocks at low tide, a mixed surface is revealed,
More detritus. Still, it is better this way
Than to have to live through a sequence of events acknowledged
In advance in order to get to a primitive statement. And the mind
Is the beach on which the rocks pop up, just a neutral

接受的意见重新指向迷宫，在选定的角落
竖立起意味深长的建筑物，像绞刑架，
穿过这一切，给风景催眠的计划，
最后变得明显。它不再是风景，而是一个高尔夫球场，
尽管聪明地留下了一点自然的点缀。
当它自行聚焦，那部分进入视野的
是生活落后的部分。它在那里，像一条胳膊。
意义的问题变得如此遥远。难道不是这"风景"——
我可以看见的我这小小的生活——在回答我
像一条狗，摇着尾巴，尽管全部的表达
不过是激动和忠诚？我曾经做过什么
想要去其他事物中漫游，对我行为的
一个解释，例如，当我知道可以拥有
这激动的庄严外壳，就像沙漠中的湖岸
因日落而闪耀？所以，如果我所有的建筑崩溃
让它高兴，我至少还能得到那种满足，知道
为了活着它不需要永恒，
喜气洋洋，困惑于它美好风度的魅力。

仿佛随着低潮时的礁石，一个混合的表面显露出来，
更多的碎石。不过，这总要胜于
不得不经受一系列预先知道的事件
为了达到一个原始的陈述。而心灵
是岩石突然出现的海滩，在他们的侮辱中

Support for them in their indignity. They explain
The trials of our age, cleansing it of toxic
Side-effects as it passes through their system.
Reality. Explained. And for seconds
We live in the same body, are a sibling again.

I think all games and disciplines are contained here,
Painting, as they go, dots and asterisks that
We force into meanings that don't concern us
And so leave us behind. But there are no fractions, the world is an integer
Like us, and like us it can neither stand wholly apart nor disappear.
When one is young it seems like a very strange and safe place,
But now that I have changed it feels merely odd, cold
And full of interest. The sofa that was once a seat
Puzzles no longer, while the sweet conversation that occurs
At regular intervals throughout the years is like a collie
One never outgrows. And it happens to you
In this room, it is here, and we can never
Eat of the experience. It drags us down. Much later on
You thought you perceived a purpose in the game at the moment
Another player broke one of the rules; it seemed
A module for the wind, something in which you lose yourself
And are not lost, and then it pleases you to play another day
When outside conditions have changed and only the game

仅仅是一个中立的支撑。他们解释

我们时代的考验,清除它有毒的

副作用,当它通过他们的系统。

现实。解释过的。我们

在同一躯体中生活了片刻,又成了同胞。

我思考这里包含的所有游戏和惩罚,

当它们进行时,画着点和星号

我们给它们强加上与我们无关的意义

把我们留在后面。但是没有任何分数,世界是个整数

和我们一样,和我们一样它既不能独立也不能消失。

一个人年轻时它似乎像一个非常陌生和安全的地方,

但既然我已经改变了,我觉得它只是古怪,寒冷

充满兴趣。沙发曾经是一个座位

不再令人迷惑,这些年按一定间隔进行的

甜蜜交谈,像一只牧羊狗

从未长大。它发生在你身上

在这个房间,在这里,我们永远不能

品尝到经验。它把我们向下拖。很久以后

你认为你在游戏中察觉到了一个目的

这时另一个游戏者打破了规则;似乎

一个为风准备的模块,你迷失其中

但并非被迫,那时它请你改天再玩

而外面的情况已经变化,只有游戏

Is fast, perplexed and true, as it comes to have seemed.

Yet one does know why. The covenant we entered

Bears down on us, some are ensnared, and the right way,

It turns out, is the one that goes straight through the house

And out the back. By so many systems

As we are involved in, by just so many

Are we set free on an ocean of language that comes to be

Part of us, as though we would ever get away.

The sky is bright and very wide, and the waves talk to us,

Preparing dreams we'll have to live with and use. The day will come

When we'll have to. But for now

They're useless, more trees in a landscape of trees.

I hadn't expected a glance to be that direct, coming from a sculpture

Of moments, thoughts added on. And I had kept it

Only as a reminder, not out of love. In time I moved on

To become its other side, and then, gentle, anxious, I became as a parent

To those scenes lifted from "real life." There was the quiet time

In the supermarket, and the pieces

Of other people's lives as they sashayed or tramped past

My own section of a corridor, not pausing

In many cases to wonder where they were—maybe they even knew.

True, those things or moments of which one

稳固，困惑而真实，像最终显示的那样。

一个人确实知道原因。我们缔结的盟约
给我们施加压力，有些人掉入了陷阱，结果
正确的方式，是直接穿过房子
从后面出去。凭借这么多的系统
当我们卷入时，仅凭其多
我们就可以在一个语言的海洋上获得自由
它逐渐成为我们的一部分，仿佛我们会离开。
天空明亮而宽阔，波浪对我们说话，
准备着我们必须以其为生和加以使用的梦。日子
将在我们需要的时候到来。但是现在
它们一无所用，只是树的风景中更多的树。

我没有料到一座时辰和思想堆积成的雕像
会投来径直的一瞥。我保留它
仅仅作为提醒，不是出于爱。我及时移动
为了变成它的另一面，然后，温和，焦虑，我变成了
那些从"真实生活"中升起的风景的主人。
在超市里，其他人生活的片断中，存在着
安宁的时刻，当他们到处走动或者大踏步地走过
我自己的那段走廊，在很多情况下
不会停下，疑惑他们置身何处——也许他们知道。
真的，那些事物，或者一个人发现自己

Finds oneself an enthusiast, a promoter, are few,
But they last well,
Yielding up their appearances for form
Much later than the others. Forgetting about "love"
For a moment puts one miles ahead, on the steppe or desert
Whose precise distance as it feels I
Want to emphasize and estimate. Because
We will all have to walk back this way
A second time, and not to know it then, not
To number each straggling piece of sagebrush
Is to sleep before evening, and well into the night
That always coaxes us out, smooths out our troubles and puts us back
    to bed again.

All those days had a dumb clarity that was about getting out
Into a remembered environment. The headlines and economy
Would refresh for a moment as you look back over the heap
Of rusted box-springs with water under them, and then,
Like sliding up to a door or a peephole a tremendous advantage
Would burst like a bubble. Toys as solemn and knotted as books
Assert themselves first, leading down through a delicate landscape
Of reminders to be better next time to a damp place on my hip,
And this would spell out a warm business letter urging us
All to return to our senses, to the matter of the day
That was ending now. And no special sense of decline ensued

是个狂热者和鼓动者的时刻,是很少的,

但是它们相当持久,

为了形式,比其他人更晚地

放弃它们的形象。有片刻忘记了"爱"

让一个人提前数里,到达悬崖或沙漠

我想强调和估计我感受到的

它的确切距离。因为

我们都必须按照这条路

再次返回,那么,不去了解它,

不去计数山艾树每一个四散的碎片

就是在黄昏前睡觉,钻进夜晚

它总是哄我们出去,解除我们的麻烦并把我们再送上床。

那些日子沉默而清晰,即将进入

一个被记住的环境。大字标题和经济

将复苏片刻,当你回头去看那堆

下面有水的生锈的弹簧床垫,然后,

就像滑向一扇门或窥视孔,一个巨大的优势

会泡沫一样爆裂。玩偶们书一般严肃而棘手

首先坚持自己的权利,被下一次会更好的暗示

牵引着穿过微妙的风景,来到我臀部的潮湿之处,

这一切将拼写出一封温暖的商业信函,催促我们

全都返回我们的感觉,回到此刻正在结束的

这一天的事情上来。没有特殊的堕落感随之发生

But perhaps a few moments of music of such tact and weariness

That one awakens with a new sense of purpose: more things to be done

And the just-sufficient tools to begin doing them

While awaiting further orders that must materialize soon

Whether in the sand-pit with frightened chickens running around

Or on a large table in a house deep in the country with messages

Pinned to the walls and a sense of plainness quite unlike

Any other waiting. I am prepared to deal with this

While putting together notes related to the question of love

For the many, for two people at once, and for myself

In a time of need unlike those that have arisen so far.

And some day perhaps the discussion that has to come

In order for us to start feeling any of it before we even

Start to think about it will arrive in a new weather

Nobody can imagine but which will happen just as the ages

Have happened without causing total consternation,

Will take place in a night, long before sleep and the love

That comes then, breathing mystery back into all the sterile

Living that had to lead up to it. Moments as clear as water

Splashing on a rock in the sun, though in darkness, and then

Sleep has to affirm it and the body is fresh again,

For the trials and dangerous situations that any love,

However well-meaning, has to use as terms in the argument

但也许会有一小段机智而疲倦的音乐

一个人带着一种新的目的感醒来：有更多的事要做

开始做事的工具刚好足够

一边等待不久就要实行的进一步的命令

无论是在受惊的小鸡到处乱跑的沙坑

还是在墙上钉着通知的村舍中的

一张大桌子上，都清晰地感到这和别的等待

非常不同。我准备处理这个

同时把有关爱的问题的日记放在一起

为许多人，同时为两个人，也为我自己

以备不时之需，这需要不同于迄今已有的。

有一天也许会发生这样的讨论

为了让我们开始感觉到它，甚至在我们

开始思考它之前，它就会在新的天气中到达

无人能够想象，但是它将发生

就像时代的发生没有导致整体的恐慌，

它将在夜里发生，早在睡眠之前和随后出现的

爱之前，把秘密吹回所有贫瘠不毛的

为它做准备的生存。时辰清澈如水

泼溅在阳光中的岩石上，尽管在黑暗中，

睡眠也必须承认它，身体再次焕然一新，

为了无论多么善意的爱

都必须在争论中习惯的

种种考验和危险的处境

That is the reflexive play of our living and being lost

And then changed again, a harmless fantasy that must grow

Progressively serious, and soon state its case succinctly

And dangerously, and we sit down to the table again

Noting the grain of the wood this time and how it pushes through

The pad we are writing on and becomes part of what is written.

Not until it starts to stink does the inevitable happen.

Moving on we approached the top

Of the thing, only it was dark and no one could see,

Only somebody said it was a miracle we had gotten past the

Previous phase, now faced with each other's conflicting

Wishes and the hope for a certain peace, so this would be

Our box and we would stay in it for as long

As we found it comfortable, for the broken desires

Inside were as nothing to the steeply shelving terrain outside,

And morning would arrange everything. So my first impulse

Came, stayed awhile, and left, leaving behind

Nothing of itself, no whisper. The days now move

From left to right and back across this stage and no one

Notices anything unusual. Meanwhile I have turned back

Into that dream of rubble that was the city of our starting out.

No one advises me; the great tenuous clouds of the desert

Sky visit it and they barely touch, so pleasing in the

那是我们生存的反身游戏,丧失了
又再次改变,一个无害的幻想一定会
日益变得严肃,并尽快简洁地陈述它的情况
危险地,我们再次在桌边坐下
这次注意到了木屑如何挤过
我们正在写字的便笺簿,变成写下的一部分。
还没等到它发臭,那不可避免的事就发生了。

继续移动,我们接近事物的顶端,
只有它是黑的,无人能够看见,
只有某人说它是个奇迹,我们已经完成了
以前的阶段,现在面对彼此矛盾的
心愿,以及对和平的希望,所以这就是
我们的盒子,我们将待在里面
只要我们觉得它很舒服,因为我们心中
破碎的欲望和外面陡峭的坡地一样空虚,
早晨会安排好一切。于是,我最初的冲动
出现,停留片刻,离去,什么
都没有留下,也没有低语。现在日子
从左向右移动,又回头穿过这个舞台
没人注意到任何异常。这时我已经返回
那个碎石的梦,那是我们出发的城市。
没人给我建议;沙漠天空上巨大稀薄的云彩
短暂逗留,它们几乎不接触,愉悦于

Immense solitude are the tracks of those who wander and continue
On their route, certain that day will end soon and that night will then fall.

But behind what looks like heaps of slag the peril
Consists in explaining everything too evenly. Those
Suffering from the blahs are unlikely to notice that the topic
Of today's lecture doesn't exist yet, and in their trauma
Will become one with the vast praying audience as it sways and bends
To the rhythm of an almost inaudible piccolo. And when
It is flushed out, the object of all this meditation will not
Infrequently turn out to be a mere footnote to the great chain
That manages only with difficulty to connect earth and sky together.
Are comments like ours really needed? Of course, heaven is nice
About it, not saying anything, but we, when we come away
As children leaving school at four in the afternoon, can we
Hold our heads up and face the night's homework? No, the
Divine tolerance we seem to feel is actually in short supply,
And those moving forward toward us from the other end of the bridge
Are defending, not welcoming us to, the place of power,
A hill ringed with low, ridgelike fortifications. But when
Somebody better prepared crosses over, he or she will get the same
Cold reception. And so because it is impossible to believe
That anyone lives there, it is we who shall be homeless, outdoors
At the end. And we won't quite know what to do about it.

各自轨迹的巨大孤独,它们继续漫游
确信白昼不久将会结束,黑夜随后降临。

但在那些看似炉渣堆的东西后面
危险在于对一切做出过于平均的解释。
那些被废话折磨的人不可能注意到
今天讲座的题目还不存在,他们在创伤中
将与大量祈祷的听众成为一体
随着几乎听不见的短笛的节奏摇摆和鞠躬。
当它泛滥开来,这沉思的对象不会
罕见地变成那伟大链条的一个纯粹注脚
克服一切困难,把大地和天空连在一起。
我们这样的评论真的有必要吗?当然,天堂很美好
关于它,啥都别说,但是我们,当我们离开
当孩子们在下午四点离开学校,我们
能抬起头面对夜晚的家庭作业吗?不,
我们即将感受的神圣宽容实际上非常短缺,
那些从桥的另一端向我们走来的人
含有戒心,不欢迎我们,来到权力的处所,
一座环绕着低低的山脊状要塞的山。但当
某人准备穿越过去之时,他或她将受到同样
冷淡的对待。因为不可能相信
任何住在那里的人,将要无家可归的是我们,
最后,在户外。我们不太了解为此要做些什么。

It's mind-boggling, actually. Each of us must try to concentrate
On some detail or other of their armor: somber, blood-red plumes
Floating over curved blue steel; the ribbed velvet stomacher
And its more social implications. Hurry to deal with the sting
Of added meaning, hurry to fend it off. Your lessons
Will become the ground of which we are made
And shall look back on, for awhile. Life was pleasant there.
And though we made it all up, it could still happen to us again.
Only then, watch out. The burden of proof of the implausible
Picaresque tale, boxes within boxes, will be yours
Next time round. And nobody is going to like your ending.

We had, though, a feeling of security
But we weren't aware of it then: that's
How secure we were. Now, in the dungeon of Better Living,
It seems we may be called back and interrogated about it
Which would be unfortunate, since only the absence of memory
Animates us as we walk briskly back and forth
At one with the soulless, restless crowd on the somber avenue.
Is there something new to see, to speculate on? Dunno, better
Stand back until something comes along to explain it,
This curious lack of anxiety that begins to gnaw
At one. Did it come because happiness hardened everything
In its fire, and so the forms cannot die, like a ruined

实际上，这令人惊异。我们都必须集中注意

他们装甲的某个细节：阴森，血红的羽毛

漂浮在弯曲的蓝色钢铁上；有罗纹的天鹅绒三角胸衣

和它更为社会化的暗示。急着去应付

附加含义的叮咬，急着挡开它。你的教训

将变成造就我们的土地

我们将回顾片刻。那里的生活是愉快的。

虽然我们虚构了它，它仍可以再次发生。

直到那时，当心。证明难以置信的

传奇故事的负担，盒中之盒，下一轮

将落在你身上。没人会喜欢你的结尾。

我们虽然有一种安全感

但我们那时没有意识到：

我们多么安全。现在，在更美好的生活的地牢，

似乎我们能够被召回，拷问

那将是不幸的，既然只有缺席的记忆

鼓舞我们，当我们活泼地来回走动

和阴森的林荫道上无情的、不安的人群一起。

那里有什么新东西可看、可思索的吗？我不知道，

最好是站在一边，直到什么东西出现，作出解释

这奇怪的缺乏焦虑开始让人

苦恼。它会出现吗，因为幸福使一切

在它的火中变硬，这样形体便不会消亡，像一座

Fort too strong to be pulled down? Arid something like pale
Alpine flowers still flourishes there:
Some reminder that can never be anything more than that,
Yet its balm cares about something, we cannot be really naked
Having this explanation. So a reflected image of oneself
Manages to stay alive through the darkest times, a period
Of unprecedented frost, during which we get up each morning
And go about our business as usual.

And though there are some who leave regularly
For the patchwork landscape of childhood, north of here,
Our own kind of stiff standing around, waiting helplessly
And mechanically for instructions that never come, suits the space
Of our intense, uncommunicated speculation, marries
The still life of crushed, red fruit in the sky and tames it
For observation purposes. One is almost content
To be with people then, to read their names and summon
Greetings and speculation, or even nonsense syllables and
Diagrams from those who appear so brilliantly at ease
In the atmosphere we made by getting rid of most amenities
In the interests of a bare, strictly patterned life that apparently
Has charms we weren't even conscious of, which is
All to the good, except that it fumbles the premise
We put by, saving it for a later phase of intelligence, and now

荒废的堡垒，坚固得无法摧毁？某种
苍白如高山雪莲似的东西仍在那里繁茂生长：
某种超乎一切的再好不过的提醒物，
它的芳香仍在关心着什么事，我们不能真的赤裸着
得到这个解释。于是一个人的倒影
试图穿过最黑暗的时间而存活，一个
预料不到的霜冻时期，我们每天早晨起来
和平常一样着手我们的工作。

虽然有些人定期离开
去拼凑童年的风景，这里以北，
我们的同类则僵硬地站在周围，绝望而机械地
等待从未到达的指令，适应
我们紧张、沉默的推测的空间，配合
天空中被压扁的、红色果实的静物
为观察的目的而将之驯服。一个人几乎满足于
和人们在一起，读他们的名字，招来
欢迎和推测，甚至无意义的音节和图表
它们来自于那些显得如此安逸的人们
在我们凭借摆脱大部分礼仪而营造的气氛里
在赤裸的、严格规划的生活情趣中，那种生活
明显拥有我们甚至意识不到的魅力，
全都是有益的，只有它在摸索我们
放置的前提，留给后来的智慧阶段，现在

We are living on it, ready to grow and make mistakes again,

Still standing on one leg while emerging continually

Into an inexpressive void, the blighted fields

Of a kiss, the rope of a random, unfortunate

Observation still around our necks though we thought we

Had cast it off in a novel that has somehow gotten stuck

To our lives, battening on us. A sad condition

To see us in, yet anybody

Will realize that he or she has made those same mistakes,

Memorized those same lists in the due course of the process

Being served on you now. Acres of bushes, treetops;

Orchards where the quince and apple seem to come and go

Mysteriously over long periods of time; waterfalls

And what they conceal, including what comes after—roads and roadways

Paved for the gently probing, transient automobile;

Farragoes of flowers; everything, in short,

That makes this explicit earth what it appears to be in our

Glassiest moments when a canoe shoots out from under some foliage

Into the river and finds it calm, not all that exciting but above all

Nothing to be afraid of, celebrates us

And what we have made of it.

Not something so very strange, but then seeming ordinary

Is strange too. Only the way we feel about the everything

我们正在靠它生活，准备长大，再次犯错，
仍然一条腿站着，同时继续出现在
一个无意义的空间，一个吻的
枯萎的田野，一种随机而不幸的观察的
绳索，依然绕在我们的脖子上，尽管我们以为
我们已把它抛在了一部不知怎么
粘在我们生活上，靠我们养活的小说里。
看到我们陷入如此糟糕的处境，任何人
都会认识到自己犯了同样的错误，
在此刻服务于你的相应过程中
记住那些同样的清单。成亩的灌木，树顶；
在很长时间中，有温柏和苹果神秘地
出现又消失的果园；一些瀑布
及其隐藏的一切，包括后来出现的——马路和车行道
为悄悄探路的、路过的汽车而铺设；
混杂的花朵；简而言之，各种东西，
使这明确的大地在我们最迟钝的时刻
出现，当一条独木舟从树叶下射出
进入河流，发现河很平静，根本不激动
尤其是没有什么可怕的，它祝贺我们
和我们用它来造就的一切。

不是什么很陌生的东西，但那看似平常的
同样也是陌生的。只有我们感受一切的方式

And not the feeling itself is strange, strange to us, who live
And want to go on living under the same myopic stars we have known
Since childhood, when, looking out a window, we saw them
And immediately liked them.

And we can get back to that raw state
Of feeling, so long deemed
Inconsequential and therefore appropriate to our later musings
About religion, about migrations. What is restored
Becomes stronger than the loss as it is remembered;
Is a new, separate life of its own. A new color. Seriously blue.
Unquestioning. Acidly sweet. Must we then pick up the pieces
(But what are the pieces, if not separate puzzles themselves,
And meanwhile rain abrades the window?) and move to a central clearinghouse
Somewhere in Iowa, far from the distant bells and thunderclaps that
Make this environment pliant and distinct? Nobody
Asked me to stay here, at least if they did I forgot, but I can
Hear the dust at the pores of the wood, and know then
The possibility of something more liberated and gracious
Though not of this time. Failing
That there are the books we haven't read, and just beyond them
A landscape stippled by frequent glacial interventions
That holds so well to its lunette one wants to keep it but we must
Go on despising it until that day when environment

而不是感觉本身是陌生的,对于我们是陌生的,
我们活着并且想继续生活在我们童年起就熟悉的
同样近视的群星之下,那时,透过窗户,我们看见它们
并马上喜欢上了它们。

我们可以回到那个原始的感觉
状态,长期以来我们认为
它是不合逻辑的,因而适合我们后来
有关宗教和移居的沉思。被恢复的一切
在被回忆时,变得比丧失还要强大;
是一个新的独立的生命。一种新的色彩。严肃的蓝。
毫无疑问。酸甜。我们必须拾起碎片
(但这些碎片是什么,如果其本身不是单独的谜,
同时也是被雨磨损的窗户?)走向一个中心票据交换所吗
爱荷华州某地,远离遥远的钟声和霹雳
它们使得这个环境易受影响,截然不同?没有人
要求我留在这里,至少我忘了他们是否这样要求过,
但是我能听见木头气孔上的灰尘,知道
更为自由和亲切的事物的可能性
尽管不是这一次。失败在于
有些书我们没有读过,就在它们之外
不断介入的冰川点缀着风景
坚守着你想占据的它的弧形空间,但是我们
必须继续轻视它,直到有一天

Finally reads as a necessary but still vindictive opposition

To all caring, all explaining. Your finger traces a

Bleeding violet line down the columns of an old directory and to this spongy

State of talking things out a glass exclamation point opposes

A discrete claim: forewarned. So the voluminous past

Accepts, recycles our claims to present consideration

And the urban landscape is once again untroubled, smooth

As wax. As soon as the oddity is flushed out

It becomes monumental and anxious once again, looking

Down on our lives as from a baroque pinnacle and not the

Mosquito that was here twenty minutes ago.

The past absconds

With our fortunes just as we were rounding a major

Bend in the swollen river; not to see ahead

Becomes the only predicament when what

Might be sunken there is mentioned only

In crabbed allusions but will be back tomorrow.

It takes only a minute revision, and see—the thing

Is there in all its interested variegatedness,

With prospects and walks curling away, never to be followed,

A civilized concern, a never being alone.

Later on you'll have doubts about how it

Actually was, and certain greetings will remain totally forgotten,

环境最终被视为一个必要但仍有报复性的对立面

抵制所有的关心和解释。你的手指沿着一根

流血的紫色线条滑下一份旧目录的纵列，抵达这海绵般的状态

把事物大声说成一个透明的感叹号

与不连续的主张相反：预先警告。于是

庞大的过去接受、循环我们对现在的报酬的主张

城市的风景再次平静，光滑

像蜡一样。怪事一旦出现

马上又变得不朽而焦虑，俯视着

我们的生活，仿佛从巴洛克尖塔上

而不是二十分钟前这里的蚊子。

过去带着我们的幸运潜逃

就像我们在涨水的河中

绕着大弯子；不去看前面

成了唯一的困境，

应该沉在那里的只在潦草的暗示里

才被提到，但明天它们将返回。

它只需要一分钟的修订，看——

那里的事物驳杂有趣，

带着前景盘绕而去，永远跟不上，

一种文明的忧虑，一个从不存在的孤独。

以后你会怀疑它的实际情况

如何，一些欢迎将被完全遗忘，

As water forgets a dam once it's over it. But at this moment

A spirit of independence reigns. Quietude

To get out and do things in, and a rush back to the house

When evening turns up, and not a moment too soon.

Headhunters and jackals mingle with the viburnum

And hollyhocks outside, and it all adds up, pointedly,

To something one didn't quite admit feeling uneasy about, but now

That it's all out in the open, like a successful fire

Burning in a fireplace, really there's no cause for alarm.

For even when hours and days go by in silence and the phone

Never rings, and widely spaced drops of water

Fall from the eaves, nothing is any longer a secret

And one can live alone rejoicing in this:

That the years of war are far off in the past or the future,

That memory contains everything. And you see slipping down a hallway

The past self you decided not to have anything to do with any more

And it is a more comfortable you, dishonest perhaps,

But alive. Wanting you to know what you're losing.

And still the machinery of the great exegesis is only beginning

To groan and hum. There are moments like this one

That are almost silent, so that bird-watchers like us

Can come, and stay awhile, reflecting on shades of difference

In past performances, and move on refreshed.

像水一旦越过就把大坝遗忘。但在这时
一个独立的精神君临。寂静
出去做一些事情,又匆忙奔向房屋
当黄昏出现,而非一个短暂的瞬时。
挖墙脚的人和走狗混同于外面的蜀葵
和荚莲属植物,它直接叠加于
一个人不太承认感觉不自在的东西上,但现在
它全部在露天里,像成功的火
燃烧在壁炉中,真的没有任何报警的理由。
甚至在时辰和日子沉默地流逝,电话
从来不响的时候,大片大片的水滴
从屋檐滴落,再没有什么秘密了
一个人可以单凭为此欣喜而活着:
战争的岁月远在过去或未来,
记忆包含一切。你看见过去的你滑倒在走廊
你决定与之再无任何关联
这样你更舒服,也许不忠诚,
但活跃。要求你了解他们失去了什么。
巨大的解经机才刚刚开始
呻吟和嗡鸣。这样的时辰
几乎是寂静的,以至于和我们一样的观鸟者
可以来停留片刻,沉思过去的表演中
差异的阴影,然后清新地继续。

801

But always and sometimes questioning the old modes
And the new wondering, the poem, growing up through the floor,
Standing tall in tubers, invading and smashing the ritual
Parlor, demands to be met on its own terms now,
Now that the preliminary negotiations are at last over.
You could be lying on the floor,
Or not have time for too much of any one thing,
Yet you know the song quickens in the bones
Of your neck, in your heel, and there is no point
In looking out over the yard where tractors run,
The empty space in the endless continuum
Of time has come up: the space that can be filled only by you.
And I had thought about the roadblocks, wondered
Why they were less frequent, wondered what progress the blizzard
Might have been making a certain distance back there,
But it was not enough to save me from choosing
Myself now, from being the place I have to get to
Before nightfall and under the shelter of trees
It is true but also without knowing out there in the dark,
Being alone at the center of a moan that did not issue from me
And is pulling me back toward old forms of address
I know I have already lived through, but they are strong again,
And big to fill the exotic spaces that arguing left.
So all the slightly more than young

但有时我们总是怀疑旧的模式

对新的感到惊奇,诗歌,穿过地板生长,

高高地立在块茎中,侵犯和粉碎

仪式的客厅,要求现在满足它的条件,

既然预备谈判终于结束了。

你可以躺在地板上,

或是没有时间过多地花在任何一件事上,

可你知道歌曲在你的颈骨里,

在你的脚跟里活跃着,没有必要

去外面跑着拖拉机的院子里寻找

空虚的空间已经出现在时间无尽的

连续统中:那空间只能由你来填满。

我想到过路障,奇怪

为什么它们不频繁出现,奇怪大风雪

越过怎样的距离才回到那里,

可它不足以拯救我,使我免于

此刻的自我选择,免于去我必须去的地方

在日落之前,在树木的掩蔽下

它真的不知道在外面的黑暗中,

我被独自留在并非我所发出的呻吟中

它拖着我返回老式的地址

我知道我已经熬过去了,但是它们再次强大起来,

大到可以填满争论留下的奇异空间。

于是所有稍微年轻一点的人

Get moved up whether they like it or not, and only
The very old or the very young have any say in the matter,
Whether they are a train or a boat or just a road leading
Across a plain, from nowhere to nowhere. Later on
A record of the many voices of the middle-young will be issued
And found to be surprisingly original. That can't concern us,
However, because now there isn't space enough,
Not enough dimension to guarantee any kind of encounter
The stage-set it requires at the very least in order to burrow
Profitably through history and come out having something to say,
Even just one word with a slightly different intonation
To cause it to stand out from the backing of neatly invented
Chronicles of things men have said and done, like an English horn,
And then to sigh, to faint back
Into all our imaginings, dark
And viewless as they are,
Windows painted over with black paint but
We can sufficiently imagine, so much is admitted, what
Might be going on out there and even play some part
In the ordering of it all into lengths of final night,
Of dim play, of love that at lasts oozes through the seams
In the cement, suppurates, subsumes
All the other business of living and dying, the orderly
Ceremonials and handling of estates,

都得到了提升，无论是否喜欢，只有
很老或非常年轻的才有说话的机会，
无论他们是在火车上还是船上，或者仅仅是一条
穿过平原的路上，从无地到无地。以后
一卷许多中青年人声音的录音带将会发行
并发现它惊人地新颖。然而，那可能与我们无关，
因为现在没有足够的空间，
足够的维度来担保任何形式的相遇
它所要求的最起码的舞台背景，为了有利可图地
在历史中掘洞，出来时有事儿可说，
甚至只是一个语调稍有不同的词
就能使它从巧妙发明的人的言行的
编年史衬幕中站出来，像一只英国号，
发出叹息，然后微弱下来
回到我们的想象之中，黑暗
像他们一样看不见，
窗户都刷了黑漆
但我们能充分地想象，承认，
外面会有什么在继续，甚至在它的要求下
扮演一定的角色，进入最后的夜晚，
进入暗淡的戏剧，透过接缝最后渗出的爱
在水泥中，流脓，包容
生与死的所有其他业务，井然有序的
仪式和不动产的处理，

Checking what does not appear normal and drawing together

All the rest into the report that will finally be made

On a day when it does not appear that there is anything to receive it

Properly and we wonder whether we too are gone,

Buried in our love,

The love that defined us only for a little while,

And when it strolls back a few paces, to get another view,

Fears that it may have encountered eternity in the meantime.

And as the luckless describe love in glowing terms to strangers

In taverns, and the seemingly blessed may be unaware of having lost it,

So always there is a small remnant

Whose lives are congruent with their souls

And who ever afterward know no mystery in it,

The cimmerian moment in which all lives, all destinies

And incompleted destinies were swamped

As though by a giant wave that picks itself up

Out of a calm sea and retreats again into nowhere

Once its damage is done.

And what to say about those series

Of infrequent pellucid moments in which

One reads inscribed as though upon an empty page

The strangeness of all those contacts from the time they erupt

Soundlessly on the horizon and in a moment are upon you

Like a stranger on a snowmobile

核实显得不正常的东西，把剩下的一切
统统纳入有一天要最后提交的报告
那一天似乎没有什么东西要恰当地接受它
我们也在疑惑是否我们也要离开，
埋葬在我们的爱中，
那爱只在很短的时间里为我们设立了边界，
然后它退回几步，再观察一回，
担心它会在这时遭遇到永恒。
当运气不佳的人在酒馆里热烈地向陌生人描绘爱情，
表面有福气的人可能意识不到正在失去它，
所以总是有少量剩下的人
他们的生命和灵魂和谐一致
他们后来知道它里面没有秘密，
阴惨的时刻，所有的生命，所有的命运
以及未完成的命运都被淹没
仿佛一个巨浪从沉静的大海中
涌起，一旦它的破坏完成
又退回虚无。
对于那一系列罕见的透明时刻
有什么可说，其中
一个人阅读铭文仿佛在一张空白页上
从那时起，所有触体的陌生感
无声地在地平线上喷发，在一个瞬间扑向你
像机动雪橇上的陌生人

But of which nothing can be known or written, only

That they passed this way? That to be bound over

To love in the dark, like Psyche, will somehow

Fill the sheaves of pages with a spidery, Spencerian hand

When all that will be necessary will be to go away

For a few minutes in order to return and find the work completed?

And so it is the only way

That love determines us, and we look the same

To others when they happen in afterwards, and cannot even know

We have changed, so massive in our difference

We are, like a new day that looks and cannot be the same

As those we used to reckon with, and so start

On our inane rounds again too dumb to profit from past

Mistakes—that's how different we are!

But once we have finished being interrupted

There is no longer any population to tell us how the gods

Had wanted it—only—so the story runs—a vast forest

With almost nobody in it. Your wants

Are still halfheartedly administered to; sometimes there is milk

And sometimes not, but a ladder of hilarious applause

No longer leads up to it. Instead, there's that cement barrier.

The forest ranger was nice, but warning us away,

Reminded you how other worlds can as easily take root

但是什么都不能了解或被写下，
仅仅是他们经过这条路吗？那被爱束缚在
黑暗中的，像灵魂一样，将设法
用一只蜘蛛般的、斯宾塞式的手填满书页
当一切变得必要，将要离开几分钟
为了返回并发现工作已经完成？
所以，它是爱情裁决我们的
唯一方式，在别人眼里我们还是老样子，
当他们随后发现，甚至无法知道
我们已经改变，我们的区别
如此巨大，看上去像一个新日子，不可能
和我们习惯应付的日子一样，就这样再次开始
我们愚蠢的循环，沉默得无法从过去的错误
获得教益——因此我们有多么不同！

但是我们一旦被打断
就不再有任何人告诉我们，众神如何
只需要它——故事于是开始——一片广阔的树林
里面几乎没有人。你的需要
仍是三心二意地予以满足；有时有牛奶
有时没有，只有一架梯子欢闹鼓掌
不再伸向它。相反，却有水泥障碍物。
护林员很好心，只是警告我们离开，
提醒你其他的世界如何能够轻松地

Like dandelions, in no time. There's no one here now
But émigrés, with abandoned skills, so near
To the surface of the water you can touch them through it.
It's they can tell you how love came and went
And how it keeps coming and going, ever disconcerting,
Even through the topiary trash of the present,
Its undoing, and smiles and seems to recognize no one.
It's all attitudinizing, maybe, images reflected off
Some mirrored surface we cannot see, and they seem both solid
As a suburban home and graceful phantasms, at ease
In any testing climate you may contrive. But surely
The slightly sunken memory that remains, accretes, is proof
That there were doings, yet no one admits to having heard
Even of these. You pass through lawns on the way to it; it's late
Even though the light is strongly yellow; and are heard
Commenting on how hard it is to get anybody to do anything
Any more; suddenly your name is remembered at the end
It's there, on the list, was there all along
But now is too defunct to cope
Which may be better in the long run: we'll hear of
Other names, and know we don't want them, but that love
Was somehow given out to one of them by mistake,
Not utterly lost. Boyish, slipping past high school
Into the early forties, disingenuous though, yet all

像蒲公英，迅速扎根。现在这里没有人

只有流亡者，以被放弃的技巧，如此靠近

水面，你可以穿过水面触摸他们。

他们能够告诉你，爱如何来而又去

如何一直来来去去，令人不安，

即使穿过现在那修剪灌木留下的垃圾，

它的毁灭，微笑着，似乎谁都不认识。

也许，它全然是装腔作势，反射在

我们看不见的镜面上的形象，似乎都很可靠

像郊区的家和优美的幻觉，安于

你能够发明的考验人的气候。但肯定

有微微沉没的记忆存留，共生，证明

曾经有过活动，尽管无人承认听说过这些。

你穿过草坪走在通往它的路上；天很晚了

即便有深黄色的光；你听到有人议论

让人多做一点点事有多么难；

突然你的名字终于被回忆起来了——

它在那里，在清单上，全都在那里

但现在已经报废，无法处理

长远看来也许更好：我们听见

其他的名字，知道我们不需要他们，但是那爱

不知怎么错误地给了他们中的一个，

却没有完全失去。孩子气地，溜过中学

进入四十年代初期，尽管没诚意，

The buds of this early spring won't open, which is surprising,

He says. It isn't likely to get any warmer than it is now.

In today's mainstream one mistakes him, sincerely, for someone else;

He passed on slowly and turns a corner. One can't say

He was gone before you knew it, yet something of that, some tepid

Challenge that was never taken up and disappeared forever,

Surrounds him. Love is after all for the privileged.

But there is something else—call it a consistent eventfulness,

A common appreciation of the way things have of enfolding

When your attention is distracted for a moment, and then

It's all bumps and history, as though this crusted surface

Had always been around, didn't just happen to come into being

A short time ago. The scarred afternoon is unfortunate

Perhaps, but as they come to see each other dimly

And for the first time, an internal romance

Of the situation rises in these human beings like sap

And they can at last know the fun of not having it all but

Having instead a keen appreciation of the ways in which it

Underachieves as well as rages: an appetite,

For want of a better word. In darkness and silence.

In the wind, it is living. What were the interruptions that

Led us here and then shanghaied us if not sincere attempts to

但这个早春的蓓蕾不会开放,他说,
这让人吃惊。天气不可能变得比现在更暖了。
在今天的主流里,一个人由衷地,把他当成了另一个人;
他缓慢地经过,拐过一个角落。一个人不能说
他在你知道它以前就走了,但有什么微温之物
挑战那从未被占据也永远不会消失的一切,
围绕着他。爱毕竟是为特权者准备的。

但还有其他什么——称它为一致的事件性,
对事物包容方式的一个普遍理解
当你的注意力分散了片刻,于是
它所有的肿块和历史,仿佛这结了硬壳的表面
始终就在周围,恰恰不是在不久前
才偶然存在的。结疤的下午是不幸的
也许,但当他们在朦胧中第一次
彼此看见,这情形内在的浪漫
像树液在这些人的身体中升起
他们最后能够体会没有它的乐趣
反而对于它未能发挥潜能且让它愤怒的方式
有了一种敏锐的鉴赏力;一个嗜好,
因为缺乏一个更好的词。在黑暗和寂静中。

在风中,它活着。是什么东西介入
把我们领到这里,然后强迫我们,如果不是真的

Understand and so desire another person, it doesn't

Matter which one, and then, self-abandoned, to build ourselves

So as to desire him fully, and at the last moment be

Taken aback at such luck: the feeling, invisible but alert.

On that clear February evening thirty-three years ago it seemed

A tapestry of living sounds shading to colors, and today

On this brick stump of an office building the colors are shaggy

Again, are at last what they once were, proving

They haven't changed: you have done that,

Not they. All that remains is to get to know them,

Like a twin brother from whom you were separated at birth

For whom the factory sounds now resonate in an uplifting

Sunset of your own choosing and fabrication, a rousing

Anthem to perpendicularity and the perennial exponential

Narration to cause everything to happen by evoking it

Within the framework of shared boredom and shared responsibilities.

Cheerful ads told us it was all going to be OK,

That the superstitions would do it all for you. But today

It's bigger and looser. People are not out to get you

And yet the walkways look dangerous. The smile slowly soured.

Still, coming home through all this

And realizing its vastness does add something to its dimension:

Teachers would never have stood for this. Which is why

Being tall and shy, you can still stand up more clearly

企图理解，不是如此渴望另一个人，那人是谁
无关紧要，然后，放弃自我，去建设我们的自我
以便能够全身心地渴望他，并在最后的时刻
被赐予这样的运气：感觉，无形而机警。
在三十三年前那个晴朗的二月黄昏
生活的织锦似乎在试验阴影的颜色，今天
这座办公楼残砖上的色彩再次变得粗糙，
终于恢复了过去的样子，证明
它们没有改变：改变的是你，
不是它们。剩下的一切就是去了解它们，
像一个你在出生时分离的双胞胎兄弟
为了他，此刻工厂的声音回荡在
你自己选择和装配的上升的日落中，一首
振奋的赞美诗，赞美正直和永久指数叙述
以唤起它来促使一切发生
在共同的厌倦和共同的责任的框架内。
快乐的广告告诉我们它将一切正常，
迷信会替你完成它。但今天
它更大更松弛。人们不会出来接你
人行道显得危险。微笑慢慢变酸。
尽管如此，穿过这一切回家
认识到它的广大确实加增了它的维度：
教师们从来不会支持这一点。这就是为什么
高大而羞怯，你仍能更明确地抗拒

To the definition of what you are. You are not a sadist

But must only trust in the dismantling of that definition

Some day when names are being removed from things, when all attributes

Are sinking in the maelstrom of de-definition like spars.

You must then come up with something to say,

Anything, as long as it's no more than five minutes long,

And in the interval you shall have been washed. It's that easy.

But meanwhile, I know, stone tenements are still hoarding

The shadow that is mine; there is nothing to admit to,

No one to confess to. This period goes on for quite a few years

But as though along a low fence by a sidewalk. Then brandishes

New definitions in its fists, but these are evidently false

And get thrown out of court. Next you're on your own

In an old film about two guys walking across the United States.

The love that comes after will be richly, satisfying,

Like rain on the desert, calling unimaginable diplomacy into being

Until you thought you should get off here, maybe this stop

Was yours. And then it all happens blindingly, over and over

In a continuous, vivid present that wasn't there before.

No need to make up stories at this juncture, everybody

Likes a joke and they find yours funny. And then it's just

Two giant steps down to the big needing and feeling

That is yours to grow in. Not grow old, the

Magic present still insists on being itself,

对你之所是的定义。你不是虐待狂
但有一天你只能相信对那定义的拆除
当事物去除了名字,当所有属性
像晶石沉入除去定义的大漩涡。
那时你必须想出什么要说的事情,
任何事,只要不超过五分钟,
在间隙中你将被冲走。那很容易。
但同时我也知道,石头房屋仍然储藏着
属于我的影子;没有什么可承认的,
没人忏悔。这段时期持续了好几年
仿佛沿着人行道边的一道矮篱笆。然后
拳头里挥舞着新定义,但这些定义显然是假的
被抛出了法庭。接下来你独自出现在
两个家伙徒步穿越美国的旧电影里。
以后降临的爱将丰富得令人满足,
像沙漠中的雨,呼唤不可想象的外交手段
直到你认为你应该离开这里,也许这个车站
是你的。随后一切都眩目地,一遍遍发生
在前所未有的连续、生动的现在中。
无需在这个接合处虚构故事,每个人
都喜欢一个笑话,他们发现你的有趣。
那么,只需两大步就能实现巨大的需要和感觉
那就是你的笑话要增长的东西。不是变老,
神奇的现在仍坚持做它自己,

But to play in. To live and be lived by
And in this way bring all things to the sensible conclusion
Dreamed into their beginnings, and so arrive at the end.

Simultaneously in an area the size of West Virginia
The opposing view is climbing toward heaven: how swiftly
It rises! How slender the packed silver mass spiraling
Into further thinness, into what can only be called excess,
It seems, now. And anyway it sounds better in translation
Which is the only language you will read it in:
"I was lost, but seemed to be coming home,
Through quincunxes of apple trees, but ever
As I drew closer, as in Zeno's paradox, the mirage
Of home withdrew and regrouped a little farther off.
I could see white curtains fluttering at the windows
And in the garden under a big brass-tinted apple tree
The old man had removed his hat and was gazing at the grass
As though in sorrow, sorrow for what I had done.
Realizing it was now or never, I lurched
With one supreme last effort out of the dream
Onto the couch-grass behind the little red-painted palings:
I was here! But it all seemed so lonesome. I was welcomed
Without enthusiasm. My room had been kept as it was
But the windows were closed, there was a smell of a closed room.

而是去参与。去生活和被生活
以这种方式把一切带向明智的结论
梦见它们的开始,并这样到达终点。

这时,在西弗吉尼亚那么大的一个地区
反对意见正爬向天空:它上升得多么迅速!
堆积的银色物质多么纤细,盘旋着
变得更细,现在似乎成了只能被称作
过量的东西。它终归在翻译中听起来更好些
那是你将读到的唯一的语言:
"我迷失了,但似乎正在回家,
穿过苹果树的五点梅花阵,但是
我越是靠近,就像在芝诺的悖论中,
家的海市蜃楼就退得更远,重新组合起来。
我能看见白窗帘在窗上拍动
花园里一棵高大的黄铜色苹果树下
那老人摘下帽子,凝视着草丛
仿佛在悲哀,为我所做的一切悲哀。
认识到机不可失,我最后一次
用尽最大的努力从梦中跋涉而出
踏上红色小围篱后面的茅草:
我曾在这里!但一切显得如此孤独。
我受到的欢迎没有热情。我的房间还是老样子
可是窗户关着,一股封闭房间的气味。

And though I have been free ever since

To browse at will through my appetites, lingering

Over one that seemed special, the lamplight

Can never replace the sad light of early morning

Of the day I left, convinced (as indeed I am today)

Of the logic of my search, yet all unprepared

To look into the practical aspects, the whys and wherefores,

And so never know, eventually, whether I have accomplished

My end, or merely returned, another leaf that falls."

One must be firm not to be taken in by the histrionics

And even more by the rigorous logic with which the enemy

Deploys his message like iron trenches under ground

That rise here and there in blunt, undulating shapes.

And once you have told someone that none of it frightens you

There is still the breached sense of your own being

To live with, to somehow nurse back to plenitude:

Yet it never again has that hidden abundance,

That relaxed, joyous well-being with which

In other times it frolicked along roads, making

The best of ignorance and unconscious, innocent selfishness,

The spirit that was to occupy those times

Now transposed, sunk too deep in its own reflection

For memory. The eager calm of every day.

But in the end the dark stuff, the odd quick attack

尽管我从此能够自由随意地

浏览,满足我的欲望,徘徊于

一个显得特别的欲望,灯光

永远不能取代我离开的那天凌晨

那悲哀的光,确信(和我今天一样)

我探求的逻辑,还完全没有准备好

去考察实际的方面,理由和原因,

因而最后也不会知道,是否我实现了

我的目的,还是仅仅带回了,另一片落叶。"

一个人必须坚定,才不被表演所欺骗

甚至还有严密的逻辑,敌人就用它

展开他的信息,像地下的钢铁战壕

到处升起它生硬、起伏的形式。

你曾经告诉别人它根本吓不倒你

仍有你自己的存在被破坏的感觉

要去忍受,要设法充分地予以照看:

可它再也没有那种隐藏的丰富了,

那种轻松、快乐的福祉

在其他时刻它与这福祉一路嬉闹,

充分利用纯真和无意识的、无知的自私,

曾经要去占据那些时刻的精神

现在被调换,过深地沉入它自己

对记忆的沉思。每天所渴望的平静。

可到最后那黑暗的材料,奇异的突袭

Followed by periods of silence that get shorter and shorter.
Resolves the subjective-versus-objective approach by undoing
The complications of our planet, its climate, its sonatinas
And stories, its patches of hard ugly snow waiting around
For spring to melt them. And it keeps some memories of the troubled
Beginning-to-be-resolved period even in the timely first inkling
Of maturity in March, "when night and day grow equal," but even
More in the solemn peach-harvest that happens some months later
After differing periods of goofing-off and explosive laughter.
To be always articulating these preludes, there seems to be no
Sense in it, if it is going to be perpetually five o'clock
With the colors of the bricks seeping more and more bloodlike
 through the tan
Of trees, and then only to blacken. But it says more
About us. When they finally come
With much laborious jangling of keys to unlock your cell
You can tell them yourself what it is,
Who you are, and how you happened to turn out this way,
And how they made you, for better or for worse, what you are now,
And how you seem to be, neither humble nor proud, *frei aber einsam*.
And should anyone question the viability of this process
You can point to the accessible result. Not like a great victory
That tirelessly sweeps over mankind again and again at the end
Of each era, presuming you can locate it, for the greater good
Of history, though you are not the first person to confuse

随后而来的是越来越短的沉默时期
解决主观对抗客观的途径，解开
我们行星的纠葛，它的气候，它的小奏鸣曲
以及故事，它坚硬丑陋的雪堆
等待被春天融化。它保留着对麻烦重重的
开始阶段的一些记忆，甚至在最初及时的
对成熟三月的暗示中，"当夜与昼变得均衡"，
甚至在数月后到来的隆重的桃子收获季
在不同的休息期和迸发的笑声之后。
这些前奏始终音色清晰，似乎没有
意义，如果它要永远停在五点钟
带着从树的褐色中渗出的越来越多血一样的
砖头颜色，然后只是变黑。但是
它与我们关系更深。当他们终于到来
用相当费力的乱响的钥匙打开你的牢门
你可以自己告诉他们它是什么
你是谁，你如何偶然成了这样，
他们如何使你，无论好坏，成了现在这样，
你如何显得，不卑不亢，自由而孤独。
如果有人怀疑这个过程的可行性
你可以指出触手可及的结果。不像一个伟大胜利
在每个时代末尾不倦地反复席卷人类，
假如为了对历史更有利
你可以定位它，尽管你不是第一个

Its solicitation with something like scorn, but the slow polishing

Of an infinitely tiny cage big enough to hold all the dispiritedness,

Contempt, and incorrect conclusions based on false premises that now

Slow you down but by that time, enchaliced, will sound attentive,

Tonic even, an antidote to badly reasoned desiring: footfalls

Of the police approaching gingerly through the soft spring air.

At Pine Creek imitation the sky was no nearer. The difference

Was microtones, a seasoning between living and gestures.

It emerged as a rather stiff impression

Of all things. Not that there aren't those glad to have

A useful record like this to add to the collection

In the portfolio. But beyond just needing where is the need

To carry heaven around in one's breast-pocket? To satisfy

The hunger of millions with something more substantial than good wishes

And still withhold the final reassurance? So you see these

Days each with its disarming set of images and attitudes

Are beneficial perhaps but only after the last one

In every series has disappeared, down the road, forever, at night.

It would be cockier to ask of heaven just what is this present

Of an old dishpan you bestowed on me? Can I get out the door

With it, now that so many old enmities and flirtations have shrunk

To little more than fine print in the contexts of lives and so much

把它的诱惑和轻蔑混淆的人，但是缓慢擦亮的
一个无限小的笼子大得足以容纳所有的沮丧，
耻辱，和建立在错误前提上的错误结论
此刻它们使你慢下来，到那时，圣餐杯将是
专门针对理由糟糕的欲望的一剂解毒剂：
穿过温柔的春天的空气小心逼近的警察的脚步声。

在"松树溪"，仿造的天空不再靠近。区别
在于微音程，生活与姿态之间的一个调味品。
它作为对万物的一个相当僵硬的印象
出现。不是不愿拥有这样
有用的记录，去增加文件夹中的
收藏。但是在需要之外，哪里还有必要
把天空携带在一个人的上衣口袋？去满足
成百万人的渴望，用比良好意愿更本质的东西
并仍然保留着最后的安慰？于是你看见
这些日子各个都有让人消除敌意的形象和态度
也许有益，但只是在每个系列中的最后一个
在夜里，永远消失在路上之后。

也许更为自大的去问问天空，你赐予我的
这个旧洗碟盆到底是什么礼物？我可以带它出门吗？
既然这么多过去的敌意和挑逗已经缩小成
生活上下文中的精美印刷品，这么多

825

New ground is coming undone, shaken out like a scarf or a handkerchief
From this window that dominates everything perhaps a little too much?
In falling we should note the protective rush of air past us
And then pray for some day after the war to cull each of
The limited set of reflections we were given at the beginning
To try to make a fortune out of. Only then will some kind of radical stance
Have had some meaning, and for itself, not for us who lie gasping
On slopes never having had the nerve to trust just us, to go out with us,
Not fearing some solemn overseer in the breath from the treetops.

And that that game-plan and the love we have been given for nothing
In particular should coincide—no, it is not yet time to think these things.
In vain would one try to peel off that love from the object it fits
So nicely, now, remembering it will have to be some day. You
Might as well offer it to your neighbor, the first one you meet, or throw
It away entirely, as plan to unlock on such and such a date
The door to this forest that has been your total upbringing.
No one expects it, and thus
Flares are launched out over the late disturbed landscape
Of items written down only to be forgotten once more, forever this time.

And already the sky is getting to be less salmon-colored,
The black clouds more meaningless (otter-shaped at first;
Now, as they retreat into incertitude, mere fins)

新的土地将毁灭，像围巾或手帕一样
在这主宰一切，也许有点过分的窗户上向外摇晃？
在坠落中我们应该注意到保护性的气流经过
随后祈祷战后有一天，可以精选
我们开始时被赋予的有限一组倒影
尝试从中大赚一笔。只有在那时，某种激进的姿态
才能获得某种意义，为它自己，不是为躺在斜坡上
喘息的我们，永远没有勇气信任我们，和我们一起出去，
不恐惧来自树顶的呼吸中某个严肃的监督人。

那交给我们的游戏计划和爱不会有任何
特殊的巧合——不，还不是思考这些事情的时机。
现在，一个人徒劳地试图把爱从它如此吻合的
对象剥离，将在某一天回忆起它。
你无妨把它给你的邻居，你遇见的第一个人，
或者把它完全抛开，正如在这样一个日子
计划把门，向这片一直养育你的树林敞开。
没有人期待它，于是
最近遭到打扰的风景发出闪光
写下的条款只是为了再次遗忘，这次是永远。

而且天空的鲑鱼色已经变浅，
乌云更无意义（起初是水獭形；
现在，当它们退回不确定中，仅仅是鱼鳍状）

And perhaps it's too late for anything like the overhaul

That seemed called for, earlier, but whose initiative

Was it after all? I mean I don't mind staying here

A little longer, sitting quietly under a tree, if all this

Is going to clear up by itself anyway.

There is no indication this will happen,

But I don't mind. I feel at peace with the parts of myself

That questioned this other, easygoing side, chafed it

To a knotted rope of guesswork looming out of storms

And darkness and proceeding on its way into nowhere

Barely muttering. Always, a few errands

Summon us periodically from the room of our forethought

And that is a good thing. And such attentiveness

Besides! Almost more than anybody could bring to anything,

But we managed it, and with a good grace, too. Nobody

Is going to hold *that* against us. But since you bring up the question

I will say I am not unhappy to place myself entirely

At your disposal temporarily. Much that had drained out of living

Returns, in those moments, mounting the little capillaries

Of polite questions and seeming concern. I want it back.

And though that other question that I asked and can't

Remember any more is going to move still farther upward, casting

也许任何大修这样的事都已经太晚了
那似乎是早先的需要，可主动权
究竟是谁的？我的意思是我不介意在这里
多留一会，安静地坐在树下，如果这一切
即将自我消除。

没有任何这个会发生的迹象，
但是我不在乎。我和我自我的各个部分保持和平
它怀疑这悠闲的另一面，摩擦它
形成一根臆测的有结的绳子，从风暴
和黑暗中隐约出现，向不存在的地方前进
几乎没有抱怨。始终有一些使命
不时地从我们深谋远虑的房间召唤我们
那是个好事情。这样的专注除外！
几乎没有任何人能把它带给任何事，
可我们设法做到了，带着一种优雅。
无人把它向我们举起。可既然你提出了问题
我要说，我不介意暂时把自己完全交给你
去处理。大部分已经排干的生命
在那些时刻，回来了，沿着委婉的问题的
毛细血管攀升，并显示出关切。我要它回来。

尽管我曾经提过又记不起来的
另一个问题正向上移动，把它巨大的影子

Its shadow enormously over where I remain, I can't see it.

Enough to know that I shall have answered for myself soon,

Be led away for further questioning and later returned

To the amazingly quiet room in which all my life has been spent.

It comes and goes; the walls, like veils, are never the same,

Yet the thirst remains identical, always to be entertained

And marveled at. And it is finally we who break it off,

Speed the departing guest, lest any question remain

Unasked, and thereby unanswered. Please, it almost

Seems to say, take me with you, I'm old enough. Exactly.

And so each of us has to remain alone, conscious of each other

Until the day when war absolves us of our differences. We'll

Stay in touch. So they have it, all the time. But all was strange.

投射在我所逗留之处,我看不见它。
但足以知道我不久将回答自己,
被进一步的疑问带走,然后返回
我度过一生的安静得惊人的房间。
它来来去去;墙壁,像面纱,再也不一样了,
然而渴望保持着原样,总是被款待
总是让人惊奇。最终,我们打断它,
催促客人离开,唯恐留下任何没有问
因而也没有回答的问题。请吧,
它几乎要说,把我带走,我够老了。真的。
于是我们都得独自留下,意识到彼此的存在
直到战争解决了我们的差异。我们将保持接触。
他们就这样,始终拥有它。但一切都是陌生的。